FREUD AND OEDIPUS

Medallion by Karl Maria Schwerdtner presented to Freud on his fiftieth birthday. PHOTOGRAPH BY DAVID NEWMAN. COPYRIGHT © 1986, FREUD MUSEUM, LONDON, ENGLAND.

PETER L. RUDNYTSKY

Freud and Oedipus

Columbia University Press

New York

The Andrew W. Mellon Foundation, through a special grant, has assisted the Press in publishing this volume.

Columbia University Press
New York   Oxford
Copyright © 1987 Columbia University Press
All rights reserved

Library of Congress Cataloging-in-Publication Data

Rudnytsky, Peter L.
    Freud and Oedipus.

    Bibliography: p.
    Includes index.
    1. Oedipus complex—History.   2. Psychoanalysis—
History.   3. Oedipus (Greek mythology)   4. Sophocles—
Criticism and interpretation.   5. German drama (Tragedy)
—History and criticism.   6. Freud, Sigmund, 1856–1939.
7. Psychoanalysts—Austria—Biography.   I. Title.
BF175.5.O33R83   1987   150.19'52   86-21532
ISBN 0-231-06352-0
ISBN 0-231-06353-9 (pbk.)

∞

Casebound editions of Columbia University Press books are
Smyth-sewn and printed on permanent and durable acid-free
paper.

Printed in the United States of America

c 10 9 8 7 6 5 4 3 2 1
p 10 9 8 7 6 5 4 3 2 1

Book design by J. S. Roberts

To my teachers

"Let the young soul ask itself, looking back on life,
'What have you really loved up to now, what has
drawn on your soul, dominated it and made it
joyful at the same time?' Consider these venerated
objects in order, and perhaps they will show you,
through their being and their sequence, a law, the
fundamental law of your true Self."

—Nietzsche, *Schopenhauer as Educator*

Contents

Preface

INTEREST IN Freud has continued un-
abated in the nearly half-century since his death. This book attempts to contribute to the history of psychoanalysis—and to the
ongoing dialogue Freud's life and work have generated—by reex-
amining Freud's epochal self-analysis in the final years of the
nineteenth century and the discovery of the Oedipus complex that
is its culmination.

Like many authors, I came to a realization of my true subject
only in the course of writing about it. This book has its proximate
origins in my unpublished 1979 Yale Ph.D. dissertation, *Siege of
Contraries: An Essay in Psychoanalytic Criticism*, in which I sought to
compare the myths of Oedipus and the Fall through readings of
Freud, Sophocles, and Milton. Even at that time it was clear to
me that it would be necessary to consider Freud's own engagement
with the Oedipus myth before undertaking any psychoanalytic
criticism of Sophocles. Also at that time I had begun to think about
the nineteenth-century antecedents of Freud's confrontation with
Oedipus, though these preliminary researches did not find their
way into the dissertation. But only when I subsequently became
aware that the Fall was really peripheral to my main concern did
Freud and Oedipus take shape in my mind.

The book that remains approaches the conjunction of names
announced in the title from three complementary perspectives—
biography, intellectual history, and Greek tragedy. In part 1 I
explore the subjective determinants of Freud's discovery of the

Oedipus complex. My organization here is thematic: I begin in chapter 1 by sifting the evidence of Freud's interest in Oedipus prior to *The Interpretation of Dreams* and showing how this interest has its roots in the unique features of Freud's family constellation; chapter 2 concentrates on Freud's crucial friendship with Fliess and on the compulsion to repeat manifested in his life; chapter 3 takes up Freud's self-analysis and attempts to reconstruct how an identification with two unnamed patients made possible his greatest discovery.

Having situated the Oedipus complex biographically in part 1, I turn in part 2 to Freud's intellectual genealogy. The plan here is straightforwardly chronological. In brief, I try to prove the existence of an "age of Oedipus," extending from Schiller to Freud, which became possible when the German Romantics rebelled against neoclassicism and took *Oedipus the King* as a paradigm for their own obsession with self-consciousness. I treat in detail three writers—Schiller, Hölderlin, and Kleist—as well as Hegel and Nietzsche and the intervening philosophical tradition. Where appropriate, I interweave biographical analysis with a critical reading of texts in which Oedipus makes an appearance. I am less concerned with tracing direct influence than with mapping the spirit of an age, but these endeavors cannot always be kept separate. A concluding chapter extends the investigation to the twentieth-century figures of Heidegger and Lévi-Strauss.

Part 3 begins with a reading of *Oedipus the King* from the retrospective standpoint of Freud's self-analysis, and proceeds—by way of an exploration of *Antigone* and *Oedipus at Colonus*—to an argument about the unity of the Oedipus cycle as a whole. In combining the methodologies of psychoanalysis and structuralism, I have not lost sight of the need for philological responsibility, and I hope that my interpretation of Sophocles will be of interest to classicists as well as to general readers. For ease of reference, I have supplied transliterations for all Greek citations. The book ends with some reflections on the bearing of my quest for psychoanalytic truth on deconstruction, and in a polemical appendix I address several attacks on psychoanalysis and the Oedipus complex.

I am well aware that, in writing this book, I have ventured into many fields outside my scholarly specializations in psycho-

analysis and Renaissance literature. My approach to psychoanalysis, moreover, concentrating as it does on the early phase of
Freud's thought, leaves out of account current theoretical developments in the areas of narcissism and preoedipal object relations,
and makes only passing mention of Lacan. But I have tried
throughout to make myself conversant with the relevant bibliographies and to base my interpretations as much as possible on
empirical evidence. I have striven for comprehensiveness, while
remembering that closure is at best provisional. By turning psychoanalysis back upon its founder, I hope both to confirm the
validity of the theory itself and to see Freud the man with realistic
detachment. The Freud I admire is in the hermeneutic tradition
of self-reflection. It is in the same spirit that I acknowledge this
book to be "a portion of my own self-analysis."

New York City
May 1986

Acknowledgments

THE APPEARANCE of a first book is the happy occasion for, if not the repayment, at least the public acknowledgment of many long-standing debts. My greatest intellectual obligation is to my present colleagues and/or former teachers in the Department of English and Comparative Literature at Columbia, whose examples have been my best precepts in literary study. An abbreviated list could not fail to include Edward W. Tayler, Steven Marcus, James V. Mirollo, Edward W. Said, John D. Rosenberg, Frank Kermode, Stephen Donadio, and P. Jeffrey Ford.

The doctoral dissertation out of which this book has grown was nurtured at Yale by the supportive direction of Harold Bloom, ably seconded by Ronald Paulson. Geoffrey H. Hartman found time to give me a reading course on Freud. While at Cambridge I benefited from George Steiner's scrupulous supervision of my work on tragedy. Gregory Nagy welcomed me into the charmed circle of his class on tragedy at Harvard. The missionary zeal of the faculty of the CUNY Latin/Greek Institute, under the direction of Floyd L. Moreland, gave me access to Sophocles in the original after only one summer. At Germantown Friends School in Philadelphia, Richard Tyre brought home the truth of his dictum, "The myths are true, we just change the names." Included in the dedication are the students at Columbia, Yale, and Harvard with whom I have discussed the ideas taken up in these pages.

I have been extremely fortunate in finding myself in the right place at the right time for psychoanalytic studies. While I was an undergraduate at Columbia, Willard Gaylin and Arnold M. Cooper began teaching courses on the history of psychoanalytic thought. At Yale a research grant funded through the generosity of Mark Kanzer enabled me to do a year of course work at the Western New England Institute for Psychoanalysis, where George F. Mahl encouraged my interest in Freud's "first phase."

Material assistance has been provided by Columbia University in the form of a Chamberlain Fellowship and of summer grants from the Council for Research in the Humanities at the initial and final stages of my work. This book could not have been completed without the unencumbered year made possible by a Mellon Faculty Fellowship at Harvard in 1983–84.

A special debt of thanks belongs to all those who read substantial portions of this work in manuscript: Steven Marcus; John D. Rosenberg; Mark Kanzer; Martin Grotjahn; James Engell; Michael Jennings; Howard Eiland; Seth Benardete; and Matthew S. Santirocco. Intellectual acuity and generosity of spirit were shown by Sandor Goodhart in his reader's report for Columbia University Press. It goes without saying that none of the individuals named here is responsible for the errors of fact, judgment, or taste that remain.

An earlier version of chapter 1 appeared in *Raritan: A Quarterly Review* (Spring 1982), 1:50–61; of chapter 8 in *American Imago* (Winter 1985), 42:413–39, copyright © 1985 by the Association for Applied Psychoanalysis; and of the appendix in *World Literature Today* (Summer 1982), 56:462–70, copyright © 1982 by the University of Oklahoma Press. I am grateful to those who granted permission to reprint. Expert technical assistance was extended by the staff at Columbia University Press. Beth Harrison compiled the bibliography.

The unwavering friendship of Kathie Plourde has sustained me during the long period of writing this book. James Bednarz saw to it that I did not forget the Renaissance in the course of pursuing my investigations of Freud.

My sister, Betsy Roslosnik, suffered me when I was most insufferable. To my late father, Ivan Lysiak-Rudnytsky, and to my mother, Joanne Benton, who proved to me that teachers make the best parents, my most abiding love.

Abbreviations

The following works are cited frequently or at widely scattered intervals throughout the text and will be documented parenthetically in abbreviated form.

F/J = *The Freud/Jung Letters: The Correspondence Between Sigmund Freud and C. G. Jung.* William McGuire, ed.; Ralph Manheim and R. F. C. Hull, trs. Princeton: Princeton University Press, 1974.

Letters = *The Letters of Sigmund Freud.* Ernst L. Freud, ed.; Tania and James Stern, trs. 1960. New York: Basic Books, 1975.

LW = Ernest Jones, *The Life and Work of Sigmund Freud.* 3 vols. New York: Basic Books, 1953–1957.

Masson = *The Complete Letters of Sigmund Freud to Wilhelm Fliess 1887–1904.* Jeffrey Moussaieff Masson, ed. and tr. Cambridge, Mass.: Harvard University Press, 1985.

Origins = Sigmund Freud, *The Origins of Psychoanalysis: Letters to Wilhelm Fliess, Drafts and Notes: 1887–1902.* Eric Mosbacher and James Strachey, trs. 1954. New York: Basic Books, 1971.

PM = G. W. F. Hegel, *The Phenomenology of Mind.* J. B. Baillie, tr. 1910. New York: Harper Torchbooks, 1967.

SE =   Sigmund Freud, *The Standard Edition of the Complete Psychological Works of Sigmund Freud.* 24 vols. James Strachey et al., eds. and trs. London: Hogarth Press, 1953–1974.

SL =   *Selected Letters of Friedrich Nietzsche.* Christopher Middleton, ed. and tr. Chicago: University of Chicago Press, 1969.

VPN =   Friedrich Nietzsche, *The Portable Nietzsche.* Walter Kaufmann, ed. and tr. 1954. New York: Viking, 1967.

PART 1: BIOGRAPHY

"One cannot help having a slightly disagreeable feeling when one comes across one's own name in a stranger. Recently I was very sharply aware of it when a *Herr S. Freud* presented himself to me in my consulting hour."

—Freud, *The Psychopathology of Everyday Life*

1
The Hero's Garb

To UNDERTAKE a biographical study of Freud is to embark upon an eminently circular enterprise. For any attempt to recount the life of the founder of psychoanalysis must necessarily come under the influence of the intellectual discipline he himself originated. Indeed, the utility of biographies of Freud may be measured by the extent to which they remain within—rather than indifferent, or actively opposed, to—a psychoanalytic perspective.[1] To turn psychoanalysis back against Freud is obviously a limit case for the theory of interpretation, but such a paradigmatic conflation of the means and object of investigation may serve to shed light on the issues at stake in any psychoanalytic study of literature. Freud's writings are notoriously interdisciplinary in nature—transgressing as they do the boundaries between fiction, autobiography, philosophy, and social and natural science—and only a hermeneutic praxis aware, as it were, of its transferential relation to Freud, its own stake in the psychoanalytic wager, can hope to do these complexities justice.

The subject of the first part of this book will be the biographical determinants of Freud's discovery of the Oedipus complex. The centrality of the Oedipus complex to Freud's thought scarcely needs to be argued. My purpose will be to explore the implications of this dynamic relation between Freud and Oedipus—between life and myth—which has had so incalculable an effect on modern culture.

In *The Interpretation of Dreams* (1900), during his first public exposition of what would later come to be known as the Oedipus complex, Freud observes parenthetically that the action of *Oedipus the King* depicts "a process that can be likened to the work of a psycho-analysis" (*SE*, 4:262–63). At the same time that he sets forth the incestuous and patricidal wishes that define the *contents* of the Oedipus complex, that is, Freud notes profoundly that the quest for psychoanalytic insight duplicates the *form* of Oedipus' self-interrogation. In no case is the parallel between the "work of a psycho-analysis" and the action of Sophocles' drama closer than in that of Freud's self-analysis. Thus, in seeking to retrace the steps by which Freud arrived at his most momentous realization—the universality of the Oedipus complex—we shall simultaneously be reflecting on the manner in which his drama of self-discovery reenacts that of Sophocles' hero.

The Medallion Incident

As Freud's paramount biographer, Ernest Jones is also the archetypal reader of Freud. My own position as an interpreter of Freud becomes inevitably a double of Jones'. It is therefore fitting that we begin this examination of Freud's engagement with the Oedipus myth by pondering an incident recounted by Jones in his classic work. In 1906, on the occasion of his fiftieth birthday, Freud was presented by a group of his adherents with a medallion, engraved on one side with his own portrait in profile and on the other with a design of Oedipus answering the Sphinx, inscribed with a line in Greek from *Oedipus the King*, "Who knew the famous riddles and was a man most mighty." When Freud read the inscription, Jones relates, he "became pale and agitated . . . as if he had encountered a *revenant*." The reason for Freud's agitation was "that as a young student at the University of Vienna he used to stroll around the great arcaded court inspecting the busts of former famous professors of the institution. He then had the phantasy, not merely of seeing his own bust there in the future, which would not have been anything remarkable in an ambitious student, but of it being inscribed with the *identical* words he now saw on the medallion" (*LW*, 2:14).

This anecdote serves as a psychoanalytic parable, which immerses us in the problem of Freud's identification with Oedipus. It shows us, first of all, that his fascination with Sophocles' hero dates back at least to his university days in the 1870s, long before the discovery of psychoanalysis or the Oedipus complex. An endeavor to establish the original moment of this identification will reveal the truth of Jones' statement that Freud's "hero's garb was in the weaving at the cradle itself" (*LW*, 2:4–5).

In the second place, the connection between earlier and later events in producing Freud's reaction must be noted. The incident on his fiftieth birthday, surely, would not have been disturbing had it not been foreshadowed by Freud's previous fantasy. The necessity of just such a relation between a "first scene" and a "second scene" in the structure of trauma is the essence of Freud's theory of "deferred action," first articulated in the posthumously published *Project for a Scientific Psychology* (1895) and given prominence in recent thought by Jacques Lacan. Freud's anxiety upon receiving the medallion because it revived the fantasy from his school days exemplifies what is described in the *Project* as "an instance of a memory exciting an affect which it had not excited as an experience" (*Origins*, p. 413). The notion that a trauma is precipitated by the conjunction of two events, which, in Jean Laplanche's words, are "linked by associative chains, but also clearly separated from each other by *a temporal barrier which inscribes them in two different spheres of meaning,*"[2] has decisive importance for our attempt to follow Freud's identification with Oedipus to its source. Every effort to establish such an original moment proves futile, because each link in the chain points beyond itself to an earlier one. As Laplanche resumes the heart of Freud's argument: "we try to track down the trauma, but the traumatic memory was only secondarily traumatic: we never manage to fix the traumatic event historically."[3]

Finally, the medallion incident illustrates both the motifs of the revenant and of fulfilled wishes in Freud's life. The return of ghosts from the past—whether of thoughts, people, or situations—is the nucleus of the psychoanalytic principle of the repetition compulsion and, like so many psychoanalytic concepts, it receives its most compelling documentation in Freud's personal history. As for the fulfillment of wishes, Freud's loss of composure upon being honored by his followers is attributable to the blurring of the boundary between inner and outer worlds, as fantasy unexpectedly becomes reality. But the capacity to achieve in reality what normally remains fantasy is what distinguishes heroes from ordinary mortals. Freud recognized this quality of heroism when he wrote of Oedipus in *The Interpretation of Dreams:* "Here is one in whom these primaeval wishes of childhood have been fulfilled, and we shrink back from him with the whole force of the repression by which those wishes have since that time been held down within us" (*SE,* 4:262–63). As the founder of psychoanalysis and himself a hero, Freud too is one "in whom these primaeval wishes of childhood have been fulfilled."

Jones concludes his account of the incident by remarking that, at his own instigation, just such a bust as Freud had imagined, complete with the inscription from Sophocles, now stands in the courtyard of the University of Vienna. In one sense, our inquiry into Freud's personal involvement with the Oedipus myth constitutes an attempt to account for the presence of this bust in the university courtyard. The "hero's garb" that begins to be woven in Freud's cradle, and is formally bestowed with the medallion on his fiftieth birthday, culminates in this adolescent wish posthumously fulfilled in reality.

"Supplements" of Oedipus

Freud adduces the story of Oedipus in *The Interpretation of Dreams* to document his contention that "it is the fate of all of us, perhaps, to direct our first sexual impulse towards our mother and our first hatred and our first murderous wish against our father. Our dreams convince us that this is so" (*SE,* 4:262). In many respects, the appearance of *The Interpretation of Dreams,* with its first public association between the names of Freud and Oedipus, marks the beginning of psychoanalysis. My interest here, however, is in showing how Freud's assertion of the universality of Oedipus' fate is itself the outgrowth of his own personal history. The posthumous publication of Freud's letters to Wilhelm Fliess from 1887 to 1904, only now available in uncensored form, has revolutionized our understanding of Freud by enabling us to study the theories and recollections contained in his works in light of his private self-analysis.[4]

The realization that Freud's discovery of the significance of the Oedipus legend is anticipated in the Fliess correspondence affords one instance of such a conceptual revolution. In itself, this fact points to the *secondary* nature of his remarks in *The Interpretation of Dreams*. What had appeared to be an original moment is transformed into the revision of a previously formulated idea. The nature of this transformation is made clear by Freud's expression of the same insight in his epochal letter to Fliess of October 15, 1897: "I have found love of the mother and jealousy of the father in my own case too, and now believe it to be a general phenomenon of early childhood. . . . If that is the case, the gripping power of *Oedipus Rex* . . . becomes intelligible" (*Origins*, p. 223).

Unlike *The Interpretation of Dreams*, where Freud's statement of the universality of the oedipal pattern is detached and impersonal, the letter to Fliess presents the discovery as a first-person confession. Certainly, the phrase "in my own case too" *(auch bei mir)* suggests that Freud has confirmed in himself a finding from his therapeutic practice, but in writing to Fliess Freud is speaking primarily as the patient in his own self-analysis. In *The Interpretation of Dreams*, however, a work intended for public scrutiny, Freud has suppressed his own identity as patient and assumed the authoritative tone of a physician pronouncing an objective truth. The progression from the Fliess correspondence to *The Interpretation of Dreams*, therefore, symbolically charts Freud's odyssey from the role of patient to that of physician, and the transformation of his self-analysis into psychoanalysis. Ultimately, however, it is as impossible to separate these roles in Freud as, in the case of Oedipus, it is to separate the identities of detective and criminal, and all Freud's psychoanalytic writings may be fruitfully read as fragments of his interminable self-analysis.

Even without the evidence of the Fliess correspondence, the medallion incident suffices to establish that Freud's preoccupation with Oedipus antedates *The Interpretation of Dreams*. One of the most startling corroborations of this identification comes in a letter written by Freud in 1885, at the age of twenty-eight, in which he informs his betrothed, Martha Bernays, that he has destroyed all his written records (excepting only family letters) of the past fourteen years:

> I have just carried out one resolution which one group of people, as yet unborn and fated to misfortune, will feel acutely. Since you can't guess whom I mean, I will tell you: they are my biographers. . . . All my thoughts and feelings about the world in general, and in particular how it concerned me, have been declared unworthy of survival. They must now be thought all over again. And I had jotted down a great deal. But the stuff simply enveloped me, as the sand does the Sphinx, and soon only my nostrils would show above the mass of paper. . . . Let the biographers chafe; we won't make it too easy for them. Let each one of them believe he is right in his "Conception of the Development of the Hero": even now I enjoy the thought of how they will all go astray. (*LW*, 1:xxii–xiii)

As Freud's future biographer, Jones understandably quotes this letter in the Preface to his three-volume work. For our purposes, however, what is most interesting here is the evidence, again long before the birth of psychoanalysis, that Freud explicitly defined his life in terms of a "Conception of the Development of the Hero." And, though it is the Egyptian and not the Theban Sphinx to which he refers, we may surmise that the hero Freud has in mind is none other than Oedipus.

Freud's decision to destroy the records of the past, combined as it is with an allusion to the Sphinx and an only half-joking avowal of his own heroic destiny, also draws attention to the persistent tension between the impulses to self-concealment and self-revelation in his work. As a justification for his own reticence, Freud was fond of quoting the following admonition from Goethe's *Faust:* "*Das beste, was Du wissen kannst,/Darfst Du den Buben doch nicht sagen*" ("The best of what you know, you must not after all tell to boys").[5] On the occasion of his final citation of these lines, upon being awarded the Goethe Prize for literature in 1930, Freud commented that Goethe "was not only, as a poet, a great self-revealer, but also, in spite of the abundance of autobiographical records, a careful concealer" (*SE*, 21:212). Throughout his career, Freud considered both Goethe and Leonardo da Vinci to be his spiritual precursors, as men of genius in whom were united the temperaments of the artist and the scientific investigator, and it is impossible not to detect a veiled self-portrait in his description of Goethe as at once "a great self-revealer" and "a careful concealer."

It has long been known that Freud destroyed all his records again in 1907 and, since the partial publication in 1971 of his letters to his adolescent friend Eduard Silberstein, it has come to light that he did so for the first time in 1877, at the age of twenty-one. Exhorting his partner in the "Academia Castellana" that they obliterate the evidence of their association, Freud wrote: "I propose that you think of a nice winter evening when we shall burn the archives in a solemn auto-da-fé."[6] Since the urge to cover up the traces of his past is itself a manifestation of his heroic ambition, Freud's sequence of repeated acts of destruction parallels his identification with Oedipus. The irony of these decisions, moreover, is that they always reinscribe the secret they are meant to conceal, as Freud's allusion to the Sphinx in the letter to Martha leaves behind a clue to his Oedipus complex.

The year 1885 was a fateful one for Freud, as in it he won a fellowship that enabled him to travel to Paris to study with the great Charcot. Two letters from that time provide further evidence of his prepsychoanalytic fixation upon Oedipus. To his fiancée's sister, Minna Bernays, he wrote: "I am under the full impact of Paris and, waxing very poetical, could compare it to a vast overdressed Sphinx who gobbles up every foreigner unable to solve her riddles" (*Letters*, p. 187). In a letter to Martha from the same period, Freud described his overwhelmed response to Charcot's presence: "I sometimes come out of his lectures as from Notre Dame, with an entirely new idea about perfection" (*Letters*, p. 185). John Gedo has commented on the connection between these references: "The equation of Charcot with Notre Dame de Paris and of Paris itself with the Sphinx whom Oedipus defeated points to the existence of an underlying repetition of the maternal aspects of the Oedipus complex behind the more obvious paternal significance of Charcot."[7]

The oedipal dimension of Freud's mention of the Sphinx in his former letter to Martha becomes unmistakable in conjunction with this reference to Paris as "a vast overdressed Sphinx" and to himself as a "foreigner" attempting to "solve her riddles." While in Paris, furthermore, Freud liked to frequent the theater despite his precarious financial situation; and, Jones reports, "*Oedipus Rex*, with Mounet-Sully in the title role, made a deep impression on him" (*LW*, 1:177).

These allusions to Oedipus and the Sphinx from 1885 in turn clarify the unconscious forces at work in a still earlier turning point in his life. Originally, Freud had planned to study law, partly as the result of a prophecy during his childhood that he would grow up to be a government minister (*LW*, 1:5). In 1873, however, Freud began to change his mind in favor of a career in medicine. The impetus for this decision came from a lecture in which he heard read "On Nature," an essay then attributed to Goethe. This rhapsodic tract begins with the following sentences: "Nature! We are surrounded by her, embraced by her. . . . We live in her midst, and yet we are strangers to her. She speaks constantly with us, but betrays not her secret to us."[8] Foreshadowing his subsequent depiction of Paris as a sophisticated Sphinx, Freud's conception of nature in maternal terms and resolve to surmount her unwillingness to "betray her secret" are also charged by an oedipal identification.

But though Freud registered in the medical department of the University of Vienna in the fall of 1873, it was not until 1875, after returning from a visit to his half-brothers who had moved to Manchester, that he definitively decided to devote his life to medical research. It appears to be more than a coincidence that it was in the summer of 1875 that Freud stopped signing his letters to Silberstein with his given Hebrew name "Sigismund" and began using the German form "Sigmund."[9] In an oedipal act of self-creation, as Gedo and Ernest Wolf have pointed out, Freud "sealed the finality of his choice of natural science by changing his given name."[10]

In the 1927 postscript to *The Question of Lay Analysis* (1926), Freud referred to the "overpowering need" he felt in his youth "to understand something of the riddles of the world in which we live and perhaps even to contribute something to their solution" (*SE*, 20:253). Even at the time of his decision to abandon law for medicine, Freud expressed the same ambition. Writing to his childhood friend Emil Fluss, Freud revealed the secret of his career change, which he had refrained from confiding for six weeks:

I shall gain insight into the age-old dossiers of Nature, perhaps even eavesdrop on her eternal processes, and share my findings with anyone who wants to learn. As you can see, the secret is not so frightful; it was fearful only because it was altogether too insignificant.[11]

Freud's wish to "gain insight into the age-old dossiers of Nature" is really one for a solution to the Sphinx's riddle, and his promise to "share my findings with anyone who wants to learn" foreshadows the founding of psychoanalysis. The tension between self-concealment and self-revelation in Freud's life is already manifested here in his withholding of his decision before imparting it. We may surmise, moreover, that his secret was "fearful" not because it was "altogether too insignificant," but because Freud dared to hope that it was altogether too momentous.

Starting with the published comments in *The Interpretation of Dreams*, we have traced a sequence of open and veiled allusions to Oedipus in Freud's life dating back to his entrance to the university in 1873. It has proved impossible to "fix the traumatic event historically" because each instance of identification has been secondary, a product of "deferred action." But two more explicit mentions of Oedipus remain to be considered. In June 1873, Freud took his *Matura* examination, the final step in his secondary education. In a letter to Emil Fluss on March 17, 1873, Freud outlined the program of study that lay before him:

I have a good deal of reading to do on my own account from the Greek and Latin classics, among them Sophocles's *Oedipus Rex*. You deprive yourself of much that is edifying if you can't read all these, but, on the other hand, you retain that cheerfulness which is so comforting about your letters.[12]

Of all the literature of classical antiquity, Freud chooses to single out *Oedipus the King* as an object of his attention. This, his earliest extant reference to Oedipus, thus shows that Freud had Sophocles' hero on his mind even before reading (in the original Greek) the tragedy that bears his name. Freud's somewhat condescending contrast between Fluss' "cheerfulness" and his own more "edifying" experience of ancient authors, moreover, implies a distinction between the sheltered lives of ordinary individuals, such as those who make up the chorus of a Greek tragedy, and his own more dangerous and exalted heroic destiny.

On June 16, 1873, Freud reported to Fluss on the outcome of his *Matura*, including his translation from Greek:

The Greek paper, consisting of a thirty-three-verse passage from *Oedipus Rex*, came off better: [I was] the only *good*. This passage I had also read on my own account, and made no secret of it. (*Letters*, p. 4)

Passages from Sophocles, being among the most difficult to translate, were reserved for the most gifted students. Freud's examiners were thus paying tribute to his ability in setting him a task for which he was so eminently prepared. As it happens, it is known which lines of *Oedipus the King* Freud was asked to translate: lines 14 to 57, the speech of the Priest, which includes a supplication to Oedipus as "the first of men, in the chances of life."[13] Like the line inscribed on the medallion,[14] about which Freud would fantasize following his matriculation at the university, the heroic image of Oedipus in this translated speech adumbrates Freud's own subsequent triumph.

In this second letter to Fluss, Freud states that he has already "read on my own account" the set passage; in the earlier letter he announces his intention of reading Sophocles. Thus, even these earliest mentions of Oedipus are "secondarily traumatic," because they point beyond themselves to a preexisting identification. Jacques Derrida, who explains the workings of memory in terms of the laying down of written traces or "supplements" in the mind, has insisted: "the supplement is always the supplement of a supplement. One wishes to go back *from the supplement to the source:* one must recognize that there is *a supplement at the source.*"[15] Each of the references to Oedipus we have noted is "the supplement of a supplement," and instead of finding a pristine original moment for Freud's preoccupation, there is only "a supplement at the source."

Freud's *Matura* also included an essay in German, and the assigned topic was again one to which he had already devoted much thought: "On the Considerations in the Choice of a Profession." Freud poured out for his examiners the same aspirations concerning a career in medicine as he had lately confided to Fluss, and was rewarded with an "excellent" for his efforts. The writing of the seventeen-year-old Freud so impressed his professor that the latter told him he had "a distinctly personal style, i.e., a style at once correct and characteristic." In imparting this morsel of praise to Fluss, Freud added:

You . . . I am sure, have until now not been aware that you are exchanging letters with a German stylist. So now I would counsel you—as a friend, not as one with a vested interest—preserve them—bind them together—guard them well—you never know![16]

It is difficult to decide whether to be struck more by the boastfulness or the accuracy of Freud's self-assessment. His urging Fluss to preserve his letters is the necessary obverse to the thrice-repeated destruction of his written records, which likewise is a manifestation of his heroic ambition. That Fluss heeded Freud's advice shows that indeed "you never know," and helps to make possible a reconstruction of the "Conception of the Development of the Hero."

The summer before taking his *Matura,* Freud returned for the first time to the town of Freiberg where he spent the first three years of his life. He and two friends stayed with the Fluss family, and in the course of the summer the seventeen-year-old Freud became infatuated with Gisela Fluss, the younger of two daughters, who was then fifteen. This adolescent passion is noteworthy in its own right, but the true crux of the episode resides in the fact, first established with the publication of the Silberstein correspondence, that Freud also developed a profound attachment to Emil and Gisela's mother, Frau Fluss. In a letter to Silberstein, Freud confessed, "it seems that I have translated esteem for the mother into friendship with the daughter."[17] Freud's first love affair is thus a profoundly oedipal experience, in which love for the mother is literally fused with—and prepares the way for—love for the girl his own age. As Freud later told Martha, who only knew of Gisela's role in the story, he had been made to "feel sentimental"[18] by the return to his birthplace. The attraction Freud felt for Frau Fluss, therefore, was itself a "supplement" for the absent mother "at the source."

While staying at the Fluss household, Freud on one occasion became intoxicated to the point of unconsciousness in an attempt to subdue the pain of an aching tooth and had to be carried to bed. When Frau Fluss asked him how he had slept the next morning, Freud reported to Silberstein, "I answered 'badly.' . . . She said laughingly, 'I came up to you twice in the night and you never noticed.' I was ashamed."[19] Freud is visited in his bedroom, at his place of origin, by a woman who is a surrogate mother. His mortification upon learning of her visit stems from more than ordinary embarrassment; the event is traumatic because it represents the symbolic fulfillment of unconscious oedipal longings.

Freud's request to Silberstein in 1877 that they destroy the records of their friendship now becomes fully intelligible. The proposed "auto-da-fé" was designed specifically to obliterate the traces of the affair of Frau Fluss, which is never mentioned again in any of Freud's writings or conversations. At the time of his joint infatuation with mother and daughter, Freud kept a daily diary, which, he told Silberstein, "I keep only for you and from which you will hear more than you actually ought to know."[20] Only in retrospect did Freud realize how true it was that he had confided to Silberstein "more than you actually ought to know." The secret behind Freud's repeated acts of destruction thus proves to be literally that of the Oedipus complex.

Freud's celebrated remarks in *The Interpretation of Dreams*, therefore, though they do usher in the psychoanalytic revolution, are themselves inscribed in the chain of "supplements" of his lifelong imitation of Oedipus. Nor was this the last time Freud added to the series. The very term "Oedipus complex," which now seems so inevitable, was not coined until 1910, under the influence of the use of the word "complex" by Jung and the Zurich school, when it appeared in Freud's paper "A Special Type of Choice of Object Made by Men." And in *Totem and Taboo* (1913) Freud extended the argument of *The Interpretation of Dreams* to claim that an actual killing of the father in a primal horde lay at the foundation of human history. At the time of writing *Totem and Taboo* Freud told Jones: "Then I described the wish to kill one's father, and now I have described the actual killing; after all, it is a big step from a wish to a deed" (*LW*, 2:354). Only in *The Ego and the Id* (1923) and later writings, finally, did Freud formally take into account the phenomenon of the "negative" Oedipus complex—involving love for the parent of the same sex and rivalry with the parent of the opposite sex—and begin to ponder the asymmetries between male and female development. Thus, not only does Freud's discovery of the meaning of the Oedipus complex proceed by means of "deferred action," but, as in the medallion incident, each new "supplement" raises the significance of the entire "associative chain" to a higher level.

The Family Constellation

In "Origins," the opening chapter of his biography, Jones terms the universality of the Oedipus complex the "greatest" of Freud's discoveries, and suggests that it was "potently facilitated by his own unusual family constellation, the spur it gave to his curiosity, and the opportunity it afforded of a complete repression" (*LW*, 1:11). But though the remarkable features of Freud's family history have been frequently commented upon, their full implications for his discovery of the Oedipus complex have not yet been appreciated.

The most salient details to remember are that when Freud's parents, Jakob Freud and Amalie Nathanson, were married in 1855, Jakob was already forty whereas Amalie was only twenty, and Jakob himself was already a grandfather by a grown son from his first marriage.[21] Indeed, both of Jakob's sons from his first marriage, Emmanuel (born 1832 or 1833) and Philipp (born 1836), were at least as old as their father's new bride. When Sigmund was born in 1856, therefore, his genealogical position was very complicated. He was, as Siegfried and Suzanne Bernfeld point out, "the eldest son of this marriage, yet at the same time he was the youngest child in his family group."[22] What is more, the other children in the extended family, Emmanuel's children John and Pauline, were actually Freud's nephew and niece—that is, "beneath" him on the family tree—though John was one year older and Pauline the same age as he.

It was not until Freud was nineteen years of age, and he visited his half-brothers in England, that he completely grasped the facts of his background. The enlightenment he received from Emmanuel is recorded in *The Psychopathology of Everyday Life* (1901):

One of my brother's admonitions lingered long in my memory: "One thing," he had said to me, "that you must not forget is that as far as the conduct of your life is concerned you really belong not to the second generation but to the third generation in relation to your father."(*SE*, 6:220)

Just as Freud was, in a manner of speaking, in the relation of grandson to his own father, so each of his generational relation-

ships was marked by a similar ambiguity. His niece and nephew
were, for practical purposes, his siblings, and his half-brothers
were old enough to be his father. This confusion is epitomized in
the fact that when his youngest sibling and only surviving brother,
Alexander, was born in 1866, it was the ten-year-old Sigmund
who chose the name, thereby arrogating to himself a paternal
function and at the same time unconsciously displacing his father
by his half-brother Philipp, since Alexander the Great—after
whom he named his brother—was the son of *Philip* of Macedon.[23]
It scarcely seems surprising that the scion of such a family tree
should have felt impelled to "gain insight into the age-old dossiers
of Nature."

The coincidence between Freud's biographical accidents of
birth and the Oedipus drama is staggering.[24] For it is the consequence of Oedipus' commission of incest with his mother that his
kinship ties display an analogous involution. Instead of the situation that obtains in a normal family, where relationships are
unequivocal and generations succeed each other diachronically,
the result of Oedipus' incest is that time is frozen and each of his
kinship ties *must have two names.* As Teiresias warns him concerning
the killer of Laius:

> He shall be shown to be to his own children
> at once brother and father, and of the woman
> from whom he was born son and husband, and of his
>   father
> sharer of the same seed and murderer.   (11. 457–60)

Edward Said has commented that the knowledge of incest "can
very correctly be described as a tangling-up of the family sequence.
. . . What overwhelms Oedipus is the burden of plural identities
incapable of coexisting within one person,"[25] and exactly the same
might be said of Freud. Because of the discrepancy between the
ages of his father and mother, there is indeed a "tangling-up of
the family sequence" and Freud is confronted by the "burden of
plural identities." There could scarcely be a more vivid illustration
of Oscar Wilde's paradoxical dictum that "Life imitates Art" than
this duplication between the three-generational kinship structures
of Freud and Oedipus.

At the close of *Leonardo da Vinci and a Memory of His Childhood*
(1910), his own speculative venture in psychoanalytic biography,

Freud asks whether one might not "take objection to the finding of an enquiry which ascribes to accidental circumstances of his parental constellation so decisive an influence on a person's fate." He dismisses this demurral, however, with the rejoinder that "if one considers chance to be unworthy of determining our fate, it is simply a relapse into the pious view of the Universe which Leonardo himself was on the way to overcoming" (*SE*, 11:136–37). Freud's recognition of the "decisive influence" of "accidental circumstances of his parental constellation" in Leonardo's case applies also to the way that his own "hero's garb," his destiny to become the discoverer of the Oedipus complex, "was in the weaving at the cradle itself." Whether it is "the fate of all of us" to experience the oedipal drama of incest and murder can only be judged by each individual on the basis of his or her own dreams. But to point out the biographical determinants of Freud's discovery in no way invalidates its claim to universality. On the contrary, it is the special circumstances obtaining in his personal history that made Freud's descent into the unconscious possible. In addition to the historical and cultural factors that converge to produce an intellectual revolution such as that achieved by Freud, the cooperation of chance in summoning the right person for the time also plays an indispensable role.

2
The Transference Neurosis

Obstinate Condolement

IN SHAKESPEARE'S *Hamlet*, Claudius reminds the grieving Hamlet that nature's "common theme / Is death of fathers," and demands to know why he alone should stubbornly "persever / In obstinate condolement."[1] A similar question arises as we focus our attention on the role of Freud's self-analysis in his discovery of the Oedipus complex. Freud writes in the Preface added in 1908 to the second edition of *The Interpretation of Dreams* that the book possessed a "further subjective significance" of which he had been unaware at the time of its original publication: "It was, I found, a portion of my own self-analysis, my reaction to my father's death—that is to say, to the most important event, the most poignant loss of a man's life" (*SE*, 4:xxvi). It is noteworthy for theory that this realization of the "further subjective significance" of his work can *only* come to Freud through "deferred action," just as our own understanding of *The Interpretation of Dreams* is transformed when it is reread against the backdrop of the Fliess correspondence.

But why should Freud have responded with such intensity to the death of his father? Sad the death of a father undeniably is, but there may be other losses of comparable gravity, and it is not immediately obvious on what grounds he refers to it so categorically as "the *most* important event, the *most* poignant loss of a man's life." In addition to the "accidental circumstances" of his birth that tie Freud to Oedipus, a second chance intervention in his personal history must, I believe, be adduced to explain the Hamletlike extravagance of Freud's reaction to the death of his father.

This chance event is the death in infancy of Freud's first sibling, Julius, who died when Freud was just under two years of age. In his letter to Fliess of October 3, 1897, immediately prior to the letter containing his interpretations of *Oedipus the King* and *Hamlet*, Freud includes the death of Julius among the memories he has unearthed from the deepest layers of his self-analysis: "I welcomed my one-year younger brother (who died within a few months) with ill wishes and real infantile jealousy, and his death left the germ of guilt in me. . . . My nephew [John] and younger brother determined, not only the neurotic side of all of my friendships, but also their depth" (*Origins*, p. 219).

Although references to his one-year-elder nephew, John, are prominent in *The Interpretation of Dreams* and elsewhere in Freud's published writings, the death of Julius—like the infatuation with Frau Fluss—is conspicuous by its absence. After the second of his famous fainting spells in Jung's presence, at the Park Hotel in Munich on November 24, 1912, Freud wrote to Ferenczi: "All these attacks point to the significance of very early experiences with death (in my case a brother who died very early, when I was a little over one year old)."[2] But this confidence was communicated to Ferenczi in a private letter, and it is consistent with Freud's suppression of any public allusion to the death of Julius that the first recorded analysis of a parapraxis, contained in a letter to Fliess of August 26, 1898, should concern the forgetting of the name Julius, but no mention of this slip is to be found in *The Psychopathology of Everyday Life*.[3]

Freud admits that he greeted the birth of Julius, his first rival for his mother's affections, "with ill-wishes and real infantile jealousy," and when these death wishes were fulfilled in reality, the psychical consequences must have been catastrophic. In "Some Character Types Met with in Psycho-Analytic Work" (1916), Freud defines a class of individuals who are "wrecked by success," who come to grief when "a deeply-rooted and long-cherished wish has come to fulfillment" (*SE*, 14:316). After his brother's death, Freud too was "wrecked by success," and left with an uncanny dread of the omnipotence of his own wishes (*LW*, 2:146). His agitation upon receiving the medallion on his fiftieth birthday, when he again experienced in reality the fulfillment of a "long-cherished wish," becomes explicable when it is seen as an unconscious reminder of the death of Julius.

By the same token, had it not happened that the death of Julius left in him the "germ of guilt," or, more literally, the "germ of reproaches" *(Keim zu Vorwürfen)*, Freud would almost certainly not have responded with such "obstinate condolement" to the death of his father. In his unconscious mind, he must have believed that his patricidal wishes had caused his father's death, just as he was responsible for that of Julius. It is a cornerstone of psychoanalytic theory that *"a wish which is represented in a dream must be an infantile one"* (*SE*, 5:553), although that infantile wish may be *"modified by being transferred on to a recent experience"* (*SE*, 5:546).[4] In obedience to the psychoanalytic principles of dream formation, accordingly, Freud's extreme response at the age of forty to his father's death may be regarded as the "day residue" or "recent experience," which is reinforced by the memory of his infantile wish for the death of Julius.

That this analogy between Freud's mourning and the structure of a dream is not an arbitrary one is shown by a dream reported by Freud to Fliess shortly after his father's death. Jakob Freud died, at the age of eighty-one, on October 23, 1896, and in his letter to Fliess of November 2 Freud narrates the "very pretty dream" he had during the night following the funeral:

I found myself in a shop where there was a notice up saying:

> You are requested
> to close the eyes.

I recognized the place as the barber's to which I go every day. On the day of the funeral I was kept waiting, and therefore arrived at the house of mourning rather late. The family were displeased with me, because I had arranged for the funeral to be quiet and simple, which they later agreed was the best thing. They also took my lateness in rather bad part. The phrase on the notice-board has a double meaning. It means "one should do one's duty towards the dead" in two senses—an apology, as though I had not done my duty and my conduct needed overlooking, and the actual duty itself. The dream was thus an outlet for the feeling of self-reproach which a death generally leaves among the survivors. (*Origins*, p. 171)

Considerable controversy surrounds the question of exactly when Freud began his "systematic" self-analysis. In his letter to Fliess of November 14, 1897, Freud himself states that there had been "no trace" (*Origins*, p. 231) of his self-analysis prior to the summer of that year, but this should not be taken too literally. In the 1908 Preface to *The Interpretation of Dreams*, on the other hand, Freud directly equates his self-analysis with his "reaction to my father's death," and it may thus be said to begin with his interpretation of this dream, which is, in fact, the first dream reported and analyzed by Freud in his letters to Fliess.[5]

In addition to following immediately upon his father's death, Freud's "close the eyes" dream precedes by almost one year his explanation to Fliess of the "gripping power" of *Oedipus the King*, and contains, as it were, the raw material of his subsequent theoretical formulation of the Oedipus complex. The parallel between the action of *Oedipus the King* and the "work" of Freud's own self-analysis consists above all in the fact that he, like Oedipus, is in unconscious possession of the truth for which he is consciously searching. The oedipal quality of the "close the eyes" dream is reinforced by its preoccupation with the theme of sight. Already in *Studies on Hysteria* (1895), in the case of Miss Lucy R., Freud had used the implicitly Sophoclean metaphor of a "blindness of the seeing eye" to describe that "strange state of mind in which one knows and does not know a thing at the same time" (*SE*, 2:117). Now, at the outset of his own self-analysis, Freud experiences the full force of this description of repression, as his quest for self-knowledge is confronted immediately by the barrier of a self-imposed injunction not to see.

The connection between Freud's responses to the deaths of his father and Julius is made apparent in his summation of the "close the eyes" dream as "an outlet for the feeling of self-reproach which a death generally leaves among the survivors," where the phrase "feeling of self-reproach" or "inclination to self-reproach" *(Neigung zum Selbstvorwurf)* foreshadows the "germ of reproaches" which Freud confesses were implanted in him by his brother's premature death. The key to the dream resides in the "double meaning" which Freud says inheres in the appeal to "close the eyes," since it may refer either to the "actual duty" of closing the eyes of his dead father or to an "apology" for failing to perform that duty. The essence of the Oedipus complex, by the same token, is the ambivalence inherent in the son's feeling toward his father— the coexistence of conscious love and reverence with unconscious hatred and desire for the father's death—and in this dream, as Didier Anzieu has perceptively remarked, "the *ambivalence* of the latent thoughts [is] expressed by the *double sense* of the manifest text."[6] The tension between Freud's pious and patricidal impulses is represented in plastic form by his simultaneous intention and inability to carry out the last rites owed to his deceased father.

Even the gesture of closing his father's eyes, moreover, is charged with ambiguity. In addition to embodying devotion to the father, the action itself may symbolize the wish to castrate and kill him. Freud writes in *Totem and Taboo* of the ritual of the totem meal that it paradoxically "offers satisfaction to the father for the outrage inflicted on him in the same act in which the deed is commemorated" (*SE*, 13:150), and this speculative reconstruction of human prehistory gains its force both from Freud's treatment of cases of obsessional neurosis and its grounding in the empirical truth of his own self-analysis.

Freud metaphorically closes his own eyes at the same time that he closes those of his father. Thus, in addition to the pivotal psychoanalytic concepts of *repression* and *ambivalence,* the dream also displays the workings of *identification.* Son and father become one through the gesture that expresses both love and hatred. In "Mourning and Melancholia" (1917), Freud prefigures his notion of the superego when he discusses in theoretical terms the process of identification with a lost object that occurs during bereavement: "Thus the shadow of the object fell upon the ego, and the latter could henceforth be judged by a special agency, as though it were the object, the forsaken object" (*SE*, 14:249). All psychoanalytic therapy is a work of mourning, an attempt to become reconciled to the loss of loved objects. Its prototype is to be found in Freud's self-analysis, which could not have taken place without the convergence between the deaths of his father and brother in producing "the feeling of self-reproach which a death generally leaves among the survivors."

Friend and Enemy

Since the initial publication of Freud's letters to Fliess in 1950, it has become a commonplace among psychoanalytically informed students that Fliess essentially served the function of an analyst in Freud's self-analysis. As Edith Buxbaum wrote in 1951, "Fliess was not only the recipient of Freud's letters reporting his self-analysis . . . but he obviously had taken the place of a transference figure toward whom Freud had developed a transference neurosis."[7] Our task in reassessing the Freud-Fliess relationship, therefore, will be to try to synthesize the implications of Freud's "transference neurosis," taking advantage of the fact that this correspondence is at last available in its entirety.

With the benefit of hindsight, first of all, it is clear that Freud's original editors did him a disservice in issuing the letters to Fliess in abbreviated form, since they thereby created the impression that matters of scandalous import were concealed in the unpublished excerpts. In reality, however, the recent edition by Jeffrey M. Masson merely rounds out and fills in—but in no way decisively alters—the picture already formed on the basis of previously available materials. What is most remarkable about this intimate correspondence, indeed, is its confirmation of Freud's essential moral decency and probity, insofar as the mingled yarn of human existence permits such judgments, for how many of us could bear to have our lives subjected to such microscopic examination?[8]

It is central to the experience of reading these letters that, with the exception of three letters from Fliess in the aftermath period of 1904, all the communications are from the pen of Freud, those by Fliess having undoubtedly been consigned to one of

Freud's strategic bonfires. The strange effect of eavesdropping on this one-sided dialogue has been compared by Ernst Kris to "listening to someone speaking on the telephone: you can only hear what one party to the conversation is saying" (*Origins*, p. 3), but surely another analogy suggests itself—that of overhearing a psychoanalysis, in which the patient does all the talking, and the analyst maintains an ideal, unbroken silence. The continuity between Freud's relationship with Fliess and those with earlier male figures in his life is exemplified by the fact that, in the cases of his correspondence with both Emil Fluss and Silberstein, Freud's letters again have been preserved whereas those of his partner have not.

In his clinical paper "The Dynamics of Transference" (1912), Freud states that the excessive emotions displayed by the patient in relation to the analyst "are made intelligible if we bear in mind that this transference has been precisely set up not only by the conscious anticipatory ideas but also by those that have been held back or are unconscious" (*SE*, 12:100). This passage serves as an exact commentary on the opening paragraph of Freud's first letter to Fliess, dated November 24, 1887, in which the keynote is struck of their entire relationship. "Esteemed friend and colleague," Freud begins:

I have a strictly business motive for writing to you to-day, but I must start with the confession that I hope to remain in contact with you, and that you left a deep impression on me, which might easily lead to my telling you frankly in what class of men I place you. (*Origins*, p. 51)

Freud's claim to have "a strictly business motive" for writing to Fliess is belied by his avowal of the "deep impression" that the latter has left on him, and his "unconscious anticipatory ideas" are revealed by his eagerness to tell Fliess "in what class of men I place you." In view of what we know of Freud's heroic ambitions, moreover, it is safe to say that the "class of men" in which he sought to place Fliess was that of the unravelers of life's riddles—the same class in which he placed himself. It forms a poignantly circular conclusion to Freud's attachment to Fliess that in the letter of April 26, 1904, in which he tried to revive contacts with his erstwhile friend by inviting him to contribute to a new journal on sexuality, but which soon led to recriminations over Freud's having divulged Fliess' cherished ideas on bisexuality, Freud again began: "If I am writing to you again after such a long interval, you surely will assume that I am prompted not by an emotional impulse but by a practical motive" (Masson, p. 460). In reality, both the grandeur and the tragedy of Freud's friendship with Fliess stem from the impossibility of disentangling—in 1904 as in 1887—the "emotional impulse" from the "practical motive."

The intensity of Freud's reaction to the death of his father, as we have already seen, is largely to be explained by the death of his brother Julius in infancy. Because of the blurring of generational lines in his family constellation, furthermore, the distinction between fraternal and paternal relationships was unclear in Freud's mind from the beginning. Both these biographical accidents are directly relevant to understanding Freud's transferential dependence on Fliess, which was composed equally of fraternal and filial aspects. Like Julius, Fliess was some two years younger than Freud, and the intertwining of Freud's feelings toward his father with those toward Fliess took place as it would in any analysis.[9]

Already in his letter of October 3, 1897 Freud expressed to Fliess his realization that "my nephew and younger brother determined, not only the neurotic side of all my friendships, but also their depth." The same insight, stripped of any reference to Julius, finds its way into a pivotal passage in *The Interpretation of Dreams.* In his commentary on the *"non vixit"* dream, Freud writes of the way that "all my friends have in a certain sense been re-incarnations" of John, adding that John himself became a revenant when he returned from England to visit Vienna during adolescence. He generalizes:

My emotional life has always insisted that I should have an intimate friend and a hated enemy. I have always been able to provide myself afresh with both, and it has not infrequently happened that the ideal situation of childhood has been so completely reproduced that friend and enemy have come together in a single individual—though not, of course, both at once or with constant oscillations, as may have been the case in my earliest childhood. (*SE,* 5:483)

Freud here acknowledges his life to be dominated by the compulsion to recreate "the ideal situation of childhood," in which

"friend and enemy" are brought together in a "single individual."
His use of the word "ideal" in this context is most appropriate,
because it suggests that infantile experience functions as the psychoanalytic equivalent of a Platonic archetype, of which "re-
incarnations" in later life are necessarily imperfect approximations.

Not only does Freud recognize his repetition compulsion intellectually, he experiences it as the dominant emotional reality
of his life. As opposed to Heinz Kohut, who believes that Freud
"did not . . . live out his transferences with his friends or family
or, what must have been most tempting, with his patients through
the formation of counter-transferences,"[10] I maintain the truth to
be precisely the reverse—that Freud "lived out his transferences"
far more intensely than most people. Freud's friendship and eventual rupture with Fliess is but the most important instance of his
reenactments of his ambivalent relations with Julius and John
throughout his adult life. His conflict-laden ties with Breuer, Adler, Jung, Rank, and numerous others may be assimilated to the
same pattern. In the *"non vixit"* dream—included among the
"absurd dreams," which in his letter of September 21, 1899 Freud
brands "the climax of my achievements in dream interpretation"
(*Origins*, p. 299)—Freud exults that he has found in Fliess a friend
to take the place of all those he has lost to death or estrangement:
"How fortunate that I have found a substitute for them and that
I have gained one who means more to me than the others could,
and that, at a time of life when new friendships cannot be easily
formed, I shall never lose his!" (*SE*, 5:486).

Freud had this crucial dream in late October 1898, but in a
matter of years his assertion that he would "never lose" Fliess'
friendship had been contradicted by events. Even intellectual insight seems to be lacking here, especially as the *"non vixit"* dream
concerns Freud's wish to outlive Fliess, and comparable misjudgments accompany the emotional crises that stud Freud's life.

The analogies between Freud's dealings with Fliess and with
later men in his life are widely recognized, but the importance of
his adolescent intimacy with Eduard Silberstein as a link between
John and Fliess has not been similarly appreciated. At the height
of their friendship, in 1875, Freud wrote to Silberstein:

I really believe we shall never part; though we became friends from free choice, we are so attached to each other as if nature would have made us blood relations. I think we are so far gone that we live in one another the whole person as he is, not only, as it was earlier, his good features. I am afraid that even if, through an unworthy deed, you should appear tomorrow completely different from the image I had conceived of you, I still could not cease to wish you well.[11]

The same fervor, the same desire to believe in the immutability of their friendship, that characterize Freud's sentiments toward Fliess are given eloquent expression here. The negative undercurrent that must accompany such effusions is also in evidence, however, as Freud hints darkly at the possibility of an "unworthy deed" on the part of his friend, if only to banish it from his mind. Like Fliess, Silberstein is a revenant of "the ideal situation of childhood," and the fused images of "intimate friend" and "hated enemy" are thus ready to spring to life in Freud's unconscious fantasy.

The same tone of hyperbolical praise for Fliess, frequently combined with an unjustified self-deprecation, found in the salutation to Freud's opening letter persists throughout most of the correspondence. Freud speaks only the literal truth when he tells Fliess in his letter of September 29, 1893, "you altogether ruin my critical faculties and I really believe you in everything" (Masson, p. 56). In the letter of November 2, 1896 reporting the "close the eyes" dream, Freud typically declares, "Perhaps I shall have a few odd things to tell you in return for your great findings and theories" (*Origins*, p. 171). On December 4, 1896 he writes, "I am busy thinking out something which would cement our work together and put my column on your base" (*Origins*, p. 172). As this phallic metaphor of male marriage suggests with unintended humor, the greatest irony of their association is that Freud for a long time regarded Fliess as the truly scientific member of their partnership. Concerning the theory of repression, Freud writes on June 30, 1896, "Perhaps you may supply me with solid ground on which I shall be able to give up explaining things psychologically and start finding a firm basis in physiology!" (*Origins*, p. 169).

The most dramatic evidence of Freud's infatuation with Fliess—and the one revelation of the letters that might be said to possess a scandalous quality—has long been known to scholars of psychoanalysis through the work of Max Schur, before its recent sensationalistic exploitation by Jeffrey Masson.[12] This is the episode of Fliess' near-fatal operation, in March 1895, on Freud's patient Emma Eckstein, in whose nose Fliess inadvertently left a half-meter strip of iodoform gauze. As Schur has convincingly shown, this event lies behind Freud's famous "Specimen Dream" of "Irma's injection" in *The Interpretation of Dreams*. Although Freud's published comments on the dream refer only to the vindication of his own "professional conscientiousness" (*SE*, 4:120), Schur argues that "the main wish behind Freud's Irma dream was not to exculpate *himself* but Fliess. It was a wish not to jeopardize his positive relationship with Fliess."[13] The sequence of Freud's letters to Fliess describing Emma's condition, indeed, clearly reveals his increasingly vigorous attempts to exonerate Fliess—and by extension himself—of any responsibility for her postoperative bleeding. Even in the initial letter of March 8, 1895, recounting the horrifying scene in which a second surgeon removed the gauze Fliess had left in Eckstein's nose, and where Freud is forced to admit "So we had done her an injustice," the emphasis falls on the fact that "this mishap should have happened to you" (Masson, p. 117); and by April 26, 1896, after Freud had taken Eckstein into analytic treatment, he imparts the happy news that "you were right, . . . her episodes of bleeding were hysterical, were occasioned by *longing,* and probably occurred at the sexually relevant times" (Masson, p. 183)—this last being a reference to Fliess' theory of periodicity. The final verdict of not guilty is delivered on January 17, 1897: "As far as the blood is concerned, you are completely without blame!" (Masson, p. 225). Exactly as Freud had vowed to Silberstein, he refuses to allow any "unworthy deed" on the part of his comrade to tarnish his idealized "image" of the latter.

But though Freud did his best to suppress his "critical faculties," the bungled operation on Emma Eckstein served as a catalyst for his doubts about Fliess, and he unconsciously rebelled against the unbounded admiration for Fliess he clung to in his conscious mind. That this is so can be seen from a letter of April 28, 1897, where Freud interprets a dream of his having to do with a telegram from Fliess reporting his address:

I felt a sense of irritation with you, as if you were always claiming something special for yourself; I criticized you for taking no pleasure in the Middle Ages. . . . As I am still doubtful about matters concerned with the father-figure, my touchiness is intelligible. The dream thus collected all the irritation with you that was present in my unconscious. (*Origins*, p. 194)

Freud's habitual excessive deference toward Fliess is here compensated for by his equally immoderate hostility. By linking his "irritation" with Fliess to "matters connected with the father-figure," moreover, Freud makes explicit that his fluctuations of mood are transferential in the clinical sense.

Despite their initial closeness, the intellectual differences and clashes of personality between the two men became increasingly acute, and by 1901 they had drifted apart, largely because of Fliess' inability to tolerate criticism and because of the incompatibility between his mystical theories of periodicity and Freud's dynamic and deterministic psychology. Ironically, it had been Josef Breuer, Freud's senior colleague and collaborator on *Studies on Hysteria*, who first introduced Fliess to Freud, and the eventual split between them reenacted in a more extreme form the earlier conflict between Breuer's static "hypnoid state" and Freud's "defense" theories of hysteria. As Freud prophetically wrote to Fliess on March 1, 1896, at a time when his relations with Breuer were at a low ebb: "That everything one enjoys in life has to be paid for so dearly is decidedly not an admirable arrangement. Will the two of us experience the same thing with each other?" (Masson, p. 175).

The complete Freud–Fliess letters permit us to see that Freud's feelings toward Breuer, as well as toward his friend and family physician Oscar Rie, depended inversely on his attachment to Fliess—as that grew closer, Breuer and Rie fell in Freud's estimation, and as Freud became disenchanted with Fliess, his opinion of the other two men was revised upward. A further disclosure of the complete correspondence is the way that Freud blamed Breuer for disturbing his relationship with Fliess by causing Fliess' wife, Ida, to believe that her husband's friendship with Freud would harm their marriage. Both this reproach of Breuer and the inverse correlation between Freud's affections for Breuer and

Fliess are articulated in the letter of August 7, 1901—a letter
singled out by the aged Freud as "very important" (Masson, p.
448) when, in 1937, he reviewed the uncannily resurfaced correspondence with Marie Bonaparte, and in which his estrangement from Fliess is definitively expressed.

If Freud's letters show the continuity between his ties with
Breuer and with Fliess, they also look ahead to the next major
male figure in his life—C. G. Jung. In the letter of April 26, 1904,
which attempted to renew contacts with Fliess, Freud included
the information that he had received "an absolutely stunning
recognition of my point of view" (Masson, p. 461) in a book
review by the Zurich psychiatrist Bleuler, director of the Burghölzli
clinic where Jung worked. Direct contacts between Freud and
Jung began in April 1906, when Jung sent Freud a copy of his
Diagnostic Association Studies, and in his dealings with Jung, Freud
exhibits the same pattern of initial idealization followed by bitter
disillusionment manifested toward Fliess. In the halcyon days, on
September 2, 1907, when he felt he had found in Jung his chosen
successor, Freud wrote of the difficulties he had faced in his earlier
years and "of the calm assurance that finally took possession of
me and bade me wait till a voice from the unknown answered
mine. That voice was yours" (*Letters,* p. 56). As with Freud's
eagerness to tell Fliess "in what class of men I place you," the
very certainty Freud expresses concerning Jung's perfect responsiveness contains the seeds of its own undoing, for in both cases
he is the victim of his "unconscious anticipatory ideas."

There can be no doubt that Freud's self-analysis following his
father's death in 1896, and culminating in the publication of *The
Interpretation of Dreams* in 1899, resulted in a taming of neurotic
elements in his personality. As Freud wrote to Fliess on March 2,
1899, "I am obviously much more normal than I was four or five
years ago" (*Origins,* p. 280). In 1901 Freud broke through a long-
standing inhibition and traveled to Rome for the first time; in 1902
he achieved a no less coveted and delayed goal in being appointed
Extraordinary Professor (i.e., Associate Professor) at the University
of Vienna. Freud reports the news of his appointment to Fliess in
a letter of March 11, 1902, which clearly marks his inner growth
as he decides to "bow to authority" (*Origins,* p. 344) and give up
his posture as permanent rebel in favor of joining the
establishment.

But though Freud did achieve a new integration in his personality after 1899, it is essential to recognize the extent to which
he continues to be governed by his "ideal situation of childhood."
After his second fainting spell involving Jung, as we have seen,
Freud in a letter to Ferenczi connected the attacks to the death of
Julius; and he wrote to Jones along similar lines: "There is some
piece of unruly homosexual feeling at the root of the matter" (*LW*,
1:317). At the time of his rupture with Adler and Stekel in 1910,
analogously, Freud confided to Ferenczi: "I had quite got over the
Fliess affair. Adler is a little Fliess come to life again. And his
appendage Stekel is at least called Wilhelm" (*LW*, 2:130). Freud's
claim that he had "got over the Fliess affair" is transparently
contradicted by his inability to view later experiences except in
terms of earlier prototypes.

Indeed, it might well be argued that the bondage of Freud's
transference neurosis becomes, not less, but more severe with the
passage of time. Part of his purpose in writing *Totem and Taboo*,
where Freud moves from the "wish" to the "deed" in describing
the killing of the father, was to hasten the expulsion of Jung from
the psychoanalytic movement. Thus, just as during his self-analysis ambivalence toward Fliess had been fused with that toward
the "father-figure," so in *Totem and Taboo*, despite having himself
become the "primal father" of psychoanalysis, Freud symbolically
acted out the murder of Jung as well as that of his own father.
Freud was abetted in the slaying by his loyal band of followers.
On March 25, 1914, Freud wrote to Abraham, enclosing a letter
from Jones, and enthusiastically detailed a plan to remove Jung
from his position as editor of the psychoanalytic *Jahrbuch:*

It is quite remarkable how each one of us is in turn seized with the
impulse to kill, so that the others have to restrain him. I suspect that
Jones himself will produce the next plan. The usefulness of cooperation
in the committee is very well illustrated by this.[14]

Like *The Interpretation of Dreams*, *Totem and Taboo* possesses a "further subjective significance" for Freud, and in addition to being a
contribution to psychoanalytic theory, must be read as "a portion
of my own self-analysis." Jung takes the place of Fliess as the
primary object of Freud's transference neurosis, simultaneously
"intimate friend" and "hated enemy," whom he must kill in
fantasy and toward whom he then experiences "the feeling of

self-reproach which a death generally leaves among the survivors."

I cannot insist too strongly that it does not invalidate psychoanalytic theory to draw attention to these patterns in Freud's life. On the contrary, the same genius that enabled him both to recover so many of his early memories and to understand theoretically the importance of infantile experience is what left Freud a lifelong prisoner of "the ideal situation of childhood." In *Beyond the Pleasure Principle* (1920), the work in which Freud elevated the repetition compulsion to the status of a theoretical postulate, he wrote of those "normal people" whose lives give the impression of "being pursued by a malignant fate or possessed by some 'daemonic' power":

Thus we have come across people all of whose human relationships have the same outcome: such as the benefactor who is abandoned in anger after a time by each of his *protégés*, however much they may otherwise differ from one another, and who thus seems doomed to taste all the bitterness of ingratitude; or the man whose friendships all end in betrayal by his friend; or the man who time after time in the course of his life raises someone else into a position of great private or public authority and then, after a certain interval, himself upsets that authority and replaces him by a new one. (*SE*, 18:22)

Each one of these ostensibly fictional sketches is transparently autobiographical, and there could be no more devastatingly accurate summary of the tragic fatality of Freud's life than his tripartite account of the "bitterness of ingratitude" tasted by the would-be "normal" man "all of whose human relationships have the same outcome."

The Eternal Triangle

In the same letter of October 3, 1897 in which he tells Fliess of the lasting effect of Julius and John on his subsequent friendships, Freud recounts a specific occurrence involving himself, John, and Pauline:

I have long known that my companion in crime between the ages of one and two was a nephew of mine who is a year older than I am and now lives in Manchester; he visited us in Vienna when I was fourteen. We seem occasionally to have treated my niece, who was a year younger, shockingly. (*Origins*, p. 219)

This same incident is described again in considerably more detail both in the autobiographical paper "Screen Memories" (1899) and in Freud's analysis of the *"non vixit"* dream in *The Interpretation of Dreams*. The link, both here and in the *"non vixit"* dream, between this particular memory and Freud's statement of the way he has continuously recreated his ambivalent relationship with John suggests that these occasions on which the two boys treated Pauline "shockingly" or "cruelly" *(grausam)* are a more complete version of the archetypal "ideal situation of childhood."

In the course of his analysis of the *"non vixit"* dream, Freud discloses the way that his anger at a present-day situation received reinforcement from infantile sources, and presents a reconstruction of the childhood scene that lies at the core of the dream:

For the purposes of dream-interpretation let us assume that a childhood memory arose, or was constructed in phantasy, with some such content as the following. The two children had a dispute about some object. . . . Each of them claimed to have *got there before the other* and therefore to have a better right to it. They came to blows and might prevailed over right. . . . However, this time I was the stronger and remained in possession of the field. The vanquished party hurried to his grandfather— my father—and complained about me, and I defended myself in the words which I know from my father's account: "I hit him 'cos he hit me." . . . From this point the dream-thoughts proceeded along some such lines as these: "It serves you right if you had to make way for me. Why did you try to push *me* out of the way? I don't need you, I can easily find someone else to play with," and so on. (*SE*, 5:483–84)

The "vanquished party" in this scene is evidently John, but Freud does not specify the "object" over which the two boys were contending. It may be inferred, however, that the dispute concerns Pauline, who, as a female coming between two males, is a substitute for the mother. In addition, Freud's concluding summary of his dream-thoughts—"Why did you try to push *me* out of the way?"—is one of the elements in the dream that point beyond

John to Freud's "ill wishes and real infantile jealousy" at the birth of Julius.[15] As the submerged figure underlying all Freud's revenants, Julius is known only through the effects of his absence—to Freud through his death, and to the reader through his excision from Freud's texts.

The importance of this primordial "childhood memory" of the struggle with John is that it shows the controlling structure of triangulation in Freud's experience. Although it involves in effect a sibling, and must be dated to the first three years of Freud's life—in "Screen Memories" it is said to take place a year later than in the letter to Fliess—the scene is wholly explicable in oedipal terms. The dispute between Freud and John is specifically over the question of priority, the claim by both boys "to have *got there before the other.*" Exactly this issue is at stake in the battle between Oedipus and Laius at the crossroads, which represent symbolically the genitals of the mother. The oedipal dimensions of this scene with John extend beyond the purely sexual sphere to evoke the controversies over intellectual priority and originality in which Freud became embroiled throughout his life.[16] When Freud proclaims that he was left "in possession of the field," his expression conflates the image of an actual rural meadow with the "field" of both intellectual and physical combat.

Freud's exultation at having been the "stronger," however, is combined with the rueful avowal that "might prevailed over right." The very moment of triumph is paradoxically also that of guilt and the formation of conscience. Thus, Freud's remorse on this occasion of his victory over John must be seen as the revival of his "germ of reproaches" at the fulfillment of his death wish against Julius. Even Freud's uncertainty as to the date of this memory—whether it took place between the ages of one and two or two and three—indicates the conflation of these two events.

Freud's ambivalence here likewise parallels the "close the eyes" dream, where the gesture of closing his father's eyes expresses both Freud's patricidal victory and his "inclination to self-reproach" at being the survivor. Many of the specific motifs of the "close the eyes" dream are repeated in the *"non vixit"* dream. The concern with arriving late at his father's funeral is echoed in the *"non vixit"* dream by a memory of having arrived late one day at the laboratory of his formidable mentor Ernst Brücke. The theme of vision is likewise reiterated in the *"non vixit"* dream, where Freud transforms his recollection of the "terrible blue eyes" by which he had been "reduced to nothing" by Brücke into a scene in which he himself "annihilated" a friend "with a look" (*SE*, 5:422). As Schur has pointed out, Freud's letter containing his interpretation of *Oedipus the King* occurs one year after, and the *"non vixit"* dream almost exactly two years after, the "close the eyes" dream; and the latter two events consequently constitute "anniversary reactions" to his father's death.[17]

If Freud's paradigmatic moment of triumph over John may be assimilated both to the death of Julius and that of his father, there is an essential continuity between preoedipal and oedipal dynamics in his personal experience. Freud recognizes this affinity in theoretical terms in *The Interpretation of Dreams*, where he first discusses "the child's death-wishes against his brothers and sisters" (*SE*, 4:255) before turning to the "dreams of the death of parents" (*SE*, 4:256) that furnish corroboration of the Oedipus complex. Too many commentators have mistakenly assumed that, because of his focus on the Oedipus complex, Freud neglected other aspects of familial conflict such as sibling rivalry or violence on the part of parents against children. Philip Rieff, for example, claims to have offered evidence of "the weakness in Freud's reconstruction of social origins" when he remarks that "the murder of the father is but one theme in the myth literature extant; the fratricide motif occurs quite as significantly as that of patricide."[18] But the reason Freud rightly gives priority to the Oedipus complex has to do with its grounding in the unconscious fantasy life of the child and not to a neglect of its permutations such as the "crime of Cain" or what might be called the "Laius complex." In the *"non vixit"* dream, Freud's justification for his retaliation against John—"I hit him 'cos he hit me"—has an exact counterpart in *Oedipus the King* in the fact that Oedipus kills Laius in self-defense. Oedipus declares that he struck back only after the old man in the carriage "on the middle / of my head came down with double prongs."[19] René Girard, who draws attention to this detail in the play, insists that "at the core of the Oedipus myth . . . is the proposition that all masculine relationships are based on reciprocal acts of violence,"[20] and Girard's concept of "reciprocal violence" certainly applies to the confrontation between Freud and John.

As in Freud's responses to the deaths of his brother and father, a crucial element in this memory concerning John is the fusion of the antithetical emotions of love and hatred. Although the antagonism between the two boys causes them to be "hated enemies," the element of identification in this triangular situation makes them into "intimate friends" as well. Beneath the manifest content of both the preoedipal and oedipal triangles, in other words, there is a latent homosexual bond between the male rivals. Jones has observed that the "erotic component" of Freud's relationship with John is "the first sign that Freud's sexual constitution was not exclusively masculine," since "to 'hunt in couples' means sharing one's sexual gratification with someone of the same sex" (*LW*, 1:11). And if Freud's relations with his male rivals are compounded of sexual desire as well as aggression, it follows that his feelings toward the female object are similarly ambivalent. That he and John behave with violence toward Pauline is made explicit in Freud's retelling of the incident in "Screen Memories":

Three children are playing in the grass. One of them is myself (between the age of two and three); the other two are my boy cousin, who is a year older than me, and his sister, who is almost exactly the same age as I am. We are picking the yellow flowers and each of us is holding a bunch of flowers we have already picked. The little girl has the best bunch; and, as though by mutual agreement, we—the two boys—fall on her and snatch away her flowers. (*SE*, 3:311)

Freud himself interprets the image of "snatching away flowers" from the girl as a symbolic defloration, but he might have added that this primordial sexual act is in effect a joint rape.

The aftereffects of Freud's tendency to form a homosexual alliance with a male counterpart at the expense of a woman who in some way is shared between them persist throughout his adult life. Clearly, the Emma Eckstein episode represents such a reenactment of the complete "ideal situation of childhood," with Fliess cast in the role of John and Emma as the victimized Pauline. (It is noteworthy in this connection that Fliess' daughter, born in 1898, was named Pauline.)[21] In his valedictory letter of August 7, 1901, Freud reproachfully informs Fliess, "I do not share your contempt for friendship between men, probably because I am to a high degree party to it. In my life, as you know, woman has never replaced the comrade, the friend" (Masson, p. 447). In view of the bearing of Freud's "not exclusively masculine" sexual orientation on his entire relationship with Fliess, it is fittingly ironic that their final quarrel in 1904 should have concerned intellectual priority to the theory of bisexuality.

An astonishing parallel to the Eckstein episode is supplied in Freud's later friendship with Jung by the story of Sabina Spielrein, which has recently come to public notice.[22] Spielrein, in brief, was a patient at the Burghölzli with whom Jung, her married physician, engaged in an affair, which he tried to claim was not improper because he was not being paid for his psychiatric services! Jung, whose duplicity throughout this scandal is awesome, did his best to conceal the facts of the matter from Freud; and when Spielrein sought to come speak to Freud in person, Freud loyally defended his Zurich colleague. Declaring in a letter of June 8, 1909 that he believed Jung "incapable of frivolous or ignoble behavior," Freud urged Spielrein to ask herself "whether the feelings that have outlived this close relationship are not best suppressed and eradicated, from your own psyche I mean, and without external intervention and the involvement of third persons" (*Symmetry*, p. 114). Freud's advice, in other words, as he wrote concomitantly to Jung, was to treat the problem as "something endopsychic" (*Symmetry*, p. 174), requiring psychological adjustment on Spielrein's part and not public chastisement of Jung. The effect of this counsel on Spielrein may be seen in a letter of June 13, 1909 in which she tells Freud that she had wanted to write to him again, "but I was warned against that by a dream in which I portrayed you as willing only to listen to your brother (that is how Dr. Jung is usually symbolized), not to me" (*Symmetry*, p. 102). Spielrein's dream is on the mark, for as in the Eckstein operation, Freud again does his best not to allow an "unworthy deed" by the latest revenant of John to color his opinion of him. Inevitably, however, as Freud grew increasingly critical of Jung's theoretical views he also took a less charitable attitude toward his conduct; and by May 8, 1913 he wrote to Spielrein, who became the author of several distinguished psychoanalytic papers, "I am glad that I am now as little responsible for his personal achievements as for his scientific ones" (*Symmetry*, p. 120).

An important connecting figure between Emma Eckstein and

Sabina Spielrein is Ida Bauer, best known as the Dora of Freud's *Fragment of an Analysis of a Case of Hysteria* (1905). As is true of the other two women, an essential issue in Freud's treatment of Dora is the conflict between her version of events and that insisted on by the male world about her. In Dora's case, the disputed event is a scene beside a lake, in which Dora claims she was propositioned by her father's friend Herr K. but which the two men attribute to her overstimulated imagination. Freud's role in the situation is quite ambiguous, for if in the course of the treatment he "came to the conclusion that Dora's history must correspond to the facts in every respect" (*SE*, 7:46), he nonetheless continued to emphasize Dora's psychic complicity in the sordid drama unfolding around her and to urge the adolescent girl that Herr K.'s scheme to cede his wife to Dora's father in exchange for her "would have been the only possible solution for all the parties concerned" (*SE*, 7:108). In this way, Freud fundamentally takes sides with the men who conspire to deny Dora's view of reality, and her decision to break off the analysis is an altogether comprehensible one.

If one aligns Dora, surrounded by her father and Herr K., with Sabina flanked by Jung and Freud, and with Emma in the hands of Fliess and Freud, and assimilates them all to Freud and John's "defloration" of Pauline in childhood, the cumulative effect is powerful and disturbing. Jane Gallop, following Luce Irigaray, has called attention to the "phallocentric pederastic economy" of psychoanalysis, in which "the girl is assimilated to a male model, male history and, 'naturally,' found lacking,"[23] and there is considerable justice to the indictment. On the other hand, however, to admit the culpable nature of the behavior of the men in question is not therefore to invalidate Freud's insights into the importance of unconscious fantasy. Dora, after all, may well have responded with repressed sexual excitement if she felt the pressure of Herr K.'s erect member against her body in an embrace prior to the scene at the lake, just as it is possible that Emma indeed had a proclivity to hysterical bleeding despite the horrors of the operation to which she was subjected. For, as Sabina Spielrein wrote in her diary on August 27, 1909, describing her embarrassed pleasure at washing exhibitionistically in front of a window. "If one wants to be completely honest—one must also be able to note things down which give a little insight into the psychology of so-called modest girls, to which category I also belong" (*Symmetry*, p. 4). Since, despite Jeffrey Masson's claims to the contrary, acceptance of the Oedipus complex does not entail a permanent turning away from the external world, perhaps feminist consciousness may be integrated with psychoanalytic theory.

It was not until 1923, as we have noted, that Freud in *The Ego and the Id* posited the existence of a "complete" Oedipus complex, and connected it to "the bisexuality originally present in children":

> a boy has not merely an ambivalent attitude towards his father and an affectionate object-choice towards his mother, but at the same time he also behaves like a girl and displays an affectionate feminine attitude to his father and a corresponding jealousy and hostility towards his mother. (*SE*, 19:33)

Once again, as with the repetition compulsion, it is clear that Freud's theoretical formulation elaborates through "deferred action" the awareness grounded in the experiential truth of his self-analysis. Because of the universal human tendency to bisexuality, Freud's "ideal situation of childhood" teaches us, sexual and aggressive impulses directed toward members of *both* sexes are inherent in the eternal triangle of the Oedipus complex.

In Hannibal's Footsteps

The figure of Oedipus stands at the center of Freud's "Conception of the Development of the Hero." His identification with Oedipus, however, is but one instance of a tendency to emulation that includes innumerable exemplars from history, literature, and myth. One other important object of identification for Freud was Hannibal. In analyzing a series of dreams concerned with his as yet unfulfilled longing to visit Rome, Freud in *The Interpretation of Dreams* describes the shattering impact of learning in his youth of an anti-Semitic attack on his father, and connects this experience to his admiration of the Carthaginian general:

At that point I was brought up against the event in my youth whose power was still being shown in all these emotions and dreams. I may have been ten or twelve years old, when my father began to take me with him on his walks and reveal to me in his talk his views upon things in the world we live in. Thus it was, on one such occasion, that he told me a story to show me how much better things were now than they had been in his days. "When I was a young man," he said, "I went for a walk in the streets of your birthplace; I was well dressed, and had a new fur cap on my head. A Christian came up to me and with a single blow knocked off my cap into the mud and shouted: 'Jew! get off the pavement!' " "And what did you do?" I asked. "I went into the roadway and picked up my cap," was his quiet reply. This struck me as unheroic conduct on the part of the big, strong man who was holding the little boy by the hand. I contrasted this situation with another which fitted my feelings better: the scene in which Hannibal's father, Hamilcar Barca, made his boy swear before the household altar to take vengeance on the Romans. Ever since that time Hannibal had had a place in my phantasies. (*SE*, 4:197)

This account is preoccupied, in the words of Freud's late paper "A Disturbance of Memory on the Acropolis" (1936), with the stirrings of "a child's criticism of his father, with the undervaluation which took the place of the overvaluation of earlier childhood" (*SE*, 22:247). The same tension between "overvaluation" and "undervaluation" reenacted in Freud's transference toward Fliess is distilled in this moving incident. The young Freud clearly reveres the occasions on which his "big, strong" father treated him as an equal and shared "his views upon things in the world we live in," yet his withering judgment of his father's humiliation is compressed in the single world "unheroic." His father's failure to measure up to heroic standards acts as a spur to his own ambitions and leads Freud to replace him in his imagination with the sterner ideal of Hamilcar Barca.

The most remarkable consequence of Freud's youthful identification with Hannibal is that it largely explains his later inhibitions about entering Rome. In "sadly turning back when I was only fifty miles from Rome," Freud writes, "I had actually been following in Hannibal's footsteps. Like him, I had been fated not to see Rome; and he too had moved into the Campagna when everyone had expected him in Rome" (*SE*, 4:196). Samuel Rosenberg has coined the useful term "reenactment syndrome" to describe Freud's tendency to respond to emotional crises by identifying, consciously or unconsciously, with a well-known personage; and on occasion, Rosenberg adds, he "went one giant step further and actually reenacted scenes, incidents, sometimes entire episodes from the lives of these real or fictional exemplars."[24] As Rosenberg summarizes the unconscious logic at work in Freud's imitation of Hannibal: "Because Hannibal *did not* enter Rome, Freud *could not.*"[25]

But as with the association between Freud's fate and that of Oedipus, his identification with Hannibal is composed of numerous "supplements." As a boy studying the history of the Punic Wars, Freud had sympathized not with the Romans but the Carthaginians, and become a partisan of the Semitic Hannibal. "To my youthful mind," Freud avows, "Hannibal and Rome symbolized the conflict between the tenacity of Jewry and the organization of the Catholic church" (*SE,* 4:196). Still earlier, Freud states, he had played with his "wooden soldiers" and affixed labels to them with the names of Napoleon's various marshals, among whom he preferred one of Jewish origin:

And at that time my declared favorite was already Masséna (or to give the name its Jewish form, Manasseh). (No doubt this preference was also partly to be explained by the fact that my birthday fell on the same day as his, exactly one hundred years later.) Napoleon himself lines up with Hannibal owing to their both having crossed the Alps. (*SE,* 4:197–98)

The coincidence between Freud's birthday and that of Masséna—a detail first recorded in the 1914 edition of *The Interpretation of Dreams*—underscores the role of chance in this series of identifications. In view of his preexisting admiration for Masséna and Napoleon, Freud's emulation of Hannibal thus becomes "a question of a transference of an already formed emotional relation on to a new object" (*SE,* 4:197).

Freud's final step backward into his childhood in analyzing his fascination with Hannibal brings together the themes of fraternal and filial rivalry and confirms the essential continuity between his preoedipal and oedipal experience. Having explored the connection between his father and Hannibal, Freud turns to his youthful quarrels with John, which we have already encountered in connection with the *"non vixit"* dream:

It may even be that the development of this martial ideal is traceable still further back into my childhood: to the times when, at the age of three, I was in a close relation, sometimes friendly but sometimes warlike, with a boy a year older than myself, and to the wishes which the relation must have stirred up in the weaker of us. (*SE*, 4:198)

Freud's ambivalence toward Fliess is a transference of his conflict between the "overvaluation" and "undervaluation" of his father, but that in turn is itself a transference of his "sometimes friendly but sometimes warlike" relations with John. The same "martial ideal," furthermore, figures in Freud's naming of his brother Alexander, with whom he claims in the "Acropolis" paper to have gone on weekly walks—an apparent confusion in memory, accompanied by a reversal of identities, of the excursions with his father mentioned in the Rome dreams.[26] Not only does this sequence of identifications show the interchangeability of Freud's unconscious crimes of Oedipus and Cain, but once again there is only "a supplement at the source."

Indeed, the regression into the past set in motion by Freud's retracing of his associations to Hannibal extends beyond his own early childhood to that of his father. Writing *The Interpretation of Dreams* in the last years of the nineteenth century, Freud thinks back to an event which occurred when he was "ten or twelve"— between 1866 and 1868—and which entails a comparison drawn by his father between that period and what he himself had experienced a generation earlier. Carl Schorske has sharpened our understanding of the political context of the various dates involved.[27] In 1895, the anti-Semitic demagogue Karl Lueger was elected mayor of Vienna, breaking the power of the progressive middle class. It was in 1867 that the new Liberal ministers were first elected in Austria—a watershed serving as the *terminus a quo* for the conversation between Freud and his father—thereby inaugurating an era in which even a young Jewish boy like Freud might entertain the hope of one day becoming a cabinet minister. The point of the anecdote told by Freud's father was precisely to contrast the current spirit of toleration with the anti-Semitic prejudice of bygone days. We may well suppose that the incident of the cap, to which Freud reacted with anger as though it had been his father's fault, represented a traumatic memory also for Jakob Freud, who hoped that his son might live to atone for it. Thus, in vowing "to take vengeance on the Romans," Freud was indirectly fulfilling his father's purpose in telling him the story and settling an old score that was as much cultural as personal. The need to look beyond Freud's individual history to the past of his father in explaining his identification with Hannibal receives a theoretical commentary in the *New Introductory Lectures on Psycho-Analysis* (1933), where Freud observes that parents "follow the precepts of their own super-egos in educating their children," and hence "a child's super-ego is in fact constructed not on the model of its parents but of its parents' super-ego" (*SE*, 22:67).

There is a memorable epilogue to the anti-Semitic attack on Freud's father contained in the memoir of Freud's eldest son, Martin. In the summer of 1901, the Freud family was vacationing in the Alpine village of Thumsee. On one occasion, Martin and his brother Ernst were subjected to anti-Semitic abuse while fishing, which they subsequently reported to their father. Freud, Martin related, "became very serious for a few moments, remarking that kind of thing could happen to us again, and that we should be prepared for it." Later that same day, the two boys had rowed their father across a lake, when they were met by the same hostile crowd as had insulted the boys earlier. Martin continues:

> Father, without the slightest hesitation, jumped out of the boat, and keeping to the middle of the road, marched towards the hostile crowd. When he saw me following him, he commanded me in so angry a voice to stay where I was that I dared not disobey. . . .
>
> In the meantime, father, swinging his stick, charged the hostile crowd, which gave way before him and promptly dispersed, allowing him a free passage. This was the last we saw of these unpleasant strangers. We never found out from where they came nor what their object had been in waylaying father.
>
> This unpleasant incident made a deep impression on me. . . . But there is no evidence that father was affected in the least. He never recalled the incident at home, and I am not aware that he ever mentioned it in any of his letters to our family or friends.[28]

Although Martin does not draw the connection between this episode of his own youth and that involving Freud and his father, there can be no doubt that Freud reacted to the latter as a repetition of the former, and that, by "taking vengeance on the Romans," he was determined to redeem in the eyes of his sons the "unheroic conduct" of his father. The "deep impression" left on Martin by his father's action parallels that left on Freud by his father's humiliation. It is one of the ironies of familial dynamics that failure on the part of the father often seems to be a precondition for greatness in the son, while the triumph of the father relegates the son to no more than "glory reflected" (the British title of Martin's memoir). As George Mahl suggests, "it could not have been an accident" that this reversal and undoing of the trauma suffered by his father enabled Freud to break the spell of his identification with Hannibal, and that—accompanied by Alexander—he "went to Rome for the first time soon afterward."[29]

In 1938, the Nazis invaded Austria, and the fate of Freud and his family hung in doubt for a time. (His four surviving elderly sisters were in fact killed in concentration camps.) There was one agonizing day when his daughter, Anna, was interrogated at Gestapo headquarters. Through international pressure Freud and his family gained permission to emigrate to England. But before leaving Vienna, he was required to sign a document that affirmed he had "not the slightest reason for any complaint" against the Gestapo. To this affidavit Freud affixed his own ironic postscript: "I can heartily recommend the Gestapo to anyone" (*LW,* 3:226). Freud's adherence to his "martial ideal" takes a quieter form in the next-to-last year of his life than when, in 1901, he single-handedly "charged the hostile crowd" at Thumsee. But who can doubt that his courage is the same in both instances, or that it reaches back, beyond the memory of his walk with his father, to his "sometimes friendly but sometimes warlike" relations with John in early childhood?

Delusions of Inferiority and Megalomania

From the beginning, Freud's relations with other males were compounded of intense ambivalance, with the result that "friend and enemy" regularly came together in a "single individual." But if Freud's attitudes toward men entail an endless series of transferences, all these "re-incarnations" of John must likewise be doubles of himself. The tension between "overvaluation" and "under-valuation" in Freud's appraisal of both his father and Fliess, in other words, reflects a contradiction in his own self-esteem. As Freud writes to Fliess on October 8, 1895, in the course of his work he feels "alternately proud and happy and abashed and miserable" (*Origins*, p. 126). On the one hand, Freud aspired to regard his life in heroic terms, but on the other he criticized himself with reproaches no less unsparing than those he directed at anyone else.

The fluctuations in Freud's opinion of himself are given vivid expression in his "open-air closet" dream, the contents of which may be savored in their entirety:

> A hill, on which there was something like an open-air closet: a very long seat with a large hole at the end of it. Its back edge was thickly covered with small heaps of faeces of all sizes and degrees of freshness. There were bushes behind the seat. I micturated on the seat; a long stream of urine washed everything clean; the lumps of faeces came away easily and fell into the opening. It was as though at the end there was still something left. (*SE*, 5:468–69)

In his associations to this dream—dating from July or August 1898—Freud tries to account for his lack of disgust at its scatological themes. In doing so, he identifies himself with three literary heroes:

> What at once occurred to me in the analysis were the Augean stables which were cleansed by Hercules. This Hercules was I. . . . The stream of urine which washed everything clean was an unmistakable sign of greatness. It was in this way that Gulliver extinguished the great fire in Lilliput—though incidentally this brought him into disfavor with its tiny queen. But Gargantua, too, Rabelais' superman, revenged himself in the same way on the Parisians by sitting astride Notre Dame and turning his stream of urine upon the city. It was only on the previous evening before going to sleep that I had been turning over Garnier's illustrations to Rabelais. And, strangely enough, here was another piece of evidence that I was the superman. The platform of Notre Dame was my favorite resort in Paris. (*SE*, 5:469)

Freud's unabashed comparison of himself to Hercules, Gulliver, and Gargantua shows the compulsive nature of his "reenactment syndrome." The residual effect of this dream is still to be seen in

Civilization and Its Discontents (1930), where Freud comments in a footnote on the "connection between ambition, fire, and urethral erotism": "Putting out fire by micturating—a theme to which modern giants, Gulliver in Lilliput and Rabelais' Gargantua, still hark back—was therefore a kind of sexual act with a male, an enjoyment of sexual potency in a homosexual competition" (*SE*, 21:90). Once more, Freud's conjectures concerning fire must be seen as a theoretical elaboration of personal experiences in his self-analysis.

The cleansing of the Augean stables is for Freud evidently a metaphor for his heroic task as founder of psychoanalysis. But though he interprets his hygienic urination as "an unmistakable sign of greatness," and asserts through his threefold identification that he "was the superman," an opposing current of feeling also emerges in the dream. Freud specifies as "the true exciting cause of the dream" an incident which had occurred the previous day. It had been "a hot summer afternoon," and that evening Freud had delivered a lecture on hysteria with which he remained extremely dissatisfied. "I was tired and felt no trace of enjoyment in my difficult work," he writes. "I longed to be away from all this grubbing about in human dirt and to be able to join my children and afterwards visit the beauties of Italy" (*SE*, 5:470). In this unpropitious mood he retired to an open-air cafe, only to have his hopes for tranquility shattered by a member of his audience:

One of my audience, however, went with me and he begged leave to sit by me while I drank my coffee and choked over my crescent roll. He began to flatter me: telling me how much he had learnt from me, how he had looked at everything with fresh eyes, how I had cleaned the *Augean stables* of errors and prejudices in my theory of the neuroses. He told me, in short, that I was a very great man. My mood ill-fitted with this paean of praise; I fought against my feeling of disgust, went home early to escape from him, and before going to sleep turned over the pages of Rabelais. (*SE*, 5:470)

The motive of the "open-air closet" dream is to fulfill the wish to be "a very great man," but when Freud is actually told that he has "cleaned the *Augean stables* of errors" he reacts with a violent "feeling of disgust." As in the medallion incident, and above all in the death of Julius, Freud's emotional agitation shows him to be "wrecked by success" upon being confronted by the fulfillment of his "deeply-rooted and long-cherished" fantasy.

The shadowy figure who approaches Freud in the cafe takes on the uncanny quality of a double, as though he were the projection of Freud's unconscious mind. As he admits, the "mood of revulsion and disgust" with which he received this homage to his greatness was replaced at night by "a mood of powerful and even exaggerated self-assertiveness" (*SE*, 5:470). The dynamics here resemble the sixteen-year-old Freud's disclaimer to Fluss that the secret of his career change was "altogether too insignificant," when it doubtless carried for him a burden of excess importance. Like a neurotic symptom, the "open-air closet" dream is an exemplary compromise formation, and Freud explains the lack of affect accompanying the dream as the result of the "mutual inhibition" of his conflicting self-appraisals:

The content of the dream had to find a form which would enable it to express both the delusions of inferiority and the megalomania in the same material. The compromise between them produced an ambiguous dream-content; but it also resulted in an indifferent feeling-tone owing to the mutual inhibition of these contrary impulses. (*SE*, 5:470)

The stalemate between Freud's "delusions of inferiority" and "megalomania" is a self-directed equivalent of his "constant oscillations" between feelings of love and hatred for all the revenants of John. Freud's emphasis on the "exaggerated" nature of his emotional swings corresponds to the "unconscious anticipatory ideas" controlling his transferential relationships from Silberstein to Jung.

The ambivalence in Freud's attitude toward his "pathological ambition" (*SE*, 4:194) receives a special fillip from the fact of his Jewishness. Freud's identification with classical heroes such as Oedipus, Hannibal, and Hercules is blended with particularly Jewish concerns in two of his dreams concerned with his longing to visit Rome. In one, Freud imagines that "someone led me to the top of a hill and showed me Rome half-shrouded in mist," to which he naturally associates the idea of "the promised land seen from afar" (*SE*, 4:194). Freud's entire career extends between the poles of his identifications with Oedipus and Moses—the primal examples of sonship and fatherhood—but this dream shows these poles to be collapsed from the outset.[30] The heroic quality of Freud's comparison of himself to Moses is balanced by a second dream, however, in which he equates his failure to arrive at Rome with the unceremonious treatment accorded the "impecunious

Jew" (*SE*, 4:195) who was constantly being thrown off the train for traveling to Karlsbad without a ticket. Thus, as Schorske has observed, "the lofty vision of Moses-Freud seeing Israel-Rome 'from afar' has its lowly analogue in the picture of the little-Jew-Christ-Freud reaching Karlsbad-Rome on a *via dolorosa.*"[31]

Such a conflict between "delusions of inferiority" and "megalomania" is doubtless to be found in some form in all human beings. What distinguishes Freud's version of this ambivalence is simply its intensity, the literalness with which he lives out his anxieties about being "a very great man." Freud introduces all four of his Rome dreams, the last of which gives rise to the discussion of the incident of his father's cap, to illustrate the way *"we find the child and the child's impulses still living on in the dream"* (*SE*, 4:191). In this context, he cites two omens of his heroic destiny that have continued to play a part in his fantasies. "At the time of my birth," he writes, "an old peasant-woman had prophesied to my proud mother that with her first-born son she had brought a great man into the world." Being a principled skeptic, Freud naturally discounts the significance of such attempts to foretell the future: "Prophecies of this kind must have been very common. . . . Nor can the prophetess have lost anything by her words" (*SE*, 4:192). But Freud immediately goes on to recollect a second omen, the prediction delivered some twelve years later by an itinerant poet that he would grow up to become a government minister, which had initially prompted him to pursue a career in law.

The remarkable thing about these events is not that they occurred, but that they left so profound an impression on Freud's memory. Ironically, despite his professions of skepticism, Freud's "Conception of the Development of the Hero" in the end vindicated all the prophecies of his greatness, thereby seeming to endow them with oracular power and to invest his life with the inevitability of a myth. Jones' statement that Freud's "hero's garb was in the weaving at the cradle itself," which I have extrapolated to refer to his family constellation, alludes specifically both to the prophecy of the "old peasant-woman" and to the fact that, like David Copperfield, the hero of his favorite novel by Dickens, Freud was "born in a caul, an event which was believed to ensure him future happiness and fame" (*LW*, 1:4). And if, in the course of his lifetime, the man predestined to heroism oscillates between "delusions of inferiority" and "megalomania," he only reinforces his identification with Oedipus, who is both "famous in the eyes of all" (l. 8) and "even to the gods / the most hateful of mortals" (ll. 1345–46).

Interminable Self-Analysis

The text of the "open-air closet" dream concludes with the remark, "It was as though at the end there was still something left." Freud's acknowledgment of the impossibility of getting completely rid of "human dirt" serves as an emblem of the inherent interminability of the analytic process. Freud, as we have seen, recognized belatedly that *The Interpretation of Dreams* formed "a portion of my own self-analysis," and the relation of *The Psychopathology of Everyday Life* to *The Interpretation of Dreams* shows that this statement holds true for the rest of his writings as well. For in the *Psychopathology* Freud not only extended his theoretical model of the mind from the private and noctural sphere of dreams to the daylight realm of social experience, as he did also in *Jokes and Their Relation to the Unconscious* (1905), but he did so in part through psychoanalytic elucidation of a number of errors he committed in *The Interpretation of Dreams.* Each of the three slips he draws attention to, moreover, has to do with criticism of his father and the "tangling-up of the family sequence."

One of these stems from his allusions to Hannibal. In the first edition of *The Interpretation of Dreams,* Freud noticed with chagrin, he had incorrectly identified Hannibal's father, not as Hamilcar Barca, but as Hasdrubal, who was in fact Hannibal's brother. As Freud's analysis in the *Psychopathology* made clear, this slip expressed his unconscious wish to be the son of his half-brother Emmanuel instead of his father:

The error of putting *Hasdrubal* instead of *Hamilcar,* the brother's name instead of the father's, occurred precisely in a context that concerned the Hannibal-phantasies of my school-years and my dissatisfaction with my father's behaviour towards the "enemies of our people." I could have gone on to tell how my relationship with my father was changed by a visit to England, which resulted in my getting to know my half-brother, the eldest son of my father's first marriage, who lived there. My brother's eldest son is the same age as I am. Thus the relations between our ages were no hindrance to my phantasies of how different things would have been if I had been born the son not of my father but of my brother. These suppressed phantasies falsified the text of my book at the place where I broke off the analysis, by forcing me to put the brother's name for the father's. (*SE,* 6:219–20)

Freud's conflation of the roles of son and brother, derived from the circumstances of his family constellation and evident in the complications of his identification with Hannibal, here takes the form of replacing his father with the more forceful Emmanuel. Alluding to Goethe's aphorism concerning Lichtenberg— "Where he makes a jest a problem lies concealed"—Freud formulates a general law of parapraxis: "where an error makes its appearance a repression lies behind it—or more correctly, an insincerity, a distortion, which is ultimately rooted in repressed material" (*SE,* 6:218). In this instance, because Freud was guilty of "insincerity" in not revealing his "suppressed phantasies," his unconscious exacted punishment by causing him to falsify "the text of my book at the place where I broke off the analysis."

Of the two other mistakes in *The Interpretation of Dreams* corrected in *The Psychopathology of Everyday Life,* one occurs in the section on "Typical Dreams" shortly before his commentary on *Oedipus the King* and *Hamlet.* As support for his views of the often antagonistic relations between fathers and sons, Freud appeals to the legend that "Kronos devoured his children, . . . while Zeus emasculated his father and made himself ruler in his place" (*SE,* 4:256). In the *Psychopathology,* however, Freud emends this to say that it was actually Kronos who castrated his father Uranus, and therefore in his previous statement he was "erroneously carrying this atrocity a generation forward" (*SE,* 6:218). Like the confusion of Hasdrubal and Hamilcar, this parapraxis is attributed by Freud to "the influence of the memory" (*SE,* 6:220) of Emmanuel, who warned him that he really belonged "not to the second generation but to the third generation in relation to your father." The third slip in *The Interpretation of Dreams* involves Freud's mistaken designation of Schiller's birthplace as Marburg instead of Marbach. This mistake, Freud explains, has to do with an interrupted train of thought "which would have contained an unfriendly criticism of my father" (*SE*, 6:219). Like the preceding two slips, this example is significant both because of its content and its context, for it is found in his analysis of the "Hollthurn" dream, whose importance to the discovery of the Oedipus complex we have yet to consider.

But perhaps the most intriguing mistake arising from the "tangling-up of the family sequence" is silently corrected by Freud in *The Interpretation of Dreams* and left unmentioned in *The Psychopathology of Everyday Life*. In the letter to Fliess of October 15, 1897, in which he first links *Oedipus the King* to *Hamlet*, Freud asks why it should be that Hamlet delays in avenging the killing of his father "when he himself so casually sends his courtiers to their death and despatches Laertes so quickly" (*Origins*, p. 224). A comparison of the parallel passage in *The Interpretation of Dreams*, where Freud refers to the way that Hamlet unhesitatingly "runs his sword through the eavesdropper behind the arras" (*SE*, 4:265), shows that in the earlier letter he has confused the brother figure, Laertes, with the father figure, Polonius.[32] In addition to documenting Freud's oedipal guilt for the death of his father, this distorted recollection of *Hamlet* attests to the continued impact of the death of Julius and to the conflation of the identities of son and brother in Freud's mind.

Looking back at *The Interpretation of Dreams*, Freud asks himself in *The Psychopathology of Everyday Life*: "How did I pass over these errors while I carefully went through three sets of proofs—as if I had been struck blind?" (*SE*, 6:218). Freud's metaphor of blindness points directly to the mechanism of repression at work in his failures of memory. No work of analysis is ever complete, because repression continues to manifest itself in the process of interpretation. Freud interprets the meanings of his dreams, but these interpretations, always incomplete, give rise to mistakes which must themselves be interpreted. And if Freud corrects these mistakes in *The Psychopathology of Everyday Life*, these corrections will likewise be incomplete, erroneous, and in need of further interpretation. This fundamental truth of psychoanalytic experience is articulated from the standpoint of hermeneutic philosophy by Hans-Georg Gadamer: "We are always within the situation, and to throw light on it is never entirely completed. . . . To exist historically means that knowledge of oneself can never be complete."[33]

The lesson that a position of complete mastery is unattainable is not one that Freud learned very well. As Jung bitterly reminded him in a letter of December 3, 1912 at the time of their rupture, during their trip to America in 1909 Freud had refused to continue with the analysis of his dreams "with your remark that 'you could not submit to analysis *without losing your authority.*' " Jung, who had received recent confirmation of Freud's continuing neurosis in his second fainting spell, added a further twist of the knife with the observation that Freud had begun *The Interpretation of Dreams,* in the dream of "Irma's injection," with the "mournful admission" of his "identification with the neurotic in need of treatment" (*F/J*, p. 526). On December 18, 1912 Jung wrote, "You know, of course, how far a patient gets with self-analysis: *not* out of his neurosis—just like you" (*F/J*, p. 535).

Jung's comments to Freud are not distinguished by either generosity or self-knowledge. In the latter letter, for example, he makes the preposterous assertion, "I am not in the least neurotic" (*F/J*, p. 535). But Jung's own embarrassing lapses do not invalidate the fundamental justice of his critique of Freud. Just as there is "something left" at the end of Freud's micturation in the "open-air closet" dream, so there always remains a residue of neurosis that continues to require—and defy—analysis. In *The Future of an Illusion* (1927), Freud holds out the possibility of an escape from neurosis. Those individuals who have been "sensibly brought up" and who "do not suffer from the neurosis" of religion, he maintains, will be able to accept that "they can no longer be the centre of creation":

They will be in the same position as a child who has left the parental home where he was so warm and comfortable. But surely infantilism is destined to be surmounted. Men cannot remain children forever. . . . We may call this *"education to reality."* (*SE,* 21:49)

Freud's evocation of a possible "education to reality" is stirring, but surely it is rather the somber lesson of psychoanalysis—exemplified in his own personal history—that a child never completely leaves the parental home, that infantilism is destined never to be fully surmounted, and that people unconsciously remain children forever.

Perhaps the most moving document in the correspondence between Freud and Jung is a letter from Jung's wife, Emma, to Freud on November 6, 1911. In it, speaking of Freud's children, she observes, "One certainly cannot be the child of a great man with impunity, considering the trouble one has in getting away from ordinary fathers," and presciently adds with reference to her husband: "And do not think of Carl with a father's feeling: 'He will grow, but I must dwindle,' but rather as one human being thinks of another, who like you has his own law to fulfill" (*F/J*, pp. 456–57). It is, ultimately, Freud's inability to regard Jung and others except with a "father's feeling"—except, that is, through the distorting mirror of his own infantile conflicts and transferences—that makes of the "education to reality" no more than eternally receding, theoretical ideal. But if Freud, who knew himself with an honesty that few have equalled, could not achieve an undistorted scientific *Weltanschauung,* who among us has escaped from bondage to the repetition compulsion? It is the persistent human tendency to make the same mistakes over and over again that renders interminable his—and our—self-analysis.

3
In
My Own Case
Too

Familiar Strangers

FREUD'S DISCOVERY of the Oedipus complex is the culminating moment in his self-analysis. Yet, as we have noted, his statement that he has found "love of the mother and jealousy of the father *in my own case too*" suggests that Freud is confirming in himself a finding from his clinical practice. Our concern in this chapter will be with two specific patients who play a decisive role in Freud's arrival at his most momentous breakthrough.[1]

The intertwining of his self-analysis with his therapeutic work is a recurrent theme in Freud's letters to Fliess. He writes on November 14, 1897:

My self-analysis is still interrupted. I have now seen why. I can only analyze myself with objectively acquired knowledge (as if I were a stranger); self-analysis is really impossible, otherwise there would be no illness. As I have come across some puzzles in my cases, it is bound to hold up the self-analysis. (*Origins*, pp. 234–35; translation modified)[2]

Freud here makes explicit the parallel between his progress in the treatment of others and of himself, and his admission that "self-analysis is really impossible" strikingly anticipates Jung's reproaches on the subject fifteen years later. But the most far-reaching implication of his recognition that he can only analyze himself "with objectively acquired knowledge," by becoming a "stranger" to himself, is the collapse of the distinction between self and other in self-analysis. Like Oedipus, who believes himself to be a stranger to Thebes, but discovers himself to be the native son of Laius and Jocasta, Freud can only uncover his most intimate secrets by a process of self-alienation. This conflation of the opposition between the "strange" and the "familiar," experienced by both Freud and Oedipus in the course of their self-analyses, receives a theoretical commentary in "The 'Uncanny' " (1919).

A second remarkable leitmotif of the letters to Fliess is the manner in which Freud seems intuitively to anticipate his own insights. This phenomenon becomes particularly insistent in the crucial months of 1897 surrounding his first formulation of the Oedipus complex. In the same letter of November 14 in which he refers to the interruption of his self-analysis, Freud comments on the way that his understanding of repression came and went beyond his conscious control: "Truth to tell, it was not entirely new; it had repeatedly shown and then withdrawn itself again; but this time it remained and saw the light of day. In a strange way I am aware of these events some time in advance" (*Origins*, pp. 230–31). Enclosing Draft N, Freud writes in his letter of May 31, 1897: "Another presentiment tells me, as if I knew already— though I do not know anything at all—that I am about to discover the source of morality" (*Origins*, p. 206). In Draft N itself, without mentioning the name of Oedipus, Freud conveys to Fliess the substance of his impending realization of the "source of morality":

> Hostile impulses against parents (a wish that they should die) are also an integral part of neuroses. . . . They are repressed at periods in which pity for one's parents is active—at times of their illness or death. One of the manifestations of grief is then to reproach oneself for their death. . . . It seems as though in sons this death-wish is directed against their father and in daughters against their mother. (*Origins*, p. 207)

Freud's awareness "in advance" of his discoveries is the obverse of the workings of "deferred action" in the unfolding of psychoanalytic theory. His paradoxical assertion that he both "knows already" and "does not know anything at all" exactly duplicates

Oedipus' "blindness of the seeing eye," and both heroes of self-knowledge find themselves in that "strange state of mind in which one knows and does not know a thing at the same time."

Both the symbiotic relation between Freud's self-analysis and his clinical work and his susceptibility to "presentiments" are in evidence in his letter to Fliess of October 31, 1895, where his two key patients are introduced for the first time:

The end of the year has got to see the end of my "bashful" case, who developed hysteria in youth and later delusions of observation, and whose almost transparent history has got to clear up certain doubtful points for me. Another man (who dares not go out into the street because of homicidal tendencies) has got to help me solve another riddle. (*Origins*, p. 131)

That Freud should speak of "solving another riddle" with the help of the patient with "homicidal tendencies" is particularly appropriate, because it is this man who will spur Freud to his discovery of the Oedipus complex. With his "bashful" case, conversely, Freud will seek to obtain confirmation of his theory of infantile sexual seduction, which leads to an attempt to verify the reality of certain "primal scenes." In complementary ways, both patients serve as pivotal doubles or alter egos of Freud.

It is appropriate that these two patients should be introduced together, because both are so deeply involved in the fate of Freud's self-analysis. But whereas Freud's "bashful" case (who is known as "E." in both *The Origins of Psychoanalysis* and the edition of Jeffrey Masson) is mentioned repeatedly throughout the letters to Fliess,[3] I am able to find no other unmistakable reference to the man "who dares not go out into the street," though he does figure prominently in *The Interpretation of Dreams* and *The Psychopathology of Everyday Life*.

Freud's treatment of E. extends from 1895 to 1900 when, Freud wrote to Fliess on April 16, he "at last concluded his career as a patient by coming to supper in my house" (*Origins*, p. 317). This five-year period coincides with that in which Freud was engaged in his most intensive self-scrutiny, and the temporal parallel between Freud's own analysis and his analysis of E. is reinforced by the uncanny resemblances between their personal histories.[4] Freud writes to Fliess on January 3, 1897:

Everything now points more and more to the first three years of life. This year I have had no further news of my patient with obsessional neurosis, whom I treated only for seven months. Yesterday I heard from [Mrs.] F. . . . that he went back to his birthplace to check the genuineness of his memories for himself, and that he got the fullest confirmation from his seducer, who is still alive (she was his nurse, now an old woman). He is said to be feeling very well; he is obviously using this improvement to avoid a radical cure. (*Origins*, p. 183)

It must be said that this passage is slightly confusing, and from the phrase "my patient with obsessional neurosis" it might seem that Freud is referring, not to E., but to the inhibited man with "homicidal tendencies," since the latter is characterized as an obsessional neurotic in *The Interpretation of Dreams* (*SE*, 4:260). But because we know from other letters of the prominent role played in E.'s history by his nurse, it may be surmised that it is he of whom Freud is speaking also in this instance.

The part played by the nurse in his childhood, moreover, closely links E. to Freud. For in his memory-laden letter to Fliess of October 3, 1897, Freud discloses that he too was seduced by his nurse in infancy:

I can only say that in my case my father played no active role, though I certainly projected on to him an analogy from myself; that my "primary originator" [of neurosis] was an ugly, elderly but clever woman who told me a great deal about God and hell, and gave me a high opinion of my own capabilities. (*Origins*, p. 219)

Here, even as he anticipates the discovery of the Oedipus complex by shifting responsibility for sexual arousal away from his father on to his own fantasies, Freud simultaneously indicts his nurse as his "primary originator" of neurosis. What is more, just as E. returned to his birthplace to verify the accuracy of his memories, so Freud sought from his mother confirmation of what he remembered concerning his nurse. Freud resembles E., that is, not only in having been seduced by his nurse but also in the process by which he obtains empirical corroboration for a reconstruction arrived at in the course of analytic work.

Freud's nurse, apparently named Monika Zajíc, remains a shadowy figure even for scholars of psychoanalysis.[5] But in addition to having been arrested for petty theft, as Freud learned from his mother (*Origins*, pp. 221–22), she seems in all probability to have initiated him into the practice of masturbation. Freud adds in a postscript to the letter of October 3 on the following day: "She was my instructress in sexual matters, and chided me for being clumsy and not being able to do anything" (*Origins*, p. 220). He writes in *Three Essays on the Theory of Sexuality* (1905): "It is well known that unscrupulous nurses put crying children to sleep by stroking their genitals" (*SE*, 7:180), and Marianne Krüll has convincingly speculated that Freud was himself pacified in this way, and then "punished with castration threats when he tried to recapture the pleasant sensation his nursemaid had first awakened in him by resorting to masturbation."[6]

The theme of masturbation forms a further specific analogy between the histories of Freud and E. In a letter of February 19, 1899, Freud tells Fliess how his "bashful" patient received his moniker:

> Do you know why our friend E. turns red and sweats whenever he sees a certain class of acquaintances, particularly at the play? He is ashamed, no doubt, but of what? Of a phantasy in which he figures as the "deflowerer" of every person he comes across. He sweats as he deflowers, because it is hard work. (*Origins*, p. 278)

Upon reading this passage, we are inevitably reminded of Freud's own "defloration" fantasy—involving himself, John, and Pauline in a dandelion meadow—in "Screen Memories." The parallels become more detailed the more closely we examine the two accounts. Freud's letter to Fliess continues by recounting the thoughts that run through E.'s mind whenever he is made to feel ashamed in a woman's presence: " 'Now the silly idiot thinks she has made me feel ashamed. If I had her in bed she'd soon see whether I felt embarrassed in front of her!' " (*Origins*, p. 278). In "Screen Memories" Freud comments on the contrast between the "boldness" of his own fantasy of defloration and the "bashfulness" and "indifference" of his actual conduct with women, and imagines himself as an eager bridegroom: " 'The most seductive part of the whole subject for a young scapegrace is the picture of the marriage night. (What does he care about what comes afterwards?)' " (*SE*, 3:316).

The fantasy recounted by Freud in "Screen Memories" is an intricate palimpsest of layers, ranging from his early childhood to his adult courtship of Martha Bernays, including specific references to adolescent visits both to his birthplace of Freiberg, where he became infatuated with Gisela Fluss (and her mother), and to Manchester, where he renewed his acquaintance with John and Pauline.[7] For our purposes, the most important component is the infantile one; and in addition to the three children, there appear in the scene "a peasant-woman with a handkerchief on her head and a children's nurse" (*SE*, 3:311). After the two boys "snatch away her flowers," Pauline runs in tears to the peasant woman, who as a consolation "gives her a big piece of black bread." John and Sigmund then discard their flowers and also ask to be given some bread; the peasant woman obliges. Freud specifies that she "cuts the loaf with a long knife."

This last detail makes it clear that the scene includes the recollection of a threat of castration—a threat which presumably came to seem real to Freud after the discovery of sexual differentiation through seeing Pauline's genitals.[8] The peasant woman holding the knife is conflated with his nurse, who both seduced him and reprimanded him for engaging in masturbation. Freud's thoughts in "Screen Memories" move easily from defloration to masturbation, since the paper ends with his interpretation of what purports to be another man's memory of "breaking off a branch of a tree" in childhood as an allusion to the German expression "to pull one out," a "very common vulgar term for masturbation" (*SE*, 3:319). The personal element of Freud's concern with masturbation is rendered unmistakable by the connection between "Screen Memories" and his March 1898 dream of the "botanical monograph," the account of which in *The Interpretation of Dreams* includes the following passage:

It had once amused my father to hand over a book with *coloured plates* . . . for me and my eldest sister to destroy. Not easy to justify from an educational point of view! I had been five years old at the time and my sister not yet three; and the picture of us blissfully pulling the book to pieces (leaf by leaf, like an *artichoke*, I found myself saying) was almost the only plastic memory I retained from that period of my life. . . . I had become a *book-worm*. I had always, from the time I first began to think about myself, referred this first passion of mine back to the childhood memory I have mentioned. Or rather, I had recognized that the childhood scene was a "screen memory" for my later bibliophile propensities. (*SE*, 4:172–73)

As various commentators have pointed out, Freud's explicit reference to his "Screen Memories" paper (cited in a footnote) reinforces the homology between the two scenes of play with a
younger female relative, in the later of which the description of
"pulling to pieces" a book—metaphorically, an "artichoke" or
flower—"leaf by leaf" is again a veiled allusion to masturbation.[9]

But though the internal links between "Screen Memories"
and the "botanical monograph" dream have often been recognized, it has not been noted how strikingly Freud's autobiographical reminiscences converge with those of E. In the letter of February 19, 1899, Freud elaborates more fully on his patient's
history:

> Moreover, he can never get over the fact that at the University he failed
> to get through in botany; so he carries on with it now as a "deflowerer."
> . . . And why was it that at Interlaken, when he was fourteen, he mas-
> turbated in such a peculiar attitude in the W.C.? It was so that he could
> get a good view of the Jungfrau [literally "maiden"]; since then he has
> never caught sight of another—or at all events not of her genitals.
> (*Origins*, p. 278)

Here are the themes both of masturbation and of beholding the
female genitals, also found in "Screen Memories." Even the relation between E.'s defloration fantasies and his failure in botany
at the university has a counterpart in Freud, who admits during
his analysis of the "botanical monograph" dream: "I never had a
specially intimate contact with botany. In my preliminary examination in botany I was also given a Crucifer to identify—and
failed to do so" (*SE*, 4:171).

The parallels between the histories of Freud and E. proceed
in tandem with the progress in their respective analyses. The
affinities come to a head in Freud's letter to Fliess of December
21, 1899:

> You remember (among the absurd dreams) my dream which so daringly
> promised an end of E.'s treatment, and you can imagine how important
> this one continuing patient has become to me. Well, the dream now
> seems to be coming true. . . . Buried deep beneath all his phantasies we
> found a scene from his primal period (before twenty-two months) which
> meets all the requirements and into which all the surviving puzzles flow.
> It is everything at the same time—sexual, innocent, natural, etc. I can
> hardly bring myself to believe it yet. It is as if Schliemann had dug up

another Troy which had hitherto been believed to be mythical. Also the fellow is feeling shamelessly well. He has demonstrated the truth of my theories in my own person, for with a surprising turn [in his analysis] he provided me with the solution of my own railway phobia (which I had overlooked). . . . My phobia, if you please, was a poverty, or rather a hunger phobia, arising out of infantile gluttony and called up by the circumstance that my wife had no dowry (of which I am proud). (*Origins*, pp. 305–6)

In exemplification of his dictum "I can only analyze myself with objectively acquired knowledge (as if I were a stranger)," Freud here asserts that his "one continuing patient" has "provided me with the solution of my own railway phobia." In her paper on E., Eva Rosenblum convincingly connects the reference to his "primal period" as "before twenty-two months" to another letter, of December 6, 1896, in which Freud tells Fliess of an unnamed patient who "still whimpers in his sleep as he did long ago in order to be taken into his mother's bed, who died when he was 22 months old" (*Origins*, p. 180). Rosenblum goes on to point out that Freud, too, experienced a separation from his mother at a slightly later age, due to her pregnancy with Anna (the sister mentioned in the "botanical monograph" dream), and to suggest that Freud's preoccupation with the termination of E.'s treatment is a reflection of his own "hunger phobia" or separation anxiety.[10] Fliess, she notes, in addition to serving as the equivalent of the analyst in Freud's self-analysis, also functions as what would today be described as the supervising analyst in Freud's treatment of E. And since Freud is in the throes of working out his own separation from Fliess at the same time that he seeks to bring E.'s treatment to a close, the two analyses are indeed inseparable, with a maternal transference underlying the struggle with the father-figure for both Freud and his patient.

In the letter of April 16, 1900, in which Freud announces the conclusion of E.'s "career as a patient," he appends a brief note of caution: "His riddle is *almost* completely solved, he feels extremely well, and his nature is entirely changed; for the moment a residue of symptoms remains. I am beginning to see that the apparent endlessness of the treatment is something of an inherent feature and is connected with the transference" (*Origins*, p. 317). The "residue of symptoms" that remains at the end of even this successful analysis corresponds to the "something left" in Freud's "open-air closet" dream. Reflected in E., Freud thus discerns the "apparent endlessness of the treatment" and the insuperability of the transference that are likewise the central lessons of his self-analysis.

In a sentence from the letter of December 21, 1899, inexplicably omitted by the editors of *The Origins of Psychoanalysis,* Freud tells Fliess that, as a reward for having assisted him in his self-analytic work, he has made E. "the present of a picture of Oedipus and the Sphinx" (Masson, p. 392), presumably in the version of Ingres.[11] Although E. assisted Freud primarily in his attempt to confirm the seduction theory by verifying the reality of infantile scenes, Freud bestows upon him the seal of psychoanalytic knowledge and the Oedipus complex. By doing so, Freud shows not only the interrelation between his oscillations concerning the validity of the seduction theory and his discovery of the Oedipus complex but also the affinity between the two patients first introduced in the letter of October 31, 1885—E. and the man with "homicidal tendencies."

But whereas E.'s importance to Freud, as I have indicated, is attested by his frequent appearances throughout the Fliess correspondence, that of the other patient can only be inferred on the basis of Freud's published works. To begin in a manner of speaking at the end, in *The Psychopathology of Everyday Life* Freud retrospectively raises the curtain on the climactic moment of his greatest discovery. Between 1895 and 1901, approximately the same period in which he treated E. and also engaged in his most intensive self-analysis, Freud regularly visited an elderly lady twice a day for the purposes of giving her a morphine injection and putting eye lotion into her eye.[12] On one occasion, Freud reports in his chapter on "Bungled Actions," he confused his two normally routine duties, and realized to his horror that he had put a few drops of morphine into her eye. Fortunately, this mistake was harmless, whereas to have administered an injection of the eye lotion would have been catastrophic. In analyzing his faulty action, Freud thinks first of the phrase *"sich an den Alten vergreifen,"* which means both "to make a blunder . . ." and "to commit an assault on the old woman." He then adds:

I was under the influence of a dream which had been told me by a young man the previous evening and the content of which could only point to sexual intercourse with his own mother. The strange fact that the [Oedipus] legend finds nothing objectionable in Queen Jocasta's age seemed to me to fit in well with the conclusion that in being in love with one's own mother one is never concerned with her as she is in the present but with her youthful mnemic image carried over from one's childhood. . . . While absorbed in thoughts of this kind I came to my patient, who is over ninety, and I must have been on the way to grasping the universal human application of the Oedipus myth as correlated with the Fate which is revealed in the oracles; for at that point I did violence to or committed a blunder on "the old woman." (*SE*, 6:178)

This passage is of the utmost interest in several respects. In the first place, it allows us to pin down the date and circumstances of Freud's realization of "the universal human application of the Oedipus myth." Because Freud communicates his interpretation of the "gripping power" of *Oedipus the King* to Fliess on October 15, 1897, this incident with the old lady must have occurred prior to that date. But since there is no mention of Oedipus in the previous letter of October 3, it seems highly probable that the events leading to his decisive revelation can be ascribed to the twelve-day interval between these two letters.

Beyond simply enabling us to reconstruct the external history of Freud's solution to the Sphinx's riddle, this inconspicuous passage in *The Psychopathology of Everyday Life* possesses profound thematic reverberations. It shows us that Freud grasps the significance of the Oedipus myth, not through a process of rational intellection, but through a nearly fatal error—an error which places him in the position of analytic patient. He is, moreover, "under the influence of a dream which had been told me by a young man the previous evening," and this "young man," as we shall see, is none other than his patient with "homicidal tendencies."

Freud's dropping of the morphine into the old lady's eye constitutes a symbolic act of incest. As his comments concerning Jocasta make clear, he is preoccupied at the time by thoughts of the way that realistic considerations of age are disregarded in the unconscious—an issue brought home to him by the confusion of generations in his family constellation. But perhaps the most note-

worthy feature of this episode is that both Freud's action and the
phrase he calls to mind, *"sich an den Alten vergreifen,"* connect his
discovery of the Oedipus complex with "an assault" on the
woman representing the mother. As we have seen in examining
the eternal triangle of Freud's "ideal situation of childhood," beneath the manifest level of hostility toward the male rival and
attraction to the female object there lies a bond of homosexual
love and heterosexual antagonism, and this pattern of unconscious hostility toward women repeats itself with such figures as
Emma Eckstein, Dora, and Sabina Spielrein.[13] It is thus consum-
mately appropriate that, although Freud should speak in his letter
to Fliess of the Oedipus complex as entailing "love of the mother
and jealousy of the father," in actual practice he uncovers its
"universal application" by reenacting his and John's "defloration" of Pauline through "doing violence to the old woman."

     Both in his self-analysis and his clinical work, Freud antici-
pated his discovery of the Oedipus complex. But only when these
two parallel lines of inquiry converged—after he found incestuous
and patricidal fantasies "in my own case too"—did Freud give
the *name* of Oedipus to the phenomena he had already described
in Draft N. That he achieves his breakthrough through a seemingly
accidental action, but one which obeys a deeper necessity, corresponds to the workings of "the Fate which is revealed in the
oracles" in the Oedipus myth. The invocation of the name of
Oedipus marks the moment when Freud claims universal validity
for his insight. He does so by linking self and other, subject and
object, into the "circle of understanding" defined by Heidegger as
the structure of all philosophical knowledge:

What is decisive is not to get out of the circle but to come into it in the
right way. This circle of understanding is not an orbit in which any
random kind of knowledge may move; it is the expression of the existential *fore-structure* of Dasein itself.[14]

Although the universality of the Oedipus complex has been chal-
lenged on anthropological or sociological grounds by revisionists
such as Malinowski or Fromm, to pose the question in these terms
is a fundamental error, for the proof of Freud's claim rests ultimately on the same self-conscious circularity elaborated by philosophical hermeneutics. Having found "love of the mother and

jealousy of the father" both in himself and in a representative other, Freud was prepared to abandon his *neurotica*—his theory of paternal seduction in childhood as the origin of neurosis—in favor of the psychoanalytic version of the hermeneutic circle known as the Oedipus complex.

Changing Carriages

But on what basis do we know that the "young man" whose dream of "sexual intercourse with his own mother" led Freud to the Oedipus complex is the same phobic patient with "homicidal tendencies" cited to Fliess in the letter of October 31, 1895? The answer to this question is contained in *The Interpretation of Dreams,* where this same individual's case is the very last one discussed before Freud launches into his commentaries on *Oedipus the King* and *Hamlet:*

> On another occasion I had an opportunity of obtaining a deep insight into the unconscious mind of a young man whose life was made almost impossible by an obsessional neurosis. He was unable to go out into the street because he was tortured by the fear that he would kill everyone he met. He spent his days preparing his alibi in case he might be charged with one of the murders committed in the town. It is unnecessary to add that he was a man of equally high morals and education. The analysis (which, incidentally, led to his recovery) showed that the basis of this distressing obsession was an impulse to murder his somewhat over-severe father. This impulse, to his astonishment, had been consciously expressed when he was seven years old, but it had, of course, originated much earlier in childhood. After his father's painful illness and death, the patient's obsessional self-reproaches appeared—he was in his thirty-first year at the time—taking the form of a phobia transferred on to strangers. A person, he felt, who was capable of wanting to push his own father over a precipice from the top of a mountain was not to be trusted to respect the rights of those less closely related to him; he was quite right to shut himself up in his room. (*SE,* 4:260)

It cannot be doubted that this patient "unable to go out into the street because he was tortured by the fear that he would kill everyone he met" is the same one mentioned in the letter to Fliess. His appearance at such a strategic point in *The Interpretation of Dreams* suggests that his "distressing obsession" bears an intimate relation to the discovery of the Oedipus complex, and accordingly enables us to conclude that this "young man" is also the same one alluded to in *The Psychopathology of Everyday Life* under whose influence Freud committed his "assault on the old woman."

Indeed, no less than that of E., the history of this Kafkan personality bears an uncanny resemblance to Freud's. His "high morals and education" are matched by Freud's own intellectual distinction and probity of character. The derivation of his phobia from "an impulse to murder his somewhat over-severe father" mirrors Freud's unconscious patricidal wishes, and the springing up of this patient's "obsessional self-reproaches" after his father's "painful illness and death" likewise has its analogue in Freud's "inclination to self-reproach" following the death of his father. The diphasic onset of his patricidal impulses—the conscious memory dating from his seventh year being superimposed on events originating "much earlier in childhood"—is paralleled by the chain of "supplements" that make up Freud's own Oedipus complex. The general classification of this patient as an obsessional neurotic, finally, accords with Freud's self-diagnosis, for, as he wrote to Jung on September 2, 1907, he regarded himself as a healthy version of "the 'obsessional' type" (*F/J*, p. 82).

But the full significance of this patient to Freud can only be measured when his second appearance in *The Interpretation of Dreams* is taken into account. In the course of his "Hollthurn" dream, dating from mid-July 1898 and taking place while Freud was traveling by train and sharing his compartment with an "aristocratic" (*SE*, 5:456) and impolite couple, Freud imagines that "I MIGHT HAVE CHANGED CARRIAGES WHILE I WAS IN A SLEEPING STATE" (*SE*, 5:455). The use of block letters underscores the importance of this feature of the dream, and Freud goes on to explain that the idea of sleepwalking "was not an original one of my own, but was copied from the neurosis of one of my patients" (*SE*, 5:457). In slightly different words, Freud summarizes once again the case of this "highly educated and, in real life, softhearted man," whose fears of being a mass murderer were temporarily allayed by locking himself into his house, until it dawned on him that "he might have left his house while he was in an unconscious state and thus have been able to commit the murder without knowing anything about it" (*SE*, 5:458). The recollection in his own dream of having "changed carriages while I was in an unconscious state," Freud adds, "was evidently intended . . . to serve the purpose of identifying me with the figure of this patient" (*SE*, 5:458).

The mechanism of identification at work here, involving one of his patients, is essentially no different from the "reenactment syndrome" displayed in Freud's emulation of heroes such as Oedipus or Hannibal. Freud himself supplies the best theoretical commentary on this process in his discussion of the "smoked salmon" dream of one of his female patients. Using the term "hysterical identification," Freud points out that this is "a highly important factor" in the formation of neurotic symptoms:

It enables patients to express in their symptoms not only their own experience but those of a large number of other people; it enables them, as it were, to suffer on behalf of a whole crowd of people and to act all the parts in a play singlehanded. (*SE*, 4:149)

As in the syllogism implied by Freud's parodying of Hannibal ("Because Hannibal *did not* enter Rome, Freud *could not*"), the key element in identification is that it "consists in the unconscious drawing of an inference" (*SE*, 4:149). Freud is at pains to insist on the *unconsciousness* of such ostensibly logical thinking:

This identification is not simple imitation but *assimilation* on the basis of similar aetiological pretension; it expresses a resemblance and is derived from a common element which remains in the unconscious. (*SE*, 4:150)

Exactly such an "*assimilation* on the basis of a similar aetiological pretension" is acknowledged by Freud in his remarks on the similarity between his own neurosis and that of the patient he has "copied" in the "Hollthurn" dream:

I knew that the root of his illness had been hostile impulses against his father and involving a sexual situation. In so far, therefore, as I was identifying myself with him, I was seeking to confess something analogous. (*SE*, 5:458)

Freud states further that his thoughts of this engaging youth, who had since been cured of his debilitating phobia, had been aroused by an "easy association" (*SE*, 5:458), since his last train journey prior to the current one had been taken in the latter's company.

As Carl Schorske has noted, it is characteristic of *The Interpre-*

tation of Dreams that, beneath its "surface organization" as a "scientific treatise," it possesses "a second, deep structure" constituting a "subplot of personal history."[15] Freud's identification with this patient with "homicidal tendencies" in the "Hollthurn" dream thus sheds unexpected light on his previous appearance in *The Interpretation of Dreams*, immediately prior to the initial mention of the Oedipus complex. For if, as I have argued, Freud's progression from the Fliess correspondence to *The Interpretation of Dreams* entails a suppression of his own identity as patient and the assumption of the tone of a physician pronouncing an objective truth, it makes sense that the patient through whom he stumbled on the Oedipus complex in the first place should literally *take his place* when he recasts his first-person confession ("in my own case too") into an impersonal generalization ("the fate of all of us perhaps") in a work intended for public scrutiny. It is this same attempt to conceal his complicity at the most crucial point in his text that Freud unwittingly reveals when he seeks "to confess something analogous" to the neurosis of his patient in the "Hollthurn" dream.

The recent work of Peter Swales has further enhanced our appreciation of the dynamics linking Freud to this anonymous individual. In the course of reviewing the quarrel between Freud and Fliess—in order to substantiate his thesis that Freud harbored the wish to murder Fliess during their final meeting at Achensee in the Alps in 1900—Swales draws attention to an incident narrated in *The Psychopatholoy of Everyday Life* in which a "young man" whom Freud meets on his travels objects during a walk together "to taking a certain path which he said was too steep and dangerous" (*SE*, 6:210). According to Swales, this episode actually involves Freud and Fliess, and reverberates with Freud's own "close personal identification" with the "highly educated" male patient we have been discussing who blamed himself for "wanting to push his father over a precipice from the top of a mountain."[16] Swales takes his reconstruction even further by correlating Freud's putative plot to murder Fliess in this manner with his second controversial hypothesis that Freud at the same period also engaged in an affair with his sister-in-law Minna Bernays. He summarizes:

In the summer of 1900, only a few weeks after their [i.e., Freud's and Fliess'] big quarrel, Freud sought to re-enact the mythical role of Oedipus by committing the crime of incest with the MOTHER—in Freud's case, with a mother-substitute in the form of his wife's sister, Minna Bernays. The corollary of this, the other side of the oedipal coin, would of course be the murder of the FATHER—in Freud's case, necessarily of a father-figure. And according to the general view of analysts, Fliess stood for Freud less as a brother than as a father symbol.[17]

The ingenuity of this argument that Freud "sought to re-enact the mythical role of Oedipus" through commission of symbolic acts of patricide and incest can scarcely be praised too highly, and I cannot attempt to do justice here to the complexity of Swales' documentation.[18] Yet I think it is important to register one fundamental objection, particularly with regard to the thesis of Freud's affair with Minna. This is that, as one who does not follow Freud in rejecting the seduction theory in favor of the Oedipus complex, Swales drastically underestimates the role of *fantasy* in mental life. His case for Freud's involvement with Minna hinges on yet another passage in the *Psychopathology* (*SE,* 6:8–14), the famous forgetting of the word *aliquis* ("someone") in a quotation from Vergil, the analysis of which leads back through an allusion to St. Januarius' miracle of the liquification of blood to a fear of having made a woman pregnant. It must be conceded that Swales' contention that this slip, despite being ascribed to "a certain young man of academic background" (*SE,* 6:8–9) whom Freud met on his holiday travels, is actually Freud's own, is indisputable.

But in reviewing the case of E., one finds in Draft L, dated May 2, 1897, the report of a "wishful dream," in which E. imagines himself arrested by a policeman for having killed a child, which he attributes to the combined effect of having once been "responsible for the abortion of a child as a result of a *liaison*" (*Origins,* p. 199) and of having practiced *coitus interruptus* in the morning prior to the occurrence of the dream.[19] At this date, there is no possibility that Freud was intimate with his sister-in-law, and yet, from all we have seen of his identification with E., it is quite likely that this abortion dream also represents an unconscious fantasy of Freud's. If, moreover, Freud was capable of fantasizing about abortion and infanticide in 1897, he was equally so in 1900; and this realization considerably weakens Swales' speculative edifice, which rests on the assumption that Freud must have forgotten *aliquis* because he actually impregnated Minna, instead of (as is highly plausible) merely feeling guilty for wishing he had done so.[20]

Returning from E. and the *The Psychopathology of Everyday Life* to the man with "homicidal tendencies," we are offered a definitive gloss on the subterranean connection between the widely dispersed references to the latter patient in *The Interpretation of Dreams* in Freud's late work *Moses and Monotheism* (1939). Arguing that the biblical story of Moses contains "indications which reveal things to us which it was not meant to communicate," he continues:

In its implications the distortion of a text resembles a murder: the difficulty is not in perpetrating the deed, but in getting rid of the traces. We might well lend the word *"Entstellung"* [distortion] the double meaning to which it has a claim but of which to-day it makes no use. It should mean not only "to change the appearance of something" but also "to put something in another place, to displace." Accordingly, in many instances of textual distortion, we may nevertheless count upon finding what has been suppressed and disavowed hidden away somewhere else, though changed and torn from its context. Only it will not be easy to recognize it. (*SE*, 23:43)

This explanation of the neglected "double meaning" of *Entstellung*—literally "displacement" and figuratively "distortion"—and of the way that what is "suppressed and disavowed" may regularly be found "hidden away somewhere else, though changed from its context," is a more elaborate version of the law of parapraxis laid down in the *Psychopathology* ("where an error makes its appearance a repression lies behind it"). It is also in the utmost degree self-reflexive. Freud's avowal that the true difficulty in committing a crime lies in "getting rid of the traces" is echoed when he apologizes for the "inartistic" form of *Moses and Monotheism* by saying, "I found myself unable to wipe out the traces [*die Spuren . . . zu verwischen*] of the history of the work's origin, which was in any case unusual" (*SE*, 23:103); and this latter passage virtually repeats Freud's addendum, in the Preface to the second edition of *The Interpretation of Dreams*, concerning his belated recognition that the book was a reaction to his father's death: "Having discovered that this was so, I felt unable to obliterate the traces [*die Spuren . . . zu-verwischen*] of the experience" (*SE*, 4:xxvi).[21] Freud's comparison of "the distortion of a text" to "a murder," therefore, is by no means a random one, and it is precisely unconscious guilt for his father's death that motivates his attempted relegation to the "Hollthurn" dream of the confession that belongs properly in his discussion of the Oedipus complex.

Two final details in Freud's account of this "case of severe obsessions accompanied by complete insight" (*SE*, 5:457) reinforce the parallels between himself and his double. In the first place, whereas in the context of the Oedipus complex Freud refers to "his father's illness and death," in conjunction with the "Hollthurn" dream he describes the patient as one who, "shortly after the death of his *parents*, began to reproach himself with having murderous inclinations" (*SE*, 5:457; italics added). This minor discrepancy, as Alexander Grinstein has suggested, doubtless arises from the circumstances of the "Hollthurn" dream, in which Freud "revenged himself on the elderly *couple* on the train."[22] Second, Freud explains that what lay behind this patient's "murderous inclinations" was "a 'Cain' phantasy, for 'all men are brothers' " (*SE*, 5:458). Like Freud's, the core of this man's neurosis consists of death wishes against his father; but his guilt takes the form of a fear of committing the fratricidal "crime of Cain." Freud has thus once again made over his patient in his own image, for it is ultimately the death of Julius he has unconsciously "perpetrated" but of which he has not succeeded "in getting rid of the traces."

Primal Scenes

The setting of the "Hollthurn" dream is an important component of his meaning. Freud surmises that the "stand-offish" behavior of the "aristocratic" couple with whom he was sharing the train compartment was due to the fact that "my arrival had prevented the affectionate exchanges which they had planned for the night" (*SE*, 5:458). The situation therefore represents for Freud the reenactment of a primal scene experience, in which he witnesses or interrupts the sexual relations of his parents. Indeed, he specifically attributes his fantasy on this occasion to "a scene of early childhood in which the child, probably driven by sexual curiosity, had forced his way into his parents' bedroom and had been turned out of it by his father's orders" (*SE*, 5:458–59). Freud's memory of this early rebuff to his "sexual curiosity" again links him to the patient whose sleepwalking neurosis he has "copied" since "the root of his [the patient's] illness" is likewise "hostile impulses against his father, dating from childhood and involving a sexual situation." The detail of "changed carriages" in the "Hollthurn" dream, in addition to cementing Freud's identification with this anonymous "young man," can be seen as an outgrowth of what Leonard Shengold has termed Freud's very brief "oedipal journey"[23] in and out of his parents' bedroom, and thus as a fantasy shaped in response to this disturbing event.

Freud's discussion of the "Hollthurn" dream implies that his intrusion into his parents' bedroom was an isolated occurrence. But authoritative research on the Freiberg period of Freud's life, his first three years, has shown that the Freud family lived in a single room, and that young Sigmund must consequently have been a frequent spectator of his parents' sexual activity.[24] It also appears probable, from the dream of "bird-beaked figures," that Freud again underwent a traumatic experience of the primal scene between the ages of nine and ten in Vienna.[25] In another connection Freud comments in *The Interpretation of Dreams* that it is "a matter of daily experience that sexual intercourse among adults strikes any children who observe it as something uncanny and that it arouses anxiety in them" (*SE*, 5:585). By "daily experience" Freud of course means his current clinical practice, but it is only slightly fanciful to apply the phrase to his own childhood in both Freiberg and Vienna.

This incident of penetrating and being evicted from his parents' bedroom probably dates from later than the Freiberg period, and it is not mentioned again in any of Freud's writings. But in his letter to Fliess of October 3, 1897, immediately after recollecting his Czech nanny, Freud refers to a second event with a direct bearing on the "Hollthurn" dream:

Later (between the ages of two and two-and-a-half) libido towards *matrem* was aroused; the occasion must have been the journey with her from Leipzig to Vienna, during which we spent a night together and I must have had the opportunity of seeing her *nudam*. . . . My anxiety over travel you have yourself seen in full bloom. (*Origins*, p. 219)

Although he does not cite this experience of seeing his mother naked on a train journey as an association to the "Hollthurn" dream—or anywhere in *The Interpretation of Dreams*—Freud's allusion to what is in effect a *different* experience of the primal scene is in all likelihood to be explained by the fact that he has the "Hollthurn" dream while he happens to be traveling on a train. Like the connection between Freud's "inclination to self-reproach" at the death of his father and the "germ of reproaches" left by the death of Julius, the "Hollthurn" dream thus provides a textbook example of the psychoanalytic theory of dream formation, since Freud's current situation—where his presence interferes with the "affectionate exchanges" planned by the couple in the train compartment—is reinforced by a memory of a pair of analogous scenes from early childhood.

Jakob Fréud left Freiberg with his family in two stages: first, when Sigmund was three, the family moved from Freiberg to Leipzig, and then, one year later, continued from Leipzig to Vienna. In addition to the two biographical accidents I have already adduced to help explain Freud's heroic destiny—his family constellation and the premature death of Julius—this uprooting from his birthplace also plays a decisive part in the development of psychoanalysis.[26] Freud thought of the first three years of life as the "prehistoric period," and because of the disruption introduced into his own life at this juncture, his Freiberg memories were, so to speak, hermetically sealed from contamination by subsequent events, and thus preserved a clarity and distinctiveness which greatly facilitated their recovery in later life.

In "Origins," Jones comments pertinently on the episode recounted by Freud in his letter to Fliess:

On the journey from Leipzig to Vienna, a year later, Freud had occasion to see his mother naked: an awesome fact which forty years later he related in a letter to Fliess—but in Latin! Curiously enough he gives his age then as between two and two and a half whereas he was in fact four years old on that journey. One must surmise that the memories of two such experiences had got telescoped. (*LW*, 1:13)

Both Jones' remarks concerning Freud's chronological confusion and his use of Latin are to the point. His suggestion that Freud mistakenly underestimates his age at the time of the journey from Leipzig to Vienna because of the "telescoping" of two similar memories accords with my own hypothesis that reminiscences of two distinct primal scenes have been conflated in the "Hollthurn" dream. The significance of Freud's retreat into Latin to communicate the "awesome fact" of seeing his mother naked is highlighted by a passage from the Dora case, where Freud asserts his right to speak openly about sex:

I call bodily organs and processes by their technical names. . . . *J'appelle un chat un chat*. I have certainly heard of some people—doctors and laymen—who are scandalized by a therapeutic method in which conversations of this sort occur. . . . The right attitude is: *"pour faire un omelette il faut casser des oeufs."* (*SE*, 7:48–49)

As Steven Marcus has observed, it is a notable irony that "in this splendid extended declaration about plain speech," Freud "feels it necessary to disappear not once but twice into French."[27] Like the French of these proverbs, the Latin of *matrem nudam* is admittedly transparent in meaning, but even the paradox of a defense that doesn't really defend may attest to the continued workings of blindness or repression.

The "anxiety over travel" to which Freud refers in his letter to Fliess is the same phobia concerning railway travel for which, in his letter of December 21, 1899, he claims to have found the "solution." This optimistic assertion is something of an exaggeration, however, for Freud's travel phobia persisted in milder form throughout his life. Hanns Sachs reports that the "only occasion" when Freud "squandered away his time unnecessarily was when he had to make a train. He was always a good deal ahead of schedule and had to wait around at the station for an hour or so."[28] At the root of this neurotic behavior is Freud's train journey from Leipzig to Vienna at the age of four. As the occasion when he literally "spent the night" with his mother, this experience takes on the quality of a fulfillment of the forbidden Oedipus wish.

In a letter to Fliess of December 3, 1897, Freud discloses an additional infantile determinant of his "anxiety over travel." He cites a memory stemming from the earlier of his two train journeys, that from Freiberg to Leipzig at the age of three:

Breslau plays a part in my childhood memories. At the age of three I passed through the station when we moved from Freiberg to Leipzig, and the gas jets, which were the first I had seen, reminded me of souls burning in hell. I know something of the context here. The anxiety over travel I have had to overcome is also bound up with it. (*Origins*, p. 237)

The "context" Freud hints at for his thoughts of "souls burning in hell" is almost certainly his recollection of his Catholic nanny, "who told me a great deal about God and hell." The themes of the primal scene and the Oedipus complex inherent in Freud's beholding his *matrem nudam* must be superimposed on his earlier traumatic experience in the station at Breslau. An oedipal interpretation of the latter event is offered by Edith Buxbaum: "The memory of the railway station was a reminder that hell and damnation await the son who covets his father's wife and who wants to kill the father for that reason."[29] In view of Freud's own explanation of his railway phobia in terms of a "fantasy of impoverishment" or a "hunger phobia," furthermore, his anxiety about being removed from his birthplace is clearly also to be connected to fears attendant upon the task of achieving separation from the mother.

It should be indisputable from the foregoing that the "Hollthurn" dream occupies a pivotal position in *The Interpretation of Dreams*, leading as it does both to a set of formative events from Freud's early childhood and to his concealment of himself behind the mask of the patient with "homicidal tendencies" in his first public discussion of the Oedipus complex. The significance of the previously noted fact that one of Freud's three parapraxes in *The Interpretation of Dreams* occurs during his analysis of this dream may now be properly appreciated. The "Hollthurn" dream takes its place beside the legend of Hannibal and the genealogy of the Greek gods (as well as the plot of *Hamlet*) as a subject sufficiently sensitive to induce Freud to commit a lapse in the course of writing about it.

"Screen Memories"
and the "Narcissistic Formation"

The frankness with which Freud disclosed his private thoughts in his letters to Fliess is attributable to his understandable confidence that they would never be read by anyone other than their intended recipient. The situation is tantalizingly similar with respect to "Screen Memories." Divided into three parts, in the first and last of which Freud presents his theoretical argument and illustrates it anecdotally, this 1899 paper contains in its middle section the analysis of an unnamed patient. Only in 1946—seven years after Freud's death—did Siegfried Bernfeld recognize the memory to be autobiographical.[30] Freud's apprehensiveness about the degree to which he had exposed himself in this paper is illustrated by the fact that when, in 1906, after the events of his early life were much more widely known than they had been in 1899, he gathered his scattered studies on psychoanalysis into a single volume, "Screen Memories" was not among them.

In his introductory note to "Screen Memories" in the *Standard Edition*, James Strachey states that the "intrinsic interest of this paper has been rather undeservedly overshadowed" by the "extraneous fact" (*SE*, 3:302) of its autobiographical character. Strachey is seriously mistaken in believing that the "further subjective significance" of "Screen Memories" is not part of its "intrinsic interest,"[31] but it remains true that, on its theoretical merits alone, the paper is a contribution of the first order. In his letter to Fliess of January 3, 1899, in which he announces that he has accomplished the "piece of self-analysis" to be included in the paper, Freud continues:

All I shall disclose to you is that the dream pattern is capable of universal application and that the key to hysteria really lies in dreams. . . . If I wait a little longer I shall be able to describe the mental process in dreams in such a way as to include the process in hysterical symptom-formation. (*Origins*, p. 271)

"Screen Memories" enables Freud to grasp the "universal application" of his method of dream interpretation to hysterical symptoms because it elaborates the key notion of compromise formation. A "screen memory" or "cover memory" *(Deckerinnerung)* occurs when a "serious or tragic" event in a person's early life is replaced by an "everyday and indifferent" (*SE*, 3:305) memory from the same period. Freud accounts for the puzzling fact that "precisely what is important is suppressed and what is indifferent retained" by the following theory:

> We shall then form a notion that two psychical forces are concerned in bringing about memories of this sort. One of these forces takes the importance of the experience as a motive for seeking to remember it, while the other—a resistance—tries to prevent any such preference from being shown. These two opposing forces do not cancel each other out, nor does one of them (whether with or without loss to itself) overpower the other. Instead, a compromise is brought about, somewhat on the analogy of a parallelogram of forces. . . . The result of the conflict is therefore that, instead of the mnemic image which would have been justified by the original event, another has been produced which has been associatively *displaced* from the former one. And since the elements of the experience which aroused objection were precisely the important ones, the substituted memory will necessarily lack those important elements and will in consequence most probably strike us as trivial. (*SE*, 3:306–7)

In the "open-air closet" dream, Freud explained that the "ambiguous dream-content" and "indifferent feeling-tone" were produced by "the mutual inhibition . . . of contrary impulses," and screen memories are constructed in identical fashion. Indeed, this brilliant demonstration that the seemingly "trivial" nature of screen memories is actually the result of a deadlocked conflict between "two psychical forces"—one "seeking to remember" a given event, the other a "resistance" against remembering—contains the nucleus of the psychoanalytic view of mental functioning.

The centrality of "Screen Memories" to psychoanalytic theory is matched by its exemplary place in Freud's self-analysis. The childhood incident recounted in the middle section of the paper, as previously noted, is the symbolic "deflowering" of Pauline by Freud and John. Here I wish to concentrate on the way that our knowledge that the memory Freud attributes to "a man of university education, aged thirty-eight" (*SE*, 3:309) is in reality one of his own drastically alters our reading of the paper. It creates, in effect, a split between what might be called the "private" and the "public" audiences of "Screen Memories." To the uninitiated "public" reader—that is, virtually everyone until the publication of Bernfeld's discovery—Freud appears in the middle section, which is cast in dialogue form, simply in the role of analyst. But to those "private" readers apprised of the paper's autobiographical dimension, Freud assumes simultaneously the guises of patient and analyst. This esoteric knowledge of Freud's dual identity in "Screen Memories" is comparable in its repercussions to the revolution effected by the Fliess correspondence on our reading of *The Interpretation of Dreams*.

At the time of its publication, only one person other than Freud possessed the secret of "Screen Memories." As the recipient of Freud's intimate letters, Fliess would have recognized the allusions that escaped those not familiar with the details of Freud's past. Fliess, therefore, was in a sense the intended audience of "Screen Memories," no less than of Freud's letters. If a contemporary "private" reading of "Screen Memories" shifts Freud from the role of analyst to that of patient, it likewise shows Fliess filling the vacated position of analyst. The fact that today anyone, and not Fliess alone, can locate the buried personal references in "Screen Memories" highlights the ironic reversal whereby—after his death—we have all become analysts of Freud.

The means by which Freud attempts to disguise his identity are of considerable interest. In his capacity as analyst, he introduces the reader to his subject, who, though his profession "lies in a very different field" from psychology, has taken an interest in psychological questions "ever since I was able to relieve him of a slight phobia by means of psycho-analysis" (*SE*, 3:309). The informed reader will immediately recognize this "slight phobia" as Freud's "anxiety over travel," and he has his imaginary patient go on to say: "I can remember two small occurrences during the railway-journey; these, as you will recollect, came up in the analysis of my phobia" (*SE*, 3:310). Without question, these "two small occurrences" are Freud's seeing his mother naked on the journey from Leipzig to Vienna and his fearful reaction to the "gas jets" at Breslau, and would have been identified by Fliess as such. A direct address to Fliess is implied by the words "you will recollect," which hark back to his earlier letters as though they were analytic sessions—as indeed they were.

As one moves from the Fliess letters, through "Screen Memories," to *The Interpretation of Dreams,* a correlation may be observed between Freud's increasingly vigorous attempts to abandon his role as patient and the severity of the distortion of his autobiographical memories. The "two small occurrences" are explicitly mentioned in separate letters to Fliess, are covertly hinted at in "Screen Memories," and in *The Interpretation of Dreams* the glimpse of *matrem nudam* and the fear of hell disappear entirely, except insofar as Freud has his "Hollthurn" dream while he is physically traveling on a train. The progressive attenuation of these two memories finds a parallel in the way that Freud *consciously* cloaks his identity as patient beneath the mask of a *fictional* character in "Screen Memories," but does so *unconsciously* through his *real* patient from the "Hollthurn" dream in *The Interpretation of Dreams.* Paradoxically, however, although Freud's efforts at self-concealment grow increasingly energetic, so do his self-revelations, and it is a curious truth that *The Interpretation of Dreams* is actually *more* intimate in its disclosures—concerning, for example, Freud's ambitions to be appointed to a professorship—than the comparatively straightforward letters to Fliess.

Freud gives the age of his fictive interlocutor in "Screen Memories" as thirty-eight, whereas he himself was forty-three at that time. But as Bernfeld has shown, this five-year discrepancy is charged with meaning for Freud:

This "round figure" expresses . . . a direct and explicit wish of Freud, who writes in his *Interpretation of Dreams* before 1899: "What are five years . . . that is no time at all for me." This remark refers to the five long years of the engagement period which he had to endure because he had not chosen a "bread-and-butter" profession.[32]

Bernfeld rightly draws attention to the five years of Freud's engagement period as one of the determinants for his seemingly random choice of his patient's age. But additional factors are at play. The passage quoted from *The Interpretation of Dreams* is taken from the dream of "1851 and 1856"—the same "absurd" dream which "obstinately promises the end of E.'s treatment." Thus, the five-year difference in ages may refer to the duration of E.'s analysis, and reinforce Freud's submerged identification with this "one persistent patient," who, we recall, shares his defloration fantasies.

But if both the age and fantasy life of Freud's double in "Screen Memories" seem inspired by E., when he is described as "a man of university education" the resemblance is rather to the patient with "homicidal tendencies," who is "of equally high morals and education."[33] As in the initial letter to Fliess of October 31, 1895, and in the underpinnings of Freud's concern with the primal scene in the "Hollthurn" dream, here in "Screen Memories" the two patients figuring so prominently in Freud's self-analysis again cannot readily be differentiated. Both come to seem to be no more than projections of facets of Freud himself. Even the statement that his imaginary analysand's profession "lies in a very different field" from his own, which Bernfeld dismisses simply as an "outright lie,"[34] may tentatively be conjectured to hint at Freud's abiding passion for archeology. Freud compares his excitement at uncovering "a scene from [E.'s] primal period" to Schliemann "once more excavating Troy," and it is attractive to speculate that he envisioned his composite alter ego as a specialist in this domain only apparently remote from psychoanalysis.[35]

Freud's endeavor to suppress evidence of his own role as patient extends beyond *The Interpretation of Dreams*. In the second of his two most important works, *Three Essays on the Theory of Sexuality*, he discusses railway travel as one of the stimulants of infantile sexuality:

A compulsive link of this kind between railway-travel and sexuality is clearly derived from the pleasurable character of sensations of movement. In the event of repression, which turns so many childish preferences into their opposite, these same individuals, when they are adolescents or adults, will react to rocking or swinging with a feeling of nausea, will be terribly exhausted by a railway journey and will protect themselves against a repetition of the painful experience by a dread of railway-travel. (*SE*, 7:242)

To the reader who has followed the allusions to Freud's own "dread of railway-travel" from the two letters to Fliess, through "Screen Memories," to the "Hollthurn" dream in *The Interpretation of Dreams*, this ostensibly impersonal elucidation of the "compulsive link . . . between railway-travel and sexuality" will clearly belong to the same series. In "On Beginning the Treatment" (1913), moreover, Freud employs the metaphor of a train ride when he counsels his fellow analysts on how to explain to their patients the rule of free association:

So say whatever goes through your mind. Act as though, for instance, you were a traveller sitting next to a window of a railway carriage and describing to someone inside the carriage the changing views which you see outside. (*SE,* 12:135)

This technical advice is anticipated in Freud's letter to Fliess of October 27, 1897, where he writes of the way his self-analytic work "hauls me through the past in rapid association of ideas; and my mood changes like the landscape seen by a traveller from a train" (*Origins,* p. 225). As in the window of the famous dream of the Wolf-Man, the "landscape" that Freud claims to be seeing outside may be interpreted as a projection of activity that is taking place within the train compartment.[36]

The paradigmatic importance of "Screen Memories" to a reading of Freud derives from the dialectical reversals whereby Freud shuttles between the roles of analyst and patient and simultaneously fills both with' (real or imaginary) other people. A theoretical account of what is taking place is suggested by "Instincts and Their Vicissitudes" (1915), where Freud explores the "component instincts" of sadism-masochism and voyeurism-exhibitionism. As both these pairs of instincts or drives *(Triebe)* lie on the boundary between sexuality and the ego, they involve the subject-object relations characteristic of the ego as well as a propulsion toward libidinal satisfaction. Both these drives, Freud states, entail "turning round . . . upon the subject's own self," since "masochism is actually sadism turned round upon the subject's own ego" and "exhibitionism includes looking at his own body" (*SE,* 14:127). At the time of writing "Instincts and Their Vicissitudes," Freud believed that sadism preceded masochism, though in "The Economic Problem of Masochism" (1924) he changed his mind and posited the existence of a primary masochism. But the crucial point is precisely the impossibility of assigning priority to either the active or the passive poles of these "component instincts," since there exists a "preliminary stage of the scopophilic instinct, in which the subject's own body is the object of the scopophilia" (*SE,* 14:132). From this "preliminary stage" or "narcissistic formation," an individual may develop either the active tendencies of sadism or voyeurism or the passive ones of masochism or exhibitionism, the former by replacing the "narcissistic object" and the latter the "narcissistic *subject*" with "another, extraneous ego" (*SE*, 14:132).

As an encounter in which the drives of curiosity and aggression are powerfully called into play, the analytic situation is eminently susceptible to the vicissitudes of "turning round upon the subject" and the "reversal from activity to passivity" (*SE*, 14:130). Although in a conventional two-party analysis both the physical setting and the transfer of money leave no doubt as to who is the patient and who the analyst, this division of labor must be seen as a derivative of the original "narcissistic formation" of self-analysis. In this sense, "Screen Memories" represents the ideal "preliminary stage" revealing the self-analytic foundation of all Freud's writings—marking, as it were, the midpoint between the letters to Fliess and *The Interpretation of Dreams*—since in it he assumes simultaneously the functions of analyst ("narcissistic subject") and patient ("narcissistic object") *and* ascribes both to "another, extraneous ego."

To some extent, this splitting of the mind into subject and object, or analyst and patient, occurs in every analytic situation. Richard Sterba has given the name "therapeutic dissociation of the ego" to the analyst's effort to draw part of the patient's ego "over to his side and to place it in opposition to the other part which in the transference is cathected or influenced from the side of the unconscious."[37] The genetic prototype for this therapeutic ego dissociation is the division within the ego itself created by the superego. Despite being "in its very essence a subject," Freud writes in the *New Introductory Lectures*, the ego "can take itself as an object, can treat itself like other objects, can observe itself, criticize itself. . . . In this, one part of the ego is setting itself against the rest" (*SE*, 23:58). The superego, in other words, may serve as the analyst within the patient, and the analyst is no more than a personification of the dissociated portion of the patient's own ego. The consequence of this interplay between subject and object is that every psychoanalysis is ultimately a self-analysis, and it is impossible to draw a firm line of demarcation between *intrapsychic* and *interpersonal*—or internal and external—reality.

Freud and Hamlet

Both in his letter to Fliess of October 15, 1897 and in *The Interpretation of Dreams,* Freud couples his remarks on *Oedipus the King* with observations on *Hamlet.* Although a juxtaposition of these works has by now become a critical commonplace, in Freud it arises out of a profound argument concerning the distinction between ancient and modern tragedy. He writes in *The Interpretation of Dreams:*

> Another of the great creations of tragic poetry, Shakespeare's *Hamlet,* has its roots in the same soil as *Oedipus Rex.* But the changed treatment of the same material reveals the whole difference in the mental life of these two widely separated epochs of civilization: the secular advance of repression in the emotional life of mankind. In the *Oedipus* the child's wishful phantasy that underlies it is brought into the open and realized as it would be in a dream. In *Hamlet,* it remains repressed; and—just as in the case of a neurosis—we only learn of its existence from its inhibiting consequences. (*SE,* 4:264)

Whereas in the Greek tragedy the underlying fantasy of incest and patricide is "brought into the open," because of the "advance of repression" in human consciousness the Oedipus complex of the modern hero can only be known "from its inhibiting consequences."

Illuminating as Freud's remarks on *Hamlet* are, they become even more so when they are applied to his own relation to the Oedipus myth. Freud, who acknowledged his "anxiety over travel" to be a phobia, likewise experienced the Oedipus complex only in a "repressed" form and inferred its existence through its "inhibiting consequences." Jacques Lacan has drawn attention to the way that *Hamlet* defines what is involved in any modern reenactment of the Oedipus myth:

> Freud himself indicated, perhaps in a somewhat *fin de siècle* way, that for some reason when we lived out the Oedipal drama, it was destined to be in a warped form, and there's surely an echo of that in *Hamlet.*[38]

In addition to commenting on the problem theoretically, Freud literally "lived out the oedipal drama," and the "warped form" in which this repetition manifests itself in his own life makes him the double of Shakespeare's archetypal modern hero. But since Freud's Hamletlike neurosis is itself a replica of that of the patient with "homicidal tendencies" through whom he discovered the Oedipus complex, there is a dovetailing of literary and biographical avenues of inquiry.

Although Freud's comments in *The Interpretation of Dreams* disclose primarily his affinity with the character of Hamlet, he also identifies with Shakespeare as playwright. Relying upon Georg Brandes' *William Shakespeare: A Critical Study* (1896), Freud advanced the thesis that "*Hamlet* was written immediately after the death of Shakespeare's father (in 1601), that is, under the immediate impact of his bereavement and, as we may well assume, while his childhood feelings about his father had been freshly revived" (*SE*, 4:265). In view of Freud's comments concerning the "further subjective significance" of *The Interpretation of Dreams* as a response to his own father's death, "we may well assume" that he saw *Hamlet* as occupying the same symbolic place in Shakespeare's life as his great work did in his own.[39] The bifold quality of Freud's resemblance to Hamlet as character and Shakespeare as author corresponds to his dual role as hero and author of *The Interpretation of Dreams*.

Freud's fascination with Shakespeare did not cease in 1900. Throughout his life he quoted freely and spontaneously from Shakespeare's plays, and in "The Theme of the Three Caskets" (1913) and "Some Character Types Met with in Psycho-Analytic Work" he offered readings of *King Lear* and *Macbeth*. But deservedly the most notorious aspect of Freud's interest in Shakespeare is his eventual conversion to the view, on the basis of a book by the unfortunately named J. T. Looney, that the plays were in fact written by the Earl of Oxford.[40] In light of the utter indefensibility of this position, which he first espoused publicly upon being awarded the Goethe Prize in 1930, Freud's susceptibility to it can only be regarded as a neurotic symptom, yet another piece of evidence for his continuing ambivalence about being "a very great man" and for the permanent incompleteness of his self-analysis. An analogous manifestation of Freud's unresolved hero complex is his attempt in *Moses and Monotheism* to deny the Jewishness of Moses, "to deprive a people of the man whom they take pride in as the greatest of their sons" (*SE,* 23:7). But though Freud's identification with Shakespeare took this bizarre turn late in life, there is a direct continuity between his final aberration and the earlier, more justified perception of a kinship between Shakespeare and himself in *The Interpretation of Dreams.*

"Sie ist eingekastelt"

In the letter to Fliess of October 15, 1897 in which he first announces his interpretations of *Oedipus the King* and *Hamlet,* Freud includes a memory from his earliest childhood that we have yet to mention. This memory weaves together various strands of his personal history and serves as a final emblem of the fatality connecting his destiny to that of Oedipus. When Freud was two and a half years of age two decisive events occurred: his nanny was exposed as a thief and dismissed at the instigation of his half-brother Philipp, and his mother gave birth to a daughter, Anna, Freud's first sibling after Julius. After suggesting that he must have preserved some recollection of his nurse's disappearance, Freud adduces and immediately interprets the following scene:

I was crying my heart out, because my mother was nowhere to be found. My brother Philipp (who is twenty years older than I) opened a cupboard [*Kasten*] for me, and when I found that mother was not there I cried still more, until she came through the door, looking slim and beautiful. What can that mean? Why should my brother open the cupboard for me when he knew that my mother was not inside it and that opening it therefore could not quieten me? Now I suddenly understand. I must have begged him to open the cupboard. When I could not find my mother, I feared she must have vanished, like my nurse not long before, I must have heard that the old woman had been locked, or rather "boxed" [*eingekastelt*] up, because my brother Philipp, who is now sixty-three, was fond of such humorous expressions, and still is to the present day. The fact that I turned to him shows that I was well aware of his part in my nurse's disappearance. (*Origins,* pp. 222–23)

Like the incident in "Screen Memories," where Freud endows the concept of "defloration" with the literal meaning of "snatching away flowers," this memory turns on the construction of a rebus. Philipp's equivocal reference to the nurse's imprisonment—*"sie ist eingekastelt"*—is understood by the young Freud to mean that she has literally been put into a cupboard. Just as a dream attempts to find visual equivalents for verbal expressions, the semantic ambiguity of Philipp's remark is given plastic form in Freud's memory.

The truth surrounding the disappearance of Freud's nurse is extremely difficult to determine. In the immediately preceding letter of October 3, where his nurse is termed his "primary originator" of neurosis, Freud states that it was not she who stole coins from his mother, but he himself who did it at her instigation. Only after verifying the memory with his mother, who told him about Philipp's role in having the nurse arrested, does Freud supply Fliess with the revised version of the episode. Marie Balmary, in her tendentious reexamination of Freud's past, has cast doubt on the entire matter of the nurse's imprisonment for theft by arguing that both her enforced disappearance and the Freud family's departure from Freiberg were attempts to suppress evidence of Jakob Freud's mysterious *second* marriage to a woman named Rebekka.[41] But it is not necessary to follow Balmary to agree that the discrepancy between the two accounts is significant, and that Freud's original fantasies are more important than the version of events subsequently elaborated on the basis of inquiries with his mother.[42]

Upon learning his mother's recollections of the story, Freud explains to Fliess how he could easily have been mistaken:

I wrote to you that she induced me to steal zehners and give them to her. In truth, the dream meant that she stole them herself. . . . The correct interpretation is: I = she. (Masson, p. 271)

Regardless of whether Freud himself or the nurse was the actual thief, the key point is their interchangeability as aggressors against his mother: "I = she." Freud's unconscious tendency to direct violence as well as love toward women, which emerges in his "assault on the old woman" at the moment of his discovery of the Oedipus complex as well as in his and John's "cruel" treatment of Pauline in childhood, here finds a prototype in Freud's early transgression against his mother. Freud himself points to the ramifications of this episode by connecting these childhood "zehners" to thoughts of "Martha's housekeeping money" and of money he receives for the "bad treatment" (*Origins*, p. 221) of his patients. Mother, wife, and patients—specifically Emma Eckstein—are drawn together as victims of Freud's hostile impulses or actions. At the same time, however, his "bad treatment" of women takes place through identification with a woman, and the equation "I = she" thus shows that Freud's misogynistic acts of aggression are no less directed against the feminine part of himself.

Along with his unusual family constellation, the death of Julius, and his family's departure from Freiberg, Freud's possession of two mothers during his earliest years is a fourth crucial biographical determinant of his heroic destiny. Indeed, the presence of the nurse in his household is an aspect of Freud's three-generational kinship structure, since, as Jones (*LW*, 1:10) points out, it made possible his fantasy of pairing her off with his middle-aged father and his mother with his half-brothers who were her chronological contemporaries. Such a doubling of parental figures is a staple feature of heroic myths, including those of Oedipus and Moses; and Leonardo da Vinci, another of Freud's revered models, likewise had two mothers.[43] Beyond conforming to this mythic pattern, Freud's polarization of the image of the mother into *"mater"* and "Nannie" has a direct bearing on his discovery of the Oedipus complex. In Jim Swan's words:

Having two such mothers, and the luck of having the "bad," ugly mother banished from his life when he was only two and a half, allows Freud to maintain a secure split between the internalized good and bad mothers. It also allows him to preserve his close relationship with his actual, very idealized mother, who, in turn, idealizes her first-born and only son.[44]

With the disappearance from his life of the nurse, who as "bad mother" forms a precursor of the punishing, castrating father, Freud is able also to banish his resentments against his mother and to consolidate the idealized image of her purely as an object of desire that forms the basis of the "positive" Oedipus complex.

Freud returned to this memory of his mother in the cupboard in a 1907 addition to the chapter on "Childhood and Screen Memories" in *The Psychopathology of Everyday Life*. In this later public

account Freud makes clear that he regarded Philipp as responsible
for his mother's confinement during childbirth just as he was for
the nurse's imprisonment: "When my mother left me a short while
later, I suspected that my naughty brother had done the same
thing to her that he had done to the nurse and I forced him to
open the cupboard [*Kasten*] for me" (*SE*, 6:51). But, in a signal
instance of "deferred action," it is only in a footnote added in
1924 that Freud explicitly connects his memory and his mother's
pregnancy with Anna:

The child of not yet three had understood that the little sister who had
recently arrived had grown inside his mother. He was very far from
approving of this addition to the family, and was full of mistrust and
anxiety that his mother's inside might conceal still more children. The
wardrobe or cupboard was a symbol for him of his mother's inside. So
he insisted on looking into this cupboard, and turned for this to his big
brother, who (as is clear from other material) had taken his father's place
as the child's rival. Besides the well-founded suspicion that his brother
had the lost nurse "boxed up," there was a further suspicion against
him—namely that he had in some way introduced the recently born
baby into his mother's inside. The affect of disappointment when the
cupboard was found to be empty derived, therefore, from the superficial
motivation of the child's demand. As regards the *deeper* trend of thought,
the affect was in the wrong place. On the other hand, his great satisfaction
over his mother's slimness can only be fully understood in light of this
deeper layer. (*SE*, 6:51–52)

Freud's "mistrust and anxiety" that the birth of his sister
might be followed by still more rivals for his mother's love associates this memory with his jealousy and guilt at the birth and
death of Julius. What Freud calls the "deeper layer" of thought—
"his great satisfaction over his mother's slimness"—is tied to his
resentment at her pregnancy, while his ostensibly "superficial"
emotion of desolation stems from his anxieties of separation. The
way that conflicting trains of thought cause the "affect of disappointment" to appear "in the wrong place" is glossed by the
comment in *The Interpretation of Dreams* that "the dream-work is at
liberty to detach an affect from its connections in the dream-
thoughts and introduce it at any other point it chooses in the
manifest dream" (*SE*, 5:465). Freud's unconscious belief that it
was Philipp who had "introduced the recently born baby into his

mother's inside" reflects the impact of his family constellation on this screen memory. As we know, his slips in *The Interpretation of Dreams* concerning Hannibal's father and the Greek gods reveal the wish to be the son of Emmanuel, but here, as in Freud's naming of Alexander, it is the unmarried Philipp who has "taken his father's place as the child's rival." Of the two half-brothers, consequently, it may be said that Emmanuel, of whom Freud always remained fond, took over the idealizing and affectionate current of Freud's feelings toward his father, whereas the "naughty" Philipp inherited the hostile components of the Oedipus complex.[45]

Freud interprets the cupboard as "a symbol of his mother's inside." But as the "box" in which his nurse was imprisoned, this womb is simultaneously a tomb or coffin. The riddle confronted by the child peering into the empty cupboard is at once that of birth and death. In *The Interpretation of Dreams*, Freud asserts that to young children disappearance is indistinguishable from death:

To children . . . being "dead" means approximately the same as being "gone"—not troubling the survivors any longer. A child makes no distinction how this absence is brought about. . . . If, during a child's prehistoric epoch, his nurse has been dismissed, and if soon afterwards his mother has died, the two events are superimposed on each other in a single series in his memory as revealed in analysis. (*SE*, 4:254–55)

Freud's mother did not literally die during his "prehistoric epoch," but she did disappear at the time of Anna's birth, when his nurse was "dismissed," and there can be no doubt that this passage comments autobiographically on the way that Freud himself "superimposed" the losses of his two mothers in early childhood.

Exactly this collapse of birth and death, the womb of Jocasta and the tomb of Antigone, is at the heart of Sophocles' Oedipus cycle. When at the age of two and a half Freud gazed into the cupboard held open by his half-brother he encountered an enigma no less daunting than that of the Sphinx, for his solution to which he was honored on his fiftieth birthday as one "who knew the famous riddles and was a man most mighty."

PART II: INTELLECTUAL HISTORY

"Who of us is Oedipus here? Who the Sphinx? It is a rendezvous, it seems, of questions and question marks."

—Nietzsche, *Beyond Good and Evil*

4
Sophocles
Unbound

"O<small>UR</small> IMAGINARY historian of literature would show that there is a compelling logical development from German Romanticism, the fountain-head of so many currents in modern literature, to the works of Sigmund Freud."[1] Our task in the second part of this book will be to substantiate these words of Erich Heller's. In part 1, I have sought to employ psychoanalytic theory to situate Freud's discovery of the Oedipus complex in the context of his own life, thereby creating a "circle of understanding" in which the method of investigation converges with its object; but I now turn from biography to intellectual history in order to study the culminating moment in Freud's self-analysis not as a personal but as a cultural phenomenon.

An examination of the works of a great writer or thinker as a self-contained whole inevitably produces a very different impression from an approach which compares that figure to predecessors and contemporaries. The former perspective naturally highlights, while the latter tends to minimize, that writer's uniqueness. In the discussion that follows, accordingly, I endeavor to redress an implicit imbalance by recognizing that Freud's thought must be seen in relation to its antecedents. But this does not mean abandoning a psychoanalytic outlook. On the contrary, too many intellectual histories of psychoanalysis, including Henri Ellenberger's erudite *The Discovery of the Unconscious*, have gone astray precisely because they have failed to acknowledge its distinctiveness, that is to say, the epistemological rupture introduced by Freud.[2] Without the impetus provided by Freud's breakthrough, on the other hand, the history to be chronicled here would have no meaning. As Nietzsche writes in *The Gay Science* (1882):

Every great human being exerts a retroactive force: for his sake all of history is placed in the balance again, and a thousand secrets of the past crawl out of their hiding places—into *his* sunshine.[3]

Each of the figures with whom we shall be concerned is sufficiently great to exert the "retroactive force" spoken of by Nietzsche, but it is that of Freud in particular which gives rise to the present inquiry.

In addition to balancing continuities and discontinuities, there is the further problem of deciding into which intellectual tradition Freud is to be placed. Beyond question, from the vast and richly complex body of Freud's work evidence may be extracted to justify seeing him in relation to any number of competing heritages. It is not, therefore, a matter of arguing that there is only one valid or true way of looking at Freud. At the same time, it may be felt that some approaches are more illuminating than others, and it is the contention of the present study that Freud is best understood, not in relation to the "international positivist tradition"[4] of his mentors Brücke or Helmholtz, or even as the connecting link between Darwin and sociobiology,[5] but rather as the heir of the movements of German Romanticism and idealistic philosophy.[6]

As William McGrath has recently established, the most decisive role in shaping Freud's philosophical outlook was played by Franz Brentano, in five of whose courses at the University of Vienna he enrolled during the years 1874–76.[7] In brief, Brentano, a Catholic who had resigned from the priesthood rather than assent to the doctrine of papal infallibility, influenced Freud by insisting on the purposiveness or "intentionality" of mental acts and by seeking to reconcile psychology and natural science through a disciplined study of what he termed "inner perception." His major work, *Psychology from an Empirical Standpoint*, appeared in 1874. Under Brentano's sway, Freud moved beyond the extreme materialism advocated by the school of Helmholtz in favor of a view that saw mental and physical phenomena as part of an unbroken continuum.

But though the connection with Brentano suffices to lift Freud out of a purely positivistic tradition, it does not go far toward situating him in the context of Romanticism or idealistic philosophy. For Brentano, whose primary allegiance was to the English empiricists, was consistently critical of Hegel and other metaphysical thinkers. In this, moreover, he was followed by Freud, who attacked with equal energy the psychology of Wilhelm Wundt, which equated mental life with consciousness, and the school of "*Naturphilosophie*," founded by Schelling, whose championing of the unconscious he regarded as wholly unscientific. In "The Claims of Psycho-Analysis to Scientific Interest" (1913), Freud summarizes what he takes to be the two positions adopted by philosophers with respect to the unconscious:

Either their unconscious has been something mystical, something intangible and undemonstrable, whose relation to the mind has remained obscure, or they have identified the mental with the conscious and have proceeded to infer from this definition that what is unconscious cannot be mental or a subject for psychology. (*SE*, 13:178)

It is in light of the judgments expressed here that one must assess a declaration such as that found in Freud's letter to Fliess on January 1, 1896:

I see that you are using the circuitous route of medicine to attain your first ideal, the physiological understanding of man, while I secretly nurse the hope of arriving by the same route at my own original objective, philosophy. For that was my original ambition, before I knew what I was intended to do in the world. (*Origins*, p. 141)

When Freud states that philosophy was his "original objective," he in all likelihood does not mean the kind practiced by Hegel or even Nietzsche, but rather the fusion of philosophical knowledge with empirical psychology exemplified by Brentano.

Thus, it must be admitted that the argument for Freud's intellectual ancestry presented here is to a large extent one that he would not himself have recognized. In partial extenuation, it may be pleaded that Brentano, despite being in many respects Wundt's antithesis, agreed with him in denying the existence of a psychical unconscious; and that Freud's defense of this idea aligns him with the Romantic tradition despite his own protestations. More radically, however, I would argue that it is from the example of psychoanalysis itself, above all, as embodied in Freud's own self-analysis, that a true sense of its nature must be derived. Thus, Freud's frequent repudiations of the attempt to equate psychoanalysis with literature and philosophy cannot override the commonality formed by their shared preoccupation with human nature and the problems of self-knowledge. As Jürgen Habermas has justly written, "psychoanalytic knowledge belongs to the category of self-reflection" because, like philosophical hermeneutics, it "derives its function in the process of the genesis of self-consciousness."[8]

Taking Freud's discovery of the Oedipus complex as a point of departure, consequently, I shall in this part undertake to show how a veritable obsession with the Oedipus myth—and with the Sophoclean drama in which it receives definitive literary representation—pervades nineteenth-century German literature and thought. My focus will be twofold: on three major Romantic writers—Schiller, Hölderlin, and Kleist—and on the philosophical tradition extending from Hegel to Nietzsche. In the final chapter, I shall examine the twentieth-century interpretations of the Oedipus myth by Heidegger and Lévi-Strauss. By documenting the centrality of *Oedipus the King* to European critical thinking since the French Revolution, I hope to prove that these last two hundred years might accurately be dubbed the "age of Oedipus."

A project in many ways parallel to the present one has recently been mounted by George Steiner. In *Antigones*, Steiner has with passion and learning explored both the afterlife of the ancient legend in Western thought and the mystery of the original Sophoclean tragedy. But Steiner's scheme of intellectual history rests on a fundamental misconception. He believes that, from roughly the 1790s to the beginning of the twentieth century, "pride of place in poetic and philosophic judgement" was held by *Antigone*, "but after 1905, and under pressure of Freudian reference, critical, interpretative focus had shifted to the *Oedipus Rex*."[9] My own view, on the contrary, is that Freud's unfolding of the Oedipus complex from *Oedipus the King*, while marking a watershed in the history of ideas, must itself be seen as the climax of a long-standing cultural preoccupation with this play. One need not, of course, deny the importance of one Sophoclean tragedy in order to build up that of another, and the widespread nineteenth-century interest in both *Oedipus the King* and *Antigone* is itself part of the larger phenomenon indelibly named by E. M. Butler "the tyranny of Greece over Germany."[10] But Steiner, in order to press his one-sided case for the centrality of *Antigone*, is led to play down those writers (Schiller, Kleist) for whom *Oedipus the King* is obviously preeminent, and to overlook the extent to which, even in those poetic thinkers he treats extensively (Hegel, Hölderlin, Heidegger), an absorption in *Antigone* is inseparable from that in *Oedipus the King*.

If one were to try to tell the whole story of Sophocles' influence from the publication of the *editio princeps* by Aldus Manutius in Venice in 1502 to the present, one would in effect be charting the intellectual history of the West since the Renaissance.[11] Fortunately, at least some foreshortening is permissible here. My thesis, in brief, is the following: until approximately the 1790s, admiration for Sophocles' *Oedipus the King* was almost always contaminated by extraneous features, above all the baleful example of Seneca (c. 4 B.C.–A.D. 65). Only when German Romantic writers and philosophers, following the lead of Lessing, were able to clear away neoclassical and Senecan excrescences, and behold Sophocles' drama afresh as a tragedy of self-knowledge, do we enter the "age of Oedipus" that reaches its apogee in Freud.

The incurable defect of Seneca's *Oedipus* is its rending of the exquisite fabric of Sophocles' plot, and reliance instead on the grossest effects of bombast and spectacle—epitomized by the narrated summoning of the ghost of Laius—to jar the audience. At the same time, the metaphysical reach of Sophocles' play is reduced to pious moralizing about the dangers of "exceed[ing] the allotted bounds."[12] Seneca's Teiresias, unlike Sophocles', does not possess the burdensome knowledge of Oedipus' guilt; necessitating the necromantic appeal to Laius, this change likewise eliminates the struggle between king and prophet as dialectically opposed "blind seers." Analogously, whereas Sophocles creates dramatic irony by having Oedipus declare at the outset to the assembled Thebans, "sick as you are, there is none / whose sickness is equal to mine,"[13] Seneca's Oedipus is apprehensive because "this pestilence, / so deadly to Cadmus' race, so widespread in its destruction, / *spares* me alone" (ll. 29–31; italics added). Examples could be multiplied, but this removal of Oedipus' avowal of suffering from the effects of the plague typifies the way that Seneca's play—whatever its other virtues—is no longer a tragedy of self-analysis.

In the vanguard of the revolt against both Seneca and French neoclassicism, as I have indicated, was Lessing, whom Freud both admired for his prose style and venerated for his espousal of tolerance toward Jews.[14] Lessing was himself building on and reacting against the work of Winckelmann, the art historian who was singly most responsible for the enthrallment of the German imagination by ancient Greece.[15] Lessing was first prompted to write his celebrated treatise *Laocoon* (1766) by Winckelmann's early pamphlet *Thoughts on the Imitation of Greek Works in Painting and Sculpture* (1755), and gave his work its title and final form following the publication of the latter's *History of Art* (1764). In *Laocoon*, Lessing strove to refute Winckelmann's equation between poetry and the visual arts, and argued for the superiority of the temporal medium of language. Despite his disagreement with Winckelmann's theoretical assumptions, however, Lessing shares with his antagonist the conviction that the character of Philoctetes constitutes a pinnacle of aesthetic achievement and, by extension, an unqualified admiration for Sophocles.

In chapter 4 of *Laocoon*, Lessing offers a devastating comparison between the dramaturgy of Sophocles and the "so-called tragedies of Seneca." Attributing the degeneration of Roman tragedy to the way that "the spectators learned in the bloody amphitheaters to misapprehend all nature," he continues:

The most tragic genius, becoming accustomed to these artistic scenes of death, had to lapse into bombast and rhodomontade. But just as little as such rhodomontades can inspire true heroism, just so little can Philoctetes' complaints make one weak. . . . He is the highest thing that wisdom can produce and art imitate.[16]

In his *Hamburg Dramaturgy* (1769), Lessing's ire is directed not against Seneca but against French neoclassicism, but the thrust of his remarks is nearly identical. Number 81 distills his attitude toward neoclassical drama, epitomized by Corneille, which he damns with faint praise by denying to it the name of tragedy:

"Various French tragedies are very fine, instructive works, which I think worthy of all praise, except that they are no tragedies."[17] Most strikingly, Lessing proceeds to couple Shakespeare with the Greek tragedians in opposition to the self-professed imitators of the ancients:

> Their authors could be nothing other than very good intellects . . . only that they are no tragic poets; only that their Corneille and Racine, their Crebillon and Voltaire have little or nothing at all of that which makes Sophocles Sophocles, Euripides Euripides, Shakespeare Shakespeare. These latter are seldom in contradiction with Aristotle's essential demands, but the former are so all the more often.[18]

The widespread current assumption that Shakespeare shares with the ancient Greek tragedians an essential kinship, which is all the more remarkable for being independent of direct influence, has its origin in the seminal criticism of Lessing.[19]

The fundamental justice of Lessing's strictures is confirmed by an examination of the plays written by Corneille (1659) and Voltaire (1719) on the subject of Oedipus.[20] As the forerunners of the German Romantics, moreover, the works of these French men of letters throw into sharp relief the innovation of those writers with whom we are principally concerned. Both Corneille and Voltaire are authors of critical essays containing commentaries on Oedipus that assist us in understanding their dramas. In his *Discourse on Tragedy* (1660), an extended meditation on Aristotle's *Poetics* and the second of his three major treatises, Corneille considers Aristotle's remarks on the subjects of pity and fear and instances the example of Oedipus to support his own view that these emotions need not be inseparable:

> If we are to believe [Aristotle], [Oedipus] has all the conditions requisite in a tragedy; nevertheless, his unhappiness excites only pity, and I do not think that any of those seeing him represented presume themselves in fear of killing their father or of marrying their mother.[21]

Beginning with the belief that Oedipus has not committed "any fault," Corneille here prophetically advances an interpretation of *Oedipus the King* that is directly opposed to Freud's claim that "Oedipus' fate moves us because it might have been ours—because the oracle laid the same curse upon us before our birth as upon him" (*SE*, 4:262)—and thereby misses the point of Sophocles' tragedy.

The extent of Corneille's departure from Sophocles is underscored by the prefatory *Examen* (1660) he appended to his own *Oedipus*, in which he tells of the difficulties he faced in selecting a theme acknowledged to be the "masterpiece of antiquity":

I will not at all conceal that after having chosen this subject, in the confidence . . . that the thoughts of Sophocles and Seneca, who have treated it in their languages, would smooth the path for me to succeed, I trembled when I considered it more closely.[22]

Corneille's juxtaposition of Sophocles and Seneca, with no sense of their incommensurability, attests to his limited understanding of Greek tragedy, and likewise supports Lessing's diagnosis of an unfortunate resemblance between French neoclassicism and the "bombast and rhodomontade" of Seneca. To make matters worse, Corneille laments in his *Examen* that "love not having any part in this tragedy, it was denuded of the principal ornaments that are needed to gain public approbation,"[23] and promises to remedy this defect in his own drama.

Corneille's *Oedipus* is in fact exactly what one might expect from his critical pronouncements—a mélange of Sophocles and Seneca, in which the focus of interest is not on Oedipus' quest for self-knowledge but on a love intrigue between Theseus and Dirce, a daughter born of the marriage of Laius and Jocasta, and on the threat posed by Dirce to the legitimacy of Oedipus' claim to the Theban throne. Emblematic of Corneille's neglect of Sophocles' essential concerns is his elimination of the character of Teiresias; following Seneca, moreover, he names the old Herdsman Phorbas and includes (Act 2, scene 3) a bloody account of the summoning of the ghost of Laius. Corneille seeks to reconcile his philosophical commitment to the doctrine of free will with the intractable constraints of the myth, but succeeds only in disrupting the Sophoclean pattern of progressive return to the past that is the soul of *Oedipus the King*. Corneille's Oedipus learns in Act 4 from Phorbas that he is the murderer of Laius, and separately in Act 5 from the Corinthian ambassador, here named Iphicrate, and Phorbas that he is the son of Laius and Jocasta and the brother of Dirce. The hint of an eventual marriage between Theseus and Dirce remains tastefully muted at the close. Indeed, the most ingenious feature of this *Oedipus* is the earlier intimation of the possibility of brother-sister incest, as Theseus pretends to be the brother of Dirce in order to take upon himself the curse that a descendant of Laius must be sacrificed to expiate his murder.

Voltaire's *Oedipus*, his first play, is deservedly overshadowed by the seven critical *Letters on Oedipus* he published in conjunction with his drama. Of these, by far the most important is the third, "Containing the Critique of the *Oedipus* of Sophocles." Not for Voltaire is the appreciation of Sophocles of Winckelmann or Lessing; rather, his third Letter is the definitive neoclassical arraignment of *Oedipus the King*, comparable in its trenchancy to Rymer's anatomy of *Othello* or Dr. Johnson on the metaphysical poets. Voltaire declares that "he knows absolutely no term to express the absurdity" of Oedipus' failure to inquire into the circumstances of his predecessor's death; he mocks Sophocles for "forgetting that the vengeance of the death of Laius is the subject of the play," since Oedipus neglects to ask the Herdsman about the murder of Laius once he has uncovered the secret of his identity; he observes that, once Teiresias confirms Oedipus' suspicions of his illegitimacy, "you will find that the play is entirely finished by the beginning of the second act,"[24] and so forth. Like the analyses of his neoclassical counterparts, Voltaire's objections address the most crucial issues of *Oedipus the King*, but at the same time reveal his utter lack of sympathy for the premises of Sophocles' artistry.

Voltaire's low opinion of Sophocles is balanced by his high regard for Corneille. "I respect much more, without doubt, this French tragedian than the Greek," he affirms in Letter 4. Voltaire astutely recognizes that in Corneille's play "the passion of Theseus makes the whole subject of the tragedy, and the sorrows of Oedipus are only an episode,"[25] but he regards the defects in both Corneille's *Oedipus* and his own—taken up in Letter 5—as due to the unavoidable thinness and implausibility of the subject matter. Like Corneille, Voltaire introduces a romantic subplot, involving a secret love between the imported character of Philoctetes and Jocasta, who is depicted as having married both Laius and Oedipus without enthusiasm. Voltaire copies as well Corneille's formula of mingling Sophocles with Seneca, eliminating the character of Teiresias, and, above all, detaching the solution of the murder of Laius from Oedipus' unraveling of the mystery of his birth. A concrete indication of the weakness of structure in Voltaire's *Oed-*

ipus is the fact that the Herdsman Phorbas makes two separate entrances—the first (Act 4, scene 2) in his capacity as witness to the murder of Laius, and the second (Act 5, scene 3), following the Messenger's revelation that Oedipus is not the son of the king and queen of Corinth, to confirm the truth concerning his parentage. Voltaire shows himself no less obtuse than Corneille to *Oedipus the King*, but whereas the latter replaced the Sophoclean drama of self-analysis with assertions of free will and heroic magnanimity, the former foreshadows his career as a freethinker with incidental attacks on religious superstition and hereditary privilege.

But though Voltaire does his best to evade the themes of incest and patricide, he cannot escape their burden altogether. As Otto Rank has suggested, it is surely significant that Philoctetes, in addition to being the beloved of Jocasta, is also accused of murdering Laius, thereby becoming a displaced double for Oedipus, much as Claudius carries out the unconscious fantasies of Hamlet.[26] Voltaire, moreover, may well have been drawn to the Oedipus myth as the subject of his first play from profound biographical motives, since it is known that he did not believe himself to be the son of his mother's husband, the tax official François Arouet, but rather of a swashbuckling musketeer and writer named Rochebrune. Even more noteworthy in this regard is the fact that it was in 1718, the year of his composition of *Oedipus*, that the twenty-two-year-old Arouet first signed himself with the self-chosen name of Voltaire.[27] Thus, like Freud's abandoning of the name of Sigismund for Sigmund at the moment of his decision to pursue a career in medicine rather than law, Voltaire seals his entry into the world of letters with an act of self-creation even as he chooses to write a play on the theme of Oedipus.

Despite these biographical considerations, however, the crucial point remains the corruption, in both Corneille and Voltaire, of the Sophoclean paradigm by extraneous romantic and Senecan elements. As an intellectual figure, Voltaire is a leading representative of the Enlightenment, but in his aesthetic ideals he remains bound to the neoclassicism of his predecessors in the theater. From this perspective, it is only with Lessing's reaction against French neoclassical as well as Senecan drama—his denial that these forms achieve the true sublimity of tragedy—that the subsequent Romantic obsession with *Oedipus the King* becomes possible.

In addition to Lessing, a second spokesman of the Enlightenment playing a pivotal transitional role in this history is Diderot. His *Rameau's Nephew*, a work in which modern consciousness may be observed giving birth to itself, is distinguished by having exerted a lasting influence on, among others, Hegel and Freud.[28] Written between 1761 and 1774 but never published during Diderot's lifetime, the work reached a European audience through Goethe's 1805 German translation. Goethe undertook this project at the instigation of Schiller, though the latter did not live to see its completion. Freud quoted from the dialogue for the first time in Lecture 21 of his *Introductory Lectures on Psycho-Analysis* (1916–17), and did so again twice subsequently. In each case, the passage chosen was that in which the character Diderot describes the impulses reigning in the mind of a young child:

> If the little savage were left to himself, preserving all his foolishness and adding to the small sense of a child in the cradle the violent passions of a man of thirty, he would strangle his father and lie with his mother. (*SE*, 16:338)

It is not difficult to understand why such a forthright statement of the essential tenets of the Oedipus complex should have appealed so strongly to Freud. Hegel, in contrast, who encountered *Rameau's Nephew* in Goethe's translation as he was writing the *Phenomenology of Mind* (1807), quotes from the work three times in his section on "Spirit in Self-Estrangement" and celebrates the paradoxical character of the Nephew as an incarnation of modern self-consciousness. In the absence of any evidence that Freud was directly influenced by Hegel, the fact that they both employ *Rameau's Nephew* to illustrate crucial aspects of their thought attests that they do participate in a common intellectual heritage.

The juxtaposition of Hegel's concept of self-conscious spirit with Freud's Oedipus complex in *Rameau's Nephew* captures the essence of what is at stake in the Romantic preoccupation with the Oedipus myth. In the aftermath of the French Revolution, which strove to do away with the past but resulted instead in a drastic intensification of the burden of history, the ubiquitous philosophical problem was how to come to terms with and surmount the barriers between consciousness and nature, subject and object, erected in the philosophy of Kant. The responses of individual thinkers—Schiller, Fichte, Schelling, Hegel, and others—

differ somewhat in emphasis, but all seek to undertake an "odyssey of consciousness" to overcome the condition of exile from
nature or self-estrangement. Charles Taylor has given the name
"expressivist anthropology" to the "new concept of self-aware-
ness" that took shape in various ways in the final decades of the
eighteenth century:

In seeing human life as expression, it rejects the dichotomy of meaning
against being; it deals once more in the Aristotelian coin of final causes
and holistic concepts. But in another respect it is quintessentially modern; for it incorporates the idea of a self-defining subjectivity. The realization of his essence is a subject's self-realization; so that what he defines
himself in relation to is not an ideal order beyond, but rather something
which unfolds from himself, in his own realization, and is first made
determinate in that realization.[29]

Taylor's explication of "self-defining subjectivity" succinctly distills the common project not only of Hegel and his contemporaries,
but also of Nietzsche and Freud. The gravitation toward *Oedipus
the King* by poets and philosophers from Schiller to Freud, in turn,
is due to its preeminence as a drama of self-unfolding, in which
(in Habermas' words) the "genesis of self-consciousness" is in-
comparably enacted.

A. W. Schlegel's compendious *Lectures on Dramatic Art and
Literature* (1808), though not remarkable for brilliance of original
insight, are extremely useful as an expression of the commonplaces of Romantic thought. In his comparison of the "sublime
creations" of the Greek tragedians to those of Seneca, for example,
he forcibly restates the views of Lessing:

The state of constant outrage in which Rome was kept by a series of
bloodthirsty tyrants, gave an unnatural character even to eloquence and
poetry. . . . But whatever period may have given birth to the tragedies
of Seneca, they are beyond description bombastic and frigid, unnatural
both in character and action. . . . With the old tragedies, those sublime
creations of the poetical genius of the Greeks, these have nothing in
common, but the name, the outward form, and the mythological materials; and yet they seem to have been composed with the obvious
purpose of surpassing them; in which attempt they succeed as much as
a hollow hyperbole would in competition with a most fervent truth.[30]

Schlegel's entire discussion of Greek tragedy is founded on the
historical scheme of Winckelmann, wherein Aeschylus incarnates

the drama in its austere beginnings, Sophocles its peak of harmonious perfection, and Euripides the softening into decadence. This same evolutionary scheme persists virtually unchanged in Nietzsche's *The Birth of Tragedy* (1872).

In his survey of the works of Sophocles in Lecture 7, Schlegel refuses to award the palm to any single play, asserting that "the whole of the tragedies of Sophocles are separately resplendent with peculiar excellencies" (p. 100). But though he does not concentrate particularly on *Oedipus the King*, Schlegel makes the important observation that "the grand and terrible character" of this drama is due to

the circumstance which, however, is for the most part overlooked; that to the very Oedipus who solved the riddle of the Sphinx relating to human life, his own life should remain so long an inextricable riddle, to be so awfully cleared up, when all was irretrievably lost. (p. 101)

The implications of this insight will be pondered more deeply by Nietzsche, as will those of Schlegel's remark that, despite the "severe conclusion" of *Oedipus the King*, "we are so far reconciled to it . . . that our feelings do not absolutely revolt at so horrible a fate" (p. 101). In defending the proposition that "a close analysis of the piece will evince the utmost propriety and significance of every portion of it" (p. 102), moreover, Schlegel draws attention to features of the play which had aroused the scorn of Voltaire— such as Oedipus' neglecting to inquire into the death of Laius— and dismisses objections to them with a Romantic stroke: "But the ancients did not produce their works of art for calculating and prosaic understandings" (p. 102). Although far less incisive than the criticism of Voltaire, Schlegel's enthusiastic appreciation in fact comes closer to capturing the spirit of Sophoclean tragedy.

One remarkable feature of the intellectual history of Germany at this period is the direct personal contact among many leading figures. As is well known, Hegel, Schelling, and Hölderlin lived together during their formative years at the seminary in Tübingen between 1790 and 1793.[31] A particularly intimate connection between A. W. Schlegel and Schelling is formed by the fact that, in 1803, the wife of the former, Caroline, divorced him to marry the latter.[32] In our own time, the "retroactive force" of Hegel has largely eclipsed the reputation of Schelling, but in his own day, the prolific Schelling, despite being five years Hegel's junior, initially seemed the more dominant thinker of the two. In essence marking a transition between the complete subjective idealism of Fichte and the dialectical system of Hegel, Schelling is praised in Hegel's first published philosophical work, *The Difference Between the Fichtean and Schellingian Systems of Philosophy* (1801), which appeared after he had joined Schelling on the faculty at the University of Jena, for contending that the dynamism of nature possessed a self-determining quality similar to that found in consciousness, and thereby revealing the underlying unity of subject and object manifested in both spheres. In the Preface to the *Phenomenology of Mind*, however, Hegel criticized Schelling in all but name for treating the concept of the Absolute as a static formula instead of as an infinitely self-differentiating process, and a break between the two men followed.[33]

Like Schlegel, Schelling is relevant in the present context because he is representative of attitudes widespread in the Romantic period. Above all, in his pronouncements on tragedy, to be found in the tenth and final letter of his *Philosophical Letters on Dogmatism and Criticism* (1795) and in the relevant sections of his posthumously published *Philosophy of Art* (1802–1803), Schelling points up how *Oedipus the King* could be viewed as a tragedy of self-consciousness. Addressed to an unnamed correspondent, who was almost certainly Hölderlin,[34] the *Philosophical Letters* show Schelling at an early stage of his thought defending his concept of spiritual freedom, which entailed a complete rejection of the external world, against the view that freedom was best conceived in terms of the plight of the tragic hero. But though he finds the solutions of art ultimately unacceptable, Schelling's insights into tragedy are extremely suggestive. Acknowledging that, "As everywhere, so Greek art is here *rule*," he observes:

It has often been asked, how the Greek reason could bear the contradictions of its tragedy. A mortal—ordained by destiny to be a criminal, himself struggling *against* destiny, and nonetheless frightfully punished for the crime, which was a work of fate![35]

The source of this contradiction in Greek tragedy, according to Schelling, lies in "the quarrel of human freedom with the power of the objective world," and he holds it to be a "*great* thought, willingly to carry also the punishment for an *unavoidable* crime."

By the *Philosophy of Art*, Schelling had moved away from his Fichtean insistence on the autonomy of consciousness and, in the *System of Transcendental Idealism* (1801), he had embraced the view that the reconciliation of subject and object was best revealed not in philosophy but in art. Thus, when he comes to treat "Of Tragedy" in the *Philosophy of Art*, Schelling restates and amplifies his earlier remarks, but without the attendant reservations. In addition, he makes explicit what could easily be inferred from his previous discussion, especially given its origin in exchanges with Hölderlin—that he took as his paradigmatic instance of tragedy Sophocles' *Oedipus the King*.

Once again, Schelling begins with the premise that the essence of tragedy is "an actual quarrel of freedom in the subject and necessity as objective," the outcome of which is that "both appear victorious and defeated in complete indifference."[36] Schelling's conception of tragedy as a collision of opposing forces, in which neither gains the upper hand, is unquestionably a source for the far better known theory of Hegel. No less prescient is Schelling's comment, reiterated here from the *Philosophical Letters*, that "the tragic person is *necessarily* guilty of a crime (and the higher the guilt is, as that of Oedipus, so much the more tragic and complicated)" (p. 695), for the same emphasis on the inevitable criminality of the tragic hero pervades the writings of Nietzsche. Like both Nietzsche and Schlegel, moreover, Schelling ponders the riddle of the "cause of the reconciliation and the harmony that lie" (p. 697) in Greek tragedy, and offers his own solution in the paradox whereby "absolute freedom is itself absolute necessity" (p. 699). And if Schelling prefigures Hegel and Nietzsche, he also anticipates Freud when he asserts that the action of tragedy must be "not merely external, but rather internal, contained within the mind itself. . . . It suffices for bad poets to contain only externally the laboriously continued action" (p. 703). Schelling's distinction between good and bad drama exactly parallels that drawn by Freud in *The Interpretation of Dreams* between the "voice within us ready to recognize the compelling force of destiny in the *Oedipus*" and the arbitrariness of most "modern tragedies of destiny" (*SE*, 4:262). The mediation of *Rameau's Nephew* needed to forge a link between Freud and Hegel is superfluous in the case of Schelling, moreover, for it is directly from the latter that Freud derives his preferred definition of the "uncanny" as *"everything that ought to have remained . . . secret and hidden but has come to light"* (*SE*, 18:224).

Schelling's discussion of tragedy has been treated with surprising harshness by recent commentators. M. S. Silk and J. P. Stern write:

> The tragic hero of Sophocles' *Oedipus Rex*, to choose Schelling's own example, is hardly the Protestant hero that Schelling makes out. It is not any external fate, but rather his own determination to search out the truth, that brings about his defeat. . . . Above all, there is no special "honour" attaching to him as an individual in respect of his "free" but "hopeless" endeavor to fight against his fate. The honour that accrues to him is the honour due to his kingship.[37]

But in attempting to denigrate Schelling, Silk and Stern only reveal the limitations in their own view of tragedy. For surely they are wrong to deny that "external fate"—whether it be symbolized by the plague or the oracle—plays no role in Oedipus' downfall. Schelling's contribution is precisely to emphasize the dialectical relation between fate and free will in *Oedipus the King*, whereby these two seemingly exclusive explanatory principles are both able to hold sway simultaneously. In this, he makes a decisive advance over Corneille, whose insistence on Oedipus' innocence registers only one half of the equation. Silk and Stern are equally wide of the mark in reducing Oedipus' dignity merely to the social fact of his kingship. Despite his commission of the most unthinkable crimes, and whatever the flaws in his character, Oedipus commands admiration for his determination to seek out the truth at all costs and his struggle against the very fate by which he is condemned, and it is to this metaphysical dimension of his heroism that Schelling has responded so profoundly.

The single most important source of intellectual inspiration for the triad of Hegel, Hölderlin, and Schelling was the poetry and philosophical writing of Schiller.[38] Born in 1759, and thus only eleven years older than Hegel and Hölderlin, Schiller provided a model for the young seminary students both in his endeavor to get beyond the duality of reason and nature enshrined in Kantianism and in his enthusiasm for the ideal of undivided sensibility embodied in Greek life and art. I shall treat Schiller in more detail in chapter 5, but here wish only to indicate that, beyond his general fascination with Greek culture, he led the way for the next generation also in his particular devotion to *Oedipus the King*. As early as 1788, Schiller had been smitten with the idea of attempting to write a tragedy in the Greek manner, but it was not until his letter to Goethe of October 2, 1797 that he openly avowed his ambition to recapture the spirit of Sophocles:

> I have been much occupied these days with searching out the material for a tragedy, which would be of the pattern of *Oedipus Rex* and furnish the same advantages to the poet. These advantages are immeasurable. . . . To this contributes that what has happened, as unalterable, is by its nature much more terrible, and the fear that something might *have happened* affects the mind completely differently from the fear that something might happen.
> The *Oedipus* is, as it were, only a tragic analysis. Everything is already there, and only remains to be unfolded. . . .
> But I fear that the *Oedipus* is its own genus and that there belongs to it no second species. Least of all would one find a counterpart to it from less legendary times. The oracle has a part in the tragedy, which absolutely cannot be replaced by anything else; and if one wanted to preserve the substance of the plot itself, with altered persons and times, what is now terrible would become ludicrous.[39]

This letter marks the culmination of the unbinding of Sophocles, which we have traced through Lessing's reaction against Voltaire and Corneille and into the Romantic period. Schiller's succinct definition of *Oedipus the King* as a "tragic analysis," in which "everything is already there, and only remains to be unfolded," sweeps aside all the peripheral Senecan and amorous material imported into the play by French neoclassicists, and strikingly looks ahead to Freud. The connection between Schiller and Freud becomes all the more remarkable when it is noted that this letter to Goethe of October 2, 1797 anticipates by almost exactly a century Freud's letter to Fliess of October 15, 1897, announcing his epochal interpretation of *Oedipus the King*. It becomes possible to view Freud's discovery of the Oedipus complex, therefore, as a cultural "anniversary reaction," completing a movement that had begun in Schiller's letter one hundred years earlier.

To reinforce the parallel, it will be recalled that Freud's father died on October 23, 1896, approximately one year before the decisive letter to Fliess. In analogous fashion, Schiller's father died on September 7, 1796, just over a year before his letter to Goethe. Thus, not only is Freud's finding "love of the mother and jealousy of the father in my own case too" (*Origins*, p. 223) a cultural revenant of Schiller's reference to *Oedipus the King* as a "tragic analysis," but it is plausible to suppose that Schiller's engagement with the Oedipus myth, like Freud's, represents a literal anniversary reaction to the death of his father. It is not necessary to pursue this line of inquiry in every case, but biographical considerations are at least implicitly relevant in any psychoanalytic study of literature. Our inquiry into intellectual history thus remains in part a venture in intellectual biography, and the complex history of Oedipus in nineteenth-century thought constitutes in two senses a genealogy of the Oedipus complex.

5
Three Romantic Case Studies

Schiller

THE CAREER of Schiller merits study both because of his intrinsic importance as a writer and because of his far-reaching influence on contemporaries and successors. The epitome of German classicism, who may also be regarded as the instigator of the Romantic movement, Schiller met and overcame the challenge of forming a positive relationship with Goethe—a task that proved insurmountable to his emulators Hölderlin and Kleist. First stricken in 1791 by the painful attacks of pleurisy to which he was to succumb in 1805, Schiller triumphed over his debilitating physical illness by continuing to exemplify in his life the spiritual equilibrium and equipoise he celebrated in his writings.

Schiller's many-sided genius expressed itself in lyric poetry and aesthetic essays, but it was above all the drama that mattered to him, and it is likewise to his plays that we must turn to document his engagement with Sophocles and the Oedipus myth.[1] The year 1788 marks a turning point in Schiller's artistic development. Already the author of four plays—*The Robbers* (1781), *Fiesko* (1784), *Intrigue and Love* (1784), and his grand tragedy in the French neoclassical manner *Don Carlos* (1787)—Schiller in 1788 came under the spell of Goethe's *Iphigenia in Tauris*, which had appeared the preceding year, and first conceived the idea of essaying a modern tragedy in the Greek manner. There is no trace of any classical influence in Schiller's works prior to that date, but so overwhelmed was he by his discovery of Greece that it led to a more than ten-year hiatus in his writings for the theater not broken until 1799 with the *Wallenstein* trilogy. Schiller in 1788 gave lyric expression to a lament for the evanescence of antiquity in "The Gods of Greece," read widely in translations of classical authors, and, despite knowing very little Greek, himself attempted translations of Euripides' *Iphigenia at Aulis* and the first 627 lines of *The Phoenecian Women*.

It appears to have been only gradually that Schiller's interest in Greek tragedy in general crystallized into the focus on Sophocles, and particularly on *Oedipus the King*, revealed in his October 2, 1797 letter to Goethe. In a letter of July 26, 1800 to J. W. Süvern, Schiller again confessed his "absolute admiration" of Sophocles' tragedies, but also the fear that "they were a phenomenon of their own times, which cannot reappear."[2] Greater or lesser traces of this "absolute admiration" for *Oedipus the King* can be discerned in Schiller's later dramas. In the *Wallenstein* trilogy, he sought to combine the pageantry and scope of Shakespeare's history plays with the Sophoclean technique of placing many crucial events in the prehistory of the action and only showing the working out of the catastrophe. A similar fusion of Shakespeare and Sophocles is found in the masterfully constructed *Mary Stuart* (1800), where, in E. M. Butler's words, "fate takes the form of the sentence of death pronounced on the heroine before the action begins" and "the very steps taken by Mary and her supporters to avert the catastrophe actually hasten its advent," all of which "is close enough to the technique of *Oedipus Tyrannus* to show where Schiller's inspiration came from."[3] In *Demetrius*, likewise, a fragment left uncompleted by Schiller at his death and potentially his greatest play, the plot centers on a pretender to the throne of imperial Russia, himself uncertain of his origins, who becomes "guiltlessly guilty" when he realizes that he is in fact not the rightful heir but is compelled to continue to press his claim lest he disillusion his supporters.

The influence of *Oedipus the King* on Schiller is still more apparent in two additional dramas. Like *Demetrius*, the first of these, *Narbonne* or *The Children of the House*, remains a fragment, begun in 1799 and extensively rewritten in drafts dating from 1804 and 1805.[4] The plot, in brief, is that Louis Narbonne secretly had his brother Pierre killed by Captain Raoul in order to take possession of the family inheritance. It is thought that Pierre's two children, Saintfoix the son and Adelaide the daughter, perished in a conflagration, but in reality they were rescued by Narbonne's trusty retainer Madelon and raised—not knowing their own origins—by a gypsy. Both children have escaped the gypsy and returned to their native city, where Saintfoix is actually reared in the household of the seemingly respectable and virtuous Narbonne. At the start of the play, Narbonne, who wishes to preserve his line by marrying Victoire, the wealthy and beautiful daughter of the bailiff, is troubled by the disappearance of a family heirloom, a piece of jewelry he had wanted to present to his betrothed.

The plot is set in motion when Narbonne, despite the warnings of Madelon that he accept his loss, insists on summoning the police to investigate the jewel theft. Young Saintfoix, suspected of the crime, attempts to flee, accompanied by Adelaide, with whom he feels a mysterious affinity. Brought before the bailiff, Adelaide has on her person another old piece of jewelry which had belonged to her mother, and for the first time Narbonne fears that these children might be the offspring of his murdered brother. He likewise comes upon Saintfoix in a love scene with Victoire, who has always shrunk from him (Narbonne) with an inexplicable dread. In the next development, the gypsy is apprehended as a possible culprit; but, in a reversal like that of the Corinthian Messenger in *Oedipus the King*, who initially enters to announce the death of Polybus but ends up disclosing that he was not Oedipus' true father, she reveals that Saintfoix and Adelaide are brother and sister. Madelon, in the position of the old Herdsman in Sophocles' play, recognizes the gypsy as the woman to whom she had illicitly sold the children, but is slain by Narbonne before she can tell what she knows. The play climaxes with the appearance of Captain Raoul, who proves to have stolen the heirloom to gain vengeance on Narbonne, whom he exposes as his brother's murderer. Saintfoix and Victoire are united in matrimony as Narbonne goes to his deserved doom.

The above summary suffices to make clear how closely Schiller has modeled his plot on *Oedipus the King*. Schiller describes the situation of *Narbonne* in the following words: "Nemesis drives a man to start and hot-headedly to pursue investigations against an enemy, until thereby his own long antiquated crime is brought to light."[5] Narbonne differs from Oedipus in that he seeks to suppress the investigation of a crime he has knowingly perpetrated, rather than to expose a deed of which he is the unwitting culprit, and Schiller's setting of a French provincial town likewise lacks the metaphysical resonance of Sophocles' Thebes. The emphasis on the brother-sister tie, at once sexual and spiritual, is reminiscent of *Antigone* and a further Romantic feature of *Narbonne*. These contrasts notwithstanding, Schiller's nineteenth-century unmasking of bourgeois hypocrisy remains a potentially remarkable dramatic recasting of *Oedipus the King*.

Of Schiller's completed works, the attempt to reproduce "the pattern of *Oedipus Rex*" culminates in *The Bride of Messina* (1803), the last of his plays save for *William Tell* (1804). Featuring a modern equivalent to a Greek chorus, the play is preceded by a brief essay, "On the Use of the Chorus in Tragedy," whose definition of the chorus as a "living wall" against artistic naturalism is cited approvingly by Nietzsche in *The Birth of Tragedy*. (A. W. Schlegel's theory of the chorus as an "ideal spectator," however, meets with Nietzsche's resounding condemnation.) Subtitled *The Enemy Brothers, The Bride of Messina* combines the themes of incest and the power of fate from *Oedipus the King* with the motif of fratricidal rivalry from Euripides' *The Phoenecian Women*.

The equivalent of the oracle, which Schiller in his October 2, 1797 letter to Goethe found so difficult to envision, is provided in this play by a curse on the family of the princes of Messina, Don Manuel and Don Cesar, brought on by their late father, who had wronged his own father by taking the woman intended to be his bride. As the Chorus intones near the end of Act I:

> Theft was it also, as we all know,
> When the former Prince's bride was brought
> To a sinful bride-bed long ago,
> For she was the bride his father sought.
> And the family's founder, fierce in his wrath,
> Poured ghastly curses on the same,
> Strewing that bride bed with seeds of crime.[6]

This curse, destined to be fulfilled in the present generation, takes the form of a conflict between the two brothers, suppressed during the lifetime of their father but renewed after his death. Their mother, Donna Isabella, has managed to reconcile them temporarily, because each has fallen in love with the same woman, who turns out to be their long-lost sister, Beatrice. Like Oedipus, Beatrice as an infant had been ordered killed by her father, as a result of a dream he had which prophesied that "She would become the murderess of both / His sons and would annihilate his race" (ll. 2351–52), but was preserved and kept in hiding by her mother, who believed a contrary prediction that "In ardent love she would some day unite / My two sons' hearts" (ll. 2366–67). In the event, Don Cesar slays Don Manuel upon discovering him in Beatrice's arms, then kills himself upon realizing that she is his sister, thereby fulfilling both halves of the paradoxical prophecy.

The flaws in *The Bride of Messina* have been penetratingly exposed by Martin Mueller. Contrary to Schiller's intention, Mueller argues, "Fate stops short of being a sufficient cause of the catastrophe and appears on closer examination as the consequence of morally culpable actions. Nor is the play's procedure genuinely analytical."[7] The play is not "analytical" because, rather than revealing past events through a process of inquiry, these past events work out their destructive consequences by interacting with present circumstances. On the question of moral culpability, whereas Oedipus commits his transgressions of incest and patricide unknowingly, *The Bride of Messina* resembles *Narbonne* in that its critical deed is "a crime by any standard," since Don Cesar claims possession of Beatrice "without even asking for her permission" and then kills his brother "without even considering whether that man has claims on the woman that might be stronger than his own."[8]

These objections are forceful, as is that to the reliance on contrived coincidences in the play, but a psychoanalytic perspective restores considerable grandeur to *The Bride of Messina* by showing how deeply Schiller explores the infantile roots of sibling rivalry and incest. Donna Isabella attempts to appease her sons' enmity by telling them that they themselves are unaware of its cause:

Think back to what first set you two at odds,
You do not know, and if you once found out,
Your childish grudge would make you blush for shame.
                                                                                    (ll. 414–16)

Far from diminishing its importance, however, this apparent lack
of motivation for the brothers' "childish grudge" is, as Rank observes, "characteristic of incestuous hatred, whose real origin is
in fact repressed."[9] That the brothers' conflict over Beatrice goes
back to desire for exclusive possession of the mother is likewise
underscored by the play. Beatrice prefers the elder Don Manuel,
though both brothers feel drawn to her by an emotion "out of the
dawn-lit days of early childhood" (l. 712); and after he has slain
Don Manuel, Don Cesar is most aggrieved because his mother
refers to his brother as her favorite:

She never loved me. At long last her heart.
Betrayed her there, when her sorrow opened it.
Her better son she called him! She has practiced
Dissimulation all her life!—And you
Are just as false as she!   (ll. 2556–60)

In addition to depicting the sexual rivalry over the sister/lover
Beatrice as a repetition of the brothers' relationship to the mother,
moreover, Schiller intimates that this fratricidal clash is a displacement and reenactment of the original oedipal transgression of the
deceased father.

Before 1788, as I have noted, there is no trace of Sophoclean
influence on Schiller's dramas. There are, nonetheless, some remarkable thematic continuities between his earlier and later
works. Schiller's first play, *The Robbers*, published when he was
only twenty-two, is closely akin to *The Bride of Messina*. Intertwining sibling rivalry and father-son conflict, *The Robbers* treats the
predicament of the virtuous but prodigal son, Karl Moor, who is
exiled from home by the machinations of his evil brother Franz,
his antagonist for the love of their cousin Amalia. *Don Carlos*,
similarly, Schiller's fourth and last play before his ten-year hiatus,
has as its kernel the love of the hero, son to the Spanish king, for
his stepmother, who—in a reversal of the pattern in *The Bride of
Messina*—had been promised to him before being preempted by
his father. Carlos confides to the Marquis of Posa in the opening
scene:

A son who loves his mother:—world-wide usage,
Nature's order, and the laws of Rome
Condemn that passion. Also, my claim comes
In fearful conflict with my father's rights.
I sense this, yet I go on loving.[10]

So pronounced are the oedipal themes of *Don Carlos*, though the incestuous desires are shifted from the natural mother to a step-mother, that Rank places the play beside *Oedipus the King* and *Hamlet* as marking the third distinct stage in the evolution of the Oedipus myth in Western literature.[11]

But, if not from Sophocles, whence is Schiller's preoccupation with oedipal conflicts derived? Certainly, other literary sources may have played a part. Significantly, however, in those fratricidal plays that lie immediately behind *The Robbers*, Leisewitz' *Julius of Taranto* (1776) and Klinger's *The Twins* (1776), the loved woman fought over by the enemy brothers, unlike Amalia, is not a blood relative.[12] Although disputed by some critics,[13] the conclusion becomes inescapable that Schiller's fascination with both oedipal themes and Sophocles' *Oedipus the King* is, like Freud's, in large measure the result of individual biographical determinants.

It would be easy to object to a biographical analysis of Schiller's works that, despite their recurrent depiction of fraternal rivalry, he, the second of four children, had no brothers. As Rank argues, however, we should "not allow ourselves to be misled" by this circumstance, since "through the explanation of the sibling complex by the parental complex, the brother-hatred in Schiller will prove to be a displacement permitted by fantasy of the guilt-accentuated father-complex."[14] In addition, there is decisive evidence to show the intensity of Schiller's attachment to his sister, Christophine, his elder by two years. In 1784, the same year in which a suitor for her hand presented himself in the person of his friend Reinwald—twenty years *her* senior—Schiller urged Christophine to come to Mannheim to manage his household. After her marriage to Reinwald, to which Schiller was vehemently opposed and which proved unhappy, the two siblings carried on a clandestine correspondence behind the back of the poet's jealous brother-in-law.[15]

A direct link between Schiller and Freud is formed by the fact that, as Freud reports in *The Interpretation of Dreams* (*SE*, 5:424), when his nephew John returned during adolescence from England on a visit to Vienna, the two boys acted the parts of Caesar and Brutus in a scene from *The Robbers*. What is more, we read in *The Psychopathology of Everyday Life* (*SE*, 6:23–24) of a memory lapse in which Freud is unable to recall the name of a friend—almost certainly, Friedrich Eckstein, the brother of Freud's unfortunate patient Emma—and thinks instead of the names Daniel and Franz, both characters in *The Robbers* (Daniel being a faithful servant of the Moor family). Freud explains this confusion by the coincidence that both he and his friend have mothers with the first name of Amalia, like the heroine of Schiller's play.[16] Finally, as Freud notes in *The Interpretation of Dreams*, "It appears that I came into the world with such a tangle of black hair that my young mother declared I was a little Moor" (*SE*, 4:337). In numerous respects, therefore, it is clear that Freud's interest in Schiller, and *The Robbers* in particular, is predisposed by personal factors.

A further dimension to the subjective relation between Freud and Schiller is provided by some noteworthy correspondences between their lives. In 1773, at fourteen, Schiller was forcibly recruited into a military academy by the tyrannical Duke Karl Eugen of Württemberg. When, in 1782, he fled from his garrison at Stuttgart, Schiller found refuge at the country estate of Henriette von Wolzogen, the mother of one of his classmates. There, the young author became enamored of a daughter, Charlotte, but also with the mother, Henriette, in whom, as Rank puts it, "he saw mother and beloved united."[17] This experience duplicates that in the life of the adolescent Freud during his visit to Freiberg, when he was simultaneously infatuated with Gisela Fluss and her mother. During his early years, Schiller regularly found himself attracted to married or otherwise maternal women. Luise Vischer, the Laura of his first poems, was a widow; and Charlotte von Kalb, who figured prominently in the lives of both Goethe and Hölderlin for similar reasons, had been married only six months when Schiller met and fell in love with her in May 1784—so much so that he urged her to divorce her husband and marry him. Similarly, when in 1788 Schiller met Charlotte von Lengefeld, whom he married two years later, he was initially enthralled by her unhappily married sister Karoline. After his marriage, he nursed the wish to maintain a household with both sisters simultaneously, as Freud did with Martha and Minna Bernays. These affinities underlie the psychological motives that independently impel Schiller and Freud to their involvement with the Oedipus myth.

In many ways, Schiller is himself the "fountain-head" of the intellectual currents that run from the German Romanticism to Freud. In a passage added in 1909 to *The Interpretation of Dreams*, Freud quotes from a 1788 letter (brought to his attention by Rank) to illustrate the similarity between his own technique of free association in dream interpretation and the "relaxation of the watch upon the gates of Reason" (*SE*, 4:103) that Schiller holds to be necessary in poetic creation. Above all, Schiller's two treatises, *Letters on the Aesthetic Education of Man* (1793) and *On Naive and Sentimental Poetry* (1795–96), are of seminal importance to subsequent thought. In the latter, Schiller sought to come to terms with his awe of both Goethe and the Greeks by equating them with the category of the "naive" and himself with that of the "sentimental" or reflective modern poet. Speaking for such alienated individuals, Schiller states, "we see in irrational nature only a happier sister who remained in our mother's house, out of which we fled abroad in the arrogance of our freedom."[18] This passage, with its imagery of the male poet ambivalently seeking to sever his attachment to his "happier sister" nature and escape his "mother's house," fuses oedipal motifs with the typical Romantic concern with the burdens of self-consciousness. Schiller's reflections prefigure those of Freud in *The Future of an Illusion*, quoted in chapter 2, where the task of "education to reality" is defined in terms of "a child who has left the parental home where he was so warm and comfortable." Schiller again adumbrates psychoanalysis in recognizing that our love for nature is "closely related to the feeling with which we mourn the lost age of childhood" (p. 103), but shares above all with Hegel the conviction that the "sentimental" poet, who no longer "functions as an undivided sensuous unity," can now "express himself only as a . . . *striving* after unity" (p. 111; italics added). Indeed, he criticizes such literary forms as the idyll precisely because they "place that purpose *behind* us, *toward* which they should, however, lead us, and hence they imbue us only with a sad feeling of loss, and not with joyous feelings of hope" (p. 149).

The gravitation toward the Oedipus myth in nineteenth-century thought is regularly accompanied by a predilection for dialectical or dualistic modes of analysis. Schiller writes at the start of the Sixteenth Letter in the *Aesthetic Education*:

From the interaction of two opposing impulses, then, and from the association of two opposing principles we have seen the origin of the Beautiful, whose highest ideal is therefore to be sought in the most perfect possible union and equilibrium of reality and form.[19]

This definition of beauty as the result of "the interaction of two opposing impulses" may be juxtaposed with Freud's announcement of his hypothesis concerning the formation of dreams in the first paragraph of *The Interpretation of Dreams*:

I shall further endeavor to elucidate the processes to which the strangeness and obscurity of dreams are due and to deduce from those processes the nature of the psychical forces by whose concurrent or mutually opposing action dreams are generated. (*SE*, 4:1)

Nietzsche, analogously, writes in the opening sentence of *The Birth of Tragedy*:

We shall have gained much for the science of aesthetics, once we perceive . . . that the continuous development of art is bound up with the *Apollonian* and *Dionysian* duality—just as procreation depends on the duality of the sexes, involving perpetual strife with only periodically intervening reconciliations.[20]

Not only is Nietzsche's cast of mind generally Schillerian, but his "Apollonian and Dionysian duality" evolves directly out of Schiller's opposition between the "naive" and the "sentimental." In the Greek festivals of Dionysus, Nietzsche affirms, "nature seems to reveal a sentimental trait; it is as if she were heaving a sigh at her dismemberment into individuals" (sec. 2), whereas "where we encounter the 'naive' in art, we should recognize the highest effects of Apollonian culture" (sec. 3). It is further evidence of the extent of Schiller's influence that the first use of the term "sublation" *(Aufhebung)*, so central to Hegel's thought, in its technical philosophical sense can apparently be traced to the Eighteenth Letter of the *Aesthetic Education*.[21]

Just as Schiller defined beauty as the "union and equilibrium of reality and form," so he strove throughout his career to reconcile his devotion to the claims of freedom with a recognition of the need for duty and legitimate authority. He remarks in the Fourth

Letter of the *Aesthetic Education*: "Man can be at odds with himself in a double fashion: either as savage if his feelings rule his principles, or as barbarian if his principles destroy his feelings" (p. 34). Recast in psychoanalytic terms, Schiller warns that the ego must learn to mediate between the conflicting and excessive demands of both the id and the superego. There is a direct development from his depiction in *The Robbers* of his equally intense desires both to rebel against and achieve atonement with paternal authority—personified in his youth by the intolerable Duke Karl Eugen—to the compromise between defiance and acceptance of the impersonal power of fate evident in his mature tragedies. Man, Schiller acknowledges in the Third Letter, finds himself constrained in various ways by a necessity over which he has no control, and he faces the challenge of "remodelling the work of need into a work of his free choice." By imagining the prospect of a different reality, he continues, man "artificially retraces his childhood in his maturity . . . and proceeds now exactly as though he were starting afresh and substituting the status of independence, with clear insight and free resolve, for the status of contract" (p. 28). In addition to inaugurating the epoch that made possible Freud's discovery of the Oedipus complex, Schiller in this passage provides an idealized definition of the aims and aspirations of psychoanalytic therapy.

Hölderlin

One of the most painfully ironic moments in German literary history is recorded by Heinrich Voss the younger, son of the leading translator of Homer, in a letter to a friend on October 29, 1804, in which he describes the mirth he shared with Goethe and Schiller at Hölderlin's expense:

What do you say to Hölderlin's Sophocles? Is the man raving or only pretending? And is his Sophocles a veiled satire of bad translators? The other evening, as I was sitting with Schiller at Goethe's, I suitably regaled them both with it. Read the fourth chorus of *Antigone*—you should have seen the way Schiller laughed. Or line 20 of *Antigone*. . . . I recommended this passage to Goethe as a contribution to his optics.[22]

The petty vanity of Voss is unmistakable, but the true tragedy of this mockery lies in the attitude of Goethe and Schiller, who had turned their backs on the Romanticism they helped to unleash. Long keeping the vulnerable Hölderlin at a distance, they regarded his poetry with unwarranted condescension. Hölderlin has, however, had his posthumous revenge, because his translations of Sophocles, over which Schiller laughed a few months before his death, have withstood the test of time far better than *The Bride of Messina* or Schiller's other more or less finished attempts to clothe *Oedipus the King* in modern dress.

As a second-generation Romantic, Hölderlin experienced still more acutely than Schiller the twin dilemmas of artistic self-consciousness and estrangement from the lost ideal of ancient Greece. The embodiment of the visionary poet, Hölderlin, with his agonizing descent into literal madness, in which he spent the last forty years of his life, likewise stands in sharp contrast to the buoyant serenity maintained by Schiller in the face of physical deterioration.

Hölderlin's obsession with Sophocles, culminating in his translations of *Oedipus the King* and *Antigone*, must be seen in the context of his own "Conception of the Development of the Hero." Already in "My Resolution," written at the age of seventeen, Hölderlin expresses his awareness that his poetic vocation condemns him to isolation even from his closest friends.[23] He declares in the second stanza:

> I flee the tender clasp of your hands, avoid
> The soulful, happy touch of a brother's lips.
> O don't be angry, friends, forgive me!—
> Look at my innermost self, then judge me!

This notion of his poetic calling is elaborated by Hölderlin in *Empedocles*, his never-completed tragedy of a failed redeemer, in his remarkable novel *Hyperion*, in his poetic odes and hymns, as well as in his translations of Sophocles and Pindar. In the second version (1799) of *Empedocles*, Hölderlin eulogizes his hero: "He who saw higher things than ever did mortal eye, / Now struck with blindness faltering picks his way" (Hamburger, p. 289). As in "The Blind Singer" (1801), the "blindness" of Empedocles is not literal, but rather a figurative reference to being deprived of sunlight and access to nature as sources of poetic inspiration, but it cannot be doubted that Hölderlin's exploration of the paradox of insight and blindness is informed at least in part by the precedent of Sophocles' Oedipus.

Freud, whose literary allegiances are to the classical German tradition of Goethe and Schiller, makes no allusions in his work to Hölderlin. In this, he is antithetical to Nietzsche, who affirmed in an essay written in 1861 at the age of seventeen that Hölderlin was his favorite poet. Casting his essay in the form of a letter to an imaginary friend, Nietzsche rebukes his correspondent for the opinion that "these vague half-mad utterances of a disrupted, broken mind made only a sad and at times repulsive impression," and reminds him that Hölderlin wrote more than poetry:

So you do not know his *Empedocles* then, this most important dramatic fragment, in whose melancholy tones reverberates the future of this unhappy poet, his grave of long madness, and not as you say in unclear talk but in purest Sophoclean language and with an inexhaustible fullness of profound ideas. (*SL*, p. 5)

This early testimonial is exceptionally poignant because, even as he discerns in *Empedocles* intimations of the "grave of long madness" in which Hölderlin's life ended, Nietzsche unwittingly prophesies, in Ronald Hayman's words, "the way that [his] own development was to run parallel to the mad poet's."[24] Nietzsche's remark on the "purest Sophoclean language" of *Empedocles*, moreover, underscores the centrality of an identification with Oedipus to both his own and Hölderlin's self-conceptions as tragic heroes.

Embedded deeply in Hölderlin's personal experience, *Hyperion* is a quintessential distillation of the Romantic themes of Hellenism, self-consciousness, and oedipal conflict. An early, fragmentary draft of the novel appeared in Schiller's periodical *Thalia* in 1794; the first volume was finally published in 1797, and the second not until 1799. In philosophical terms, *Hyperion* shows Hölderlin's effort to come to terms with the radical idealism of Fichte, whose lectures at Jena he attended in the winter of 1794–95, and thus stands as a pendant to Schelling's *Philosophical Letters*, written at just this time. In one of the work's most famous passages, the protagonist Hyperion, an eighteenth-century Greek struggling to recapture the spirit of his country's classical past, laments to his friend Bellarmin:

Oh, man is a god when he dreams, a beggar when he thinks; and when inspiration is gone, he stands, like a worthless son whom his father has driven out of the house, and stares at the miserable pence that pity has given him for the road.[25]

This description of the imagination in exile, with its striking inversion of the parable of the prodigal son, brings together familial imagery and the problem of consciousness in what appears to be a heightened reformulation of Schiller's characterization of the "sentimental" poet as one who has deserted nature "in our mother's house, out of which we fled abroad in the arrogance of our freedom."

The personal note in *Hyperion* is sounded by Hölderlin's portrayal of Schiller as the protagonist's tutor Adamas and, above all, by his transformation of his ill-fated love for Susette Gontard into Hyperion's passion for Diotima:

After that, I never managed to see Diotima alone. There was always some third person to intrude on us, separate us, and the world lay between her and me like an unbounded emptiness.[26]

In addition to its biographical origins, however, *Hyperion* possesses a prominent literary antecedent both for its epistolary form and for its exploration of the theme of forbidden love in Goethe's *The Sorrows of Young Werther* (1774). To Hyperion's dismay at the intrusion of a third party between himself and Diotima one may compare Werther's letter to Lotte just prior to committing suicide:

Oh, I knew that you loved me, knew it when I met your first soulful glance, with the first pressure of your hand, and yet, when I was away from you, when I saw Albert at your side, I despaired again, in a fever of doubt.[27]

The close parallel between the situations in Goethe's *Werther* and Hölderlin's "Greek *Werther*" does not invalidate the attempt to understand Hölderlin's—or, for that matter, Goethe's—choice of subject matter in biographical terms, but points up rather the perenially complementary relations between individual and cultural history.

Hölderlin was born in 1770 in the town of Lauffen on the Neckar, where his father managed estates belonging to the Lutheran church. After the father's death in 1772, a sister was born. Hölderlin's mother remarried in 1774, and the family moved to

Nürtingen, where the new stepfather was mayor. A half-brother was born in 1776, but in 1779 Hölderlin lost a father for the second time with the death of his stepfather. As we have already seen in Schiller's case, Hölderlin's personal history bears certain noteworthy points of resemblance to Freud's. Hölderlin's departure from his birthplace at the age of four is analogous to Freud's uprooting from Freiberg at the age of three; and, still more importantly, Freud's early experience of loss with the death of Julius, which intensified his later guilt-ridden reaction to the death of his father, finds a more extreme counterpart in the conjunction between the premature deaths of Hölderlin's father and stepfather.

The aftereffects of Hölderlin's repeated traumatic fulfillment of unconscious oedipal death wishes may be discerned both in his friendship with Schiller and in his tragic love for Susette Gontard. Hölderlin first met Schiller in the autumn of 1793, when he was interviewed by the latter for the post of private tutor to the son of Charlotte von Kalb, an old flame of Schiller's. Already at Tübingen, Hölderlin had revered Schiller and sought, with uncanny success, to imitate his poetry; and after their acquaintance, Hölderlin was conscious of feeling filially dependent on Schiller. He wrote to his mother from Jena on February 22, 1795, after leaving his post in the von Kalb household at Waltershausen: "Schiller really concerns himself so paternally with my affairs that I recently had to confess to this great man I did not know how I had deserved that he should take such an interest in me."[28] But, as in Freud's transferential attachment to Fliess, the negative pole of such enthrallment could not be suppressed indefinitely. It finds expression in Hölderlin's letter to Schiller of June 30, 1798:

> Therefore may I confess to you that I am at times in secret struggle with your genius, in order to secure my freedom from it, and that the fear of being completely dominated by you has frequently hindered me from approaching you calmly.[29]

Because of his infantile fears of abandonment, Hölderlin's devotion to Schiller possessed an all-consuming quality, wherein if he could not be everything to his idol he believed himself to be nothing. Hölderlin consequently found himself torn between the intolerable alternatives of remaining in Schiller's vicinity or of parting from him.[30]

Inasmuch as it was Schiller who had introduced Hölderlin

into the von Kalb household, a situation with unmistakably oedipal overtones arises in Hölderlin's relations with the still charming
Charlotte, heightened by this free spirit's lackluster marriage to a
retired military officer. Recent research, moreover, has documented that, while at Waltershausen, Hölderlin engaged in an
affair with Wilhelmine von Kirms, Charlotte's domestic companion, a widow (like his mother) and some ten years his senior,
which resulted in the clandestine birth in July 1795 of a daughter,
who died of smallpox the following year. If Hölderlin's attraction
to Charlotte von Kalb forms the main plot, as it were, and his
physical liaison with Wilhelmine von Kirms the subplot, of his
domestic drama at Waltershausen, a final wrinkle is added by the
fact that the pedagogical difficulties Hölderlin used as an excuse
for leaving his post stemmed from his inability to control or tolerate the masturbatory activities of his young charge—an externalized equivalent to his own phallic transgressions in fantasy and
reality.[31]

Involved as this period at Waltershausen is in its own right,
its greatest significance is as a preamble to Hölderlin's subsequent
enthrallment by Susette Gontard. Only one year older than Hölderlin, Susette was married to a considerably older businessman,
known for his irascibility, and the mother of four children. The
oedipal structure of this household arrangement, in which Hölderlin again served as tutor from December 1795 to the autumn
of 1798, is thus transparent. The fact that he and Susette never
consummated their love seems only to have added to its intensity,
for it is immortalized as a true communion of souls in *Hyperion*.

In December 1801, more than a year after his final parting
from Susette Gontard and six months after an unanswered letter
to Schiller pleading for support of a plan to come to Jena as a
lecturer in Greek literature, Hölderlin set out on a solitary journey
to the south of France. In an earlier epigram "Sophocles" (1799),
Hölderlin had concisely defined the paradox of the Greek dramatist's tragic serenity: "Many have tried, but in vain, with joy to
express the most joyful; / Here at last, in grave sadness, wholly I
find it expressed" (Hamburger, p. 71). But it is above all the great
poems of this later period, including "Bread and Wine," "Ger-
mania," and "The Only One," that show the obstacles facing
Hölderlin in his project of resuscitating ancient Greece as well as

the increasing strain in his attempt to reconcile his devotion to the Greek gods with the imperious demands of Christ. The claims of Christianity were personified in Hölderlin's life by his mother, from whom he sought to guard the secret of his paganism, but to whom he eventually capitulated.[32] The first pronounced signs of Hölderlin's incipient mental derangement emerged after his return home from Bordeaux, where he believed that the ruins and "athletic" people had brought him into contact with the spirit of Greece. A letter written in the autumn of 1802 to Casimir Ulrich von Böhlendorff indicates that the onset of Hölderlin's madness was accompanied by a deepening of his conception of himself as a tragic hero:

The mighty element, the fire of heaven and the silence of the people, their life in nature, their confinedness and their contentment, moved me continually, and as one says of heroes, I can well say of myself that Apollo has struck me.[33]

As in *Empedocles* and "The Blind Singer," Hölderlin again describes himself as metaphorically blinded by "the fire of heaven," only now the consequence of being struck by Apollo is an all too literal journey into madness.

Among the final literary labors completed by Hölderlin prior to his insanity were translations of *Oedipus the King* and *Antigone*, which were published with accompanying brief critical essays on each play in 1804. "We call this work a translation," writes Karl Reinhardt, "but we must be clear that we are concerned with something worlds apart from any merely literary-humanistic achievement."[34] Begun as early as 1796 and, other than *Hyperion*, the only works of his seen by Hölderlin into print, these translations from Sophocles are at once culminating documents in Hölderlin's spiritual autobiography and representative testimony of the centrality of the Oedipus myth to the German Romantic period as a whole.

In his critical "Observations" (*"Anmerkungen"*), obscure even in German, Hölderlin extends his consideration of tragedy, previously expounded in the "Argument for *Empedocles*" (1799), as based on the conflict between the simultaneous needs for fusion and separation between god and man, and once more struggles with the problem of renouncing his loyalty to the Greek gods in favor of Christ. In addition to their intrinsic importance, Hölderlin's commentaries have a historical interest in providing a bridge between the Sophoclean interpretations of Schelling and Hegel. When, for example, Hölderlin asserts that the tragedy of *Antigone* depends on the fact that "between Creon and Antigone, the formal and the counter-formal, the balance is maintained too equally,"[35] there is an immediate connection both to Schelling's formulation, in the contemporary *Philosophy of Art*, that in tragedy freedom and necessity "both appear victorious and defeated in complete indifference" and to Hegel's reading of the play, where the deadlock between Creon and Antigone serves to show that "both are equally right, and, hence, in their opposition (which comes about through action) are equally wrong" (*PM*, p. 743). The use of Sophocles to expound a fundamentally dialectical outlook is common to all three scholars of the Tübingen seminary, but the inflection given by Hölderlin to what he terms the "highest impartiality of the two opposed characters" in *Antigone* is uniquely conditioned by his experience as a practicing poet.

As a poet and not a philosopher, moreover, Hölderlin, whose knowledge of Greek far exceeded that of Schiller, is exceptionally attuned to Sophocles' language.[36] Hölderlin possesses to an unparalleled degree the poet's belief in the life-giving and death-dealing power of words. "The *Greek-tragic word is death-effective*," he writes oracularly in "Observations on *Antigone*," "because the body which it seizes really kills" (5:269). Complementing his linguistic responsiveness is Hölderlin's attempt, in both commentaries, to specify with virtually scientific precision the means by which a tragic effect is produced. Speaking of the benefits rendered to ancient tragedy by "lawful calculations and other techniques" which "can always reliably be repeated," Hölderlin in "Observations on *Oedipus*" draws a profound analogy between the function of a caesura in individual lines of verse and the "counter-rhythmic interruptions" (5:196) marked in both plays by Teiresias, whose divinely sanctioned interventions serve as a fulcrum balancing the two unequal units of the action. This focus upon the laws of tragic art brings Hölderlin into relation with Freud, who likewise sought to understand intellectually the "gripping power" of *Oedipus the King*, rather than merely experiencing it passively.[37]

Hölderlin's identification with Sophocles' tragic heroes lends a sense of urgency to his exegeses of both *Oedipus the King* and *Antigone*. Concerning *Antigone*, he writes:

It is a great expedient of the secretly working soul that at the highest consciousness it evades consciousness and, before the present god really seizes it, greets the latter with bold and blasphemous words, and thus preserves the holy, living possibility of spirit. (5:267)

Butler is surely right to see in this passage a reflection by Hölderlin on his own encroaching madness, and to suggest on the basis of it that "some shattering experience had preceded his collapse, and that he had almost consciously taken refuge from it in insanity."[38] In "Observations on *Oedipus*," Hölderlin beautifully explains that Oedipus' downfall arises because he "*interprets* the oracle *too infinitely*," and thereby "is tempted *to enormity*" (5:197). He locates this "too infinite" interpretation at the moment when Oedipus asks "in *particular*" about the injuction of the oracle to purify the land, and thereby first learns about the murder of Laius. According to Hölderlin, *Oedipus the King* shows that "knowledge, when it has broken its barriers, . . . excites itself to know more than it can bear or grasp" (5:198); and in thus perceiving a link between excessive knowledge and derangement or "enormity" *(nefas)* Hölderlin, like Schelling, looks ahead to Nietzsche.

Even during the period of his insanity, the better part of which—from 1807 until his death in 1843—Hölderlin spent under the benevolent care of a carpenter named Zimmer in Tübingen, he continued to write, occasionally showing flashes of his former genius. The most overwhelming piece composed by Hölderlin during his last phase is the prose poem "In lovely blueness" (1823), which concludes:

If someone looks into a mirror, a man, and in it sees his image, as though it were a painted likeness; it resembles the man. The image of man has eyes, whereas the moon has light. King Oedipus has an eye too many perhaps. The sufferings of this man, they seem indescribable, unspeakable, inexpressible. If the drama represents something like this, that is why. Like brooks the end of something sweeps me away, which expands like Asia. Of course, this affliction, Oedipus has it too. . . . And immortality amidst the envy of this life, to share in that, is an affliction too. But this also is an affliction, when a man is covered with freckles, to be wholly covered with many a spot! The beautiful sun does that: for it rears up all things. It leads young men along their course with the allurements of its beams as though with roses. The afflictions that Oedipus bore seem like this, as when a poor man complains that there is something he lacks. Son of Laios, poor stranger in Greece! Life is death, and death is a kind of life. (Hamburger, pp. 603–5)

In a voice spoken from beyond "his grave of long madness," Hölderlin here comments definitively on the "affliction" of his poetic vocation with which he wrestled throughout his creative life. Hölderlin sees in the "indescribable, unspeakable, inexpressible" sufferings of Oedipus a "mirror" for his own fate, and his allusion to "an eye too many" refers back to the "Observations," where Oedipus is said to precipitate his destruction by "too infinite" acts of interpretation. The "freckles" left by the "beautiful sun" that "leads young men along their course with the allurements of its beams as though with roses," analogously, clearly evoke the "fire from heaven" by which Hölderlin claims to have been smitten in the letter to von Böhlendorff as well as the figurative "blindness" suffered by Empedocles for having seen "higher things than ever did mortal eye." If, moreover, the "you" in the question "But what comes over me when I think of you now?" can only be his Diotima, then Hölderlin's entire passage exquisitely blends the themes of forbidden love and tragic introspection inherent in the Oedipus myth.

When Wilhelm Waiblinger, Hölderlin's early biographer, visited the poet for the first time in 1822, he noted in his diary that Hölderlin "speaks always of suffering, when he is intelligible, of Oedipus, of Greece."[39] Recorded shortly before the writing of "In lovely blueness," Waiblinger's observations condense the themes not only of that prose poem but of Hölderlin's poetic career as a whole. In "Observations on *Oedipus*," Hölderlin meditates autobiographically on Oedipus' "despairing struggle to come to himself, the roughshod, almost shameless striving to become master of his own, the foolish-wild searching after a consciousness" (5:199), and it is he himself who is the eternal Romantic "son of Laios, poor stranger in Greece."

Kleist

Heinrich von Kleist took his own life, at the age of thirty-four, in a shocking double suicide, in which he shot his terminally ill companion, Henriette Vogel, in the heart before shooting himself in the mouth. On the day of his death, November 21, 1811, Kleist wrote to his cousin Marie:

For this my life, the most tormented of any that anyone has ever lived, I can now at last thank Him, since he makes it good through the most glorious and sensual of deaths. O if only there were something I could do to assuage the bitter pain that I shall cause you. . . . Can it console you that I never would have exchanged you for this woman if she had wanted nothing more than to live with me? . . . The decision that she came to in her soul, to die with me, drew me, I cannot tell you with what inexpressible and irresistible force, to her breast. . . . A tumult of joyousness, never experienced before, gripped me, and I cannot conceal from you that her grave is more precious to me than the beds of all the empresses of this world.[40]

This climactic event, which reminds us of Freud's screen memory of his mother's pregnancy and his nurse being "boxed up" in its crossing of the opposites of the "bed" and the "grave," provides the vantage point from which Kleist's life and art can be retrospectively comprehended.[41] It points to the existence of a profound incestuous fixation, which in turn illuminates the preoccupation with the Oedipus myth in his dramatic work.

Kleist's suicide is both the obverse of and counterpart to Hölderlin's withdrawal into madness. No less tragic than that of Hölderlin, Kleist's end differs from the lyric poet's in its violence and deliberateness. The self-destruction of both younger writers forms a pointed contrast to Schiller's unflagging optimism and, still more, to the Olympian detachment cultivated by the later Goethe.

Although Hölderlin and Kleist do not appear to have been aware of each other's existence, a striking parallel between their careers is formed by their common struggle with the sage of Weimar. The ill-starred nature of Hölderlin's relations with Goethe is symbolized by the fact that, at their first meeting in November 1794, Hölderlin failed to recognize the great man to whom he had been introduced.[42] On August 21, 1797, Goethe wrote to Schiller following a meeting with Hölderlin: "I have especially advised him to write short poems."[43] It was, as we have seen, Schiller whose role in Hölderlin's life was decisive and finally catastrophic, but Goethe cannot be said to have offered him much encouragement.

Whereas the painful shyness and awkwardness exhibited by Hölderlin in his dealings with Goethe foreshadow his insanity, Kleist's bloody end is in keeping with the open defiance of Goethe expressed in his oath of 1803, "I shall pluck the wreath from his brow!"[44] Kleist was certainly a most troublesome individual, and inflicted on Goethe the ambivalent burden of his unbounded admiration and intense jealousy, but Goethe for his part was unjust in his treatment of Kleist. Flinging Kleist's *Kate of Heilbronn* (1806) into the fire, he termed it the embodiment of "accursed perversity" (*Abyss*, p. 177); when he did accept Kleist's sublime metaphysical comedy *The Broken Jug* (1806) for the Weimar theater, he ruined it by dividing the continuously flowing action into three distinct parts; and upon being sent *Penthesilea* (1807), which in its violence and frenzy now seems uncannily close to the spirit of Greek tragedy, Goethe rejected it with the insult that he would have been "more pleased to have something from the heart" (*Abyss*, p. 180). As Philip B. Miller has observed, Goethe, the "frequent champion of the safely third-rate, was strikingly consistent in rejecting the best of the new generation," and there is "more than a suggestion of unseemly professional jealousy" in his disdain not only of Hölderlin and Kleist but also of Caspar David Friedrich, now agreed to have been the foremost painter of the period, whose canvases Goethe recommended be "smashed against a table" (*Abyss*, p. 177).

As is true of Hölderlin, Freud's lack of interest in the work of Kleist is balanced by the passionate admiration of Nietzsche. And just as Nietzsche designated Hölderlin as his favorite poet at the age of seventeen, so it was in anticipation of his fifteenth birthday that he confided to his diary the thought that he might like to receive an edition of Kleist.[45] Nietzsche's most extended discussion of Kleist occurs in *Schopenhauer as Educator* (1874), the third of his four *Untimely Meditations*, where he couples him with Hölderlin: "Our Hölderlin and Kleist, and many others like them, were destroyed by their abnormality and could not endure the climate of so-called German culture."[46]

Nietzsche's responsiveness to marginal figures such as Hölderlin and Kleist, at a time when the reputation of both writers stood far lower than it does today, points up the fact that his own "abnormality" made available to him domains of experience beyond the reach of the more conventional Freud. Indeed, Freud's own identification with Goethe takes on a new dimension of significance in light of the latter's encounters with Hölderlin and Kleist. For Freud, like Goethe, exhibited his share of "professional jealousy" in his dealings with colleagues and followers; and he found his Kleist in Victor Tausk, one of his most brilliant and unstable pupils, who likewise ended his life with a pistol, in a suicide for which Freud—no less than Goethe in the case of Kleist—bore at least indirect responsibility.[47]

As is well known, Kleist's career as a writer began in response to what Nietzsche, who compares him in this regard to Schopenhauer, terms the "devastation and despair of all truth . . . experienced as an effect of the Kantian philosphy."[48] Kleist himself conveys the essence of his "Kant crisis" in his famous letter of March 22, 1801 to his fiancée Wilhelmine von Zenge:

> If everyone saw the world through green glasses, they would be forced to judge that everything they saw *was* green, and could never be sure whether their eyes saw things as they really are, or did not add something of their own to what they saw. And so it is with our intellect. We can never be certain that what we call Truth is really Truth, or whether it does not merely appear so to us. If the latter, then the Truth that we acquire here is *not* Truth after our death, and it is all a vain striving for a possession that may never follow us into the grave. (*Abyss*, p. 95)

Insofar as a confrontation with the Kantian legacy was the constitutive problem for the diverse proponents of "expressivist anthropology" in the Romantic period, the very extremity of Kleist's breakdown makes his situation representative, as will be his subsequent obsessions with self-consciousness and the Oedipus myth.

Once launched on his career as a writer, Kleist's most important project was his tragedy *Robert Guiscard*. Begun in 1802, portions of *Robert Guiscard* were read aloud by Kleist in 1803 to Christoph Martin Wieland, the eminent poet and novelist, then seventy years of age. The extent to which Wieland was impressed by Kleist's unfinished work is made clear by his letter to Wedekind of April 10, 1804:

> If the spirits of Aeschylus, Sophocles, and Shakespeare were to collaborate in creating a tragedy, the outcome would be equivalent to Kleist's *Death of Guiscard the Norman*, if the whole proves equal to what he then read to me. From that moment on, it was clear to me that Kleist was born to fill the wide gap in our dramatic literature which, at least in my opinion, even Goethe and Schiller have failed to fill.[49]

It is understandable that Kleist should have revered the man who believed him capable, where Schiller and Goethe had fallen short, of reviving the spirit of authentic tragedy in Germany. Noteworthy, too, is Wieland's characterization of *Robert Guiscard* as a blending of Shakespeare and the Greeks, for such an alchemical fusion had been Schiller's goal in *Wallenstein* and other historical dramas, and was originally prescribed in the criticism of Lessing.

Both internal and external evidence confirms that *Robert Guiscard* was composed under the immediate influence of *Oedipus the King*.[50] In June 1803, Kleist, who did not know Greek, checked out of the Dresden library a volume of Sophocles' tragedies in translation, including *Oedipus*.[51] *Robert Guiscard*, of which only the first ten scenes survive, is set in the eleventh century during the siege of Constantinople by the Normans, led by Guiscard. Not only, as in *Oedipus the King*, is there a plague in the Norman camp, but it emerges that Guiscard himself is infected, though he attempts to conceal this fact from his anxious warriors. At the outset, Guiscard feels confident that he will survive the plague, probably because of a prophecy that he would die at Jerusalem, but it is likely that Kleist intended to contrive a Sophoclean irony based on the revelation that the place where the Normans had pitched their camp was formerly named Jerusalem. Guiscard, moreover, had come to power many years earlier by deposing his brother, and a theme evidently to be developed in the course of the play was to have been the rivalry between Guiscard's son, Robert, and nephew, Abelard, who seeks to press his legitimate claim to the throne.

In July 1803, Wieland wrote to Kleist with words of encouragement: "Nothing is impossible for the sacred muse who inspires you. You *must* complete your *Guiscard*, though the entire Caucasus, and Mount Atlas as well, were weighing upon you" (*Abyss*, p. 151). But precisely because Kleist identified his poetic ambition so completely with *Robert Guiscard*, he was unable to bring it to completion. Instead of plucking the wreath from Goethe's brow, he found himself forced to confront his own humiliation. Kleist's despair is revealed in a letter of October 3, 1803 to his half-sister Ulrike:

I have labored five hundred consecutive days, with most of the nights thrown in, in my single purpose: to wrestle down yet one more wreath of fame to place beside the many already achieved by our family: now our saintly guardian goddess calls to me: Enough! . . . It was hell that gave me this half-talent of mine: heaven grants a whole one or none at all. (*Abyss*, pp. 151–52)

Following his acknowledgment of failure, Kleist set out on a headlong trip to Paris, then unsuccessfully sought to join a group of conscripts to fight in the war against Napoleon, and finally suffered one of the prolonged nervous breakdowns he underwent during the course of his brief life.

But Kleist's debacle with *Robert Guiscard* was at least partially offset by *The Broken Jug* and *Penthesilea*, two plays he did manage to finish, both of which may be regarded as reactions to the abortion of his magnum opus. The connection between *Robert Guiscard* and *The Broken Jug* is especially clear because, like the tragedy, the comedy was begun in 1802 and under the spell of Kleist's fascination with *Oedipus the King*.[52] Kleist conceived the idea for *The Broken Jug* in response to a literary competition with several friends, the object of which was to account for the scene in a copperplate engraving of the same title by Jean-Jacques Le Veau, depicting a village court of justice. In his Preface, appended only to a manuscript version of the play, Kleist states explicitly that he saw in this seemingly innocuous tableau intimations of *Oedipus the King*:

One noticed thereon, first, a judge who sat gravely on the seat of justice; before him stood an old woman, who held a broken jug; . . . the accused, a young peasant; . . . a girl, who probably figured in this matter; . . . and the court clerk (he had perhaps scrutinized the girl a moment ago) looked mistrustfully at the judge from the side, as Creon did at Oedipus at a similar opportunity [when the question was, who killed Laius?].[53]

The indebtedness to *Oedipus the King* signalled in the Preface to *The Broken Jug* is amply borne out by the play itself. Kleist's comedy resembles Schiller's unfinished *Narbonne* in depicting the involuntary self-incrimination of a knowingly guilty culprit, but what Nietzsche in *The Birth of Tragedy* says of Sophocles' design in *Oedipus* could with equal justice be applied to the artistry of Kleist: "As a poet he first shows us the marvelously tied knot of a trial, slowly unraveled by the judge, bit by bit, for his own undoing" (sec. 9). In other words, Kleist in *The Broken Jug* achieved what Schiller in *The Bride of Messina* had been unable to manage—a genuinely "analytical" plot, where "everything is already there, and only remains to be unfolded."

To symbolize his identification with Oedipus, Kleist's protagonist Justice Adam has a club foot—the left, traditionally associated with sin. The offense of which Adam is guilty is the attempted seduction of the country maiden, Eve, under the pretext of a forged document stating that her betrothed, Ruprecht, will be sent on military duty to Indonesia, if Eve does not comply with Adam's demand for sexual favors. During a visit to Eve's chamber the previous night, Adam had hung his wig on a jug belonging to Eve's mother, Mrs. Martha, which then shattered when Adam was forced to escape hastily through a window as Ruprecht broke in upon them, and thus becomes the object of litigation in the next day's court proceedings. Ruprecht himself is the prime suspect, having been found in Eve's room, and the name of a former suitor, Cobbler Letrecht, is also put forward, but Eve is unable to disclose the truth for fear of Adam's retaliation. The play opens the morning after Adam's escapade, and his ultimate unmasking is assured both by the suspicions of Court Clerk Light, Adam's Creon, who covets his office, and by the arrival of District Judge Walter, whose name in German suggests "power" or "Lord," and who refuses to tolerate Adam's obfuscations.

Kleist enhances the controlling analogy between *The Broken Jug* and *Oedipus the King* in various ingenious ways. As in *Robert Guiscard*, where he probably meant to use the device of an unexpectedly fulfilled prophecy, Kleist here creates an effect of dramatic irony through the dream recounted by Adam to Light just prior to the entrance of Walter:

> Hm. I had this dream: a plaintiff seized
> And hailed me into court, and there I stood
> And at the same time there I sat as justice
> On the bench, scolding, tongue-lashing
> My other self—then sentenced me to irons.
>
> (3.269–73)

This dream, the equivalent to the oracle in *Oedipus the King*, forewarns the spectator of what is to occur; and its imagery is echoed near the close of the play when Adam shamelessly attempts to convict Ruprecht—"His stiff neck I hereby sentence to wear /

Irons" (11.1876–77)—only to have his villainy finally exposed by Eve, who exhorts her beloved: "Earn your irons, Ruprecht! Go. Pitch him down / From his tribunal" (11.1898–99). In a parody of Oedipus' exile from Thebes, Adam is last seen fleeing across the landscape, and a ritual purification of the blight upon the courtroom has taken place.

A pivotal moment in the action of the drama is the arrival of Mrs. Bridget, a Kleistian counterpart to the Messenger of Sophoclean tragedy. Like the Corinthian Messenger in *Oedipus the King*, as Martin Mueller has noted, Mrs. Bridget "performs two functions," for she is "summoned to testify about the identity of a man she saw in the garden with Eve," but when she appears, "she carries with her a wig found under Eve's window,"[54] which of course belongs to Justice Adam. In addition, Mrs. Bridget's theory that the jug was broken by the devil, like the Messenger's announcement to Oedipus of the death of Polybus, initially furnishes Adam with a source of comfort, though the evidence she brings contributes to his eventual downfall. Finally, just as in *Oedipus the King*, to Voltaire's exasperation, the revelation of Oedipus' identity causes the issue of Laius' murder to be shunted into the background, so by the end of *The Broken Jug* the exposure of Adam's perfidy leads to a general forgetting of the lawsuit over the jug, save by Mrs. Martha, who in the last lines of the play vows to seek justice in the great court of Utrecht.

But though *The Broken Jug* is a brilliant transposition of *Oedipus the King* to a comic register, the symbolism of the names makes plain that Kleist likewise intends his play to be a witty commentary on the myth of the Fall. The action begins with Adam and Light exchanging a rapid-fire series of puns on the idea of falling, as Adam seeks to explain away the injuries incurred in his illicit adventure, which fully exploits Kleist's reliance on biblical typology, and likewise—through references to Adam's club foot—equates him with both his namesake and Oedipus. By the end of the play, however, the perfidious Adam is identified rather with Satan, and Ruprecht, whose refusal to believe unquestioningly in Eve's purity is depicted as a form of moral blindness, takes over the role of fallen Adam, while Walter lives up to his name as the "Lord" who drives the recreant Justice Adam from his Edenic refuge. Kleist's dovetailing of the myths of Oedipus and the Fall is an aesthetic tour de force, but it is grounded on the philosophical realization that both explanatory paradigms are assimilated in the Romantic period to the travails of consciousness.

In *Penthesilea*, Kleist takes as his classical subtext not *Oedipus the King* but Euripides' *Bacchae*. No less than *The Broken Jug*, however, this story of the deadly confrontation between Achilles and the Amazonian queen is, in Philip Miller's words, "in an allusory way *about* the impossibility of completing *Guiscard*" (*Abyss*, p. 1), as well as a dramatization of Kleist's collision with Goethe.[55] Both matters of urgent concern to Kleist are brought together in Penthesilea's outburst to her companion Prothoe:

> Should I—'twere madness but to think of it—
> Cease now to dog him? I who still for five
> Long days of toil and sweat have sought his fall? . . .
> What! Am I not so greatly to complete
> What is so fair begun? May I not seize
> The laurel wreath that flutters o'er my head?
>
> (5.707–9, 713–15)

No less than her creator, Penthesilea desires "so greatly to complete / What is so fair begun," and her reference to "five / Long days of toil" clearly echoes the "five hundred consecutive days" for which Kleist laments to Ulrike that he has labored over *Robert Guiscard*. Her aspiration to "seize / The laurel wreath" likewise alludes at once to the "wreath of fame" mentioned in the same letter and to Kleist's boast that with *Robert Guiscard* he would "pluck the wreath" from Goethe's brow.

Penthesilea is a drama that takes literally the metaphorical equation between eros and the death instinct. As Agave does to her son Pentheus in the *Bacchae*, Penthesilea slays and rends the body of her beloved Achilles while in a state of Dionysian fury, and only later comes to a shattering realization of what she has done. "Literally bitten? Bitten to death?" she bewails to Prothoe, "Not kissed to death?"[56] She continues:

> Then it was a blunder. Kisses [*Küsse*], bites [*Bisse*],
> They rhyme; and whoever loves right from the heart,
> Can easily catch hold of one for the other.   (p. 284)

This "rhyming" of kissing and biting expresses Kleist's conflation of violence and love, and the difference between the two is no more than a "blunder" *(Versehn)* or Freudian slip. Kneeling before the corpse of Achilles, Penthesilea berates herself further for the parapraxis she has committed:

> You dear, sweet bridegroom, forgive me.
> By Diana, I have merely misspoken,
> Because I am not master of these rash lips.
> Now I'll say to you clearly what I meant:
> This it was, beloved, and no more. (p. 284)
> *She kisses him.*

Penthesilea's word for "misspoken" *(versprochen)* echoes the *ver-* prefix of *"Versehn,"* which is likewise used repeatedly by Freud in his subtitle to *The Psychopathology of Everyday Life: Forgetting* [*Vergessen*], *Slips of the Tongue* [*Versprechen*], *Bungled Actions* [*Vergreifen*], *Superstitions, and Errors.* When Penthesilea declares that she is "not master of these rash lips," her equivocal language refers simultaneously to her inability to speak her mind clearly and to the confusion that causes her to "catch hold of" *(greifen)* biting instead of kissing.

With the benefit of hindsight, Penthesilea's union in death with Achilles takes on the macabre quality of a rehearsal for the double suicide with which Kleist ended his life. The resemblance between the fates of character and author reaches its apogee in Penthesilea's lines to her slain enemy beloved:

> By Jupiter! I want to die in the opinion
> That my bloody kisses were dearer to you
> Than the pleasure-moistened ones of any other
> woman. (p. 285)

Just as Kleist prefers Henriette Vogel's "grave" to "the beds of all the empresses of this world," so Penthesilea wants her "bloody kisses" to be "dearer" to Achilles "than the pleasure-moistened ones of any other woman." Both Kleist's life and art are marked by the violent joining of antitheses. His existence is the *"most* tormented" that anyone has ever known, but it is redeemed by "the *most* glorious and sensual of deaths." It was, Kleist tells Marie, *because* Henriette was willing to die with him that he found himself irresistibly drawn to her. In psychoanalytic terms, as Hellmuth Kaiser has explained, the "tumult of joyousness" felt by Kleist at this crossing of death and love is due to the unconscious belief that "the grave is precisely a substitute for the bed and therewith also for the body of the mother."[57] In dying with Henriette—who, to compound the symbolism, was afflicted with cancer of the uterus—Kleist joins the marriage bed with the deathbed and, like Oedipus, reenters the body of his mother.

Although our primary concern is with Kleist's dramas, the way that an unconscious violation of the incest taboo underlies his aesthetic yoking of opposites may be briefly illustrated by his famous novella *The Marquise of O——* (1807). This tale of inexplicable pregnancy, which hovers between religious allegory and pornography, contains near the end a brief scene of reconciliation between the Marquise and her father the Commandant, narrated from the perspective of the Marquise's mother:

Finally she opened the door and peered in—and her heart leaped for joy: her daughter lay motionless in her father's arms, her head thrown back and her eyes closed, while he sat in the armchair, with tear-choked, glistening eyes, and pressed long, warm and avid kisses on her mouth: just as if he were her lover! . . . He hung over her as if she were his first love and held her mouth and kissed it.[58]

Seemingly peripheral to the main action, which focuses on the ambivalent feelings of the Marquise toward the Count who is both a "devil" and an "angel," this erotic epiphany intimates that incestuous desire is in fact at the heart of Kleist's haunting story.[59]

In the first of two series of epigrams published in his ill-fated journal of the arts, *Phoebus* (1808–9), Kleist includes a meditation on "The *Oedipus* of Sophocles":

> Horror, from which the sun hides itself! To the same woman
> To be at once son and husband, and brother to his children.[60]

The immediately succeeding epigram, "The Areopagus," is evidently autobiographical, and gains particular force when read as a commentary on *Penthesilea*:

> Let his tired heart have its way! Out of putrefaction's
> Realm he gladly beckons forth flowers of beauty.

Next Kleist presents a satirical reflection of the possible complicity of the Marquise in her own violation:

> This novel is not for you, my daughter. In
> unconsciousness!
> Shameless buffoonery! She only, I know, kept her
> eyes shut.

Taken as a sequence of free associations, these three epigrams show the connection in Kleist's mind between the explicit representation of incest in *Oedipus the King* and the paradoxes and reversals in his own *Penthesilea* and *The Marquise of O———*.

It is striking that Kleist portrays his own imaginative autobiography in *Penthesilea* through an identification with the character of the Amazonian heroine. Just as his shooting of Henriette makes literal the deadly assault on the female sexual partner symbolically enacted by Freud both in childhood and at the moment of discovering "the universal human application of the Oedipus myth," so Kleist openly experiences the homosexual attraction that lurks beneath every "positive" Oedipus complex. On January 7, 1805 he writes nostalgically to Ernst von Pfuel, his friend from military service who in 1848 became Prime Minister of Prussia:

You restored the age of the Greeks in my heart; I could have slept with you, my dear boy; so entirely did my soul embrace you! I had often, as I watched you stepping into the lake at Thun, contemplated your handsome body with almost *maidenly* feelings. (*Abyss*, p. 159)

These "maidenly feelings" find their way into *Penthesilea*, and upon completion of the play he writes in late autumn 1807 to Marie von Kleist that "it is the women who are guilty of the total decline of our stage," and "the Greek conception of theater could never have developed if women had not been excluded from it" (*Abyss* p. 175). The references to Greece in the letters both to Pfeul and to Marie point up the extent to which Kleist's own homosexual leanings fit into a tradition that, since the flamboyant Winckelmann, has formed a more or less submerged component of "the tyranny of Greece over Germany."[61]

Little is known concerning Kleist's earliest years, but even the bare facts of his family history help fill in somewhat a psychoanalytic portrait of the artist. His father, like many of the poet's ancestors a high-ranking Prussian military officer, died in 1788, when Kleist was eleven years of age. Prior to marrying Kleist's mother, he had been married to a much younger woman, with whom he had two daughters, including Kleist's favorite Ulrike. Kleist himself was the third of five siblings and the first boy. The death of his mother followed in February 1793, and it is this loss, rather than that of his father, which seems to have affected Kleist most deeply. He writes to his aunt, Auguste von Massow, in March 1793, thanking her for assuming the role of surrogate mother:

All of this, pain and joy, is natural so soon after such an unhappy event; the best solacer of all griefs, time, will by and by console me too, but I shall never forget the cause of it. (*Abyss*, p. 17)

A later letter of July 28–29, 1801 to Adolphine von Werdeck, a lady of the Prussian royal court in whose house Kleist had been received as a guest six years previously, allows us to speculate that it is ultimately his separation from the mother's breast that he "shall never forget":

Ah, love weans us of its joys like a mother smearing wormwood on her breast. And yet the remembrance even of the bitterness is sweet. No, it is no misfortune to have lost a happiness; it is only a misfortune no longer to remember it. (*Abyss*, p. 117)

Both letters to his aunt and to Adolphine von Werdeck display the fusion of opposites—"pain and joy," "bitterness is sweet"— that typify Kleist's art and erotic experience. The hypothesis that Kleist is impelled most deeply by the need to regain the maternal breast receives corroboration from the suicide letter to Marie von Kleist, where he declares that Henriette's decision to die with him drew him, "I cannot tell you with what inexpressible and irresistible force, *to her breast' (an ihre Brust)*. When it is added that Kleist in all likelihood never consummated a sexual relationship with a woman, and that his closest emotional ties were, first, with his half-sister Ulrike and, later, with his cousin by marriage Marie, fifteen years his senior, the conclusion indeed seems incontrovertible that Kleist remains dominated by incestuous attachments—the memory of a mother's love he finally recaptured in the perfect constancy of his death with Henriette.

Kleist's homosexual orientation makes it possible to define his life in terms of his major friendships with other men: Christoph Ernst Martini, his tutor until the age of eleven, to whom in a letter of March 18, 1799 Kleist confided his decision to leave the military profession to pursue "ideal virtue" (*Abyss*, p. 21) as a student; Ludwig Brockes, his companion during the journey to Würzburg in 1800; the painter Heinrich Lohse, whom Kleist met in Dresden in 1801; Pfeul and Otto Ruhle von Lilienstern, the latter also a comrade from the Potsdam military regiment who went on to become Inspector General of Prussian Military Schools; and Adam Müller, his collaborator on publishing activities beginning in 1807. Frequently, changes of direction in Kleist's life may be correlated with shifts in his emotional loyalties, as when his abandonment of a scholarly career coincides with the supplanting of Martini by Brockes.[62] Even the Würzburg journey—an occurrence no less veiled in mystery than Nietzsche's alleged visit to a brothel in Cologne where he may have contracted syphilis—which has been explained as a secret spy mission but with greater likelihood was intended to correct a medical condition (perhaps phimosis) that impeded his marriage, may simply have had as its primary motivation the need to secure the intimate companionship of an idealized older friend such as Brockes. Kleist's notorious "Kant crisis," by the same token, may well have been precipitated by Brockes' enforced departure from Berlin early in 1801.[63]

But though the erotic dimension of Kleist's relations with men is often explicit, he, like Freud, regularly fuses in the same person an "intimate friend" and "hated enemy." "And you think I might love a woman? And cannot even keep a friend?" (*Abyss*, p. 140), Kleist protests to Lohse after a bitter quarrel. This mixture of antithetical emotions is no less explosive in his dealings with women. "You, for example, my dear, my best Ullrique," Kleist writes to his half-sister on January 12, 1802, "how could I so intensely love you and, often in the same moment, injure your most delicate feelings?" (*Abyss*, p. 142). Even more pronouncedly bisexual than Freud, Kleist confirms the psychoanalytic lesson that attraction and hostility toward members of both sexes are inherent in the triangular structure of the Oedipus complex.

In more unstable fashion, Kleist also shares with Freud the character trait of driving ambition, with its oscillation between the extremes of "delusions of inferiority" and "megalomania." He partakes, too, of the mania for self-concealment that frequently accompanies a hero complex. Kleist constantly torments Wilhel-

mine with hints of the real purpose of his Würzburg journey, but
never satisfies her curiosity. (After the breaking off of her pro-
tracted engagement with Kleist, Wilhelmine von Zenge married
Wilhelm Traugott Krug, Kant's successor in the chair of philosophy at Königsberg.) Freud's repeated destruction of his personal
records is paralleled by Kleist's burning of the manuscript of *Robert
Guiscard* and complete obliteration of his documents, both personal
and literary, prior to his suicide.[64]

If the secret at once concealed and revealed by Freud's attempts to eliminate the traces of his past is that of the Oedipus
complex, the same is true of Kleist, whose life is punctuated by
involvements in triangular situations.[65] The intensity of Kleist's
clashes with Lohse is largely explained by the circumstance that
he was deeply attracted both to the painter's fiancée, Caroline von
Schlieben, and to her younger sister Henriette. The story has
survived of an occasion when, in deep depression over her lover's
failure to write, Caroline declared to Kleist, "If the situation does
not soon change, I'll go mad," to which the latter replied: "Quite
right, that is the best thing you could possibly do, and if you
happen to regain your sanity, I'll get a pistol and shoot us both
dead. That much I can do for you" (*Abyss*, p. 104). Apocryphal
but also highly credible is the account of a quarrel between Kleist
and Adam Müller over Sophie von Haza, who, after obtaining her
divorce in 1808 from another man, became the latter's wife. While
walking with a lady on the Brühl Terrace in Dresden, Kleist is said
to have cried out: "I must have Müller's wife; if he refuses to step
aside, he must die!" Later that day, the story continues, Kleist met
Müller on the Elbe Bridge and threatened to throw him into the
river.[66] Not least of the erotic satisfactions of Kleist's suicide was
that in Henriette Vogel he found a woman, as he wrote to Marie
von Kleist, "who for my sake is prepared to leave a father who
worships her, a husband generous enough to have relinquished
her to me, a child lovely as and lovelier than the morning sun"
(*Abyss*, p. 203). This complete oedipal triumph is compounded by
that fact that Marie herself must have felt, in Joachim Maass'
words, "a truly feminine hatred of his companion in death."[67]

The Prince of Homburg (1810), Kleist's last and greatest play,
would have perished in the general conflagration prior to his
suicide had not a manuscript copy fortunately been sent to Marie

von Kleist. With its implicity oedipal themes, this psychological drama of a soldier with the soul of a poet completes the circle begun with *Robert Guiscard* and brings to a culmination Kleist's literary autobiography.[68] The play opens with the young hero, who is in the service of the Elector of Brandenberg, sleepwalking in a garden on the night prior to a major battle against the Swedes. The continuity of this work with Kleist's earlier career is evinced by the fact that, while somnambulating, the Prince is "weaving his own splendid wreath of fame" (1.1) from a laurel tree. In order to test him, the Elector—like Achilles, a revenant of Goethe—removes the wreath from the Prince's hands and gives it to his niece Natalie, with whom the Prince is secretly in love. As this happens, the Prince whispers in his sleep, "Natalie! My tender maid! My bride!" and likewise refers to the Elector, actually his cousin, as "my father!" and to the Elector's wife as "my mother." Appalled at the Prince's reveries, the Elector concludes the scene with the words: "Into the void with you, Sir Prince of Homburg! / Back into the darkness!"

The crux of the action takes place in Act 2 when the Prince, despite explicit orders to the contrary, attacks the army of Swedes prior to receiving a signal and wins a smashing victory. What is more, it appears that the Elector has died in battle, which permits the Prince to make a declaration of love to Natalie:

> O Lady! I shall undertake your charge!
> I'll stand, an angel with a flaming sword,
> Beside your orphan'd throne! (2.6)

Subsequently, however, it emerges that the Elector has not been killed, news to which the Prince responds with an equivocal expression of both joy and sorrow: "Like gold, your word falls heavy on my heart" (2.8). In Act 3, the Prince, despite being condemned to death for his disobedience, retains a confident belief that the Elector will do him no harm:

> I'm sure of it! I'm dear to him, I know it,
> Dear as a son. . . .
> Am I not everything I am through him? (3.1)

It is only when his companion, Count Hohenzollern, asks whether he might have "done anything, / Be it on purpose or unconsciously," to offend the Elector, and the Prince learns that Natalie has been promised in marriage to the Swedish king Karl Gustav, that he is overcome with terror at his impending execution. By making the Prince aware of his interference with the Elector's plans for Natalie, Hohenzollern's question forces him also to confront the unconscious determinants of his previous conduct—desire for the death of his surrogate father and usurpation of his claims to the forbidden love object. As Kaiser has perceptively written:

The hero has taken upon himself the guilt not merely of *one* offense, but rather of two—a manifest one, the insubordination in battle, and a secret one, the Oedipus deed. . . . As long as for the Prince the matter is limited only to his official offense, he feels himself, although guilty according to the precepts of the law, innocent before his own conscience, and therefore he can look forward to the future with a clear conscience. . . . As the consciousness of his own love to the Elector upholds the belief in the Elector's fatherly love, so the dawning consciousness of father-hate threatens the ego of the hero with the danger of losing the father's love.[69]

Both the power of *The Prince of Homburg* and the vehemence of the Prince's emotional swings can only be understood in light of this "secret" familial drama underlying the "manifest" concern with military justice.

As the action unfolds, the Prince becomes increasingly reconciled to his fate—in large measure because he secures a promise from the Elector not to marry Natalie to the Swedish king—and he even ratifies his own death sentence when an offer of clemency is extended to him. The final scene of the drama is a mirror image of the first. The Prince walks in the garden, blindfolded, awaiting the burst of gunfire that will transport him to immortality, not knowing that he has been spared by the Elector. "Has it struck, my final hour of pain?" (5.11), he wonders, in words that equate death with the fulfillment of his joys. "It has! Hail, and God bless you! You are worthy!" Captain Stranz replies, as he unbinds the Prince's eyes; and when Natalie places a laurel wreath on his head, he falls down in a faint. "Heavens! He'll die of rapture!" Natalie exclaims, in words that remind us how closely *The Prince of Homburg*, no less than *Penthesilea*, prefigures Kleist's own suicide. The Prince, like Freud in the medallion incident, is "wrecked by success," as the drama ends with a real gratification of every fantasy expressed during his initial sleepwalking scene. As a result of this massive wish fulfillment, the boundary between dream and waking, internal and external worlds, is completely obliterated. To the Prince's cry, "No, tell me! Is it a dream?" Colonel Kottwitz replies, "A dream, what else?" thereby inducing the audience to share in the Prince's confusion of fantasy and reality.

In addition to the oedipal configurations of its plot, *The Prince of Homburg* anticipates psychoanalysis in its depiction of unconscious mental processes. Kleist's use of the motif of sleepwalking enables him to reveal to the audience the thoughts of the Prince unavailable to his conscious mind. After the Prince awakens from his trance, moreover, he finds that the name of Natalie "has slipped my mind" (1.4), a lapse evidently serving to indicate the illicit nature of his passion for her. Striking confirmation of Kleist's pre-Freudian discovery of the unconscious is provided by his essay "On the Gradual Fabrication of Thoughts While Speaking" (1805):

Whenever you seek to know something and cannot find it out by meditation, I would advise you, my dear and very clever friend, to talk it over with the first person you meet. He need not be especially brilliant, and I do not suggest that you *question* him; no, *tell* him about it. (*Abyss*, p. 218)

Kleist, whose remarks on this topic are doubtless affected by the fact that he himself suffered from a speech defect, here recommends the therapeutic technique of spontaneous talk to which Freud would give the name of free association. That Kleist urges his friend to direct his unpremeditated discourse at "the first person you meet" corresponds to Freud's advice that the analyst cultivate a certain anonymity in order to facilitate the formation of a transference by the patient. When Kleist goes on to write that "it is not *we* who 'know'; it is rather a certain condition, in which we happen to be, that 'knows' " (*Abyss*, p. 222), it is likewise clear that Freud's concept of the id (*das Es*), which he inherited from Nietzsche by way of Georg Groddeck, is familiar to him in all but name.

As *The Prince of Homburg* culminates the preoccupation with *Oedipus the King* evident since Kleist's earliest works, so "On the Marionette Theater" (1810), now recognized as a central document of Romantic thought, distills his meditations on self-consciousness, the other issue of overriding concern to Kleist in the decade following his "Kant crisis."[70] Cast in the form of a dialogue between the author and the leading member of a dance company, "On the Marionette Theater," like *The Broken Jug*, is an allegory of the "first stage of human culture" recounted in "the third chapter of the Book of Genesis" (*Abyss*, p. 214). According to Kleist's interlocutor, the consequence of the Fall is that humanity is tormented by a self-consciousness which lifts it above the harmony of the natural world while preventing it from attaining the perfection of divinity. The curse of affectation, says the dancer, "appears when the soul *(vis motrix)* is located at any point other than the center of gravity of a movement" (*Abyss*, p. 213), and it is because marionettes are "incapable of affectation" that they display an agility paradoxically superior to that of human performers. The character Kleist himself recounts an anecdote—a striking exemplification of Lacan's theory that the ego is formed by means of a "mirror stage"[71]—of a young man possessed of "marvelous grace," who on one occasion was reminded by "a glance in a large mirror" of his own resemblance to the statue of the Spinario. But when he sought unsuccessfully to duplicate the illusion of removing a thorn from his foot, he underwent an "inconceivable transformation," with the result that an "iron net" forever interfered with "the free play of his gestures" (*Abyss*, pp. 214–15).

But though man has been banished by self-knowledge from a condition of pure spontaneity, Kleist joins Schiller in affirming that the sole recourse is to persist in a "striving after unity." "Paradise is locked and bolted and the Cherub is behind us," the dancer observes. "We must make a journey around the world to see if a door has perhaps been left open" (*Abyss*, pp. 213–14). Having "traversed the infinite," he elaborates, grace "will return to us once more, and so appear most purely in that bodily form that has either no consciousness or an infinite one, which is to say, either in the puppet or a god" (*Abyss*, p. 216). To this the authorial persona responds with amusement: "That means that we would have to eat of the tree of knowledge a second time to fall back into the state of innocence." Kleist, for whom the Oedipus myth is interchangeable with that of the Fall, in discerning that the only way to recover paradise is through a repetition of forbidden knowledge, points to the converging parallels between the "journey around the world" of consciousness demanded by both psychoanalysis and Hegelian philosophy.

6
Hegel

$\mathbf{A}$ S BOTH the widespread influence of Schiller and the intimate personal association of Hegel, Hölderlin, and Schelling at Tübingen attest, it is impossible to disentangle philosophy from literature in the German Romantic period. In shifting our attention from the three imaginative writers dealt with in the previous chapter to Hegel, therefore, we alter the focus of our inquiry but not its essential subject matter. Despite his own quarrels with the antirational impulses of Romanticism,[1] Hegel remains incontestably not only the most powerful but also the most representative thinker of his age.

It is, above all, the problem of self-consciousness that stands at the center of Hegel's philosophy. Inasmuch as we ended our study of Kleist by noting the convergence of the myths of Oedipus and the Fall in his work, it is appropriate to begin our examination of Hegel with the following passage from his posthumously published *Aesthetics* (1835):

> With this solution of the riddle in his own person he [Oedipus] has lost his happiness as Adam did when he came to the knowledge of good and evil. The seer now, he blinds himself, resigns the throne, exiles himself from Thebes, just as Adam and Eve were driven away from Paradise, and wanders away a helpless old man.[2]

No less explicitly than Kleist in *The Broken Jug*, Hegel brings together the figures of Adam and Oedipus, and our investigation into the role of the Oedipus myth in his thought is, in effect, an attempt to understand the inevitability of this juxtaposition.

Hegel offers an extended commentary on the story of the Fall in the lesser *Logic* (1817) that forms the first part of his *Encyclopedia of the Philosophical Sciences*. Combating the typically Romantic belief that "the only way of being reconciled and restored to peace is to surrender all claims to think and know," Hegel argues that "the step into opposition, the awakening of consciousness, follows from the very nature of man."[3] In this radical reinterpretation, Adam's defiance of God's prohibition against eating from the Tree of Knowledge, far from being sinful, is the heroic beginning of the universal human odyssey of consciousness. A direct parallel to Schiller's criticism of the idyll for leading one backwards instead of forwards emerges when Hegel declares:

The harmoniousness of childhood is a gift from the hand of nature: the second harmony must spring from the labour and culture of the spirit. And so the words of Christ, "Except ye *become* as little children," etc., are very far from telling us that we must always remain children. (*Logic*, p. 43)

And just as Hegel's preference for the "second harmony" of spirit is congruent with Schiller's advocacy of a "striving after unity," so the manner in which he suggests self-division may be overcome echoes the recommendation of Kleist:

But this position of severed life has in its turn to be suppressed, and the spirit has by its own act to win its way to concord again. The final concord is spiritual; that is, the principle of restoration is to be found in thought, and thought only. The hand that inflicts the wound is also the hand which heals it. (*Logic*, p. 43)

Since "the hand that inflicts the wound" is in this instance specifically the one that plucks the forbidden fruit, Hegel's solution for healing the "severed life" induced by the Fall coincides with Kleist's conviction that "we would have to eat of the tree of knowledge a second time to fall back into the state of innocence."

The Hellenism that Hegel shares with so many of his contemporaries was doubtless augmented by his friendship with Hölderlin and Schelling, but its roots reach back before his arrival at the Tübingen seminary in 1788 to his thorough grounding in the classics acquired at the Stuttgart gymnasium.[4] During the summer of that year Hegel studied Sophocles' *Oedipus at Colonus*. In the words of his first biographer, Karl Rosenkranz:

The reading of Sophocles he continued unabated for several years. He also translated him into German and later, probably under the influence of his friendship with Hölderlin, tried to render not only the dialogues but even the choruses metrically, but was not particularly successful. As the still extant translations show, he occupied himself most with *Antigone*, which to him represented the beauty and profundity of the Greek spirit most perfectly.[5]

Despite his vocation as a philosopher, Hegel derived his conception of ancient Greece above all from tragedy; and, as Rosenkranz' comments suggest, in this reverence for tragedy Sophocles was inevitably accorded pride of place.

The admiration for Greek tragedy revealed in Hegel's youthful efforts at translation is underscored by a series of radical theological essays written between 1793 and 1799, but not published until after his death.[6] In the earliest of these, the fragments on *Folk Religion and Christianity* (1793), Hegel unfavorably contrasts those who seek consolation for misfortune through belief in an afterlife with the superior acceptance of destiny on the part of the Greeks: "What can an Oedipus demand as recompense for his undeserved sufferings, since he believed himself to stand in service under the mastery of fate?" (*HTJ*, p. 70). In a similar vein, he writes in *The Positivity of the Christian Religion* (1795) that

in everything great, beautiful, noble, and free they [the heathen] are so far our superiors that we can hardly make them our examples but must rather look up to them as a different species at whose achievements we can only marvel. (*ETW*, p. 153)

As Dominique Janicaud has observed, Hegel's encounter with the great works of the classical past is informed by the paradox that "even while being fundamentally superior to the Greeks, we must recognize what they have had that is unsurpassable,"[7] and in this ambivalent relation to antiquity Hegel's situation is essentially the same as that of Christian epic poets such as Dante or Milton.

The continued veneration of ancient Greece in Hegel's mature thought receives definitive expression in his 1809 lecture "On Classical Studies," delivered during his tenure as rector of the gymnasium at Nuremberg. Speaking of Greece and Rome, Hegel affirms: "While the first paradise was that of human *nature*, this is the second, the higher paradise of the human *spirit*" (*ETW*, p.

325). Just as it is necessary to overcome the "severed life" caused by the Fall through persisting in the quest for knowledge, so our estrangement from the "second paradise" of the classical world can only be surmounted by increasingly rigorous study of the ancients:

This world separates us from ourselves, but at the same time it grants us the cardinal means of returning to ourselves: we reconcile ourselves with it and thereby find ourselves again in it, but the self which we then find is the one which accords with the tone and universal essence of mind. (*ETW*, p. 328)

In Hegel's model, the internally divided modern individual returns from the journey to the ancient world with his own experiences attuned to the "universal essence of mind," exactly as Freud completed a hermeneutic circle when he found his own predicament mirrored in that of Oedipus.

There is a pronounced shift in Hegel's attitude toward Christianity from *The Positivity of the Christian Religion* to *The Spirit of Christianity and Its Fate* (1799). Whereas in the former work Hegel attacked Christianity as an institutional religion, which he found lacking when measured against both Greek "folk religion" and Kant's ethical doctrine, by the latter essay he came to view the teachings of Jesus as the embodiment of a moral beauty in keeping with the Greek spirit, while the legalism of both Kantian philosophy and Judaism became the target of his scorn.[8] Despite Hegel's revaluation of Christianity and concomitant disparagement of Judaism, however, he continues in *The Spirit of Christianity* to hold up Greek tragedy as a permanent standard of value: "The great tragedy of the Jewish people is no Greek tragedy; it can rouse neither terror nor pity . . . it can arouse horror alone" (*ETW*, pp. 204–5).

A probing discussion of tragedy in *The Spirit of Christianity and Its Fate* arises out of Hegel's contrast between the concepts of punishment and fate. According to Hegel, punishment is the form of retribution inflicted specifically by *law*, which always remains in a relation of externality to the transgressor, with the result that no genuine reconciliation can follow from it. Fate, on the other hand, occurs within the "orbit of life," and hence "life can heal its wounds again; the severed, hostile life can return into itself again and annul the bungling achievements of a trespass" (*ETW*, p. 230). Implicit in Hegel's notion of life "healing its wounds again" is once more the model of the Fall, in which the "step into opposition" is ultimately overcome. Because life exists within every individual, the penalty exacted for an offense under the dispensation of fate "is the equal reaction of the trespasser's own deed, of a power which he himself has armed, of an enemy made an enemy by himself" (*ETW*, p. 230). Hegel's emphasis on the "equal reaction" of life to a crime brings him very close to Freud's idea of the revenant. With particular reference to murder, Hegel contends: "Destruction of life is not the nullification of life but its diremption, and the destruction consists in the transformation into an enemy," which means, as T. M. Knox explains in a note, that "the murderer thinks he has killed his victim. But he has only turned life into an enemy, only produced a ghost to terrify him" (*ETW*, p. 229). An identical insight into the revenant, no less relevant to Freud's life than to psychoanalytic theory, is expressed more directly by Nietzsche in *Daybreak* (1881): "He who intends to kill his enemy should consider whether this is not precisely the way to make his enemy immortal to him."[9]

Hegel cites the example of Macbeth and the ghost of Banquo in his analysis of the workings of fate, and, as he will do again in the *Phenomenology of Mind*, he discerns a connection between Shakespeare's villainous hero and Greek tragedy. Although he does not mention Oedipus by name, Hegel clearly has him in mind when he proceeds to elaborate his distinction between fate and punishment:

> But fate has a more extended domain than punishment has. It is aroused even by guilt without crime, and hence it is implicitly stricter than punishment. Its strictness often seems to pass over into the most crying injustice when it makes its appearance, more terrible than ever, over against the most exalted form of guilt, the guilt of innocence. (*ETW*, pp. 232–33)

Hegel's evocation of Oedipus in terms of "the most exalted form of guilt, the guilt of innocence," recasts Schelling's formulation of four years earlier, in his *Philosophical Letters on Dogmatism and Criticism*, concerning the mortal "frightfully punished for the crime, which was a work of fate." But even as he engages in a dialogue with his prodigious colleague from Tübingen, Hegel anticipates the direction of his own future thought when he goes on to insist that "the honor of a pure soul is all the greater the more con- ⌐ciously it has done injury to life in order to maintain the supreme values" (*ETW*, p. 233). Here, Hegel is unquestionably thinking of *Antigone*; and, though he rates the heroism of Antigone higher than that of Oedipus, it is noteworthy that he defines the power of fate in the two tragedies in complementary terms.

As *The Interpretation of Dreams* does for Freud, the *Phenomenology of Mind* marks the emergence of Hegel's mature philosophy. But just as Freud's royal road to the unconscious draws upon his private letters and drafts to Fliess, so Hegel's royal road to absolute spirit is embedded in his posthumously published early theological writings. The similarity between the positions of these two landmark texts in the careers of their authors underscores the inevitability of choosing the *Phenomenology of Mind* as the focal point for a comparison between Hegelian philosophy and psychoanalysis.[10] What is at stake in such a juxtaposition has been discerned by Jean Hyppolite:

To reread thus the *Phenomenology* would consist in envisaging the totality of this difficult and sinuous work as the veritable Oedipus tragedy of the human spirit in its entirety, with perhaps this difference that the final unveiling—what Hegel names "absolute knowledge"—remains ambiguous and enigmatic.[11]

Just as Freud's discovery of the Oedipus complex is inextricably bound up with the realization that the action of *Oedipus the King* "can be likened to the work of a psycho-analysis" (*SE*, 4:262), so Hegel's allusions to *Oedipus the King* and *Antigone* are indications of the way that the form of his work as a whole discloses "the veritable Oedipus tragedy of the human spirit in its entirety." Because the *Phenomenology of Mind* is itself in the highest degree a self-analytic text, it may be read as a thematic commentary on the voyage of introspection by which Freud arrived at the Oedipus complex.

Above all, Hegel in the Preface to the *Phenomenology* makes explicit use of the metaphor of the journey likewise employed by Kleist in "On the Marionette Theater": "To reach the stage of genuine knowledge, or produce the element where science is

found—the pure conception of science itself—a long and laborious journey must be undertaken" (*PM*, p. 88). In arguing for the
necessity of such "a long and laborious journey" to arrive at
"genuine knowledge," Hegel anticipates Freud in attacking those
who would provide a short-cut to the analytic process. One must,
says Hegel, obtain "the result along with the process of arriving
at it" (*PM*, p. 69); philosophers who seek to grasp the absolute
through intuition without the exertions of reason demand "not
so much *insight* as *edification*" (*PM*, p. 72); and most com-
prehensively:

The goal to be reached is the mind's insight into what knowing is.
Impatience asks for the impossible, wants to reach the goal without the
means of getting there. The *length* of the journey has to be borne with,
for every moment is necessary; and again we must *halt* at every stage.
(*PM*, p. 90)

Paul Ricoeur has justly remarked that Hegel's quest entails a "teleology" because of its progressive movement toward the future,
whereas Freud's is an "archaeology" defined by a regressive ex-
cavation of the past; but since past and future exist in dialectical
relation, we may "find in Freud an inverted image of Hegel."[12]
The "length of the journey" is the same in either case; one must
"halt at every stage," whether or not one calls them by the psychoanalytic name of "fixation points"; and Freud and Hegel are
united in their opposition to the merchants of consolation who
proclaim "the triumph of the therapeutic."[13]

Hegel's conception of the *Phenomenology of Mind* in terms of a
journey is directly tied to the work's self-analytic structure. When
he writes in the Preface that "everything depends on grasping the
ultimate truth not as *Substance* but as *Subject* as well" (*PM*, p. 80),
Hegel articulates a fundamental truth not only of his philosophy
but also of psychoanalysis. To read the works of Freud without
an awareness of their autobiographical component is to eliminate
the dimension of "subject" from psychoanalytic theory. Because
the Preface to the *Phenomenology* was written only after the rest of
the work had been completed, it stands—albeit on a much larger
scale—in the same relation to the body of the text that the Preface
of the second edition, where Freud speaks retrospectively about
the "further subjective significance" of his book as "a portion of

my own self-analysis," does to *The Interpretation of Dreams*. Containing the gist of what is to follow, the Preface to the *Phenomenology* both opens and closes the hermeneutic circle that Hegel, well before Heidegger, teaches us to be the form of understanding: "It [true reality] is the process of its own becoming, the circle which presupposes its end as its purpose, and has its end for its beginning" (*PM*, p. 81).

No less than in Freud's self-analysis, the drama in the *Phenomenology of Mind* consists of a discovery of what one has already known. Freud, as we have seen in part 1, could "only analyze myself with objectively acquired knowledge (as if I were a stranger)," was filled with "presentiments" and aware "in advance" of his breakthroughs, and generally found himself "in that strange state of mind in which one knows and does not know a thing at the same time." Exactly this paradoxical condition of simultaneous knowledge and ignorance is inherent in Hegel's endeavor. The affinities between his thought and psychoanalysis are once again best described by Hyppolite:

The philosopher must not substitute himself for ordinary consciousness . . . but rather *follow* it in its theoretical and practical experiences . . . until the point where, in what Hegel calls absolute knowledge, the ordinary consciousness will finally say, "But what you have just discovered—I knew it all along." (A little bit as Oedipus says it at the end of that immense quest which leads him to such tragic results.) It is only when ordinary consciousness recognizes itself in philosophic consciousness, and the latter in the former, that psychoanalysis will be achieved, that science will be alive, and ordinary consciousness will be scientific.[14]

This uniting of "ordinary consciousness" and "philosophic consciousness" occurs for Oedipus at the moment that he realizes himself to be the son of Laius and Jocasta, and it is reenacted by Freud at the culmination of his self-analysis when he discovers "love of the mother and jealousy of the father in my own case too" and achieves the "absolute knowledge" of the Oedipus complex.

The phrase "in my own case too," as I have argued, points specifically to the anonymous patient with "homicidal tendencies" through whom Freud came to fathom "the universal human application of the Oedipus myth." That he should attain this insight by identification with a "stranger" who is a second self is superbly glossed by Hegel: "A self having knowledge *purely* of itself in the absolute antithesis of itself . . . is knowledge *in universal form*" (*PM*, p. 86). Thus, just as he defends the constructive circularity of Freud's theory, Hegel corroborates its claim to universality:

The task of conducting the individual mind from its unscientific standpoint to that of science had to be taken in its general sense; we had to contemplate the formative development of the universal individual, of self-conscious spirit. (*PM*, p. 89)

Like Freud, Hegel conflates ontogeny and phylogeny, and relies in his appeal to the notion of a "universal individual" on the precedent of Sophocles' Oedipus.

The "long and laborious journeys" of both Hegel and Freud, moreover, resemble *Oedipus the King* in turning on experiences of reversal and frustration. Hegel refers in a famous phrase from the Preface to the *Phenomenology* to "the labour of the negative" (*PM*, p. 81), and likewise confronts the power of death: "But the life of mind is not one that shuns death, and keeps clear of destruction; it endures death and in death maintains its being" (*PM*, p. 93). In language that pertains to Freud as much as to Hegel, Habermas characterizes the way that progression in the *Phenomenology of Mind* occurs through "the destructions of false consciousness":

As shown by the prototypical area of experience in life history, the experiences from which one learns are negative. The reversal of consciousness means the dissolution of identifications, the breaking of fixations, and the destruction of projections.[15]

Not only did Freud's self-analysis arise in response to his father's death but its pivotal event—the abandonment of the seduction theory—was indeed a *peripeteia* or "reversal of consciousness." Hegel's celebrated dialectic of master and slave, by the same token, originates in "a life-and-death struggle" (*PM*, p. 232), and its unexpected outcome is the ultimate ascendancy of the slave over the master.

Hegel is not normally thought of as a philosopher of the unconscious.[16] In point of fact, however, the *Phenomenology of Mind* most closely resembles psychoanalysis in its recognition of a realm within the mind that is not directly accessible to consciousness. Again in the Preface Hegel writes:

What is "familiarly known" is not *properly known*, just for the reason that it is *"familiar."* When engaged in the process of knowing, it is the commonest form of self-deception, and a deception of other people as well, to assume something to be familiar, and give assent to it on that very account. Knowledge of that kind, with all its talk, never gets from the spot, but has no idea that this is the case. (*PM*, p. 92)

This declaration that what is "familiarly known" *(das Bekannte)* may not be "properly known" *(erkannt)* will become one of the recurrent commonplaces in nineteenth-century German philosophy. The same awareness underlies Freud's exploration of the collapse of the distinction between the "strange" and the "familiar" in "The 'Uncanny.'" The goal of the odysseys of consciousness undertaken in both psychoanalysis and Hegelian philosophy, therefore, may be defined indifferently as a process of "defamiliarization" or of making what is unconscious conscious.

Hegel, furthermore, connects the concept of the unconscious to that of dynamic repression when he describes the "flight from the actual world" attempted by faith: "Such flight from the realm of the present is, therefore, directly in its very nature a dual state of mind" (*PM*, p. 513). The reference to "flight from the realm of the present" prefigures Breuer and Freud's apothegem in *Studies on Hysteria* that *"hysterics suffer mainly from reminiscences"* (*SE*, 2:7), and in *Inhibitions, Symptoms and Anxiety* (1926) Freud specifically equates repression with flight. Because of the spiral structure of the *Phenomenology of Mind*, what takes place at any given stage of development is reenacted in countless forms; and one may take as representative of the "dual state of mind" Hegel's analysis of how an individual's pursuit of purely private satisfaction comes into conflict with necessity:

Consciousness, therefore, through the experience in which its truth ought to have been revealed, has instead become to itself a riddle; the consequences of its deeds are to it not really its own deeds. (*PM*, p. 388; translation modified)

For Hegel no less than Freud, the quest to uncover the truth is inseparable from the "riddle" of self-blinding or repression, and it is only out of such Sophoclean "reversals of consciousness" that one can win through to a higher level of awareness.

Although it is clear from the foregoing quotations that the *Phenomenology of Mind* is informed throughout by an oedipal paradigm, it is when Hegel turns his attention to tragedy that his anticipation of Freud comes most sharply into focus. Hegel discusses tragedy at two key points in the *Phenomenology*—first, in the portion of the section on "Spirit" entitled "Ethical Action"; and second, near the end of the work, in that subdivision of "Religion" devoted to "The Spiritual Work of Art." In Hegel's mature system, it should be acknowledged, art stands as the lowest of the three realms (the other two being religion and philosophy) in which "absolute spirit" manifests itself. It is likewise true that Greece comes to play a more subordinate role than it did in his early unpublished tracts.[17] Representative of his later views is Hegel's statement that the thought of the universal "did not gain its full recognition till the days of Christianity. The Greeks, in other respects so advanced, knew neither God nor even man in their true universality" (*Logic*, p. 227). Despite this theoretical revision, however, Hegel remained constant in his emotional attachment to both art—the highest form of which he believed to be tragedy— and Greek culture, and the Sophoclean cast of his thought continues to be unmistakable.

Hegel's interpretation of tragedy rests in an important way upon the equivocation in the German word *Geist* that allows it to be translated as either "mind" or "spirit." Already in his discussion of fate in *The Spirit of Christianity*, where he speaks of "the equal reaction of the trespasser's deed," Hegel elides the difference between what takes place in the "mind" of the individual transgressor and in the "spirit" of the cosmic force outside of him. This ambiguity recurs in the *Phenomenology*, as may be seen in the parallel Hegel draws between the sundering in internal and external reality:

> There arises in this way in consciousness the opposition between *what is known* and *what is not known*, just as, in the case of substance, there was an opposition between the *conscious* and the *unconscious*. (*PM*, p. 486)

This sundering, Hegel explains, is brought about merely through *action*—the step into self-consciousness—and thus is tantamount to the Fall of Man:

> For the latter [self-consciousness], just in that it is a self to itself, and proceeds to act, lifts itself out of the state of *simple immediacy*, and itself

sets up the *division into two*. By the act it gives up the specific character of ethical life, that of being pure and simple certainty of immediate truth. . . . By the act it thus becomes *Guilt*. For the deed is its doing, and doing is its inmost nature. And the *Guilt* acquires also the meaning of *Crime*. (*PM*, p. 488)

W. H. Auden has observed of Freud that he "differs both from Rousseau who denied the Fall . . . and also from the theological doctrine which makes the Fall the result of a deliberate choice, man being therefore morally responsible."[18] These words may be applied without modification to Hegel, whose reinterpretation of the Fall in both the *Phenomenology* and the *Logic* turns precisely on the insistence that "the step into opposition, the awakening of consciousness, follows from the very nature of man."

Hegel's analysis of the "division into two" fostered by self-consciousness serves to highlight the connection in his thought between the myths of Oedipus and the Fall. The equation he posits between act, guilt, and crime elaborates Schelling's assertion that "the tragic person is *necessarily* guilty of a crime," although in Hegel's revisionary reading Adam, like Oedipus, is held to exhibit the "most exalted" form of the "guilt of innocence." Because for Hegel the essence of action is to replace "simple immediacy" by a "double form" (*PM*, p. 488), the consequence of any deed is, as it were, to create a "repressed" domain within the universe, which will in due course redound upon the perpetrator. As Hegel's allusions to "what is not known" *(des Nichtgewußten)* and "the unconscious" *(Bewußtlosen)* make clear, his concept of self-consciousness is indeed the "inverted image" of the psychoanalytic postulate of the unconscious; and it is as the representative hero of "ethical self-consciousness" (*PM*, p. 489) that he portrays the figure of Oedipus.

Hegel prefaces his interpretation of *Oedipus the King* with an elaboration of his general theory of what is at stake in any decision to take action:

The decision, however, is *inherently* something negative, which plants an "other" in opposition to it, something foreign to the decision, which is clear knowledge. Actual reality, therefore, keeps concealed within itself this other aspect alien to clear knowledge, and does not show itself to consciousness as it fully and truly is. (*PM*, p. 490)

In the immediately ensuing German text, Oedipus again is not cited by name, but his exemplary status as the embodiment of deluded "consciousness" is only made more telling by Hegel's ellipsis:

[In the story of Oedipus] the son does not see his own father in the person of the man who has insulted him and whom he strikes to death, nor his mother in the queen whom he makes his wife. In this way a hidden power shunning the light of day, waylays the ethical self-consciousness, a power which bursts forth only after the deed is done, and seizes the doer in the act. For the completed deed is the removal of the opposition between the knowing self and the reality over against it. . . . In this truth, therefore, the deed comes to the light;—it is something in which a conscious element is bound up with what is unconscious, what is peculiarly one's own with what is alien and external:—it is an essential reality divided in sunder, whose other aspect consciousness experiences and finds to be its own aspect, but as a power violated by its doing, and roused to hostility against it. (*PM*, p. 490; brackets added)

All the parallels between Hegel and Freud come to a head in this passage. The failure of Hegel's Oedipus to recognize his mother and father provokes "a hidden power shunning the light of day" *(eine lichtscheue Macht)* to overtake him, and the action of the tragedy depicts "the removal of the opposition between the knowing self and the reality over against it." Hegel again explicitly recognizes the existence of "what is unconscious" *(das Unbewußte),* and his analysis of the convergence of "what is peculiarly one's own" *(dem Sein)* with "what is alien and external" *(das Nichtseiende)* catches the essence of the uncanny. Indeed, his description of the way that consciousness discovers the "other aspect" of reality to be its "own aspect" but now "roused to hostility against it" conforms exactly to the psychoanalytic model of the "return of the repressed."

As he had done in *The Spirit of Christianity,* Hegel couples his exegesis of *Oedipus the King* with that of *Antigone.* He virtually repeats his earlier affirmation that "the honor of a pure soul is all the greater" if it chooses consciously to do "injury to life" when he writes in the *Phenomenology:*

But the ethical consciousness is more complete, its guilt purer, if it *knows beforehand* the law and power which it opposes, if it takes them to be sheer violence and wrong. (*PM*, p. 491)

Antigone differs from Oedipus in the deliberateness of her violation of "essential reality." But the problem of the "division into two" is present in both cases, even though the tragic collision in *Antigone* takes place between two distinct characters—Antigone and Creon—and that in *Oedipus the King* is located in the mind of Oedipus himself. In "The Spiritual Work of Art," Hegel contends that the duality of the sexes corresponds to the "two powers" of the "ethical substance":

the ethical substance by its very principle broke up, as regards its *content*, into two powers—which were defined as *divine* and *human* law, law of the nether world and law of the upper world, the one the *family*, the other *state sovereignty*, the first bearing the impress and *character of woman*, the other that *of man*. (*PM*, p. 739)

Antigone, as representative of the "nether world," "divine law," and "family," stands in opposition to Creon, the spokesman for the "upper world," "human law," and "state sovereignty." That this polarity might be redefined as that between "the unconscious" and "the conscious" becomes unmistakable when Hegel writes:

The higher and lower right come to signify in this connexion the power that knows and reveals itself to consciousness, and the power concealing itself and lurking in the background. (*PM*, p. 740)

But though womankind, "the everlasting irony in the life of the community" (*PM*, p. 496), incarnates the unconscious of male authority, because of the "double form" of reality even Antigone's nobility is tainted by "one-sidedness" (*PM*, p. 487). It may consequently be said of both her and Creon no less than of Oedipus that "the agent finds himself thereby in the opposition of knowing and not knowing" (*PM*, p. 739).

As he does with Antigone, Hegel draws the fates of Eteocles and Polyneices into Oedipus' orbit. Either of Oedipus' two sons might, in his view, "with equal right take possession of the community" (*PM*, p. 493), but because the "single soul" of government "does not admit of a duality," the rivals fall into conflict, and "their equal right in regard to the power of the state is destructive to both, for they are equally wrong" (*PM*, p. 439). The "equal right" and "equal wrong" of Eteocles and Polyneices is another version of that attributed by Hegel to Antigone and Creon, and both of these in turn are a variation on the "guilt of innocence" of Oedipus.

Hegel's meditation on the human psyche is tied to a profound awareness of the duplicities inherent in language. In "The Spiritual Work of Art" he returns to his association between Oedipus and Macbeth in *The Spirit of Christianity* and, in a burst of syncretism, adduces also Orestes and Hamlet as tragic heroes who are confronted by "the double-tounged, equivocal character" (*PM*, p. 740) of oracular pronouncements. The Ghost in *Hamlet*, the Witches in *Macbeth*, and the Sphinx's riddle in *Oedipus the King* are "in nothing different" from the Delphic oracle:

But the commands of this truth-speaking god, and his proclamations of what *is*, are really deceptive and fallacious. For this knowledge is, in its very principle, directly not knowledge, because *consciousness* in acting is inherently this opposition. (*PM*, p. 740)

Apollo is a "truth-speaking god" who embodies the "aspect of light" (*PM*, p. 740), but he immediately becomes "deceptive and fallacious" when he enters the domain of language. This paradox, a demonstration of reality's "double form," adumbrates Nietzsche's assertion of the inseparability of Apollo and Dionysus. And just as psychoanalysis distinguishes between "manifest" and "latent" content in interpreting dreams, so Hegel, realizing that repression leads to a condition where "knowledge is . . . directly not knowledge" *(Wissen ist . . . unmittelbar das Nichtwissen)*, warns against being taken in by the "manifest and obvious meaning" (*PM*, p. 740) of language as a whole.

Although Hegel's affinities with psychoanalysis are most evident in his two sections dealing with Sophoclean tragedy, important anticipations of Freud may be found throughout the *Phenomenology of Mind*. For Hegel, as for Freud, "self-consciousness is the state of *Desire* in general" (*PM*, p. 220), and it is the fate of desire that plays a decisive role in the evolution of culture.[19] Hegel likewise confronts squarely the inescapability of conflict in human life, and his outlook is fundamentally dualistic:

Regarding this play of forces, however, we saw that its peculiarity lay in this, that the force which is *awakened into activity* by another force is just on that account the *inciting agency* for this other force, which thereby itself only then becomes an inciting force. (*PM*, p. 194)

This passage, which might be taken as an abstraction of the psychoanalytic theory of the instincts, belongs to that tradition of dialectical thought whose outlines we have already traced from Schiller to Freud. Indeed, the very term *"aufheben"*—borrowed, as we recall, from Schiller—that forms the mainspring of Hegel's system has a "twofold meaning," since "to supersede is at once *to negate* and *to preserve"* (*PM,* pp. 163–64), and is thus an illustration of Freud's thesis that "primal words" possess "antithetical meanings."

As Hegel's primordial myth of the struggle between master and slave most vividly exemplifies, the entire *Phenomenology of Mind* is in essence a two-character drama. What is more, it is ultimately impossible to determine whether these constantly metamorphosing characters are two separate individuals or two aspects of a single psyche.[20] As Hegel writes in "Lordship and Bondage":

> This process of self-consciousness in relation to another self-consciousness has in this manner been represented as *the action of one alone.* But this action on the part of the one has itself the double significance of being at once *its own action* and *the action of that other* as well. (*PM,* p. 230)

Hegel's blurring of the line of demarcation between internal and external reality corresponds to Freud's notion of the "narcissistic formation," in which an individual may replace either the role of subject or object within his own fantasy by "another, extraneous ego" (*SE,* 14:132). Since, as I have argued in chapter 3, the "narcissistic formation" provides a theoretical model for the analytic situation, which elevates self-analysis to a position of ontological primacy as the "preliminary stage" of any two-party analysis, Hegel's dramatization of the interchangeability of *interpersonal* and *intrapsychic* experience confirms the status of the *Phenomenology* as—like "Screen Memories"—an exemplary self-analytic text.

Whereas the *Phenomenology of Mind* depicts the process of Hegel's voyage of introspection, the *Logic* sets forth the results of the journey in systematic form. It is, therefore, instructive to see how many of the points of contact between Hegel and Freud from the *Phenomenology* are found apodictically restated in the later work. The conviction expressed in the Preface to the *Phenomenology* that knowledge has a circular structure is reiterated in the Introduction to the *Logic:*

The very point of view, which originally is taken on its own evidence only, must in the course of the science be converted to a result—the ultimate result in which philosophy returns into itself and reaches the point with which it began. In this manner philosophy exhibits the appearance of a circle which closes with itself, and has no beginning in the same way as the other sciences have. (p. 23)

Just as the *Logic* shares with the *Phenomenology* the attempt to "reach the point with which it began," so Hegel again maintains that knowledge is a matter of becoming genuinely aware of what is ostensibly "familiar":

But things thus familiar are usually the greatest strangers. Being, for example, is a category of pure thought: but to make "is" an object of investigation never occurs to us. (*Logic*, p. 40)

And even as he conflates the "strange" and the "familiar," Hegel justifies the procedure by which we have turned psychoanalysis back upon Freud himself:

The forms of thought must be studied in their essential nature and complete development: they are at once the object of research and the action of that object. Hence they examine themselves: in their own action they must determine their limits, and point out their defects. (*Logic*, p. 66)

Properly understood, psychoanalysis, like Hegelian philosophy, is "at once the object of research and the action of that object." In allowing for the self-analytic dimension of Freud's works, we have seen that they do indeed "examine themselves" and "determine their limits." If the "retroactive force" of Freud has caused us to see in Hegel a precursor of psychoanalysis, in making explicit the principles of psychoanalytic investigation, Hegel reminds us that Freud might equally well be included within his own system.

One of the most celebrated passages in the *Logic* is Hegel's statement of the relation between contingency and necessity:

From such circumstances and conditions there has, as we say, proceeded quite another thing, and it is for that reason that we call this process of necessity blind. If on the contrary we consider teleological action, we have in the end of action a content which is already foreknown. This activity therefore is not blind but seeing. . . . Necessity is blind only as long as it is not understood. (p. 209)

Hegel's use of the metaphor of blindness and vision resonates with Sophoclean overtones. That this discussion of "teleological action" is indeed grounded in Sophocles is confirmed by the posthumously published *Lectures on the Philosophy of Religion* (1832). Avowing that the "moral justice" of destiny is "expressed in the noblest form in the tragedies of Sophocles," Hegel continues: "The destiny of individuals is represented as something incomprehensible, but necessity is not a blind justice; on the contrary, it is recognized as the true justice."[21] For Oedipus, who gropes in ignorance to find the murderer of Laius, the action of his drama would doubtless seem "incomprehensible," but to the spectator observing the working out of a "foreknown" outcome the same process reveals the guiding hand of "true justice." Because of this spiritual logic manifested in Sophocles' tragedies Hegel terms them "the eternal patterns or models of the moral notion" (p. 264).

In addition to amplifying the blindness metaphor in the *Logic*, Hegel's examination of Sophocles in *Lectures on the Philosophy of Religion* shows the consistency with which he adhered to the interpretation of the Oedipus myth put forward in the *Phenomenology of Mind*. Beginning with the theme of collision in *Antigone*, where Antigone and Creon "both end in injustice just because they are one-sided, though at the same time they both obtain justice too," Hegel turns to *Oedipus the King*:

> We have another example of collision in the case of Oedipus, for instance. He has slain his father, is apparently guilty, but guilty because his moral power is one-sided; that is to say, he falls into the commission of this horrible deed unconsciously. He, however, is the man who solved the riddle of the Sphinx; he is the man distinguished for his knowledge, and so a kind of balance is introduced in the shape of a Nemesis. He, who is so gifted for knowledge, is in the power of what is unconscious, so that he falls into a guilt which is deep in proportion to the height on which he stood. Here, therefore, we have the opposition of the two powers, that of consciousness and unconsciousness. (p. 265)

Like both Schlegel and Nietzsche, Hegel connects Oedipus' solving of the Sphinx's riddle with his commission of the crimes of incest and patricide. The pattern of repetition whereby Oedipus "falls into a guilt which is deep in proportion to the height on which he stood" is the temporal corollary to a law of double meanings, since

Oedipus is simultaneously "distinguished for knowledge" and "in the power of what is unconscious." Hegel again looks ahead to psychoanalysis in dividing the mind into "the opposition of two powers, that of consciousness and unconsciousness." As he remarks of Oedipus in the *Aesthetics*: "it was what was unknown that was the actual and essential deed, namely the murder of his own father."[22]

Of the lecture cycles published after his death, that on the *Philosophy of History* (1837) is the most useful for charting the outcome of Hegel's lifelong preoccupation with Oedipus. Already in the *Phenomenology of Mind* Hegel had sought "to contemplate the formative development of the universal individual, of self-conscious spirit," and this task is transferred to the stage of history in the *Philosophy of History*. Just as in the *Phenomenology*, moreover, specific allusions to the figure of Oedipus reinforce the larger design of the *Philosophy of History* as "the veritable Oedipus tragedy of the human spirit in its entirety."

Hegel's predilection for circular thinking, which we have noted both in the *Phenomenology* and in the *Logic*, reappears yet again in the theoretical Introduction to the *Philosophy of History*:

What I have said thus provisionally, and what I shall have further to say, is, even in reference to our branch of science, not to be regarded as hypothetical, but as a summary view of the whole; the result of the investigation we are about to pursue; a result which happens to be known to *me*, because I have traversed the entire field.[23]

Having arrived at the standpoint of "philosophic consciousness," Hegal informs the "ordinary consciousness" of his reader or listener of "the result of the investigation we are about to pursue." It is as if Teiresias were talking to Oedipus or, more precisely, as if Oedipus, upon the discovery of his identity, were talking to himself as he was at the beginning of the play. The circularity of Hegel is thus a function of the *retrospective* quality of his investigation, a quality best formulated in the famous metaphor from the Preface to the *Philosophy of Right* (1821):

As the thought of the world, it [philosophy] appears only when actuality is already there cut and dried after its process of formation has been completed. . . . The owl of Minerva spreads its wings only with the falling of the dusk.[24]

Hegel's "owl of Minerva" presides as well over the labors of Freud, whose analytic interventions typically occur after the "process of formation has been completed." Although Hegel adds that philosophy "always comes on the scene too late to give" instruction,[25] this attitude may be regarded not so much as the antithesis of the curative aims of analysis, but as the counterpart to the therapeutic pessimism also found in Freud's later writings.

Just as Hegel's orientation toward the past in the *Philosophy of History* is in keeping with psychoanalytic theory, so too is his understanding of the relation of the past to the present:

we have, in traversing the past—however extensive its periods—only to do with what is *present;* for philosophy, as occupying itself with the true, has to do with the eternally present. Nothing in the past is lost for it, for the idea is ever present; spirit is immortal; with it there is no past, no future, but an essential now. This necessarily implies that the present form of spirit comprehends within it all earlier steps. (*PH,* p. 79)

The psychoanalyst, like the Hegelian philosopher, "in traversing the past" has "only to do with what is present," since a patient's narrative of his previous experiences must be interpreted in light of the *transference* exhibited in the current analytic situation. Freud, who spoke of the "timelessness" of the unconscious, would doubtless concur with Hegel that the "present form" of an individual's personality "comprehends within it all earlier steps." This realization that "nothing in the past is lost," articulated theoretically by both Freud and Hegel, is integral to *Oedipus the King,* where at the moment of "absolute knowledge" Oedipus' past returns to engulf his present.

As in the *Phenomenology of Mind,* the "long and laborious journey" narrated in the *Philosophy of History* is conceived in terms of a quest for self-knowledge:

But for spirit, the highest attainment is self-knowledge; an advance not only to the intuition, but to the thought—the clear conception of itself. This it must and is also destined to accomplish; but the accomplishment is at the same time its dissolution, and the rise of another spirit, another world-historical people, another epoch of universal history. (*PH,* p. 71)

The irony whereby the "accomplishment" of a culture "is at the same time its dissolution," as Hayden White has observed, at once characterizes "the enigma of human existence as a riddle" and is "yet another way of indicating the essentially Comic nature of the whole historical quest."[26] Hegel refers earlier to the *"cunning of reason"* to describe the way that the historical process "sets the passions to work for itself, while that which develops its existence through such impulsion pays the penalty, and suffers loss" (*PH*, p. 33). Another version of the dictum that "necessity is blind only as long as it is not understood," the notion of the "cunning of reason" enables Hegel to reconcile his design of portraying "a theodicy . . . so that the ill that is found in the world may be comprehended" (*PH*, p. 15) with his unflinching recognition that "the history of the world is not the theatre of happiness. Periods of happiness are blank pages in it" (*PH*, p. 26). Because the individual caught up in the flux of history is unlikely to grasp the relation between his selfish pursuits and the design of providence, reality once again conceals an "aspect alien to clear consciousness"; or, as Hegel phrases his argument for the unconscious on this occasion, in every action "something further may be implicated than lies in the intention and consciousness of the agent" (*PH*, p. 28).

Hegel's belief that "the highest attainment is self-knowledge" links him not only to Freud but also to Nietzsche. A no less powerful bond between these three thinkers is their common devotion to the idea of the hero. "But by my love and hope I beseech you," Nietzsche's Zarathustra exhorts a noble youth, "do not throw away the hero in your soul!" (*VPN*, p. 156). In *Moses and Monotheism,* while acknowledging the modern tendency to explain historical events in terms of "general and impersonal factors," Freud unabashedly argues that the ascendancy of monotheism among the Jews is due to "the transcendent influence of a single personality" (*SE*, 23:107–8). In precisely the same spirit, Hegel proclaims in the *Philosophy of History:*

World-historical men—the heroes of an epoch—must, therefore, be recognized as its clear-sighted ones; their deeds, their words are the best of that time. Great men have formed purposes to satisfy themselves, not others. . . . Their fellows, therefore, follow these soul-leaders; for they feel the irresistible power of their own inner spirit thus embodied. (*PH*, pp. 30–31)

Because this shared emphasis by Hegel, Nietzsche, and Freud on the dynamic force of the individual personality itself arises from their own stature as "world-historical men," what each has to say about the hero is implicitly applicable to the other two. Thus, when Hegel writes that a hero is activated by "an unconscious impulse that occasioned the accomplishment of that for which the time was ripe" (*PH*, p. 30), he elucidates the way that the accidents of Freud's personal history converged with the historical conditions of the nineteenth century to give birth to psychoanalysis.

The Sophoclean motifs in the *Philosophy of History* are brought out at the start of the work proper, where Hegel recurs to the imagery of blindness:

Imagination has often pictured to itself the emotions of a blind man suddenly becoming possessed of sight, beholding the bright glimmering of the dawn, the growing light, and the flaming glory of the ascending sun. (*PH*, p. 103)

It is not surprising that Hegel should invoke the journey of the sun to symbolize "the course of history, the great day's work of spirit" (*PH*, p. 103). What is unusual is that he complicates it with the description of "a blind man suddenly becoming possessed of sight." This "reversal of consciousness" is accompanied by yet another, for Hegel proceeds to draw a contrast between the physical and intellectual sun:

The history of the world travels from East to West, for Europe is absolutely the end of history, Asia the beginning. . . . Here rises the outward physical sun, and in the West it sinks down: here consentaneously rises the sun of self-consciousness, which diffuses a nobler brilliance. (*PH*, pp. 103–4)

The "nobler brilliance" of this "sun of self-consciousness," which rises in the west where the "outward physical sun" sets, recalls Hegel's description of ancient Greece and Rome as "the higher paradise of the human *spirit*" in "On Classical Studies." It is, he reiterates in the *Philosophy of History*, among the Greeks—the first European people—that "spirit became introspective, triumphed over particularity, and thereby emancipated itself" (*PH*, p. 222).

Although Hegel recognizes that "the *historical* transition takes place when the Persian world comes in contact with the Greek," he accounts for the "inward or ideal transition" (*PH*, p. 221) from oriental to Greek civilization in more poetic fashion. Whereas "the spirit of the Egyptians presented itself to their consciousness in the form of a *problem*," he explains:

The Greek Apollo is its solution; his utterance is: *"Man, know thyself."* In this dictum is not intended a self-recognition that regards the specialities of one's own weaknesses and defects; it is not the individual that is admonished to become acquainted with his idiosyncrasy, but humanity *in general* is summoned to self-knowledge. (*PH*, p. 220)

Later in his discussion Hegel asserts—as he will again in the *Logic*— that the Greeks, "since they had not attained an intellectual conception of themselves, did not yet realize spirit in its universality" (*PH*, p. 250), but this disclaimer is contradicted by the statement that in Apollo's injunction "humanity *in general* is summoned to self-knowledge."

Having established that the "inward or ideal transition" from east to west is symbolized by the relation to Egypt to Greece, Hegel proceeds to offer a specific mythological illustration of this shift of self-knowledge from "problem" to "solution":

Wonderfully, then, must the Greek legend surprise us, which relates, that the Sphinx—the great Egyptian symbol—appeared in Thebes, uttering the words: "What is that which in the morning goes on four legs, at midday, on two, and in the evening on three?" Oedipus, giving the solution, *Man*, precipitated the Sphinx from the rock. (*PH*, p. 220)

Already in the *Phenomenology of Mind* Hegel had introduced his interpretation of the Sphinx, just prior to treating Greek religion under the rubric "Religion in the Form of Art," as an artifact in which self-consciousness is on the point of discovering itself:

The artificer, therefore, combines both [outer and inner being] by blending the forms of nature and self-consciousness; and these ambiguous beings, a riddle to themselves—the conscious struggling with what has no consciousness, the simple inner with the multiform outer, the darkness of thought mated with the clearness of expression—these break out into the language of a wisdom that is darkly deep and difficult to understand. (*PM*, p. 707)

When these passages are considered together, it is clear that in both the *Phenomenology of Mind* and the *Philosophy of History* Hegel equates the solving of the Sphinx's riddle with the advent of Greek culture, and thus sees Oedipus as the hero who raises humanity to self-consciousness. Steven Marcus has remarked of Freud's self-analysis that in it "the classical instruction to know thyself was brought into historical and momentous conjunction with *Oedipus Rex*,"[27] but this "historical and momentous conjunction" is already to be found in Hegel's self-analysis of the human spirit.

Oedipus' "solution and liberation of that Oriental spirit" embodied in the Sphinx means that "the inner being of nature is thought, which has its existence only in the human consciousness." But Hegel does not overlook the vicissitudes of Oedipus' fate:

But that time-honored solution given by Oedipus—who thus shows himself possessed of knowledge—is connected with a dire ignorance of the character of his own actions. The rise of spiritual illumination in the old royal house is disparaged by connection with abominations, the result of ignorance; and that primeval royalty must—in order to attain true knowledge and moral clearness—first be brought into shapely form, and be harmonzied with the spirit of the beautiful, by civil laws and political freedom. (*PH*, pp. 220–21)

As in his *Lectures on the Philosophy of Religion*, Hegel depicts Oedipus as at once "possessed of knowledge" and in "dire ignorance of the character of his own actions," which is to say that he discerns the connection between his vanquishing of the Sphinx and unwitting commission of the "abominations" of incest and patricide. The progression of the "old royal house" from such unspeakable beginnings to "true knowledge and moral clearness," culminating in *Oedipus at Colonus*, is for Hegel a paradigm for the history of the world, which "is nothing but the development of the idea of freedom" (*PH*, p. 456).

For his sixtieth birthday, in 1830, Hegel was given a medal by his pupils, which on one side bore his portrait and on the other an allegorical representation: on the left, a seated male figure reading from a book, behind whom an owl crouches upon a pillar; on the right, a woman holding fast to a towering cross; and between the two, facing the seated figure, is a naked genius, whose arm points toward the elevated cross.[28] This medal might be taken as an emblem of everything that separates Hegel from Freud. Above all, the reconciliation between philosophy and theology implied by the genius bridging the owl and the cross accurately reflects the degree to which Hegel's mature system is religious in intention, or, in his own words, a "true *theodicy*, the justification of God in history" (*PH*, p. 457). Freud's universe, by contrast, is altogether without transcendence, and he—like the hermeneutic philosophers otherwise so deeply influenced by Hegel—would have little patience with the idea of "absolute knowledge." But these differences, though real, do not override the more important continuities between them. Just as for Freud the attempt to uncover origins always comes up against Derrida's "supplement," so even for Hegel "absolute knowledge" always remains an elusive ideal, in practice (in Hyppolite's words) "ambiguous and enigmatic." We may define the relation between Freud and Hegel by saying that, although it is impossible to imagine Freud as the recipient of Hegel's medal, Hegel might fittingly have been honored by the medallion presented to Freud on his fiftieth birthday—a design of Oedipus answering the Sphinx, inscribed with the words "Who knew the famous riddles and was a man most mighty."

7
Between Hegel
and Nietzsche

SÁNDOR FERENCZI begins his 1912
paper "The Symbolic Representation of the Pleasure and Reality
Principles in the Oedipus Myth" with an extended quotation from
a November 11, 1815 letter from Schopenhauer to Goethe, of
which the following portion is printed in italics:

It is the courage of making a clean breast of it in face of every obstacle
that makes the philosopher. He must be like Sophocles' Oedipus, who,
seeking enlightenment concerning his terrible fate, pursues his indefa-
tigable enquiry, even when he divines that appalling horror awaits him
in the answer. But most of us carry in our hearts the Jocasta, who begs
Oedipus for God's sake not to enquire further; and we give way to her,
and that is the reason why philosophy stands where it does.[1]

As its title suggests, the chief purpose of Ferenczi's paper is
to integrate Schopenhauer's definition of the philosopher with
Freud's recent "Formulations on the Two Principles of Mental
Functioning" (1911), in order to propose that Oedipus "represents
the reality-principle in the human mind," whereas Jocasta "is the
personification of the pleasure-principle, which, regardless of objective truth, wants nothing else than to spare the ego pain" (p.
221). Ferenczi takes his comparison of Oedipus and Jocasta to its
logical conclusion when he makes the misogynous generalization
that "in women the tendency to repression . . . prevails; in men

the capacity for objective judgement and for tolerating painful insight" (p. 222).

Ferenczi's paper is of interest here because it marks in an exemplary way a crossroads of three avenues of inquiry: in the first place, by pointing to Schopenhauer's allusion to Oedipus, he makes a contribution to the intellectual history of psychoanalysis; second, he elaborates Freud's theoretical ideas; and third, he offers a psychoanalytic commentary on *Oedipus the King*. Ferenczi's paper is the first to advance the by now standard interpretations that the meaning of Oedipus' name "Swollen Foot" is linked to the phallus and that his self-blinding is a symbolic castration. These three aspects of Ferenczi's essay are not, of course, radically distinct. The misogyny revealed in his own thought, for example, is undeniably one of the legacies bequeathed to psychoanalysis by nineteenth-century philosophers such as Schopenhauer, and it may indeed be rooted in the deeply ingrained sexism of ancient Greek culture as expressed in Sophocles' tragedy.

Of the three facets of "The Symbolic Representation of the Pleasure and Reality Principles in the Oedipus Myth," it is the first—the intellectual historical—that is most relevant to our present purpose. What I propose to do in this chapter is to provide a bridge between my more extended examinations of Hegel and Nietzsche by briefly discussing, first Schopenhauer, and then two transitional figures—Eduard von Hartmann and J. J. Bachofen. I shall also consider what comes "between" Hegel and Nietzsche in the sense of Nietzsche's own attitude toward Hegel as a precursor and toward the history of philosophy generally. In pursuing our oedipal thread through the labyrinth of nineteenth-century German thought, we shall have occasion to note what is, after all, not a surprising finding. Since, as we know from Harold Bloom, the "anxiety of influence" that governs intellectual as well as literary history is itself structured by the Oedipus complex,[2] it frequently happens that the burden of writers' indebtedness to their precursors is exhibited with particular acuteness in the course of their exegeses of the Oedipus myth.

An example of this phenomenon is provided by Ferenczi's attempt to determine why it was that "the Oedipus myth immediately occurred to Schopenhauer when he wished to illustrate by a simile the correct psychical attitude of the scientist" (p. 218).

Deploying biographical arguments, he notes that the occasion of the letter was that, in 1815, the twenty-seven-year-old Schopenhauer found himself recognized for the first time "by a man of Goethe's greatness and standing" (p. 219). The letter consequently begins on a note of gratitude and deference completely uncharacteristic of the "proud, self-confident" young philosopher. Schopenhauer's relation to Goethe, Ferenczi adds, is inevitably a filial one, since "heroes of the spirit" such as Goethe become " '*revenants*' of the father for countless men, who transfer to them all the feelings of gratitude and respect that they once shewed to their bodily father" (p. 220). (Ferenczi's argument is strengthened when it is noted that Schopenhauer's mercantile father had died in 1805, probably as a result of suicide.) The subsequent reference to the Oedipus myth, therefore, "may well have been an unconscious reaction against this—perhaps rather extravagant—expression of gratitude towards the father" (p. 220). The hostile component of Schopenhauer's ambivalence emerges at the end of his letter. Brusquely addressing the venerable Goethe "as an equal," Schopenhauer "lays a eulogizing emphasis on the unusual value of his book" (p. 220), *The World as Will and Idea* (1818), and insists that if Goethe does not respond immediately to his request for assistance, he will turn elsewhere in his effort to find a publisher.

Thus, in Ferenczi's analysis, Schopenhauer's allusion to Oedipus is itself the manifestation of an oedipal dynamic, the full import of which he is himself unaware. Although Schopenhauer recognizes that the resistances to the search for truth are primarily "not of an intellectual, but of an affective nature" (p. 216), and his association to Sophocles' hero shows his "unconscious perception" that the greatest of these resistances stems from an "infantile fixation on the hostile tendencies against the father and on incestuous ones toward the mother" (p. 218), explicit comprehension of this harsh truth was beyond even his discernment. While writing his letter to Goethe, Ferenczi concludes, Schopenhauer "was himself dominated . . . by affects that would have debarred this insight" (p. 219).

The oedipal underpinning of Schopenhauer's encounter with Goethe is still more apparent in his dealings with Hegel, his mighty opposite in nineteenth-century German philosophy. The nature of their relationship may best be illustrated anecdotally. When, in

1820, Schopenhauer—whose *The World as Will and Idea* attracted little notice at the time of its publication—began teaching philosophy at the University of Berlin, he elected to give his lecture at exactly the same time as the most popular course offered by Hegel, then at the height of his renown.[3] The implacably stubborn Schopenhauer delivered his lectures to an empty room and, when given the choice between changing his hours or canceling his course, he decided instead to resign his position as university lecturer!

But though Schopenhauer had only disdain for the optimism and teleological thinking of Hegel, he was in some respects more closely akin to his antagonist than he cared to admit. He writes in *Parerga and Paralipomena* (1851):

> The two main requirements for philosophizing are: firstly, to have the courage not to keep any question back; and secondly, to attain a clear consciousness of anything that *goes without saying* so as to comprehend it as a problem. (*EA*, p. 117)

A clear reprise of his definition of the philosopher in the letter to Goethe, Schopenhauer's assertion that one must learn to "comprehend as a problem" what "goes without saying" is a restatement of the Hegelian topos that "what is 'familiarly known' is not *properly known*, just for the reason that it is *'familiar.' "* In his conception of the philosopher as an Oedipus possessing "the courage of making a clean breast of it in face of every obstacle," moreover, Schopenhauer aligns himself equally with Hegel and Freud. Just as Hegel undertook in the *Phenomenology of Mind* a mapping of "the veritable Oedipus tragedy of the human spirit in its entirety," and Freud from his youth saw himself as an Oedipus resolved to make nature (or the Sphinx) "betray her secret," so Schopenhauer urges:

> And finally [observe] the poet, and even more the philosopher, in whom thought has attained such a degree that, neglecting individual phenomena *in* existence, he stands in wonder before *existence itself*, before this mighty sphinx, and makes of it his problem. (*EA*, p. 173)

The fact that Hegel and Schopenhauer are intellectual antipodes only heightens the significance of their independent emulation of the same Sophoclean prototype, and corroborates the hypothesis that the entire period of post-Kantian philosophy in Germany constitutes an "age of Oedipus."

No one was more aware of the subterranean affinities between Schopenhauer and Hegel than Nietzsche. Discussing the traditional enmity between German and English conceptions of philosophy, he writes in *Beyond Good and Evil* (1886):

in their fight against the English-mechanistic doltification of the world, Hegel and Schopenhauer were of one mind (with Goethe)—these two hostile brother geniuses in philosophy who strove apart toward opposite poles of the German spirit and in the process wronged each other as only brothers wrong each other.[4]

Walter Kaufmann comments in a footnote to this passage that "Hegel, who was then very famous and influential, never wronged Schopenhauer, who was young, unknown, and deliberately provocative; but Schopenhauer attacked Hegel after his death in the strongest terms, in print." Although factually accurate, Kaufmann's correction misses the point of Nietzsche's characterization of Hegel and Schopenhauer as "hostile brother geniuses," which is to depict intellectual history as an interlocking structure of oedipal and sibling rivalries, and simultaneously to reconstruct his own philosophical genealogy.

A similar portrayal of Hegel and Schopenhauer as "opposite poles" of "one mind" is found in the important section "On the old problem: 'What is German?' " from Book 5 of *The Gay Science*. In this miniature sketch of the history of German philosophy, Nietzsche first invokes Leibniz and Kant before turning to Hegel, whom he praises for having been the first to introduce "the decisive concept of 'development' into science":

We Germans are Hegelians even if there had never been any Hegel, insofar as we (unlike all Latins) instinctively attribute a deeper meaning and greater value to becoming and development than to what "is."[5]

Immediately after this tribute to Hegel, however, Nietzsche proceeds to cite Schopenhauer as the fourth great German philosopher, whose achievement was to recognize the "ungodliness of existence":

As a philosopher, Schopenhauer was the *first* admitted and inexorable atheist among us Germans: This was the background of his enmity against Hegel. *(ibid.)*

Once again, Kaufmann intervenes editorially with the disclaimer, "This explanation seems rather implausible." But as in the passage from *Beyond Good and Evil*, Kaufmann's historical scruples lead him to overlook the deeper truth that Nietzsche is using "retroactive force" to create a myth of intellectual history, whereby he himself emerges as the heir of both Hegel and Schopenhauer. When, on the verge of madness, Nietzsche in *Ecce Homo* (1888) looked back to *The Birth of Tragedy*, he concluded that his first book "smells offensively Hegelian, and the cadaverous perfume of Schopenhauer sticks only to a few formulas."[6] Although he now wishes to repudiate his indebtedness altogether, Nietzsche again points to the origins of his thought in the two dominant philosophers of the previous generation.

There is, however, a pronounced difference between the nature of Nietzsche's relation to Schopenhauer and to Hegel. As the tribute in *Schopenhauer as Educator* makes clear, Nietzsche looked upon Schopenhauer with a feeling of personal reverence. Writing in 1874 nine years after first coming upon a copy of *The World as Will and Idea* in a Leipzig bookstore, Nietzsche remains under the spell of his admiration: "I belong to those readers of Schopenhauer who know quite definitely after reading the first page that they will read every page and will listen to every word he had to say."[7] After lamenting that in Schopenhauer "I only found a book, and that was a great lack," Nietzsche continues:

And thus I made all the more effort to see beyond the book and to picture the living man whose great testament I had to read, the man who promised to make only those his heirs who wished to be and were capable of being more than just his readers: namely, his sons and pupils. (p. 17)

As these passages vividly demonstrate, Nietzsche's attachment to Schopenhauer is transferential in the strict psychoanalytic sense, that is, governed by a filial model and approached with "unconscious anticipatory ideas." Like Freud's similar friendships with Fliess, Jung, and others, moreover, Nietzsche's initial subservience to Schopenhauer gave way eventually to a revolt against his authority; but even after his intellectual emancipation from Schopenhauer, Nietzsche continued to respect him as the incarnate ideal of a philosopher who *"voluntarily takes the pain of truthfulness upon himself"* (p. 43).

Nothing comparable to this depth of feeling for Schopenhauer the "living man" enters into Nietzsche's attitude toward Hegel. It is, therefore, all the more paradoxical that, in terms of the history of philosophy, it is Hegel rather than Schopenhauer who must be regarded as his dominant precursor. As R. J. Hollingdale has suggestively observed, although Nietzsche may be said to "come after" Schopenhauer in a chronological sense,

one would do better to say that Nietzsche came after Hegel, inasmuch as Hegel summarized and brought to completion a tradition which had lasted two millennia and it was this tradition which constituted his real "predecessor."[8]

But though the personal element is lacking, the oedipal dynamic present in Nietzsche's enchantment and ultimate disillusionment with Schopenhauer is no less powerful in his confrontation with the philosophical tradition epitomized by Hegel.

In Book 5 of *The Gay Science*, Nietzsche initiates an attack directed unmistakably against Hegel when he writes: "Here is a philosopher who fancied the world was 'known' when he had reduced it to the 'idea.' " The criticism continues:

How easily these men of knowledge are satisfied! Just have a look at their principles and solutions of the world riddle with this in mind! . . . For "what is familiar is known": on this they are agreed. . . . Error of errors! What is familiar is what we are used to; and what we are used to is most difficult to "know"—that is, to see as a problem; that is, to see as strange, as distant, as "outside us." (sec. 355)

It is a signal irony that the same words Nietzsche uses to denounce Hegel—"what is familiar is known" (*"was bekannt ist, ist erkannt"*)—are themselves an unwitting echo of Hegel's declaration in the Preface to the *Phenomenology of Mind* that what is "familiarly known" (*das Bekannte*) is not "properly known" (*erkannt*) by virtue of its very familiarity.[9] Like Schopenhauer, Nietzsche repeats this central insight of nineteenth-century German philosophy without realizing that it draws him into Hegel's orbit. Having undoubtedly repressed his memory of reading the famous Hegelian passage, Nietzsche himself experiences the confusion of the "strange" and the "familiar" that is the essence of the uncanny. The manner in which Nietzsche's implicit critique of Hegel is subverted by the cryptomnesic fragment of Hegel in his own text shows Nietzsche to be subjected to Freud's law of parapraxis: "where an error makes its appearance a repression lies behind it—or more correctly, an insincerity, a distortion, which is ultimately rooted in repressed material" (*SE,* 6:218).

The anxiety of influence exhibited by Nietzsche in his response to Hegel carries over to his attitude toward Eduard von Hartmann. Although little read and known today, in his own time von Hartmann was a celebrity. His major work, *Philosophy of the Unconscious* (1868), published when von Hartmann was only twenty-six, became a best-seller; by 1882, it had gone through nine editions in Germany alone, had already been translated into French, and in 1884 it was translated into English.[10] The dominant impulse in von Hartmann's thought is the attempt to reconcile Hegel's optimistic vision of history as the unfolding of a rational plan with Schopenhauer's pessimistic insistence on the dominance of the will in human nature, with Schopenhauer's will now renamed as the unconscious. Von Hartmann's conviction that, in Stanley Hall's paraphrase, "this is the best of all possible worlds, but at the same time worse than none at all,"[11] is intellectually confused; but this very lack of clarity is an indication of von Hartmann's centrality as a conduit of the main currents of philosophical thought in the nineteenth century.

Nietzsche's attitude toward von Hartmann is consistently disparaging. In "On the old problem: 'What is German?' " from *The Gay Science,* Nietzsche condemns von Hartmann together with two other obscure contemporaries for their trivialization of the legacy of Schopenhauer's pessimism:

Neither Bahnsen nor Mainländer, not to speak of Eduard von Hartmann, gives us any clear evidence regarding the question whether Schopenhauer's pessimism, his horrified look into a de-deified world that had become stupid, blind, mad, and questionable, his *honest* horror, was not merely an exceptional case among Germans, but a German event. (sec. 357)

Nietzsche's dismissal of von Hartmann is understandable on intellectual grounds, but it is plausible to suggest that his animus toward the latter is accentuated by the fact that he saw in von Hartmann a debased parody of his own philosophical endeavor. Concerning Hegel and Schopenhauer, von Hartmann writes in *Philosophy of the Unconscious:*

How closely the two philosophers are connected is rendered evident by the undesigned coincidence that the principal works of both philosophers appeared in the year 1818, when one at the same time recalls the utterance of Hegel, "where several philosophers synchronously appear, they will represent different aspects of a single soul."

As certainly as Schopenhauer was incapable of comprehending Hegel, so certainly must Hegel, if he had known him, have shrugged his shoulders over Schopenhauer; both stood so far from one another, that every point of contact was wanting for mutual recognition.[12]

Von Hartmann here foreshadows Nietzsche's view of Hegel and Schopenhauer as "hostile brother geniuses" and "opposite poles" of "one mind," and in thus advancing an identical scheme of the history of German philosophy he implicitly calls into question Nietzsche's originality.

As the culminating figure in German Romantic philosophy and a foremost exponent of the concept of the unconscious, von Hartmann might have been expected to appeal to Freud. But, like Nietzsche, Freud did not welcome intellectual doubles, and he virtually ignored his predecessor's work.[13] Nonetheless, a study of *Philosophy of the Unconscious* allows us to discern the state of European thinking on the unconscious prior to the revolutionary change brought about by Freud.

In many respects, the anticipations are startling indeed. Most importantly, for both von Hartmann and Freud, acceptance of the unconscious entails the corollary that self-knowledge is at least as problematic, if not more so, as knowledge of other people. In von Hartmann's words:

This much, however, we have seen . . . that this peculiar essence which we ourselves are is still more remote from our consciousness and the sublimated ego of pure self-consciousness than anything else in us; that we can most easily get to know this deepest core of ourselves in the same way as we come to know other men, namely, by inferences from action. (*PU*, 1:264)

The same anti-Cartesian postulate is expressed thus by Freud in *The Psychopathology of Everyday Life:*

It can in fact be said quite generally that everyone is continually practising psychical analysis on his neighbors and consequently learns to know them better than they know themselves. The road whose goal it is to observe the precept γνῶθι σεαυτόν ["know thyself"] runs *viâ* the study of one's own apparently accidental actions and omissions. (*SE*, 6:211)

What these "inferences from action" reveal as "this deepest core of ourselves" is indicated by von Hartmann's enumeration of the deceptions practiced by the unconscious upon our conscious assessment of our behavior and motives:

That we very often do not know what it is we really will . . . every one will probably have had opportunity of observing in himself and others. In these doubtful cases we often naively think that we are willing what appears to us good and laudable, *e.g.*, that a sick relation whose heir we are to be, may not die, or that in a collision between the common weal and our individual weal the former is preferred, or that an engagement formerly entered into may be kept, or that our rational conviction and not our inclination and passion may gain the day. This belief may be so strong that afterwards, if the decision falls out contrary to our supposed will, and yet no grief but an unbounded joy takes possession of us, we do not know how to give over astonishment at ourselves, because we are now suddenly aware of disillusion, and learn that we unconsciously have willed the contrary of what we had imagined. (*PU*, 1:252–53)

Von Hartmann's shrewd cynicism gives him an intuitive grasp of the notion of ambivalence. To his catalogue of conflicts between our "supposed" and "true" wills, one may compare Freud's illustration of the universal "tendency to forget what is disagreeable" again in *The Psychopathology of Everyday Life*:

Finding fault with one's wife, a friendship which has turned into its opposite, a doctor's error in diagnosis, a rebuff by someone with similar interests, borrowing someone else's ideas—it can hardly be accidental that a collection of instances of forgetting, gathered at random, should require me to enter into such distressing subjects in explaining them. (*SE*, 6:144)

The strongly autobiographical cast to the "distressing subjects" supposedly "gathered at random" by Freud suggests that there may be a personal dimension to those enumerated by von Hartmann as well, and both authors use the hypothesis of the unconscious to strip away the veil of illusion and unmask the fundamentally selfish impulses governing all human conduct.

Philosophy of the Unconscious is divided into three major sections: "The Manifestations of the Unconscious in Bodily Life," "The Unconscious in the Human Mind," and "Metaphysic of the Unconscious." Von Hartmann most closely approximates Freud in the second section, where he marshals empirical evidence to prove the existence of an unconscious region in the mind. But in "Metaphysic of the Unconscious" he gives free reign to mystical speculation, as he contemplates the end of human history. For von Hartmann, the apocalypse consists of a universal "overcoming" of the "instinctive will to live" (*PU,* 3:138), a "temporal end of the world-process" which is at the same time "the complete victory of the logical over the alogical" (*PU,* 3:131). This call for a rational mass suicide is the preposterous outcome of von Hartmann's amalgam of Hegel and Schopenhauer. But though such eschatological fantasies cannot be taken seriously by psychoanalysis, it is noteworthy that von Hartmann invokes the figure of aged Oedipus from *Oedipus at Colonus* to preside over his vision of the senescence of humanity:

> There is only one difference between it and the individual. Hoary humanity will have *no heir* to whom it may bequeath its heaped-up wealth, no children and grandchildren, the love of whom might disturb the clearness of its thought. Then will it, imbued with that sublime melancholy which one usually finds in men of genius, or even in highly intellectual old men, hover like a glorified spirit over its own body, as it were, and as Oedipus at Colonus, feel in the anticipated peace of non-existence the sorrows of existence as if they were *alien* to it, no longer *passion,* but only a self-*compassion.* (*PU,* 3:117)

Like the medal given to Hegel on his sixtieth birthday, von Hartmann's Oedipus is a measure of the distance between himself and Freud. And yet, the fact remains that von Hartmann preceded Freud both in his exploration of the unconscious and in his use of the Oedipus myth to exemplify his theory, just as he anticipated Nietzsche's claim to be the philosophical heir of Hegel and Schopenhauer. No less than the reference to Oedipus in Schopenhauer's letter to Goethe, therefore, this epiphany of Oedipus near the end of *Philosophy of the Unconscious* may be taken as an emblem of the paradigms that shape the burdens of influence in all forms of creative endeavor.

If Nietzsche's enmity toward von Hartmann is attributable at least in part to intellectual rivalry, the same explanation holds for the lack of any mention in his works of J. J. Bachofen, the Swiss jurist and historian of Roman law, best remembered as the theorist of matriarchy. The tendentious nature of Nietzsche's silence concerning Bachofen is confirmed by several converging lines of argument. In the first place, Nietzsche upon his arrival in Basel in 1869 came to know Bachofen personally, and during the next several years was a frequent guest in the latter's home.[14] Bachofen, moreover, was born in 1815, only two years later than Nietzsche's prematurely deceased father. Most importantly, Bachofen appears to be the immediate, if unacknowledged, source of Nietzsche's celebrated polarity of Apollo and Dionysus.[15] On June 18, 1871, as he was completing *The Birth of Tragedy*, Nietzsche checked out of the Basel library Bachofen's first major work, *An Essay on Ancient Mortuary Symbolism* (1859), which proclaims "the close ties between Dionysus and Apollo,"[16] and where he would have read that Dionysus

leads everything back to unity, to peace, and to the *philia* of primal life. Slaves as well as free men take part in all mysteries, and all barriers fall before the god of material lust, barriers which political life would raise in time to ever greater heights.[17]

In *The Birth of Tragedy*, Nietzsche wrote of the effects of Dionysian transport:

Now the slave is a free man; now all the rigid, hostile barriers that necessity, caprice, or "impudent convention" have fixed between man and man are broken. Now, with the gospel of universal harmony, each one feels himself not only united, reconciled, and fused with his neighbor, but as one with him, as if the veil of *māyā* had been torn aside and were not merely fluttering in tatters before the mysterious primordial unity.[18]

Nietzsche's Hindu terminology is Schopenhauerian in inspiration, but this passage is otherwise a close paraphrase from *Ancient Mortuary Symbolism*. In a letter of April 6, 1867, to Carl von Gersdorff, Nietzsche had declared that he looked upon books as "so many tongs which pinch out the nerve of independent thought" (*SL*, p. 22), and this distaste for reading that might endanger his own originality receives concrete expression in Nietzsche's covert appropriation of Bachofen's ideas.

As in the case of von Hartmann, there is a close parallel between the neglect of Bachofen by Nietzsche and by Freud. Indeed, so shadowy is the presence of Bachofen in Freud's work that Henri Ellenberger incorrectly states that Freud "never mentions Bachofen."[19] But in *Totem and Taboo*, after speaking of the incest taboo introduced by the fraternal clan following the killing of the primal father, Freud adds: "Here, too, may perhaps have been the germ of the institution of matriarchy, described by Bachofen, which was in turn replaced by the patriarchal organization of the family" (*SE*, 13:144). Despite this reference, Freud—whose psychology in general neglects the mother in favor of the father— is evidently made uncomfortable by Bachofen's thesis concerning the priority of matriarchy. Several pages later, he admits: "I cannot suggest at what point in this process of development a place is to be found for the great mother-goddesses, who may perhaps in general have preceded the father-gods" (*SE*, 13:149).

A second, this time implicit, allusion to Bachofen occurs in *Moses and Monotheism*, where Freud invokes Aeschylus' *Oresteia* to argue that the shift from matriarchy to patriarchy represents "an advance in civilization, since maternity is proved by the evidence of the senses while paternity is a hypothesis, based on an inference and a premise" (*SE*, 23:114). Bachofen, who offers an extended discussion of the *Oresteia* in his masterwork *Mother Right* (1861), asserts in the Introduction that whereas the "mother's connection with the child is based on a material relationship" and "is accessible to sense perception," that of the father "can never, even in the marital relation, cast off a certain fictive character," from which he concludes: "the triumph of patriarchy brings with it the liberation of the spirit from the manifestations of nature, a sublimation of human existence from the laws of material life" (p. 109). As in *Totem and Taboo*, Freud in *Moses and Monotheism* is unquestionably drawing upon Bachofen's ideas; but, like Nietzsche, he does not confront the implications of his indebtedness to the latter.

Bachofen's own thought is distinctly Hegelian in origin. In the Introduction to his last major book, *The Myth of Tanaquil*

(1870), Bachofen relies on the notion of dialectic to explain the movement of history:

> An extreme can only be explained in terms of its opposite, which provokes resistance; an extreme hetaerism engenders a no less extreme puritanism. It is no paradox but a great truth borne out by all history that human culture advances through the clash of opposites. (p. 227)

Bachofen's emphasis on the "clash of opposites" as the dynamic force in culture aligns him with the great nineteenth-century tradition of dialectical analysis. Applying this point of view to the relations between the sexes, Bachofen writes in *Mother Right*:

> The realm of the idea belongs to the man, the realm of material life to the woman. In the struggle between the two sexes that ultimately ends with the victory of the man, every great turning point is connected with an exaggeration of the preceding system. (p. 150)

This equation of the two sexes with conflicting ethical principles— the "realm of the idea" being masculine and "material life" feminine—is plainly derived from Hegel. Bachofen's insistence that the battle of the sexes "ends with the victory of the man" points, however, to an important tension in his attitude toward matriarchy. On the one hand, he writes fervently and eloquently of the merits of this earliest phase of civilization; but, on the other hand, he espouses the conviction that the superseding of matriarchy by patriarchy was not only necessary but desirable. Bachofen's belief that humanity is engaged in a "triumphant journey upward from the depths, from the night of matter to the light of a celestial-spiritual principle" (*MR*, p. 185) is itself profoundly Hegelian. Although this teleological outlook has little appeal to modern readers, its insufficiencies do not invalidate what is of permanent value in the concept of dialectic.

In *Mother Right*, Bachofen puts forward a detailed interpretation of the Oedipus myth to substantiate his contention that the human race is advancing toward "a celestial-spiritual principle." Oedipus, in Bachofen's scheme, represents "the intermediary stage of human development," that is, the marriage bond or matriarchy proper, midway between "motherhood without marriage" and "conjugal father right" (p. 179). To readers of Hegel it will not come as a surprise that Bachofen's treatment of the Oedipus myth appears in the chapter on "Egypt" or that he regards Oedipus as a hero whose experience defines an epochal moment in human history:

Oedipus marks the advance to a higher stage of existence. He is one of those great figures whose suffering and torment lead to a higher human civilization, who, themselves still rooted in the older state of things, represent the last great victim of this condition and by this same token the founder of a new era. (pp. 181–82)

Like Hegel, Bachofen concentrates upon Oedipus' encounter with the Sphinx as the crucial episode in this transition to "a higher human civilization." Bachofen considers the Sphinx to be "an embodiment of tellurian motherhood . . . the feminine right of the earth in its dark aspect as the inexorable law of death," and notes that in her riddle "man is considered only in his transient aspect, mortality" (p. 181). In Oedipus, "the male principle takes on independent significance side by side with the female" (p. 182), but because the overcoming of the Sphinx leads also to a new dignity for woman within the shelter of marriage, Oedipus is revered "as the institutor of her higher condition" and becomes "her benefactor, her redeemer" (p. 183).

Bachofen has little to say about problems of individual identity, and, as practitioners of analytical psychology have recognized, he is in fact closer in spirit to Jung than to Freud.[20] Like Jung, Bachofen holds religion to be the "one mighty lever of all civilization" (*MR*, p. 85), and not—as Freud maintained—the collective equivalent to an individual neurosis. By the same token, when Bachofen declares that "The dependence of the different stages of sexual life on the cosmic phenomena is no freely constructed parallel, but a historical phenomenon, an idea conceived by history itself" (*MR*, p. 115), he again adopts a mystical standpoint alien to that of psychoanalysis, which would instead see the "cosmic phenomena" of myths as projections of human "sexual life." Despite such contrasts, however, Bachofen and Freud belong to the same tradition, and it often requires no more than a modification of emphasis to render the two outlooks compatible.[21] The equation between Oedipus' name and identity as "Swollen Foot" and an erect penis, for example, which Ferenczi interprets psychoanalytically in sexual terms, is adduced by Bachofen as proof of "the religious ideas underlying the mythical figure of Oedipus": "The swollen foot from which he takes his name shows him to be an embodiment of the male fecundating principle, which in its tellurian-Poseidonian aspect is not infrequently associated with the foot or shoe" (*MR*, p. 180).

Most generally, Bachofen shares with Freud the conviction that "myth must form the starting point for any serious investigation of ancient history" (*MR*, p. 75). In *The Myth of Tanaquil*, he prefigures Freud's argument that "historical" (or psychical) truth may be as valid as "material" (or external) truth:

> But to deny the historicity of a legend does not divest it of value. What cannot have happened was nonetheless thought. External truth is replaced by inner truth. Instead of facts we find actions of the spirit. (p. 213)

When Bachofen goes on to compare the transformations undergone by a myth through time to alterations in an ancient monument, and suggests that "its original form is never fully concealed, the cracks and gaps can never be so completely filled in as to frustrate all insight into its original character" (*MT*, p. 216), he relies upon the same archeological metaphor regularly employed by Freud to illuminate the process of reconstruction of the past undertaken in psychoanalytic therapy.

Nietzsche, too, proclaims in *The Birth of Tragedy* that the "entire domain of myth" belongs to "Dionysian truth" (sec. 10). This assimilation of myth to the category of the Dionysian leads Nietzsche to assert that, prior to Euripides, "all the celebrated figures of the Greek stage—Prometheus, Oedipus, etc.—are mere masks of this original hero, Dionysus" (sec. 10). Bachofen not only precedes Nietzsche in his veneration of myth, he also provides a precedent for his pairing of Oedipus and Dionysus. In *Mother Right*, Bachofen stresses the incest that Oedipus commits not with Jocasta but with Mother Earth:

> In this stage of the natural principle, as many myths show, the mother is seen also as the wife, even as the daughter of the man who fecundates her: each generation of men in turn fecundates the maternal matter of earth. The son becomes husband and father, the same primordial woman is today impregnated by the grandfather, tomorrow by the grandson. (p. 180)

The conflation of generational roles attributed here to Oedipus is a variation upon that ascribed by Bachofen to Bacchus (or Dionysus) in *Ancient Mortuary Symbolism*:

The phallic god striving toward the fertilization of matter is not the original datum: rather, he himself springs from the darkness of the maternal womb. He stands as a son to feminine matter. . . . Matter, the mother who bore him to this light, now becomes his wife. Bacchus is both the son and husband of Aphrodite. Mother, wife, sister merge into one. Matter takes all these attributes by turns. (p. 30)

Both Oedipus and Dionysus are for Bachofen incarnations of the "male fecundating principle" or "phallic god," who assume interchangeably the identities of "son and husband" or "husband and father" in relation to "the maternal matter of earth."

Like von Hartmann, who also draws upon the philosophy of Schopenhauer, Bachofen establishes the connections between the thought of Hegel and Nietzsche. Nonetheless, the assumption that, in Gilles Deleuze's words, "There is no possible compromise between Hegel and Nietzsche"[22] is one of the conventional pieties of modern intellectual life. As in my juxtaposition between Hegel and Freud, I do not mean to overlook the very real differences between Nietzsche and Hegel. Hegel, after all, held that the real is the rational, was thoroughly systematic, sought to reconcile theology with philosophy, and at his death in 1831 was an acclaimed member of the faculty of the University of Berlin. Nietzsche, by contrast, denied that existence had any rational purpose, distrusted systems, proclaimed his atheism, and left his university post at Basel to become the hermit of Sils Maria. Indeed, it may be justified to speak of an epistemological break introduced by Nietzsche—no less than by Freud—and to credit him, as Heidegger has done, with initiating the "overturning" of the metaphysical tradition of which Hegel is the last great exponent.[23] Despite these important considerations, however, Deleuze's insistence that there are no grounds for comparison between Hegel and Nietzsche is a polemical simplification that does not withstand careful scrutiny.

In addition to the indirect links forged by mediating figures such as von Hartmann and Bachofen, there is the more decisive question of the impact of Hegel on Nietzsche's own thought. We have already noted how Nietzsche's mockery of Hegel for assuming that "what is familiar is known" rebounds upon himself. A second possible instance of Nietzschean amnesia concerning the reading of Hegel occurs in section 9 of *The Birth of Tragedy*. This section, which contains Nietzsche's most extended interpretation of the Oedipus myth, is prefaced by a general discussion of the nature of the hero in Sophoclean tragedy. To evoke the Dionysian depths beneath the Apollonian lucidity of Sophocles' characters, Nietzsche imagines "a phenomenon that is just the opposite of a familiar optical phenomenon":

> When after a forceful attempt to gaze on the sun we turn away blinded, we see dark-colored spots before our eyes, as a cure, as it were. Conversely, the bright image projections of the Sophoclean hero—in short the Apollonian aspect of the mask—are necessary effects of a glance into the inside and terrors of nature; as it were, luminous spots to cure eyes damaged by gruesome night.

Hayden White has commented that Nietzsche's "brilliant reversal of figures" in this passage is "reminiscent of the sun Metaphor at the beginning of Hegel's *Philosophy of History*."[24] But if Nietzsche's optical metaphor is "reminiscent" of Hegel's, may it not also be a direct echo of the latter? In the *Philosophy of History*, it will be recalled, Hegel not only pictured "the emotions of a blind man suddenly becoming possessed of sight," but coupled this image with his own "brilliant reversal" of the "sun of self-consciousness" that rises in the west. This concern with vision and blindness is implicitly Sophoclean in the *Philosophy of History*, and becomes explicitly so in Nietzsche's reinterpretation. If it is possible to speak here of the repressed presence of Hegel in Nietzsche's text, then this unconscious borrowing illustrates the workings of the anxiety of influence in a specifically oedipal context.

Nietzsche's most sustained polemic against Hegel's philosophy of history, as well as against von Hartmann, is to be found in *On the Use and Disadvantage of History for Life* (1874), the third of his *Untimely Meditations*. Nietzsche directs his ire above all against the vanity inherent in Hegel's teleological model of historical development, and many of his sallies are quite devastating. He shrewdly notes that "for Hegel the apex and terminus of history coincided in his own Berlin existence," and scoffs: "The personality and the world process! The world process and the personality of the flea-beetle!"[25] In their attitudes to history, if anywhere, it should be possible to admit the existence of a complete incompatibility between Hegel and Nietzsche.

The complication, however, is that not all Nietzsche's pronouncements on teleology are easily reconciled with those in *On the Use and Disadvantage of History*. In *Twilight of the Idols* (1888), in fact, he reveals an understanding of the relation between "the personality and the world process" no less self-centered than that of Hegel. In a philosophical parable "How the 'True World' Finally Became a Fable," Nietzsche uses the metaphor of a dawning and rising sun to chart in six stages "The History of an Error." The climactic sixth stage comes about when Zarathustra abolishes the metaphysical fiction of a "true world": "Noon; moment of briefest shadow; end of the longest error; high point of humanity; INCIPIT ZARATHUSTRA" (*VPN*, p. 486). This equation of historical progression with the movement of the sun again recalls the *Philosophy of History*; and, as Werner Dannhauser has remarked, implicit in Nietzsche's vignette is the notion that Zarathustra's "is a true teaching because it appears at a privileged moment in time when truth becomes possible."[26] The persistence in Nietzsche's own thought of the belief in teleology he had condemned in Hegel, betrayed by his use of figurative language, underscores his continued dependence on the philosophical tradition that constitutes his "real 'predecessor.'"

At the outset of *Beyond Good and Evil*, Nietzsche stigmatizes *"the faith in opposite values"* as the "fundamental faith of the metaphysicians," and responds by doubting "whether there are any opposites at all" (sec. 2). Seizing on this point, Deleuze argues that "dialectic thrives on oppositions because it is unaware of far more subtle and subterranean differential mechanisms" and that, "wherever dialecticians see antitheses or oppositions," Nietzsche shows "there are finer differences to be discovered."[27] It is incontestable that Nietzsche is frequently critical of dialectic. The problem once again, however, is that he himself exhibits an addiction to "opposite values" as incurable as that of any metaphysician. Nietzsche's dichotomies appear in manifold guises—master morality and slave morality, Dionysus and the Crucified, Dionysian and Romantic forms of suffering—but they all reveal a tendency

toward "antitheses or oppositions." In what remains the most
penetrating psychological study of Nietzsche, Lou Andreas-Salomé suggests compellingly that he "describes his own ego" in
the slave morality of *On the Genealogy of Morals* (1887) and delin-
eates his ideal "antitype" in the "joyful, instinctually confident,
unconcerned" morality of the master.[28] In view of Nietzsche's
own reliance on polarities even as he questions "whether there
are any opposites at all," one may justly apply to him what he
says of his persona Zarathustra in *Ecce Homo*: "In every word he
contradicts . . . in him all opposites are blended into a new unity"
(*"Zarathustra,"* sec. 6).

The difficulty of clearly distinguishing between Hegel and
Nietzsche becomes still more acute when it is asked which of the
two is the more idealistic or materialistic. Hegel, of course, is
conventionally thought to be the proponent of idealism, whose
dialectic received a materialist revision at the hands of Marx and
Engels. And yet it is Nietzsche and not Hegel who delivers the
following ringing defense of idealism in *Twilight of the Idols*:

Let us get rid of a prejudice here: idealizing does not consist, as is
commonly held, in subtracting or discounting the petty and inconse-
quential. What is decisive is rather a tremendous drive to bring out the
main features so that the others disappear in the process. (*VPN*, p. 518)

To this statement, which might serve as a justification of Hegel's
procedure in the *Philosophy of History*, one may contrast Hegel's
own insistence in the Introduction to that work on the empirical
foundation of his historical method:

We must proceed historically—empirically. Among other precautions
we must take care not to be misled by professed historians who . . . are
chargeable with the very procedure of which they accuse the philosopher—introducing *a priori* inventions of their own into the records of
the past.[29]

Just as it is nearly impossible to differentiate between Hegel and
Nietzsche in terms of idealism and materialism, so it is highly
debatable whom to call the optimist and whom the pessimist. One
would assume that Hegel, whose entire system is explicitly a "true
theodicy," must be the more optimistic, except that he does give
full weight to "the labour of the negative" in both individual
experience and history. Nietzsche, on the other hand, who ad-

vocated a "pessimism of strength" that is tantamount to a profound optimism, seems to be positively Hegelian in his declaration in *The Gay Science*: "I want to learn more and more to see as beautiful what is necessary in things. . . . *Amor fati*: let that be my love henceforth!" (sec. 276). Like Hegel, in short, Nietzsche affirms the virtue of necessity and arrives at a comic perspective by assimilating and going beyond the truths of tragedy.[30] In his own words from *The Gay Science*: "the short tragedy always gave way again and returned into the eternal comedy of existence" (sec. 1).

My attempt to document continuities between Hegel and Nietzsche is in the service of the larger project of situating Freud in the context of nineteenth-century thought. One of the most important common elements in the outlooks of Hegel, Nietzsche, and Freud, as we noted in the preceding chapter, is an emphasis on the "world-historical man" or hero. The extent of the affinity between them is highlighted by a literary allusion that recurs in all three writers. Describing the way that dreams draw upon not only recent wishes but also those of the distant past, Freud says of the latter in *The Interpretation of Dreams*: "They are not dead in our sense of the word but only like the shades of the Odyssey, which awoke to some sort of life as soon as they had tasted blood" (*SE*, 4:249). He subsequently employs the same simile to refer to the "indestructibility" (*SE*, 5:553) of unconscious memories. Through this analogy, Freud equates the psychoanalytic discovery of the "timelessness" of the unconscious with Odysseus' descent to the underworld in Book 11 of the *Odyssey*.

In a discussion of epic poetry, Hegel in the *Phenomenology of Mind* invokes the same motif as he elaborates upon his theory of the consequences of taking action:

Acting disturbs the peace of the substance, and awakens the essential being; and by doing so its simple unity is divided into parts, and opened up into the manifold world of natural powers and ethical forces. The act is the violation of the peaceful earth; it is the trench which, vivified by the blood of the living, calls forth the spirits of the departed, who are thirsting for life, and who receive it in the action of self-consciousness. (*PM*, p. 733)

Hegel here reiterates his thesis that action itself constitutes the primordial "division into two" that is represented mythologically by the Fall. For both Hegel and Freud, the "blood of the living" is inhabited by "the spirits of the departed." Like their shared enthusiasm for *Rameau's Nephew*, Hegel's illustration of the "action of self-consciousness" with the same passage from the *Odyssey* later used by Freud to explain the workings of the unconscious exemplifies the converging conceptions of the mind in his philosophy and psychoanalysis.

Between Hegel and Freud, Nietzsche in *Mixed Opinions and Maxims* (1879) alludes twice to the same Homeric topos for his own purposes. In the first instance, he acknowledges that ancient texts are inevitably distorted when they are interpreted according to the spirit of a later age, but holds such active misreadings to be preferable to the aridity of purely "historical" scholarship:

These works can only survive through our giving them our soul, and our blood alone enables them to talk to *us*. Real "historical" discourse would talk ghostly speech to ghosts. We honour the great artists less by that barren timidity that leaves every word, every note as it is than by energetic endeavours to aid them continually to a new life.[31]

In the final aphorism of the volume, Nietzsche gives a more personal meaning to the theme of Odysseus' journey to Hades, by using it to speak of his encounters with the thinkers who have most influenced him:

I too have been in the underworld, like Odysseus, and I shall yet return there often; and not only sheep have I sacrificed to be able to talk with a few of the dead, but I have not spared my own blood. (*VPN*, p. 67)

Unlike Freud, for whom the ghosts of the past are primarily the experiences of childhood, or Hegel, for whom they are "natural powers and ethical forces," Nietzsche's revenants are the immortal writers of his cultural heritage. But these three conceptions of the "underworld" are ultimately interchangeable, for Nietzsche's coming to terms with previous philosophers is an integral part of his quest for self-knowledge, Hegel's "ethical forces" themselves entail "an opposition between the conscious and the unconscious," and Freud's search for lost time proceeds by means of his identification with classical heroes such as Oedipus and Odysseus.

Nietzsche's disparagement of the "barren timidity" of conventional scholarship, and his championing of the reading of ancient works in light of contemporary concerns, is a defense of his own procedure in *The Birth of Tragedy*. His major opponent in the controversy following the publication of that work was the great classical scholar Ulrich von Wilamowitz-Moellendorff, who upheld the ideal of objectivity in interpretation. As late as 1908, when Wilamowitz delivered a lecture at Oxford on "Greek Historical Writing," he continued to settle old scores with Nietzsche, for his own use of the motif from the *Odyssey* is a direct, if thinly veiled, attack on Nietzsche through a revision of the first of his two aphorisms:

It may be that Mr Dryasdust [i.e., sober scholarship] is no very agreeable companion, but he is indispensable. It is the curse of ancient historical writing that it neglected him. Very famous persons have tried to do the same in our days. . . . We know that ghosts cannot speak until they have drunk blood; and the spirits whom we evoke demand the blood of our hearts. We give it to them gladly; but if they then abide our question, something from us has entered into them, something alien that must be cast out . . . in the name of truth![32]

The connection between psychoanalysis and the tradition of nineteenth-century philosophy is epitomized by the shared opposition of Hegel, Nietzsche, and Freud to the position of Wilamowitz. For Wilamowitz, as a philologist, the problem is to exorcise the distortions introduced by the "blood of our hearts" in order to be able to understand ancient texts accurately. For Freud and his philosophical precursors, on the other hand, to whom the study of the ancient world is not an end in itself but a means to self-knowledge, the emphasis is precisely the reverse: the impossibility of banishing the ghosts of the past that continue to live in the blood of the present. Whether it stems from the personal or the cultural past, all three modern "heroes of the spirit" recognize, the revenant is "something alien" that can never be "cast out" from life itself.

8
Nietzsche

During TWO meetings of the Vienna Psychoanalytic Society in 1908, Freud declared that the "degree of introspection" reached by Nietzsche "had never been achieved by anyone, nor is it likely to be again," but also that he "does not know" the latter's work, because his "occasional attempts at reading it were smothered by an excess of interest."[1] Taken together, these seemingly contradictory statements define the fundamental paradox of Freud's relation to Nietzsche. Although it might be expected that Freud's admiration for Nietzsche's depth of self-knowledge would lead him to read the latter with special care, it in fact provides a motive for Freud *not* to become familiar with Nietzsche's work. As the extraordinary phrase "smothered by an excess of interest" makes clear, it is precisely because Nietzsche poses so grave a threat to his own originality that Freud is compelled to avoid his influence by the most energetic efforts at repression.[2]

Freud's avowal that he "does not know" Nietzsche's writings, furthermore, is called into question by the series of provable links between himself and Nietzsche.[3] From the correspondence between Freud and his adolescent friend Eduard Silberstein, it is known that in 1873, during his first year at the University of Vienna, the seventeen-year-old Freud had read Nietzsche's published work, which at that date certainly included *The Birth of Tragedy* and probably also the first two *Untimely Meditations*.

While at the university, it will be recalled, Freud studied

philosophy with Franz Brentano, and during the same period he joined the Reading Group of Viennese German Students (Lese-verein der deutschen Studenten Wiens), a radical society which took Schopenhauer, Nietzsche, and Wagner as its inspirational leaders.[4] During the first three months of 1884, Freud's friend Josef Paneth, later to be immortalized as the deceased "friend and opponent" of the *"non vixit"* dream, with whom he had attended Brentano's lectures, became well acquainted with Nietzsche in Nice, and kept Freud informed of his impressions. In 1900, Freud again turned his thoughts to Nietzsche, for he wrote to Fliess on February 1, "I have just acquired Nietzsche, in whom I hope to find words for much that remains mute in me, but have not opened him yet" (Masson, p. 398).

Freud must have "opened" his Nietzsche before the two meetings of the Vienna Psychoanalytic Society in 1908, which were devoted specifically to *On the Genealogy of Morals* and *Ecce Homo*, for it would scarcely be possible to discuss these works without having read them. And during the very meeting of the Vienna Society in which Freud professed his ignorance of Nietzsche, he revealed his knowledge, when in response to the observation of Paul Federn that "Nietzsche has come so close to our views that we can only ask 'Where has he not come close?' " Freud retorted that "Nietzsche failed to recognize infantilism as well as the mechanism of displacement."[5]

Four years later, in 1912, Lou Andreas-Salomé arrived in Vienna to study psychoanalysis, thereby forging what Freud near the end of his life referred to as "the only real bond between Nietzsche and himself" (*LW*, 3:213). Despite its disingenuous quality, Freud's statement does suggest the degree to which the presence of Andreas-Salomé provides the feminine component of an oedipal triangle involving Nietzsche and himself. And in 1926, when Otto Rank completed his painful break from Freud, he sent his former mentor for his seventieth birthday an elegantly bound set of Nietzsche's works—at once an expression of gratitude for all Freud had done for him, but also a defiant reminder of Freud's unacknowledged debt to his philosophical precursor.[6] Finally, in 1934, when Arnold Zweig disclosed his intention of writing a novel based upon the life of Nietzsche, the idea for which occurred to him "because in you I recognized the man who has carried out

all that Nietzsche first dreamed of," Freud raised numerous objections, including the admission that "perhaps the relationship
you establish between Nietzsche and me also plays a part in my
reasons."[7]

Freud's oedipal struggle to resist Nietzsche's influence takes
on an added dimension of significance in light of Nietzsche's own
identification with Oedipus as an exemplary hero of self-knowledge.[8] In an essay on Nietzsche no less searching than his two
studies of Freud, Thomas Mann has written that in Nietzsche's
early works "the young thinker . . . throws prophetic glances
ahead to his own fate that seems to lie before him like an open
book of tragedy."[9] An exact counterpart to Nietzsche's own divi-
nation that in the "melancholy tones" and "purest Sophoclean
language" of Hölderlin's *Empedocles* "reverberates the future of the
unhappy poet," Mann's observation receives its strongest confirmation from the interpretation of the Oedipus myth put forward
by Nietzsche in *The Birth of Tragedy*:

> It is this insight that I find expressed in the horrible triad of the Oedipus'
> destinies: the same man who solves the riddle of nature—that Sphinx
> of two species—also must break the most sacred natural orders by mur-
> dering his father and marrying his mother. Indeed, the myth seems to
> whisper to us that wisdom, and particularly Dionysian wisdom, is an
> unnatural abomination; that he who by means of his knowledge plunges
> nature into the abyss of destruction must also suffer the dissolution of
> nature in his own person.[10]

Just as Oedipus "plunges nature into the abyss of destruction" by
solving the Sphinx's riddle, only to discover that he incarnates
that riddle in himself, so Nietzsche in his first book offers an
intellectual analysis of the meaning of Oedipus' fate, the full truth
of which he will realize as he experiences the "dissolution of
nature" through his own tragic journey into madness.

Virtually every detail of Nietzsche's interpretation may be
brought into relation with earlier nineteenth-century philosophy.
His perception of the connection between Oedipus' solving of the
Sphinx's riddle and his commission of incest and patricide recalls
similar comments by both A. W. Schlegel and Hegel. In particular,
Nietzsche's insistence that a solving of the "riddle of nature" (*das
Rätsel der Natur*) entails a breaking of "the most sacred natural

orders" (*die heiligsten Naturordnungen*) brings together repetition in the temporal sphere with a law of antithetical meanings, exactly as does Hegel's reference to Oedipus in *Lectures on the Philosophy of Religion* as simultaneously "distinguished for knowledge" and "in the power of what is unconscious." No less Hegelian is Nietzsche's statement that "the contradiction at the heart of the world" revealed in tragedy is one of "a clash of different worlds, e.g., of a divine and human one, in which each, taken as an individual, has right on its side, but nevertheless has to suffer for its individuation, being merely a single one beside another" (sec. 9). Nietzsche's belief that Dionysian wisdom is an "unnatural abomination," moreover, is in the direct tradition both of Hölderlin's observation that Oedipus is "tempted to enormity" by his "too infinite" interpretation of the oracle's injunction to purify Thebes and of Schelling's dictum, applied specifically to Oedipus, that "the tragic person is *necessarily* guilty of a crime."

Nietzsche's awareness of double meanings and repetition links him also to psychoanalysis, but he most closely anticipates Freud in the attention he gives to the centrality of incest in the Oedipus myth. Indeed, he prefaces his remarks about "the horrible triad of Oedipus' destinies" by invoking "a tremendously old popular belief . . . that a wise magus can only be born from incest," which he then brings to bear on "the riddle-solving and mother-marrying Oedipus" to conclude that "where prophetic and magical powers have broken the spell of past and future, . . . some enormously unnatural event—such as incest—must have occurred earlier, as a cause" (sec. 9). In point of fact, of course, Oedipus' incest follows rather than precedes his defeat of the Sphinx; but in thus disregarding chronology, Nietzsche underscores the insight that Oedipus' "unnatural abomination" takes priority "as a cause" of his ability to solve the "riddle of nature."

Nietzsche's discussion of "the most sorrowful figure of the Greek stage, the unfortunate Oedipus," in section 9 of *The Birth of Tragedy* is set in the context of his elucidation of the synthesis of Apollonian and Dionysian principles characteristic of Greek tragedy at its height.[11] Although he asserts that Oedipus and other heroes are "mere masks" (sec. 10) of Dionysus, it is noteworthy that Nietzsche's most extended analyses of tragedy are devoted to

Oedipus the King and *Oedipus at Colonus*. By the same token, despite the fact that his loyalty to Wagner, who saw himself as a second Aeschylus, caused Nietzsche to embrace in theory the view that Aeschylus embodied the purest form of Greek tragedy, in *The Birth of Tragedy* commentary on *Prometheus Bound* is actually subordinated to that on the two Oedipus plays.[12] In 1879, three years after his break with Wagner, Nietzsche wrote to Peter Gast, the young composer upon whom he placed unreasonably high expectations: "After Aeschylus came Sophocles! I do not want to give you any clearer indication of my hopes" (*SL*, p. 170). This analogy, wherein the younger Gast, as Sophocles, exceeds his forerunner Wagner-Aeschylus, brings out into the open the way that Nietzsche's own identification with Sophocles diverts him from his official devotion to Wagner's Aeschylus in *The Birth of Tragedy*.

The chief polemical purpose of Nietzsche's meditation on Oedipus is to counteract the debased notion of "Greek cheerfulness" stemming ultimately from Winckelmann. Despite his critical attitude, however, Nietzsche in fact closely resembles Schelling and other commentators in attempting to account for the extraordinary harmony that accompanies—and mitigates—the suffering of Sophoclean tragedy. In this regard, Nietzsche makes the comment, previously quoted in connection with Kleist's *The Broken Jug*, that "as a poet, [Sophocles] first shows us a marvelously tied knot of a trial, slowly unraveled by the judge, bit by bit, for his own undoing." His exegesis in *The Birth of Tragedy* continues:

The genuinely Hellenic delight at this dialectical solution is so great that it introduces a trait of superior cheerfulness into the whole work, everywhere softening the sharp points of the gruesome presuppositions of this process. (sec. 9)

Nietzsche's remarks concerning the "superior cheerfulness" induced by the "dialectical solution" of *Oedipus the King* bear a striking resemblance to Freud's aside in his letter of October 3, 1897 to Fliess: "You see how the old liking breaks through again. I cannot give you any idea of the intellectual beauty of the work" (*Origins*, p. 220). Because Freud's self-analysis itself reenacts *Oedipus the King*, Nietzsche's interpretation of that play—like Hegel's "long and laborious journey" in the *Phenomenology of Mind*—may be read also as a gloss on Freud's discovery of the Oedipus complex. Nietzsche goes beyond Freud in the attention he gives to the "divine counterpart of the dialectic" in *Oedipus at Colonus*, and to the religious dimension of Greek tragedy generally, but there can be no doubt that *The Birth of Tragedy* provides a crucial connecting link between psychoanalysis and previous explorations of the Oedipus myth in nineteenth-century thought.

The interest in Oedipus exhibited by Nietzsche in *The Birth of Tragedy* is carried forward in his subsequent writings. Since its posthumous publication, the fragment "On Truth and Lie in an Extra-Moral Sense" (1873) has gained notoriety principally as a statement of Nietzsche's philosophy of language, but it also contains one of his most passionate declarations on the difficulty of self-knowledge:

> What, indeed, does man know of himself! Can he even once perceive himself completely, laid out as if in an illuminated glass case? Does not nature keep much the most from him, even about his body, to spellbind and confine him in a proud, deceptive consciousness . . . ? She threw away the key; and woe to the calamitous curiosity which might peer just once through a crack in the chamber of consciousness and look down and sense that man rests upon the merciless, the greedy, the insatiable, the murderous, in the indifference of his ignorance—hanging in dreams, as it were, upon the back of a tiger. In view of this, whence in all the world comes the urge for truth? (*VPN*, p. 44)

Nietzsche's reference here to the "calamitous curiosity which might *peer* just once through a crack in the chamber of consciousness" echoes the metaphor in *The Birth of Tragedy* of "a *glance* into the inside and terrors of nature" as well as the admiration accorded to Schopenhauer in *The Gay Science* for his "horrified *look* into a de-deified world that had become stupid, blind, mad, and questionable."[13] Although Oedipus is not mentioned by name, Nietzsche's reliance on optical imagery suggests that he has Sophocles' hero in mind in his evocation of the dangers of an unbridled "urge for truth."

Through its description of humanity as "hanging in dreams . . . upon the back of a tiger," this powerful excerpt from "On Truth and Lie" adumbrates the aphorism "Dreams and Responsibility" from *Daybreak*, a representative work from Nietzsche's positivistic "middle" period. He exhorts his readers:

You are willing to assume responsibility for everything! Except, that is, for your dreams! . . . Nothing is *more* your own than your dreams! . . . And it is precisely here that you rebuff and are ashamed of yourselves, and even Oedipus, the wise Oedipus, derived consolation from the thought that we cannot help what we dream! From this I conclude that the great majority of mankind must be conscious of having abominable dreams. . . . Do I have to add that wise Oedipus was right, that we really are not responsible for our dreams—but just as little for our waking life, and that the doctrine of freedom of the will has human pride and feeling of power for its father and mother? Perhaps I say this too often, but at least that does not make it an error.[14]

If "On Truth and Lie" reveals that Nietzsche, like Freud, is engaged in a descent to the unconscious, this aphorism from *Daybreak* confirms that he likewise divined that the royal road to it lay through dreams. Nietzsche alludes to precisely those lines from *Oedipus the King* where Jocasta attempts to reassure Oedipus that "many men before now even in dreams / have lain with their mother"[15]—lines later quoted by Freud in *The Interpretation of Dreams* in support of his contention that "the legend of Oedipus sprang from some primordial dream-material" (*SE*, 4:263). In insisting that nothing is "more our own" than our "abominable dreams," Nietzsche comes preternaturally close to Freud; but his final twist—that we are not responsible even for our waking life— outdoes Freud in the radicality of its attack on "freedom of the will."

Nietzsche's ongoing preoccupation with Oedipus receives its most searching elaboration in his masterpiece *Thus Spoke Zara-thustra.*[16] In "Zarathustra's Prologue," which precedes part 1 of the work, there is an incident involving a tightrope walker which has a direct bearing on Zarathustra's subsequent destiny. When the tightrope walker reaches "the exact middle of the course," a "jester" suddenly follows him on to the rope. "Foreward, lame-foot!" the jester cries, until finally:

he uttered a devilish cry and jumped over the man who stood in his way. This man, however, seeing his rival win, lost his head and the rope, tossed away his pole, and plunged into the depth even faster, a whirlpool of arms and legs. (*VPN*, p. 131)

The jester's identification of the tightrope walker as "lamefoot" is unmistakably oedipal. The jester prefigures the dwarf representing the "spirit of gravity" whom Zarathustra must vanquish in the climactic episode of "The Vision and the Riddle" in part 3. Here, the jester's "jumping over" the tightrope walker signifies the initial defeat of the aspiring overman, through the loss of a specifically oedipal struggle over priority. The tightrope walker's "plunge into the depth" dramatizes the threat of the abyss which accompanies Zarathustra—and Nietzsche—on his quest for self-knowledge.

Part 2 of *Thus Spoke Zarathustra* begins with "The Child and the Mirror," in which Zarathustra, after "months and years" of solitude, feels a renewed longing to share his teachings with humanity. He is "shaken" by a dream of a child carrying a mirror, for when he looks into the mirror, "it was not myself I saw, but a devil's grimace and scornful laughter" (*VPN*, p. 195). This "devil's grimace and scornful laughter" symbolize primarily the distortions that endanger Zarathustra's teaching, but the child may also personify both Zarathustra's own regression to an infantile state and the spirit of the future toward which he wishes to lead humanity. Zarathustra's distress upon gazing into the mirror, like the incident of the young man who fancied his resemblance to the Spinario in Kleist's "On the Marionette Theatre," conforms to Lacan's theory of the "mirror stage" in the formation of the ego, which holds that the ego is from its inception constituted by a sense of self-alienation epitomized by a child's beholding of its own reflection in a mirror. After the dream, however, no longer frightened, Zarathustra leaps up "as a seer and singer who is moved by a spirit" (*VPN*, p. 195). The pairing of the words "seer" and "singer" seems to echo *Oedipus the King*: the play is filled with imagery of sight, and at line 36 the Sphinx is termed a "harsh singer." This important preparatory episode thus combines a sensitivity to the mental processes studied more formally by psychoanalytic theory with haunting resonances of the text of Sophocles.

Zarathustra brings himself to the verge of proclaiming the doctrine of eternal recurrence, finally disclosed in "On the Vision and the Riddle," at the end of part 2 in "On Redemption." His meditation on the relation of will to time is justly famous:

> To redeem those who lived in the past and to recreate all "it was" into a "thus I willed it"—that alone should I call redemption. Will— that is the name of the liberator and joy-bringer; thus I taught you, my friends. But now learn this too: the will itself is still a prisoner. Willing

liberates; but what is it that puts even the liberator himself in fetters? "It was"—that is the name of the will's gnashing of teeth and most secret melancholy. Powerless against what has been done, he is an angry spectator of all that is past. The will cannot will backwards; and that he cannot break time and time's covetousness, that is the will's loneliest melancholy. (*VPN*, p. 260)

Although Heidegger has argued that "revenge is the will's aversion to time, and that means ceasing to be, its transience,"[17] this interpretation must be rejected. Nietzsche is not disturbed by time's transience, but specifically by the fixity and immutability of the past.

Because of the impossibility of "willing backwards," the will itself is "in fetters" and preyed upon by "most secret melancholy." This sense of powerlessness and of the meaninglessness of existence, however, is overcome at a stroke by the doctrine of eternal recurrence, which involves the simple but miraculous expedient of performing what had just been deemed impossible—"to recreate all 'it was' into a 'thus I willed it.' " Nietzsche's own claims notwithstanding, the idea of eternal recurrence is far from being a scientific hypothesis, but is rather a desperately defensive effort to deny the oppressiveness of the past through an exertion of "creative will." As Stephen Donadio has lucidly explained:

Faced with this unendurable prospect [i.e., the impossibility of retroactive will], what Nietzsche characteristically proceeds to do is to reverse the terms of the situation, to move from one state of affairs to its implied antithesis: for the man who is totally impotent he substitutes the man who is all-powerful.[18]

Not to be heard at this point in *Thus Spoke Zarathustra* is the cautionary admonition from *Daybreak* that "the doctrine of freedom of the will has human pride and feeling of power for its father and mother." Since what Nietzsche seeks to do is to recreate his own past, his project is ultimately the oedipal one of becoming his own father and begetting himself.

The oedipal implications of Nietzsche's concept of eternal recurrence are fully brought out in "On the Vision and the Riddle," the very title of which echoes Zarathustra's earlier identification with the seer Teiresias and the Sphinx. Zarathustra recounts his battle with the "spirit of gravity," described as "half dwarf, half mole, lame, making lame" (*VPN*, p. 268), who stands before him at a gateway inscribed "Moment" (*VPN* p. 270). As in the earlier scene with the jester and tightrope walker, the fact that the dwarf is addressed as "lamefoot" (*VPN*, p. 270) underscores the oedipal nature of the encounter. The dwarf, who is also termed "my devil and archenemy" (*VPN*, p. 270), is not an independent being, but an externalized portion of Zarathustra's own psyche, an incarnation of the "devil's grimace" he saw previously upon looking into the child's mirror in the dream.

The gateway of the present moment is depicted as a crossroads. "Behold this gateway, dwarf!" exclaims Zarathustra. "It has two faces. Two paths meet here; no one has yet followed either to its end" (*VPN*, p. 269). The riddle of time posed by the "two paths" of past and future lends the gateway the enigmatic quality of the Sphinx; but, as in the Oedipus myth, the crossroads may be interpreted also as the maternal genitalia, where the father and son meet in a struggle for priority. Zarathustra calls out: "Stop dwarf! It is I or you! But I am the stronger of us two: you do not know my abysmal thought. *That* you could not bear!" (*VPN*, p. 269). The conflict between time and will, expressed abstractly in "On Redemption," is here enacted in plastic form, with Zarathustra, or the will, insisting that he is "stronger" than the paternal force of the past embodied in the dwarf.

As Zarathustra formulates his doctrine of the eternal recurrence of the present moment, the gripping power of the action increases in intensity. "And this slow spider, which crawls in the moonlight, and this moonlight itself, and you and I in the gateway," he asks, "must we not eternally return?" (*VPN*, p. 270). Suddenly, as Zarathustra grows afraid of "the thoughts behind my thoughts" (*VPN*, p. 271), he hears the howling of a dog, and then recalls when he had heard a similar howling in the past: "Yes, when I was a child, in the most distant childhood: then I heard a dog howl like this." It was, he adds, "in the stillest midnight," just when "the full moon, silent as death, passed over the house . . . as if on another's property" that the dog howled from terror, "for dogs believe in thieves and ghosts" (*VPN*, p. 271).

Zarathustra's encounter with a paternal figure in the present leads to an association to a memory from his "most distant childhood." This recollection may, in a clinical psychoanalytic sense, be termed a "screen memory," and specifically one of the primal scene. The terrified howling of the dog is a projection of the child's response to the noctural spectacle of parental intercourse. The reference to the moon "as if on another's property" depicts the child's anguished recognition of the conflict between his own desire for the mother and the sexual prerogative of the father. Even Zarathustra's assertion that the moon "stood still" may be taken as a reversal into the opposite of the violent motion in the scene, just as Freud interpreted the "immobility" of the wolves in the tree of the dream of the Wolf-Man as the representation of an identical transformation (*SE*, 17:35).[19]

This regression to "most distant childhood" is followed by yet another hallucinatory occurrence in the present. Zarathustra, now alone "among wild cliffs . . . in the bleakest moonlight," again hears a howling dog and sees a man lying before him: "A young shepherd I saw, writhing, gagging, in spasms, his face distorted, and a heavy black snake hung out of his mouth" (*VPN*, p. 271). As is made clear by the important section "The Convalescent" in part 3, the shepherd is himself an externalized double of Zarathustra. That the shepherd appeared to have been "asleep" when the snake "crawled into his throat" indicates that the scene is a continuation of the previous screen memory, and the description of the snake as "heavy" associates it with the "spirit of gravity" or paternal authority. The snake is, in particular, a symbol of the father's penis, which Zarathustra longs both to incorporate and to sever. Overcome by "nausea and pale dread," Zarathustra cries out to the shepherd: "Bite! Bite its head off! Bite!" (*VPN*, p. 271). In "The Convalescent," Zarathustra interprets the snake as an expression of his "great disgust with man," but he also provides corroboration for an explanation of his "nausea" as a response to the primal scene:

Naked had I once seen both, the greatest man and the smallest man. . . . And the eternal recurrence even of the smallest—that was my disgust with all existence. Alas! Nausea! Nausea! Nausea! (*VPN*, p. 331)

As H. Miles Groth has observed, Zarathustra's memory of having seen "the greatest man and the smallest man" refers both to "the father and the young Zarathustra, but also to the father's large penis compared to the boy's smaller organ, when the boy had witnessed the father naked."[20] Zarathustra's (or Nietzsche's) re-action to this childhood trauma is transmuted into the philosophical doctrine of eternal recurrence.

Taken together, the shepherd, the dog, and Zarathustra constitute a fraternal clan, which accomplishes the castration of the primal father. After biting off and spitting out the head of the snake, the shepherd bursts into triumphant laughter: "No longer shepherd, no longer human—one changed, radiant, *laughing*! Never yet on earth has a human being laughed as he laughed" (*VPN*, p. 272). This collective vanquishing of the "spirit of gravity" incarnated first by the dwarf and then by the phallic snake is greeted by unnatural laughter marking the victory of "creative will" and the success of Zarathustra's fantasy of self-generation.

In *Beyond Good and Evil*, Nietzsche sought to present in more systematic fashion the doctrines of the overman and of eternal recurrence he had figured forth imaginatively in *Thus Spoke Zarathustra*. It is, therefore, not surprising that the oedipal themes implicit in the imagery of *Thus Spoke Zarathustra* are matched by prominent overt references to Oedipus in *Beyond Good and Evil*. The work commences with an investigation into the "will to truth" that has characterized philosophy until Nietzsche's own day. Insisting that "we should finally learn from this Sphinx to ask questions, too," Nietzsche continues with a defense of the possible value of "untruth":

> The problem of the value of truth came before us—or was it we who came before the problem? Who of us is Oedipus here? Who the Sphinx? It is a rendezvous, it seems, of questions and question marks.[21]

Nietzsche's interrogative style of "questions and question marks" aptly conveys the break with classical philosophy signaled by his willingness to call into doubt the "value of truth." But the extent to which even his rejection of metaphysics remains within the tradition of the quest for self-knowledge is revealed by his invocation of Oedipus in the opening section of his work.

In addition to his identification with Oedipus, as we have noted in the previous chapter, Nietzsche saw Odysseus' descent to the underworld as a prototype for his philosophical mission. The two heroes, Oedipus and Odysseus, are brought together in a climactic passage of *Beyond Good and Evil*:

To translate man back into nature; to become master over the many vain and overly enthusiastic interpretations and connotations that have so far been scrawled over that eternal basic text of *homo natura*; to see to it that man henceforth stands before man as even today, hardened in the discipline of science, he stands before the *rest* of nature, with intrepid Oedipus eyes and sealed Odysseus ears, deaf to the siren songs of old metaphysical bird catchers who have been piping at him all too long, "you are more, you are higher, you are of a different origin!"—that may be a strange and insane task, but it is a *task*—who would deny that? (sec. 230)

In the face of Nietzsche's eloquence, it seems almost ungenerous to point out that his appeal for a "hardened" reading of "that eternal basic text of *homo natura*" contains a factual error: in the *Odyssey*, Odysseus has his ears *unsealed* as, tied to the mast, he listens to the Sirens' song. This slip, doubtless caused by an association of the Sirens with the character of Papageno in Mozart's *The Magic Flute*, reflects Nietzsche's desire that man become "deaf" to the allures of "old metaphysical bird catchers." It does not, however, diminish the force of his recognition, reminiscent of the glimpse through the "crack in the chamber of consciousness" in "Of Truth and Lie," that "intrepid Oedipus eyes" and "sealed Odysseus ears" are indispensable prerequisites for his "strange and insane task" as a philosopher.

Nietzsche's query, "Who of us is Oedipus here? Who the Sphinx?" echoes a recurrent refrain in his work. Already in *The Birth of Tragedy* he had commented that Oedipus, who "plunges nature into the abyss of destruction," must be prepared to pay with "the dissolution of nature in his own person." The same equation between hero and antagonist is signaled in *Thus Spoke Zarathustra* by the use of the term "lamefoot" *(Lahmfuß)* to refer both to the tightrope walker and to the dwarf. In a direct echo of *The Birth of Tragedy*, Nietzsche writes in *Beyond Good and Evil*: "Whoever fights monsters should see to it that he does not become a monster. And when you look long into an abyss, the abyss also looks into you" (sec. 146). The culmination of this motif, and also the terminus of Nietzsche's interest in Oedipus, is to be found in *Ecce Homo*, which opens with the words:

The good fortune of my existence, its uniqueness perhaps, lies in its fatality: I am, to express it in the form of a riddle, already dead as my father, while as my mother I am still living and becoming old.[22]

In this passage, written shortly before falling into the "abyss" of madness, Nietzsche lives out the consequences of his oedipal identification, as he transforms the "fatality" of his life into a version of the Sphinx's riddle.

On one level, Nietzsche's statement that he is "already dead as my father, while as my mother I am still living and becoming old," is simply a factual record of the circumstances of his existence in 1888. But if this "good fortune" is subjected to psychoanalytic interpretation, Nietzsche's "riddle" may be taken as a confession of his unconscious complicity in the crimes of incest and patricide. On the other hand, the configuration of the absent father and dominant mother suggests also the pattern of the "negative" Oedipus complex found in men whose sexual constitution is predominantly homosexual. In either case, it is clear that Nietzsche's engagement with the Oedipus myth demands to be set in the context of his personal history.

In our poststructuralist era, Nietzsche is often thought to have helped make it impossible to speak about the "author" of a literary or philosophical text. And yet, in September 1882, when Lou Salomé wrote to Nietzsche proposing "the reduction of philosophical systems to personal records of their authors," he hailed this as "truly the notion of a sister soul."[23] He subsequently appropriated the idea in *Beyond Good and Evil*: "Gradually it has become clear to me what every philosophy so far has been: namely the personal confession of its author and a kind of involuntary and unconscious memoir" (sec. 6). In explicitly sanctioning the biographical mode of exegesis that likewise inheres in the assumptions of psychoanalysis, Nietzsche invites us to search for the genetic roots of the preoccupation with Oedipus revealed by his "involuntary and unconscious memoir."

Nietzsche's riddling self-definition in *Ecce Homo* presents his philosophy, in effect, as a search for his dead father. For Freud, as we know, the death of his father was "the most important event, the most poignant loss" of his life, and the impetus behind his self-analysis. As has already proven variously to be the case with Schiller, Hölderlin, and Kleist, Nietzsche's use of the Oedipus myth is grounded in some remarkable parallels with the life of Freud. Their common bond of filial loss is reinforced by a second crucial similarity: like Freud's, Nietzsche's response to his father's death is compounded by the untimely death of a brother.

Nietzsche's father, a Lutheran pastor, died at the age of thirty-six in 1849, when young Fritz was just four years of age. The death of Nietzsche's brother, Joseph, followed some six months later in January 1850. Some indication of Nietzsche's state of mind is afforded by a dream from that period recorded in an autobiographical sketch written at the age of fourteen:

I heard the church organ playing as at a funeral. When I looked to see what was going on, a grave opened suddenly, and my father arose out of it in a shroud. He hurries into the church and soon comes back with a small child in his arms. The mound on the grave reopens, he climbs back in, and the gravestone sinks back over the opening. The swelling noise of the organ stops at once, and I wake up. In the morning I tell the dream to my dear mother. Soon after that little Joseph is suddenly taken ill. He goes into convulsions and dies within a few hours.[24]

One noteworthy fact about this dream is that it took place *before* the death of his baby brother. Thus, the fate of being "wrecked by success" through the fulfillment of infantile death wishes, found also in Freud's response to the death of Julius, is even more prominent in the case of Nietzsche. But in addition to disclosing unconscious hostility toward both his father and brother, Nietzsche's dream points out to the existence of his negative Oedipus complex, through a sense of identification with a sibling who is united with the absent and beloved father.

Just as Freud's intensely ambivalent reaction to the death of his father is largely explained by the infantile substrate of the "germ of reproaches" left by the very early death of Julius, so it is the conjunction between the deaths of his father and brother that prepares the way for Nietzsche's identification with Oedipus. (The history of repeated experiences of death in childhood brings Nietzsche even more closely into relation with his "favorite poet" Hölderlin, who at the age of two lost his father, and his stepfather seven years later.) Unlike Freud, however, Nietzsche was not *forty* but *four* years of age at the time of his father's decease, and this discrepancy helps to account for a fundamental contrast in character between the two men. Freud, for all his neurotic traits, was unquestionably sane, whereas Nietzsche, even before his final breakdown, reveals a mind on the edge of psychosis. In comparing the lives and thought of Freud and Nietzsche, a parallel emerges with striking consistency: Nietzsche duplicates the tendencies of Freud, but in a more *exaggerated* form, indicative of arrest at a more *primitive* stage of development, caused by the deaths of first his father and then his brother, at the height of his own oedipal phase. Following the deaths of his father and brother, Nietzsche was left in a household comprised entirely of women. In addition to his mother, young Fritz was surrounded by his grandmother, two maiden aunts, an elderly maid, and his sister, Elizabeth, nearly two years his junior. This rearing in a matriarchal environment doubtless contributed to the preponderance of homoerotic components in Nietzsche's sublimated sexual constitution: he is not known to have consummated a relationship with a member of either sex. In particular, the close bond between Nietzsche and his sister, who was to exert so baleful an influence on his later life and reputation, was evident at an early age, since the six-year-old Elizabeth was already given to saving everything the eight-year-old Fritz committed to paper for her "treasure drawer."[25] Shortly after his brother's death, Nietzsche and his family moved from the small village of Röcken, where his father had been pastor, to the cathedral city of Naumburg. This sequence is closely analogous to the migration of Freud's family from Freiberg to Leipzig to Vienna, and to that of Hölderlin's family from Lauffen on the Neckar to Nürtingen; and in Nietzsche's case, too, it must have had the effect of preserving his earliest memories (those revealed in *Thus Spoke Zarathustra*) with utmost distinctness.

Between 1858 and 1864 Nietzsche attended the famous boarding school at Pforta, and during this period the signs of his subsequent heroic destiny begin to become apparent. In October 1861 Nietzsche wrote his prophetic letter to an imaginary friend expressing his admiration for Hölderlin. This was followed in March 1862 by his first "philosophical" essay, "Fate and History," which contains the avowal:

To dare to launch out on the sea of doubt without compass or steersman is death and destruction for undeveloped heads; most are struck down by storms, very few discover new countries. From the midst of this immeasurable ocean of ideas, one will often long to be back on firm land.[26]

Nietzsche's proclamation of his willingness "to launch out on the sea of doubt without compass or steersman" foreshadows all the subsequent statements concerning his "strange and insane" task as a philosopher. During this Pforta period, in 1864, Nietzsche wrote an essay specifically devoted to *Oedipus the King*, in which he looks ahead to *The Birth of Tragedy* by arguing that *"Oedipus Rex* in its idea necessarily requires completion and reconciliation in *Oedipus at Colonus."*[27] In 1870, after assuming his professorship of classical philology in Basel, Nietzsche delivered a course of undergraduate lectures on *Oedipus*, though the notes for these remain unpublished.[28] Like that of Freud, therefore, Nietzsche's "Conception of the Development of the Hero," centering on Oedipus, is composed of numerous "supplements" antedating its appearance in his published work.

The greatest intellectual crisis of Nietzsche's early manhood was his abandonment of Christianity, which took place gradually during his years at Pforta and became irrevocable with his refusal to take communion at Easter in 1865. Following that decision, Nietzsche on June 11, 1865 wrote in a well-known letter to his sister:

Faith does not offer the least support for a proof of objective truth. Here the ways of men part: if you wish to strive for peace of soul and pleasure, then believe: if you wish to be a devotee of truth, then inquire. (*VPN*, p. 30)

The contrast in this letter between "devotees of truth" and those who desire "peace of soul and pleasure" parallels that in "Fate and History" between the "very few" who "discover new countries" and the "undeveloped heads." Most strikingly, Nietzsche's distinction between heroic and unheroic individuals also conforms to that patronizingly made by Freud in his letter to Emil Fluss of March 17, 1873, between his own "edifying" experience of *Oedipus the King* and other Greek and Latin classics in their original languages and his friend's "comforting cheerfulness." For both Freud and Nietzsche, as indeed for Hölderlin in "My Resolution," an awareness of their exceptional destinies is tied to a self-imposed "splendid isolation" from lesser mortals.

Nietzsche's crisis of faith was intensified by the fact that his father had been a pastor. As R. J. Hollingdale has intelligently observed, to renounce belief in a life after death "may, if your father is dead, become a sort of parricide,"[29] particularly if he happens to have been a pastor. Having lost his father (and brother) once in early childhood, in other words, Nietzsche symbolically killed him a second time by denying him immortality. The sense of danger associated in his mind with the "urge for truth" arises directly out of the personal issues at stake in his repudiation of Christianity.

In 1864, Nietzsche enrolled as a student of theology at Bonn, but the following year he moved to Leipzig and, in the aftermath of his refusal of communion, changed his field from theology to philology. Both professional decisions were made under the sway of the eminent philologist Albrecht Ritschl, whom Nietzsche followed to Leipzig. Fittingly, it was within two weeks of his arrival, in October 1865, that Nietzsche came across Schopenhauer's *The World as Will and Idea* in a bookstore, and felt mysteriously compelled to take it home. Although it had been published in 1818, *The World as Will and Idea* only became widely known in the 1850s, following a pessimistic reaction against the dominant trends in Hegelian and neo-Hegelian philosophy. As we have seen, Nietzsche's sole regret in his discovery of Schopenhauer was that in *The World as Will and Idea* he "only found a book, and that was a great lack." Precisely this deficiency was remedied when, in November 1868, two months prior to receiving the unexpected news of his appointment to a professorship at Basel, Nietzsche first met Richard Wagner.

If the effects of transference are conspicuous in Nietzsche's veneration of Schopenhauer, in his worship of Wagner they are overwhelming. Indeed, in *The Birth of Tragedy* Nietzsche drew upon Schopenhauer's philosophy to glorify Wagner's achievement in music at the expense of his own discipline of philology, thereby curtailing himself in relation to both his father figures simultaneously. As Ronald Hayman has argued:

Though, consciously, he was content to recognize Wagner as a paragon of artistic genius, superior to all his contemporaries, Oedipal forces were at play. . . . Towards Wagner, Nietzsche was not conscious of feeling envy, only loving admiration, but he had sacrificed his artistic ambitions on the altar of philology and become impotent as a composer, while Wagner was still at the height of his powers. . . . There was no possibility for Nietzsche to set himself up as a rival to his surrogate father. At most he could aspire to a mastery over words comparable to Wagner's mastery over music, but he was masochistically disparaging words as inferior.[30]

The "oedipal forces" aroused in Nietzsche's relations with Wagner were reinforced by the coincidence that Wagner was born in 1813, the same year as Nietzsche's deceased father. Above all, however, at Tribschen, where Nietzsche became a frequent house-guest, the fifty-six-year-old composer lived with the thirty-one-year-old Cosima von Bülow, the illegitimate daughter of Franz Liszt, who had already borne Wagner two children and in 1869 was pregnant with a third, although she had not yet obtained a divorce from her husband, the conductor Hans von Bülow. The oedipal dynamics inherent in Nietzsche's jealousy of Wagner's attainments were reinforced by the presence of Cosima, who completed the triangle. For most of his life, Nietzsche succeeded in repressing his attraction to Cosima. Only in January 1889, after the outbreak of his madness, did he declare his passion. He then wrote in a letter to Cosima: "Ariadne, I love you. Dionysus"; and in the asylum at Jena he said on March 27, 1889: "My wife, Cosima Wagner, has brought me here."[31]

Nietzsche's unorthodoxy in *The Birth of Tragedy* earned him the opprobrium of virtually the entire world of classical scholarship. In particular, his championing of Wagner's cause led to an estrangement between himself and his former mentor Ritschl. When Ritschl did not write to him following the publication of his book, Nietzsche on January 30, 1872 sent a letter in which he asserted that his "manifesto . . . surely . . . challenges one least of all to keep silence," and added: "I thought that if you ever met with anything promising in your life, it might be this book." Upon receipt of this communication, Ritschl perspicuously wrote in his journal: "Amazing letter from Nietzsche (= megalomania)" (*SL*, p. 93). It seems inevitable that Ritschl should have been, in Silk and Stern's words, "the first surprised recipient" of Nietzsche's "new openness,"[32] since his exaggerated positive transference toward Wagner left only negative feelings for the superseded Ritschl. That it was Wilamowitz who led the orthodox attack on Nietzsche further highlights the oedipal patterns of intellectual history, since, at twenty-four, he was four years Nietzsche's junior and had followed in his footsteps as the outstanding pupil in

classics at Pforta; and when Nietzsche enrolled at Leipzig under
Ritschl, Wilamowitz remained at Bonn with Otto Jahn, Ritschl's
enemy.[33] Interestingly, one of the few philologists to defend *The
Birth of Tragedy* was the distinguished scholar Jacob Bernays, himself a pupil of Ritschl's and the uncle of Freud's wife, Martha.

The triangle formed by Nietzsche, Wagner, and Cosima has
a close counterpart in that, lasting only for the latter six months
of 1882, involving Nietzsche, Paul Rée, a Jewish moral philosopher five years his junior, and the twenty-one-year-old Lou Salomé, except that Nietzsche was now in the dominant position.
In this "Trinity," as Lou called it, no less than in the earlier triangle,
powerful homoerotic currents played their part—as the famous
photograph of Lou holding a whip over the two men pulling a
cart attests—but ultimately each man wanted Lou for himself.
After in effect ceding Lou to Rée in November 1882, Nietzsche
wrote in a letter: "As soon as we come to love something totally,
the tyrant in us (which we are only too glad to call 'our higher
self') says 'Sacrifice just *that* to me.' And we do, but it is torture,
like being roasted over a slow fire."[34] Nietzsche's reaction on this
occasion—external surrender accompanied by a turning of aggression against the self—repeats that exhibited during his revolt
against Wagner in 1876, when, as Walter Kaufmann observes,
"Instead of coming out into the open, his aversion first manifested
itself in migraine headaches and vomiting which served Nietzsche
as an excuse to stay away from Wagner after he had moved to
Bayreuth."[35]

Nietzsche learned of Wagner's death on the same day in
February 1883 that he delivered part 1 of *Thus Spoke Zarathustra*
to the printer. Once again, his "first reaction was physical illness:
he was in bed for several days. His second reaction was relief—
unmistakably filial."[36] In *Beyond Good and Evil*, Nietzsche foreshadows Freud's theory of the repetition compulsion: "If one has
character one also has one's typical experience, which recurs
repeatedly" (sec. 70). The masochism revealed by Nietzsche's
ever-recurring "typical experience" bears out the justice of Andreas-Salomé's contention that his celebration of master morality
is a compensation for his own identification with the standpoint
of the slave.

In addition to his other difficulties, Nietzsche's involvement with Lou led to jealousy on the part of his sister and to open conflicts with his mother, who called him "a disgrace to his father's grave."[37] This insult wounded Nietzsche in the most vulnerable region of his psyche, and the ensuing rift between himself and his mother and sister was never fully healed. The latter exacerbated matters by her growing involvement with the anti-Semite Bernhard Förster, whom she married in 1885. Nietzsche, again the victim in a triangular situation and, in Hayman's words, "losing the one woman who might once have been expected to devote her life to him,"[38] refused even to attend the ceremony. The death of Wagner, coming between the writing of the first two parts of *Thus Spoke Zarathustra*, likewise revived all Nietzsche's oedipal conflicts, and its effects, superimposed on those of the events of 1882, are registered in the deepening conflicts with the "spirit of gravity" in the later portions of the work.

As Nietzsche's most important object of transference, Wagner plays a part in his life comparable to that of Fliess in the self-analysis of Freud. In "On the Friend" from part 1 of *Thus Spoke Zarathustra*, an implicit meditation on his conflict-ridden ties with both Wagner and Rée, Nietzsche writes:

> Our faith in others betrays in what respect we would like to have faith in ourselves. Our longing for a friend is our betrayer. And often love is only a device to overcome envy. . . . In a friend one should have one's best enemy. . . . What is the face of a friend anyway? It is your own face in a rough and imperfect mirror. (*VPN*, p. 168)

This passage recalls the *"non vixit"* dream in *The Interpretation of Dreams*, where Freud admits that he has often succeeded in reproducing the "ideal situation of childhood" where "intimate friend" and "hated enemy" came together in a "single individual" (*SE*, 5:483). In accordance with Nietzsche's tendency to go to greater extremes than Freud, however, Wagner remained a lifelong obsession of his in a way that Fliess did not for Freud. Being literally old enough to be Nietzsche's father, and a composer of world renown, Wagner was in reality a far more formidable figure than Fliess, who (like Julius) was somewhat younger than Freud. But just as Fliess' age is no barrier to his assuming the place of the father in Freud's transference neurosis, so, as Nietzsche's "best enemy," the paternal Wagner could simultaneously be looked upon as a friend and even a substitute for the dead brother Joseph.

In his discussion of the *"non vixit"* dream, Freud cites as a literary precedent for his experience of antithetical emotions toward a single person the relationship of Brutus and Caesar in Shakespeare's *Julius Caesar*. He adds, as we have seen in chapter 5, that he "really once did play the part of Brutus" (*SE*, 5:424) during adolescence, when he and his elder nephew John—who had himself become a revenant by returning to Vienna from England on a visit—enacted a scene, not from Shakespeare's play, but from Schiller's *The Robbers* before an audience of children. It is more than a coincidence that Nietzsche should likewise have taken Brutus as a model for his struggle against Wagner. Declaring that "before the whole figure and virtue of Brutus Shakespeare prostrated himself," Nietzsche elaborates in *The Gay Science:*

Independence of the soul!—that is at stake here. No sacrifice can be too great for that: one must be capable of sacrificing one's dearest friend for it, even if he should also be the most glorious human being, an ornament of the world, a genius without peer—if one loves freedom as the freedom of great souls and he threatens this kind of freedom. (sec. 98)

Drawing on this passage, Kaufmann has coined the term "Brutus crisis"[39] to refer to Nietzsche's repeated attempts to secure "independence of the soul" by rebelling against men and thinkers he had formerly admired. Here Nietzsche clearly imputes to Shakespeare his own "prostration" before Brutus, while seeing in Caesar a portrait of Wagner, the "dearest friend" and "genius without peer" whom he had "sacrificed" to preserve his own "freedom."

The parallel between the identifications with Brutus of both Nietzsche and Freud becomes still more remarkable when it is set in the context of a third allusion to the Brutus–Caesar relationship. Schiller, too, underwent a "Brutus crisis," for he describes his ambivalent feelings toward Goethe, whose confidence he had not yet gained, in a February 2, 1789 letter to Gottfried Körner in the following terms:

It is a wholly astonishing mixture of hatred and love that he has aroused in me, a feeling not entirely unlike that which Brutus and Cassius must have had against Caesar. I could kill his spirit and then love him again from my heart.[40]

As the author of *The Robbers*, in which Freud literally "played the part of Brutus," Schiller stands directly behind the *"non vixit"* dream, as he does behind so much of nineteenth-century thought. The continuity between the "mixture of hatred and love" experienced by Schiller, Nietzsche, and Freud toward their respective Caesars illustrates at once the intellectual antecedents of psychoanalysis and the universality of the laws of mental life codified by Freud. The endlessly receding dialectic between art and life—and between filial and fraternal relationships—revealed by the "supplements" to the Brutus theme may be traced back to the classical period. It completes the pattern to recollect that Caesar himself, who in his youth composed a lost tragedy entitled *Oedipus*, looked upon Brutus as his natural son, and is reported to have cried out in Greek, upon being stabbed to death by his protégé, "And you, my son?"[41]

The eccentricity of Nietzsche's reading of *Julius Caesar* prepares us for the fact that, like Freud, he came to doubt that Shakespeare was the author of his plays. Nietzsche differs from Freud only in assigning Shakespeare's laurels, not to the Earl of Oxford, but to Bacon. "And let me confess it," he writes in *Ecce Homo*, "I feel instinctively sure and certain that Lord Bacon was the originator, the self-tormentor of this uncanniest kind of literature" ("Clever," sec. 4). No more than Freud's is Nietzsche's skepticism about Shakespeare's identity a considered scholarly judgment. Rather, like their identifications with Brutus, both men's doubts represent a neurotic symptom resulting from their uncannily similar hero complexes. When Nietzsche proclaims in *Ecce Homo*, "I have been told that it is impossible to put down one of my books—that I even disturb nightly rest" ("Books," sec. 3), one is again inevitably reminded of Freud, who in *On the History of the Psycho-Analytic Movement* (1914) also identified himself, in Hebbel's words, as "one of those who have 'disturbed the sleep of the world'" (*SE*, 14:21).

One of the constitutive features of Freud's identity, as I have tried to show, is a drastic fluctuation in his self-appraisals between "delusions of inferiority" and "megalomania." An even more unstable version of the same tension is exhibited by Nietzsche. As early as 1872 Ritschl detected signs of "megalomania," and before his collapse, Nietzsche was regularly given to asseverations such as that in *Ecce Homo:* "I am no man, I am dynamite" ("Destiny," sec. 1). The opposite of such manic boasts is the depression evident in a letter written on Christmas Day, 1882, to Franz Overbeck: "My lack of confidence is now immense—everything I hear makes me feel that people despise me" (*SL*, p. 199). By the same token, Freud undeniably viewed the circumstances of his origins—his Jewishness, his native city of Vienna—with strongly mixed emotions, but Nietzsche carried his "family romance" to the delusory lengths of denying his German identity. "Consider my name: my forebears were Polish aristocrats," he writes in December 1882 to Heinrich von Stein, and continues with only apparent inadvertence: "As for 'the hero':—I do not think so highly of him as you do. All the same, it is the most acceptable form of human existence, particularly when one has no other choice" (*SL*, p. 197). In language that melds Nietzsche and Freud, Lou Andreas-Salomé observes that "the heroic and all-too-human elements lie close together, especially for the psychoanalyst," and it is she who pays most fitting tribute to the connection between both men's genius and neurosis: "Confronted by a human being who impresses us as great, should we not be moved rather than chilled by the knowledge that he might have attained his greatness only through his frailties?"[42]

As a result of his struggle to break free from the influence of Schopenhauer and especially Wagner, Nietzsche engaged in a sustained meditation on the problem of discipleship. Although he never abandoned the view expressed in *Schopenhauer as Educator* that "only he who has first given his heart to some great man receives the *first consecration of culture*,"[43] he became increasingly aware of the necessity for a disciple to leave behind his erstwhile master and to follow himself. Most importantly, just as Nietzsche refused to restrict his own "independence of the soul," so he extended the same freedom to his own admirers. In his most famous statement of this attitude, at the close of part 1 of *Thus Spoke Zarathustra*, Zarathustra exhorts his overly deferential followers:

> One repays a teacher badly if one always remains nothing but a pupil. And why do you not want to pluck at my wreath?
>
> You revere me; but what if your reverence tumbles one day? Beware lest a statue slay you.
>
> You say you believe in Zarathustra? But what matters Zarathustra? You are my believers—but what matter all believers? You had not yet

sought yourselves: and you found me. Thus do all believers; therefore all faith amounts to so little.

Now I bid you lose me and find yourselves; and only when you have denied me will I return to you. (*VPN*, p. 190)

The importance of this passage, the imagery of which recalls the motif of "plucking the wreath" that runs obsessively through Kleist's works, is attested by the fact that Nietzsche chose to reprint it at the beginning of *Ecce Homo*. Through Zarathustra Nietzsche recognizes that the young philosopher must be permitted to undergo what psychoanalysis would call a "dissolution of transference" if he is to become a master in his own right.

If there is an analogy between Freud's ambivalent attachment to Fliess and that of Nietzsche to Wagner, there is an even closer replica of the Nietzsche-Wagner tie in Freud's encounter with Jung, except that Freud as the considerably older man is now cast in the inhibiting role of Wagner. There is, consequently, a devastating irony in the fact that, on the eve of their rupture, Jung in his letter of March 3, 1912 should have quoted to Freud just this passage from part 1 of *Thus Spoke Zarathustra*, bracketed by the avowals: "I would never have sided with you in the first place had not heresy run in my blood" and "This is what you have taught me through psychoanalysis. As one who is truly your follower, I must be stout-hearted, not least towards you" (*F/J*, pp. 491–92).

In the letter in which he responded to Jung's quotation from Nietzsche on the need for intellectual independence, Freud committed a revealing slip of the pen. He professed to be in "full agreement" with Jung, but went on to write: "But if a third party were to read this passage, he would ask me *why* I had tried to tyrannize you intellectually, and I should have to say: I don't know" (*F/J*, p. 492).[44] Freud's "why," as the editor notes, is an obvious lapse for "when," but it is precisely the mystery of his need to "tyrannize intellectually" over others that Freud was unable to fathom. Despite leading a far more tormented life than Freud, Nietzsche nonetheless managed to achieve a generosity of spirit that the latter could not match. Had Freud been a better Nietzschean, he might have issued the warning: "One repays a teacher badly if one always remains nothing but a pupil" to his own followers, instead of hearing it flung back at him as a reproach by his most promising disciple. And even as we rely upon the teachings of Freud to understand Nietzsche, let us likewise heed Nietzsche's admonition on the dangers of reverence, lest—in confusing an intellectual commitment to psychoanalysis with an idolatry of Freud—a statue slay us.

9
After
Freud

$\mathbf{T}$HE PURPOSE of this part has been to
set Freud in an intellectual context by examining treatments of
the Oedipus myth in nineteenth-century German literature and
philosophy. Since I have undertaken a study of Freud's antecedents, an appraisal of the numerous twentieth-century dramatiza-
tions of the Oedipus theme, from Hugo von Hofmannstahl's *Oedipus and the Sphinx* (1905) to Jean Cocteau's *The Infernal Machine*
(1934) and beyond, written after psychoanalysis began to have
an impact on modern culture, lies beyond my purview.

Despite my focus on the intellectual origins of psychoanalysis,
however, two twentieth-century commentaries on the Oedipus
myth warrant consideration by way of an epilogue. The first of
these, by Heidegger, is clearly pertinent, since Heidegger in so
many respects represents the culmination of the tradition, beginning with Hegel and Hölderlin and extending through Nietzsche,
that I have traced here. The second, that of Lévi-Strauss, is the
most famous post-Freudian interpretation of the Oedipus myth,
and poses in economical form the question of the relations between structuralism and psychoanalysis.

Heidegger

Martin Heidegger is probably the most important philosopher of the twentieth century. In his work, initially an extension of the phenomenology of Husserl, idealism is transformed into existential philosophy, a meditation on Being. The study of Heidegger is complicated by the notorious "turn" in his thought after *Being and Time* (1927), following which he sought to emancipate himself entirely from the assumptions of metaphysics. In our own time, Derrida has defined his own project of deconstruction largely in terms of a revolt against Husserl and Heidegger, and it may be said that the postmodern era begins in this movement beyond Heidegger.

Clearly, it will not be possible for me to do justice to Heidegger's complexities in a brief discussion. What I shall attempt to do, however, is to integrate Heidegger's exegesis of *Oedipus the King* with those of Freud and his nineteenth-century precursors. My focus will be on *An Introduction to Metaphysics* (1935), a work that marks the transition between Heidegger's earlier and later thought.

As we have seen throughout this second part, a study of the Oedipus myth is tied to the problem of the "anxiety of influence," that is, a writer's struggle with the weight of tradition. This problem is particularly acute in Heidegger's case, because he insists so strongly on his own originality. In *An Introduction to Metaphysics*, for example, he claims that "in *Sein und Zeit* the question of the meaning of being is raised and developed *as a question* for the first time in the history of philosophy."[1] As a general principle, psychoanalysis teaches us to be skeptical about the very idea of a "first time," and Heidegger's assertion seems particularly dubious when it is recollected that Hegel *does* make being a question in the *Logic*: "Being . . . is a category of pure thought, but to make 'is' an object of investigation never occurs to us." Hegel, moreover, anticipates Heidegger's teaching concerning the circular structure of knowledge. These and other connections need to be weighed against the genuine transformations wrought by Heidegger in his use of earlier concepts, but they do serve to undermine Heidegger's exaggerations of his own uniqueness.[2]

It is, ultimately, Heidegger's language—what Adorno has branded his "jargon of authenticity"[3]—that tells most heavily against him. Proclaiming in a typical passage that his philosophy marks "a new beginning," which "is possible," Heidegger continues:

But we do not repeat a beginning by reducing it to something past and now known, which need merely be imitated; no, the beginning must be begun again, more radically, with all the strangeness, darkness, insecurity of a true beginning. Repetition as we understand it is anything but an improved continuation with the old methods of what has been up to now. (*IM*, p. 39)

Implicit in such a pronouncement is a retreat from the historical consciousness that is the most vital legacy of nineteenth-century thought. As Hans-Georg Gadamer has written of the French Revolution:

The Revolution's radical attempt to make the Enlightenment's faith in reason the basis of religion, state, and society had the counter effect of bringing historical relativity and the power of history into general awareness; for history is that which decisively rebutted the presumptuous excesses of the Revolution's "new beginning."[4]

At the close of the epoch we have surveyed, Heidegger repeats the doctrine of the "new beginning" promulgated by the French Revolution at its outset. And just as history has checked the "presumptuous excesses" of the Revolution in the political sphere, so it has chastened the hyperbole in Heidegger's philosophical rhetoric of originality.

Heidegger's belief in repetition as a forward-looking and not a backward-looking phenomenon links him unmistakably to Kierkegaard.[5] Through his pseudonym Constantine Constantius, Kierkegaard in *Repetition* (1843) draws a fundamental distinction between recollection and repetition:

When the Greeks said that all knowledge is recollection they affirmed that all that is has been; when one says that life is a repetition one affirms that existence which has been now becomes. . . . Recollection is the pagan life-view, repetition is the modern life-view; repetition is the *interest* of metaphysics, and at the same time the interest upon which metaphysics founders.[6]

Kierkegaard's definition of repetition as "the interest upon which metaphysics founders" is an attack on the seeming impersonality of Hegel from the standpoint of his own commitment to a radical subjectivity. Yet, no less than Hegel's "teleology," Kierkegaard's progressive view of repetition is the "inverted image" of Freud. As a nineteenth-century philosopher obsessed by self-knowledge, Kierkegaard has his own place in the history I have sought to chronicle. He writes in *The Sickness unto Death* (1849):

The law for the development of the self with respect to knowledge, in so far as it is true that the self becomes itself, is this, that the increasing degree of knowledge corresponds with the degree of self-knowledge, that the more the self knows, the more it knows itself.[7]

But though Kierkegaard thoroughly understands "the pagan life-view," he differs from the other figures we have examined in being, in Arnold's terms, an adherent of Hebraism rather than Hellenism. Hence, he is, as it were, in the intellectual world we are exploring but not of it. And yet, as we shall see in part 3, his interpretation of *Antigone* in volume 1 of *Either/Or* (1843) is unjustly overshadowed by Hegel's better-known reading of the play.

Despite his own protests to the contrary, Heidegger carries forward the idealistic and Romantic traditions of the nineteenth century. One of my central arguments has been that, before Schiller could define *Oedipus the King* as a "tragic analysis," it was necessary to "unbind Sophocles" by liberating Greek tragedy from Senecan and neoclassical admixtures, a process initiated by Lessing and carried forward by a wide range of writers. It is noteworthy that Heidegger shares an antipathy to Latin models no less vehement than that of Lessing or A. W. Schlegel:

What happened in this translation from the Greek into the Latin is not accidental and harmless; it marks the first stage in the process by which we have cut ourselves off and alienated ourselves from the original essence of Greek philosophy. (*IM*, p. 13).

Heidegger is referring specifically to the distortions introduced when Greek philosophical terms were rendered into their supposed Latin equivalents, but he might have been defining the metamorphosis of Sophoclean into Senecan tragedy.

This analogy may be taken further since, just as it was the Latin and not the Greek terms which passed through Christianity into the mainstream of Western philosophy, so for millennia it was predominantly through the distorting mirror of Roman copies that the knowledge of Greek tragedy was transmitted to posterity. With almost mystical fervor, Heidegger maintains that "along with German the Greek language is (in regard to its possibilities for thought) at once the most powerful and spiritual of languages" (*IM*, p. 57). Whatever the validity of Heidegger's statement about the Greek and German languages as a metaphysical proposition, it accurately registers the affinity between these two cultures, of which his own work is a conspicuous late manifestation. At the same time that he seeks to recover "the original essence of Greek philosophy," particularly as represented by the pre-Socratics Parmenides and Heraclitus, Heidegger discerns a dialectical unity between philosophy and tragedy:

This poetic thinking forms a body with the contrary aspect, the thinking poetry of the Greeks and particularly that poetry in which the being and (closely related) being-there of the Greeks was in the truest sense created: the tragedy. (*IM*, pp. 144–45)

Exactly like his forerunners in nineteenth-century literature and philosophy, when Heidegger seeks to exemplify the "being-there of the Greeks" the "thinking poetry" to which he turns is preeminently that of Sophocles.

If Heidegger shares with Hegel and others a focus on Greek tragedy, he likewise blends his interest in the Oedipus myth with the paradigm of an odyssey of consciousness. *Being and Time* begins by announcing that its task is essentially one of self-analysis: "We are ourselves the beings to be analyzed. The Being of any such entity is *in each case mine.*"[8] By *An Introduction to Metaphysics*, Heidegger is less concerned with particular "beings" than with the ground of "Being," but he remains "embarked on the great and long venture of demolishing a world that has grown old and of rebuilding it authentically anew" (*IM*, pp. 125–26). As opposed to the other sciences, where the object "is always in some way present," philosophy "has no object to begin with," and is "a process which must at all times achieve being . . . anew" (*IM*, p. 85). Heidegger's definition of philosophy as a self-generating process of destruction and recreation accords both with psychoanalytic treatment and with Hegel's realization that "substance" cannot be divorced from "subject." Like many of Heidegger's works, *An Introduction to Metaphysics* was originally delivered in the form of lectures, and Heidegger—addressing his audience as though its members embodied the "ordinary consciousness" and he the Hegelian "absolute consciousness"—draws attention to this fact in urging that "the listener should take the different steps in the process after and with the lecturer" (p. 85).

No less than that of Hegel or Kleist, Heidegger's "great and long venture" is a secularized transposition of the myth of the Fall. Paradoxically, Heidegger himself is at pains to deny this connection. In *Being and Time*, he refuses to "take the fallenness of Dasein as a 'fall' from a purer and higher 'primal status' " (p. 220). Despite this disavowal, George Steiner has justly maintained that Heidegger's effort to lead man back from inauthentic to authentic being in fact conforms to a theological model:

The "positivity of fallenness" in Heidegger's analysis is an exact counterpart to the *felix culpa* paradox, to the doctrine which sees in Adam's "happy fall" the necessary precondition for Christ's ministry.[9]

In true Romantic or Hegelian fashion, Heidegger begins by recognizing that man exists in a condition of "severed life," and that only "the hand that inflicts the wound" is able to restore wholeness. Once again, Heidegger's protests should not obscure the truth that—like Nietzsche—his greatest achievement is to extend the great classical tradition of systematic self-scrutiny.

Heidegger commences his quest in *An Introduction to Metaphysics* by posing the question: "Why are there essents, why is there anything at all, rather than nothing?" (p. 1). This question, which is for Heidegger "first," though "not in a chronological sense" (p. 1), in turn "encounters the search for its own why" (p. 5). Like Oedipus, for whom the solution to the Sphinx's riddle of man in the abstract leads to the further riddle of his own identity and origins, Heidegger's single question "recoil[s] . . . upon itself"

and becomes double: "Why the why?" (p. 5). Only those questions to which there are no finite answers are for Heidegger worth
asking, and he continues by expounding what it means really to
open the question of being:

a daring attempt to fathom this unfathomable question by disclosing
what it summons us to ask, to push our questioning to the very end.
Where such an attempt occurs there is philosophy. (p. 8)

Heidegger's definition of philosophy as a willingness "to push our
questioning to the very end" plainly reveals him to be a scion of
Oedipus.

One noteworthy feature of Heidegger's thought is the absence
of any discussion of sexuality.[10] From a psychoanalytic perspective, this omission suggests that sexual themes must be present,
but in a repressed form. In a brilliant article, Theodore Thass-
Thienemann has shown how Heidegger's preoccupation with the
contrast between "essents" and "nothing" may be traced to its
infantile roots.[11] Heidegger writes in "What Is Metaphysics?"
(1929):

Where shall we seek Nothing? Where shall we find Nothing? In
order to find something, must we not know beforehand that it is there?
Indeed we must! First and foremost we can only look if we have pre-
supposed the presence of a thing to be looked for.[12]

To this passage Thass-Thienemann juxtaposes that by Freud in
"The Infantile Genital Organization" (1923):

We know how [male] children react to their first impressions of the
absence of a penis. They disavow the fact and believe that they *do* see a
penis, all the same. . . . and they then slowly come to the emotionally
significant conclusion that after all the penis had at least been there
before and had been taken away afterwards. (*SE*, 19:143–44)

Since the word "no-thing" symbolically and etymologically represents "the very concrete aspect of the female genitals connected
with the notion that there is something missing,"[13] Heidegger's
relentless questioning may be viewed as a sublimated expression
of the discovery of sexual differentiation with its attendant castration fantasies.

As in Hegel's *Phenomenology of Mind*, the oedipal paradigm of

An Introduction to Metaphysics is implicit in the structure of the work as a whole, but emerges with particular prominence when Heidegger turns his attention directly to tragedy. It is not an accident when, in his section on "Being and Appearance," where Heidegger seeks to explore the "unity and conflict" of these powers in early Greek thought, he declares, "Let us consider the *Oedipus Rex* of Sophocles" (p. 106). Basing his discussion to a large extent on his own follower Karl Reinhardt's *Sophocles* (1933), Heidegger expounds:

At the beginning Oedipus is the savior and lord of the state, living in an aura of glory and divine favor. He is hurled out of this appearance, which is not merely his subjective view of himself but the medium in which his being-there appears; his being as the murderer of his father and desecrator of his mother is raised to unconcealment. (p. 106)

No less than Schelling, Nietzsche, or Freud, Heidegger disregards the social fact of Oedipus' kingship to concentrate on the process of "unconcealment" in the tragedy. Indeed, since he insists that Oedipus' identity is actually that of "the murderer of his father and desecrator of his mother," Heidegger's analysis of *Oedipus the King* as a drama depicting the "disclosure of being" is substantially in accordance with the assumptions of psychoanalysis.[14]

Heidegger continues by commenting on Oedipus' investigation into the murder of Laius:

With the passion of a man who stands in the manifestness of glory and is a Greek, Oedipus sets out to reveal this secret. Step by step, he must move into unconcealment, which in the end he can only bear by putting out his own eyes, i.e., by removing himself from all light, by letting the cloak of night fall round him, and, blind, crying out to the people to open all doors that a man may be manifest to them as what he *is*. (*IM*, pp. 106–7)

Crucial to a psychoanalytic view of the mind is a recognition of the tension between the impulses to self-concealment and to self-revelation. Heidegger forcefully shows how Oedipus embodies this dialectic, since his unwitting "move into unconcealment" necessitates "putting out his own eyes," which in turn leads to the further disclosure of throwing open the palace doors so "that a man may be manifest . . . as what he *is*." Like the double-edged exegeses of Hegel and Nietzsche, Heidegger's reading of *Oedipus the King* illuminates as well the fundamental issues at stake in Freud's self-analysis.

Heidegger does not conclude his meditation on the somber note of Oedipus' self-blinding. He reminds us of Oedipus' undaunted heroism:

> But we cannot regard Oedipus only as the man who meets his downfall; we must see him as the embodiment of Greek being-there, who most radically and wildly asserts its fundamental passion, the passion for disclosure of being, i.e., the struggle for being itself. (*IM*, p. 107)

As for Heidegger it is in tragedy that the "being-there of the Greeks was in the truest sense created," so it is Oedipus whom he finds "the embodiment of Greek being-there." This recognition of Oedipus' paradigmatic status confirms Heidegger's place at the apex of the tradition extending from Schiller to Freud. His description of Oedipus as the man who "most radically and wildly" exemplifies the Greek "fundamental passion" for knowledge, moreover, echoes his own earlier resolve "to push our questioning to the very end," and hence reinforces Heidegger's identification with Oedipus. Of all his great nineteenth-century predecessors, it was Hölderlin (followed by Nietzsche) to whom Heidegger felt most closely akin, and he proceeds to invoke the reference to Oedipus' "eye too many" from "In lovely blueness": "This eye too many is the fundamental condition for all great questioning and knowledge and also their only metaphysical ground" (*IM*, p. 107). Heidegger bears witness to his own possession of an "eye too many" by his "great questioning" in *An Introduction to Metaphysics* and *Being and Time*.

Following his interpretation of *Oedipus the King*, Heidegger examines in more general terms the relations between being, nonbeing, and appearance. He proposes that "the man who holds to being as it opens round him and whose attitude toward the essent is determined by his adherence to being, must take three paths" (*IM*, p. 110). Having placed philosophy at the crossroads, Heidegger implicitly again equates the philosopher with Oedipus, who faces the necessity of making a choice: "Thought at the beginning of philosophy was the opening and laying-out of the three paths" (*IM*, p. 110). Since "it is with this decision that history begins," this inaugural moment also takes on some connotations of the Fall: "Accordingly decision means here no judgment and choice, but a separation in the above-mentioned togetherness of being, unconcealment, appearance, and nonbeing" (*IM*, p. 110). In view of the interpenetration of the three realms, however, "a truly sapient man is therefore not one who blindly pursues a truth, but only one who is always cognizant of all three paths, that of being, that of nonbeing, and that of appearance" (*IM*, p. 113). Whether intended as such or not, Heidegger's distinction between the man "who blindly pursues a truth" and his "truly sapient" counterpart, who "is always cognizant of all three paths," precisely registers the evolution of Oedipus from *Oedipus the King* to *Oedipus at Colonus*.

A further illustration of the way that Heidegger's discourse appears to be an extended commentary on Sophocles, even in the absence of overt mention of his plays, is provided in the section on "Being and Thinking." Here, in the context of a discussion of Heraclitus and Parmenides, Heidegger spells out three postulates guiding his philosophical investigation:

1. The determination of the essence of man is *never* an answer but essentially a question.

2. The asking of this question and the decision in this question are historical, and not merely in a general sense; no, this question is the very essence of history.

3. The question of what man is must always be taken in its essential bond with the question of how it stands with being. The question of man is not an anthropological question but a historically meta-physical question. (*IM*, p. 140).

Translated into the terms of the Oedipus myth, Heidegger's three propositions may be reformulated as follows: 1) the solution to the Sphinx's riddle leads not to an answer but to a further riddle; 2) Oedipus' quest is an investigation into his own origins; and 3) the universality of Oedipus' fate "is not an anthropological question" but depends ultimately on the "historically meta-physical" proof of the hermeneutic circle. From Heidegger's second tenet, that the question of being "is the very essence of history," it is clear that his occasional claims for an apocalyptic "new beginning" do not tell the entire story.

It is striking that Heidegger's remarks on *Antigone* are more celebrated than those on *Oedipus the King*. In actuality an extended exegesis of the sublime first stasimon (the "ode on man"), inserted as a parenthesis within a still larger meditation on a maxim of Parmenides concerning the identity of being and thinking, the reading of *Antigone* unquestionably shows Heidegger at the height of his literary powers, but nonetheless cannot be removed from the overarching framework supplied by the Oedipus myth. In this pairing of Antigone and Oedipus, as I have urged in opposition to Steiner, Heidegger follows the precedent of Hegel and Hölderlin.

If Heidegger limits his discussion of *Antigone* to the first stasimon, this exegesis is itself to a large extent centered on the first two lines:

> polla ta deina, k'ouden an-
> thrōpou deinoteron pelei.[15]
>
> There are many strange things, but nothing
> that walks is stranger than man.

"In these first two verses the poet anticipates," Heidegger comments. "He will spend the rest of the poem in catching up with himself" (*IM*, p. 148). This unfolding of the first two lines, finally, is concentrated on the single word *deinon* ("strange"), and, as applied to man, *ouden deinoteron* ("nothing stranger"): "Man, in one word, is *deinotaton*, the strangest. This one word encompasses the extreme limits and abrupt abysses of his being" (*IM*, p. 149).

Translated by Hölderlin first as *"Gewaltge,"* and later as *"Ungeheuer"* (*"Ungeheuer ist viel. Doch nichts / Ungeheuerer, als der Mensch"*), *deinon* is rendered by Heidegger as *"unheimlich."* This, it brings matters full circle to note, is also Freud's word for what we know in English as the "uncanny." Echoing his earlier observations on the fate of Oedipus, Heidegger writes:

Everywhere man makes himself a path; he ventures into all realms of the essent, of the overpowering power, and in so doing he is flung out of all paths. Herein is disclosed the entire strangeness of this strangest of all creatures. (*IM*, p. 151)

Heidegger does not limit himself to Freud's psychological conception of the uncanny, but seeks to define it as "the basic trait of the human essence" (*IM*, p. 151); but this is only to extend, and not to repudiate, Freud. The crossing of the "strange" and the "familiar" is the same in both cases: "The strangeness, the uncan-niness of these powers resides in their seeming familiarity" (*IM*, p. 156). Heidegger, in fact, most closely resembles Hegel in his reformulation of the master-trope of the strangeness of the osten-sibly familiar, as he does also in his treatment of the schism in the realm of appearance:

The self-manifestation of the apparent belongs immediately to being and yet again (fundamentally) does not belong to it. Therefore appearing must be exposed as mere appearance, and this over and over again. (*IM*, p. 113)

The notion of the unconscious here, cast in the language not of idealism but of existentialism, recalls Hegel's remarks concerning the way that "ethical self-consciousness" is waylaid by "a hidden power shunning the light of day" and that "the agent finds himself thereby in the opposition of knowing and not knowing." And as Heidegger alchemically fuses Freud and Hegel, so his declaration, "And yet the truth is that everyone is remotest from himself" (*IM*, p. 70), is an unacknowledged borrowing from Nietzsche's *The Gay Science:* "Everybody is farthest away—from himself."[16]

In a luminous late essay ". . . Poetically Man Dwells . . ." (1954), the title of which is taken from "In lovely blueness," Heidegger returns to Hölderlin's image of Oedipus' "eye too many," upon which he had brooded in *An Introduction to Metaphysics:*

For dwelling can be unpoetic only because it is in essence poetic. For a man to be blind, he must remain a being endowed by nature with sight. A piece of wood can never go blind. But when man goes blind, there always remains the question whether his blindness derives from some defect and loss or lies in an abundance and excess. In the same poem that meditates on the measure for all measuring, Hölderlin says: "King Oedipus has perhaps one eye too many." Thus it might be that our unpoetic dwelling, its incapacity to take the measure, derives from a curious excess of frantic measuring and calculating.[17]

It is itself a "measure" of the "turn" in Heidegger's thought that, twenty years after *An Introduction to Metaphysics,* he now cites Oedi-pus' "eye too many," not as a precondition for "all great ques-tioning and knowledge and also their only metaphysical ground," but as a stigma betraying "a curious excess of frantic measuring

and calculating." But since only a man can experience the contradiction between "poetic" and "unpoetic" dwelling, Heidegger's
use of Oedipus' second sight—at once blindness and visionary
power—to refer both to "defect and loss" and "abundance and
excess" is not so much a rejection of his earlier celebratory view
as its necessary completion. As if in illustration of his own principle
that "a piece of wood can never go blind," Heidegger combines
his sublime self-interrogations in *An Introduction to Metaphysics* with
the never-retracted endorsement of "the inner truth and greatness" (p. 199) of the National Socialist movement. In his incarnation of the paradoxical duality of the human condition, Heidegger lives out the "strangest" consequences of his identification
with Sophocles' hero, and marks the close of the "age of Oedipus."

Structuralist Oedipus

Heidegger and Lévi-Strauss represent antipodes in twentieth-century thought. Heidegger, the phenomenologist of time and being,
is the heir of Lessing in insisting on the irreducible horizon of
temporality in human experience. Lévi-Strauss, by contrast, proclaims himself an "archaeologist of space,"[18] and hails music and
mythology as "instruments for the obliteration of time."[19] Yet,
like Hegel and Schopenhauer in an earlier age, these "hostile
brother geniuses" of temporal and spatial analysis are joined by
subterranean affinities. Both Heidegger and Lévi-Strauss, for example, define their positions through bitter controversies with
Sartre.[20] Both mount critiques of the traditional metaphysical conception of the subject. And yet, like Heidegger, Lévi-Strauss has
himself undergone searching reappraisal by Derrida, who finds
structuralism, no less than phenomenology, to be entrapped within
a "metaphysics of presence."[21] Thus, the entry into the poststructuralist era inevitably entails also a move beyond Lévi-Strauss,
who joins Heidegger as a final spokesman for the "age of Oedipus."

In one important respect, Lévi-Strauss' concern with the
Oedipus myth differs from that of all the figures we have studied.

For he, unlike the German tradition from Schiller through Hei-degger, concentrates not on Sophocles' tragedy *Oedipus the King*, but on the Oedipus *myth* in a general sense. Indeed, Lévi-Strauss specifically rejects the attempt to canonize the Sophoclean—or, for that matter, any other—version of the myth. He writes in "The Structural Study of Myth" (1955) that mythological studies have been hampered by "the quest for the *true* version, or the earlier one," and proposes instead that "we define a myth as consisting of all its versions; or, to put it otherwise, a myth remains the same as long as it is felt as such."[22] Thus, "not only Sophocles, but Freud himself, should be included among the recorded versions of the Oedipus myth on a par with earlier or seemingly more 'authentic' versions" (SSM, p. 217).

Much of what, from a psychoanalytic standpoint, may be objected to in Lévi-Strauss is condensed in these statements. For, as we have seen, it is the self-analytic *form* of *Oedipus the King* that provides a decisive precedent for Freud's discovery of the Oedipus complex, and is integral to the greatness of the tragedy. It cannot be accidental, as Alister Cameron has noted, that the Oedipus plays of Seneca, Voltaire, and the rest are referred to by the names of their authors, "but there is only one *Oedipus*."[23] Similarly, I have argued, the "retroactive force" of Freud's reliving and re-telling of Sophocles in the Oedipus complex grants his version an imaginative, if not a temporal, priority that enables it to be legit-imately called "true" or "authentic." Ironically, Lévi- Strauss him-self testifies to the authority of Freud and Sophocles in the very act of denying that their accounts should be accorded special status. My own brief for Sophocles and the Oedipus complex should not be taken to mean that there is nothing to be learned from other poets and philosophers of the myth. But it is to affirm that a comparative study of legendary materials ought not to be confused with the egalitarian belief that no version may be deemed better or more definitive than any other.[24]

In point of fact, Lévi-Strauss has interpreted the Oedipus myth in print on only two occasions: in "The Structural Study of Myth" and again more briefly in "The Scope of Anthropology" (1960), his inaugural address upon assuming the chair of social anthro-pology at the Collège de France. But the importance of these references cannot be gauged by their frequency. "The Structural

Study of Myth" is unquestionably Lévi-Strauss' best-known essay, and rightfully so, since it contains his only sustained analysis of a myth generally familiar to students of Western culture, and also presents succinctly many of the cardinal tenets of his thought.[25] Thus, an evaluation of Lévi-Strauss' reading of the Oedipus myth leads directly to an assessment of structuralism as a whole.

Lévi-Strauss stands in an oblique relation to the tradition of German idealistic thought. In his autobiographical narrative *Tristes Tropiques* (1955), he accounts for his interest in, and approach to, anthropology in terms of the formative influence of three allied disciplines—psychoanalysis, Marxism, and (only initially surprising in this company) geology:

All three demonstrate that understanding consists in reducing one type of reality to another; that the true reality is never the most obvious; and that the nature of truth is already indicated by the care it takes to remain elusive. (*TT*, p. 50).

The lesson imbibed by Lévi-Strauss from these modes of cognition that "the true reality is never the most obvious" makes structuralism the heir of Freud and Marx in positing a fundamental opposition between *latent* and *manifest* content in whatever body of data is under observation. (For Marx, the distinction might be between a nation's economic order and its political institutions, and for Freud between a covert sexual meaning and an individual's apparently innocuous dream, but the principle is the same in both cases.) As Lévi-Strauss declares, he seeks to uncover a "master-meaning, which may be obscure but of which each of the others is a partial or distorted transposition" (*TT*, p. 48). He faults phenomenology precisely because, rather than accepting a disjunction between surface and depth, it postulates "a kind of continuity between experience and reality" (*TT*, p. 50). A concrete instance of Lévi-Strauss' hermeneutic method is afforded by the Oedipus myth, where, after arranging its "mythemes" or units of narrative into thematic groupings, he announces:

We may now see what it means. The myth has to do with the inability, for a culture which holds the belief that mankind is autochthonous . . . , to find a satisfactory transition between this theory and the knowledge that human beings are actually born from the union of man and woman. (SSM, p. 216)

There is, plainly, a great danger of arbitrariness and simplification in such a quest for an all-encompassing "master-meaning," even if one admits in theory the usefulness of the distinction between latent and manifest content; and deconstructionists would go further and say that Lévi-Strauss' belief in a hidden Truth is the ultimate metaphysical delusion.

As Lévi-Strauss' acknowledgment of the precedent of psychoanalysis makes clear, he is well versed in the writings of Freud. Indeed, it often seems as though Lévi-Strauss' purpose in structuralism is to reformulate the teachings of psychoanalysis at a more abstract level of generality. His anthropology, for example, is the most vigorous post-Freudian reassertion of "the universal presence of an incest taboo,"[26] which Lévi-Strauss takes to mark the passage from nature to culture. With reference to the Oedipus myth, Lévi-Strauss cleverly suggests that Freud's interpretation may be included within his own, since "it is still the problem of understanding how one can be born from two: How is it that we do not have only one procreator, but a mother plus a father?" (SSM, p. 217). In putting the issue thus, Lévi-Strauss allows us to hear, in his claim that the Oedipus myth answers the question "born from one or born from two?" (SSM, p. 216), both his own method of binary analysis—applied to the categories of "autochthony *versus* bisexual reproduction" (SSM, p. 217)—and Freud's model of the Oedipus complex as the discovery of sexual difference through male or female forms of castration anxiety.

Along similar lines, Lévi-Strauss argues in a footnote that the Sphinx constitutes "the personification of a female being with an inversion of the sign," and is thus "a phallic mother par excellence" (SSM, p. 231)—thereby rejoining a psychoanalytic interpretation of the Sphinx originally put forward by Otto Rank.[27] When he proposes that every myth may be expressed in terms of a complicated algebraic formula, Lévi-Strauss adds that the formula gains significance because "Freud considered that *two traumas* (and not one, as is so commonly said) are necessary to generate the individual myth in which a neurosis consists" (SSM, p.

228). At the same time that he appropriates the psychoanalytic concept of "deferred action," Lévi-Strauss defines the reciprocal relation between himself and Freud, since if neurosis is an "individual myth," this implies that myth or religion is—as Freud would have it—a "collective neurosis."

Marxism being an offshoot of Hegelianism, Lévi-Strauss through his study of Marx is indirectly in touch with the whole of German idealism. Surprisingly, however, he nowhere (to my knowledge) discusses his connection with Hegel, the philosopher whose thought—apart from his teleological view of history—most closely anticipates his own. Lévi-Strauss' approach to myth in terms of binary oppositions and their mediation is in all essentials a reprise of Hegel's dialectic. He writes:

We need only assume that two opposite terms with no intermediary always tend to be replaced by two equivalent terms which admit of a third one as a mediator; then one of the polar terms and the mediator become replaced by a new triad, and so on. (SSM, p. 224)

In addition to thus providing a Baedeker to the *Phenomenology of Mind*, Lévi-Strauss unexpectedly converges with Hegel in his analysis of kinship relations. According to Lévi-Strauss, there are three minimal requirements for the formation of a *"unit of kinship"*:

In order for a kinship structure to exist, three types of family relations must always be present: a relation of consanguinity, a relation of affinity, and a relation of descent—in other words, a relation between siblings, a relation between spouses, and a relation between parent and child.[28]

In the *Phenomenology*, Hegel explores the competing claims of exactly these "three types of family relations":

Amongst the three relationships, however, of husband and wife, parents and children, brothers and sisters, the relationship of husband and wife . . . is not inherently self-complete; similarly, too, the second relationship, the reverent devotion of parents and children to one another. . . . An unmixed intransitive form of relationship, however, holds between brother and sister. (*PM*, p. 474)

As Hegel's preference for the "unmixed intransitive" relationship between brother and sister makes clear, a recollection of *Antigone* hovers beneath this anatomy of kinship ties. This evocation of Sophocles is only one example of the way that a comparison of

Lévi-Strauss to his precursors remains anchored in the Oedipus myth.

As Lévi-Strauss' most immediate twentieth-century forebears are Durkheim and Mauss, so in the nineteenth century he is closest to Ferdinand de Saussure. From Saussure's structural linguistics he borrows both the notion of the arbitrary nature of the sign and the distinction between *langue*—the structure of language—and *parole*—language as it is actually spoken: "*langue* belonging to a reversible time, *parole* being non-reversible" (SSM, p. 209). With characteristic boldness, Lévi-Strauss contends that "myth belongs to the same category as language," that is, that "mythological time . . . is both reversible and non-reversible, synchronic and diachronic" (SSM, pp. 210, 211).

Together with his emphasis on binary oppositions, this reliance on the dichtomy between *langue* and *parole*, or between synchronic and diachronic aspects of meaning, lies at the heart of Lévi-Strauss' method of structural analysis. It has also been the chief target of those who would attack or modify his theories. As Terence S. Turner contends, "The basic problem with Lévi-Strauss' concept of myth structure is that it used a phonological model for a syntactic structure," and further, "synchrony ends up completely eclipsing diachrony."[29] Turner's reminders that we need to pay more attention to the diachronic dimension of myth and that "the sequential pattern of narrative, although it is an irreversible form of temporal organization, is not 'diachronic' in the sense of [chaotic] historical time,"[30] are undoubtedly justified. And yet, it may be interposed in Lévi-Strauss' defense, first, that the contrast between synchronic and diachronic readings retains its usefulness and, second, that his view of myth as simply a higher-order linguistic phenomenon points to the importance of language as the prototype for, in Lacan's terms, the Symbolic order as a whole.

The test of Lévi-Strauss' generalizations comes when he turns to the specific example of the Oedipus myth. It must be conceded that his interpretation does not hold up very well under careful scrutiny. In his famous chart, which is too well known to warrant reproduction here, Lévi-Strauss arranges what he takes to be the most important incidents or details from the myth in four vertical columns. (Diachronic or chronological order is retained by disregarding the columns and reading the horizontal rows from left to right and from top to bottom.) It is an immediate drawback that three out of the eleven events cited by Lévi-Strauss concern the character of Cadmus, Oedipus' ancestor, and thus are external not only to Sophocles' drama but even, arguably, to the story of Oedipus.[31] More significantly, as Brian Vickers has noted, Lévi-Strauss' neat disposition of the myth into four symmetrical columns is only achieved by "leav[ing] out whole sections of the myth"—Oedipus' exposure, rescue, adoption, flight from Corinth, and the like—and "it suppresses crucial details of knowledge, intention, and motive."[32] There is, finally, a vitiating circularity to Lévi-Strauss' whole procedure, since when he writes that "all the relations belonging to the same column exhibit one common feature which it is our task to discover" (SSM, p. 215), he has, as it were, loaded the dice by presupposing the results he wishes to obtain.

Lévi-Strauss defines his four columns in the following terms: 1) _"overrating of blood relations"_; 2) _"underrating of blood relations"_; 3) _"denial of the autochthonous origin of man"_; and 4) _"persistence of the autochthonous origin of man"_ (SSM, pp. 215, 216). As his critics have shown, there are numerous difficulties with Lévi-Strauss' classificatory scheme. Under "overrating of blood relations," for example, Lévi-Strauss includes both Oedipus' marrying of his mother Jocasta and Antigone's unlawful burial of Polyneices (as well as Cadmus' search for his sister Europa, ravished by Zeus). But, unlike Oedipus' incestuous marriage with Jocasta, where kinship ties are admittedly "more intimate than they should be" (SSM, p. 215), both Antigone's burial of her brother and Cadmus' search for his sister may well be regarded simply as "affirmations of ordinary kinship obligations in the face of the efforts of others to undermine or 'underrate' them."[33]

Similarly, the third column, "denial of the autochthonous origin of man," lists two "mythemes": Cadmus' killing of the dragon and Oedipus' killing of the Sphinx. (There is a small, but telling, factual error even here, since the Sphinx is not killed by Oedipus, but rather commits suicide.) Various objections may be raised. Turner asks, for example, "why should the destruction by men of autochthonous monsters be interpreted to mean the 'denial of the autochthonous origin of _man_'?"[34] What is more, both the dragon slain by Cadmus and the Sphinx, ostensibly symbols of man's earth-born origins, are not "autochthonous beings, as the birth of each did result from the union of male and female."[35] Conversely, Lévi- Strauss supports his category of "the persistence of the autochthonous origin of man," not with episodes from the myth, but with an etymological analysis of the names of Labdacus (= lame), Laius (= left), and Oedipus, (= swollen foot), all of which "refer to *difficulties in walking straight and standing upright*" (SSM, p. 215). But even accepting Lévi-Strauss' etymologies, the problem is that lameness or impairments in walking are found in numerous other Greek heroes (i.e., Philoctetes, Achilles, and Jason) who have nothing to do with autochthony.[36] Lévi-Strauss asserts that "it is a universal characteristic" in mythology that men born from the earth "either cannot walk or they walk clumsily" (SSM, p. 215); but, in the absence of evidence from Greek sources, he points only to two examples from North American Indian mythology to attest to this supposedly "universal characteristic."

All these individual challenges to Lévi-Strauss' analysis of the Oedipus myth are grounded in the *arbitrariness* of his method. He seems himself to be susceptible to the caveat concerning structural linguistics which he articulates in *The Savage Mind* (1962):

It identifies pairs of oppositions made up of phonemes but the *spirit of each opposition remains largely hypothetical*; it is *difficult to avoid a certain impressionism* in the preliminary stages, and several possible solutions to the same problem remain open for a long time.[37]

In order for Lévi-Strauss' attempt to tell us "what it means" to be truly convincing, he must demonstrate that his synchronic grouping of plot elements depends on something less "hypothetical" than the "impressionism" of the individual interpreter.

Despite the disappointing results in the case of the Oedipus myth, however, it would be a mistake to dismiss structuralist theory completely. In particular, just as the distinction between diachronic and synchronic meaning remains indispensable apart from its questionable application in particular instances, the same holds for Lévi-Strauss' model of binary analysis. The most sweeping justification of Lévi-Strauss' outlook is offered by Edmund Leach:

Binary oppositions are intrinsic to the process of human thought. Any description of the world must discriminate categories in the form "*p* is what not–*p* is not." An object is alive or not alive and one could not formulate the concept "alive" except as the converse of its partner "dead." So also human beings are male or not male, and persons of the opposite sex are either available as sexual partners or not available. Universally these are the most fundamentally important oppositions in all human experience.[38]

Certainly, the forms taken by binary oppositions may vary in different cultures, and there may be other, more elaborate ways of processing information, but Leach's statement that "binary oppositions are intrinsic to the process of human thought" remains empirically true and theoretically significant. His suggestion that "the most fundamentally important oppositions" are those between life and death, male and female, and potential sexual partners who are and are not subject to the incest taboo likewise carries conviction.

Leach's formulation has the virtue of returning Lévi-Strauss to the dialectical tradition in which, as we have seen, he belongs. Lévi-Strauss' discussion of mediation in myths leads to an explanation of the "ambiguous and equivocal character" of "tricksters"—represented in North American Indian stories by the coyote or raven—in terms of their "position halfway between two polar terms" (SSM, p. 226). In this instance, Lévi-Strauss' attempt to generalize on the basis of a limited sample is completely persuasive:

Not only can we account for the ambiguous character of the trickster, but we can also understand another property of mythical figures the world over, namely, that the same god is endowed with contradictory attributes—for instance, he may be *good* and *bad* at the same time. (SSM, p. 227)

Lévi-Strauss' view of myth as serving to provide "a logical model capable of overcoming a contradiction" (SSM, p. 229) leads him to an understanding of key psychoanalytic concepts such as ambivalence and compromise formation from a perspective complementary to Freud's. Oedipus, sacred and accursed, stranger to Thebes and native son, is assuredly "endowed with contradictory attributes" and "good and bad at the same time."

In addition to his disregard of Sophocles' tragedy in favor of a broader survey of the Oedipus myth, Lévi-Strauss differs from

Freud in a second major respect. Whereas Freud sees man as a creature dominated by instincts and impulses, Lévi-Strauss—in typically French or Cartesian fashion—highlights the importance of rationality and intellect. "Contrary to what Freud maintained," he asserts in *Totemism* (1962), "social constraints, whether positive or negative, cannot be explained, either in their origin or in their persistence, as the effects of impulses or emotions."[39] To the psychoanalytic critic, Lévi-Strauss' exclusive concentration on "intellectual operation" at the expense of "inarticulate emotional drives" (SSM, p. 207) is a serious failing. But though Lévi-Strauss rejects Freud, it is not necessary for psychoanalysis to exclude structuralism, since Lévi-Strauss' conception of myth as impelled by a tendency to "overcome contradiction" invests his system with an implicit dynamic motive comparable to Freud's pleasure principle.

Although far less well known than that in "The Structural Study of Myth," Lévi-Strauss' interpretation of the Oedipus myth in "The Scope of Anthropology" avoids the many pitfalls of the former and goes beyond it in that it deals with the role of the incest prohibition in the narrative.[40] Beginning typically with an apparently unrelated North American Indian story of incest between brother and sister, where, however, "the precautions taken to avoid incest make incest, in fact, unavoidable" (p. 21), Lévi-Strauss connects this first similarity to the Oedipus myth with the further fact that the brother in the Indian story has a "double personality," just as Oedipus is "thought dead and yet alive, condemned child and triumphant hero" (pp. 21–22). For both these reasons, Levi-Strauss concludes that "the incest between brother and sister" in the Iroquois myth constitutes "a permutation of the Oedipal incest between mother and son" (p. 21).

To clinch his comparison, however, Lévi-Strauss needs to find in the Indian story an analogue to the Sphinx episode, which he does in the reference to a sorceress as "mistress of the owls," since owls are known "to ask riddles which the hero must answer under pain of death" (pp. 21, 22). Having documented that "the same correlation between riddles and incest" exists in two wholly heterogeneous cultures, Lévi-Strauss stunningly adduces Percival as an "inverted Oedipus," since—instead of committing incest and solving riddles—he both abstains from sexual intercourse and "does not even knuw how to ask questions" (pp. 22–23). Thus, he arrives at a general formulation:

Between the solution of the riddle and incest, a relation exists, not external and of fact, but internal and of reason. . . . Like the solved riddle, incest brings together terms meant to remain separate: The son is joined with the mother, the brother with the sister, *in the same way as the answer succeeds, against all expectations, in rejoining the question.* (p. 23)

Once again, as in his interpretation of the Sphinx as a "phallic mother," Lévi-Strauss' definition of Percival as an "inverted Oedipus" unknowingly echoes comments already made by Rank.[41] Above all, however, Lévi-Strauss' recognition that Oedipus' "marriage with Jocasta does not arbitrarily follow the victory over the sphinx" (p. 24) endorses the similar conclusions reached by Schlegel, Hegel, and Nietzsche.

In an essay wittily entitled "If Oedipus Had Read His Lévi-Strauss," Anthony Burgess writes:

If Oedipus had read his Lévi-Strauss, he would have known [after solving the riddle of the Sphinx] that incest was on its way. The man who solves the insoluble puzzle has, symbolically, disrupted nature. Since incest is the ultimate perversion of nature, nature is shocked to death. To the "primitive" mind, the puzzle and the sexual taboo have an essential factor in common—the knot that it is dangerous to untie since, untying it, you are magically untying the knot that holds the natural order together.[42]

Even more directly than the above-quoted passage from "The Scope of Anthropology," which it seems to paraphrase, Burgess' summary points to the remarkable parallel between Lévi-Strauss' view of the link between "riddle and incest" and Nietzsche's commentary on "the horrible triad of Oedipus' destinies" in *The Birth of Tragedy*: "the same man who solves the riddle of nature—that Sphinx of two species—also must break the most sacred natural orders by murdering his father and marrying his mother."[43]

The full resonance of Nietzsche's description of "that Sphinx of two species" (*jener doppelgearteten Sphinx*) emerges when it is placed at once in a structuralist and a psychoanalytic context. On a literal level, of course, Nietzsche refers to the hybrid composition of the Sphinx from a woman's head and breasts and the body of a lion (often with wings and a conspicuous tail). But if the Oedipus myth answers the question "born from one or born from two?" this depiction of the "riddle of nature" as an ambiguous creature corroborates Lévi-Strauss' preoccupation with binary oppositions. From a psychoanalytic perspective, however, the Sphinx's conflation of a woman's upper body and animal's hind quarters reflects not simply an "intellectual operation" but also "inarticulate emotional drives." As Thass-Thienemann explains, "The small child is familiar with the head and breasts of the mother, but the lower body, always kept covered, represents the mystery of the Unknown."[44] Thus, the Sphinx's "two species" supports at once a structuralist reading of the Oedipus myth in terms of "autochthony *versus* bisexual reproduction" and a psychoanalytic reading in terms of sexual difference and castration anxiety.

Seen yet again from a slightly different standpoint, the Sphinx's "juxtaposition of heterogeneous components in a single body" is taken by Turner as a mirror image of Oedipus' anomalous status within "the social body of the family,"[45] where he joins together incompatible kinship ties. Finally, if attention is shifted from the composition of the Sphinx to her riddle, it is impossible to discount the speculation of the psychoanalytic anthropologist Géza Róheim, who interprets the "being with the indefinite number of legs" delineated in the riddle as a manifestation of the "combined body" glimpsed by the child in parental intercourse, "father and mother in one person."[46] In addition to all its other meanings, therefore, "that Sphinx of two species" is a symbolic embodiment of the primal scene.

If, for Lévi-Strauss, myths and their heroes possess "an ambiguous and equivocal character" as a result of their attempt to mediate between conflicting categories, the same may be said of structuralism itself. On the one hand, Lévi-Strauss sometimes seeks to align structuralism with science, and claims that "progress in comparative mythology depends on the cooperation of mathematicians" (SSM, p. 219). More often, however, he mocks such scientific pretensions by stating that his attempts at interpretation should be regarded as those of a "street peddler, whose aim is not to achieve a concrete result, but to explain, as succinctly as possible, the functioning of the mechanical toy which he is trying to sell to the onlookers" (SSM, p. 213). Lévi-Strauss' characterization of himself as a "street peddler," and of structuralism as a "mechanical toy," looks ahead to his praise of the *"bricoleur"* or "handyman" in *The Savage Mind*.

Just as I take what is most valuable in psychoanalysis to be, not its connections with nineteenth-century biology and positivism, but its participation in the traditions of Romanticism and idealistic philosophy, so I believe Lévi-Strauss' imperishable contributions to be his flashes of poetic insight and his rehabilitation of dialectical analysis. In the "Overture" to *The Raw and the Cooked* (1964), Lévi-Strauss reiterates his contention that "myths are themselves based on secondary codes" isomorphic with those of language, and adds that his work is intended as "a tentative draft of a tertiary code," that is, as a "myth of mythology" (*RC*, p. 12). For Lévi-Strauss, as for Hegel in the *Logic*, the "forms of thought" to be examined by philosophy or structuralist anthropology are "at once the object of research and the action of that object."

The Raw and the Cooked is the first of four volumes in Lévi-Strauss' *Introduction to a Science of Mythology*. Thus, as the introductory summation to an encyclopedic treatise, the "Overture" to *The Raw and the Cooked* parallels the Preface to the *Phenomenology of Mind*. Lévi-Strauss might have been describing the *Phenomenology* as well as his own work when he refers to its form as that of a "spiral," which "will go back over previous findings and incorporate new objects only in so far as their examination can deepen knowledge that had previously existed only in rudimentary form" (*RC*, p. 4). No less Hegelian in temper is Lévi-Strauss' avowal that he has sought "to attain a level at which a kind of necessity become apparent, underlying the illusions of liberty" (*RC*, p. 10). Both Freud and Hegel, moreover, would surely concur with Lévi-Strauss that "the starting point of the analysis must inevitably be chosen at random, since the organizational principles . . . are contained within it and only emerge as the analysis progresses" (*RC*, p. 3). A counterpart to the realization of the arbitrariness of the starting point is an acceptance that the task of interpretation can never be completed:

And so we see that the analysis of myths is an endless task. Each step forward creates a new hope, realization of which is dependent on some new difficulty. The evidence is never complete. (*RC*, p. 5)

Like his precursors in the study of Oedipus, Lévi-Strauss is engaged in "a long and laborious journey," a confrontation with alien modes of thought that is at the same time an interminable self-analysis.[47]

As structural anthropology is a "myth of mythology," so its founder is a consummate hero or "trickster." Lévi-Strauss recounts in *Tristes Tropiques* how, in attempting to emigrate from France to the United States during World War II, he was suspected as a traitor both by the Vichy government and by the American authorities—truly an illustration of "ambiguous and equivocal character." Comparing his belated discovery of America with that of earlier travelers, Lévi-Strauss laments: "I am subject to a double infirmity: all that I perceive offends me, and I constantly reproach myself for not seeing as much as I should" (*TT*, p. 34). An identical "double infirmity" accompanies Oedipus on his quest for self-knowledge. As he retraces his past, Lévi-Strauss, like Oedipus, comes to the realization that "events without any apparent connection . . . suddenly crystallize into a sort of edifice which seems to have been conceived by an architect wiser than my personal history" (*TT*, p. 34). And Lévi-Strauss reveals the subjective dimension of his understanding of "deferred action" when he writes: "twenty years of forgetfulness were required before I could establish communion with my earlier experience, which I had sought the world over without understanding its significance or appreciating its essence" (*TT*, p. 39).

In his anthropological travels, Lévi-Strauss literalizes the Romantic metaphor of a "journey around the world" of consciousness. But whereas when Hegel writes, "This world separates us from ourselves, but at the same time it grants us the cardinal means of returning to ourselves," he means the *ancient* world, Lévi-Strauss undergoes his process of self-estrangement and self-recovery at the hands of the primitive societies of the New World. This contrast accords with his emphasis on the comparative study of versions of the Oedipus myth, as opposed to the exclusive concentration of Freud and his predecessors on *Oedipus the King*. But as Hegel and Freud returned from their intellectual odysseys to ancient Greece with a self "which accords with the tone and universal essence of mind," so Lévi-Strauss regards anthropology as a means of "linking up at opposite ends with world history and my own history" and thereby disclosing "the rationale common to both" (*TT,* p. 51). That Lévi-Strauss' journey likewise entails the uncanny collapse of the distinction between the "strange" and the "familiar," self and other, becomes clear when he reflects on the "hidden motives underlying ethnic curiosity" in *The Savage Mind:*

The fascination exercised over us by customs apparently far removed from ours, the contradictory feelings of proximity and strangeness with which they affect us, stem perhaps from the fact that these customs are very much closer to our own than they appear and present us with an enigmatic image that needs deciphering.[48]

No less than the pilgrims of the German Romantic tradition, Lévi-Strauss' "ethnic curiosity" is impelled ultimately by a desire to undo the Fall, to heal the "wound" of consciousness by recapturing a state of innocence. He leaves us with a final image of the twin obsessions of nineteenth-century thought—Oedipus in the Garden of Eden.

PART III: GREEK TRAGEDY

O three roads and hidden vale,
oak-coppice and narrow mountain-pass
                        in triple ways,
that drank mine own blood of my father
from my hands, do you still remember
what deeds I wrought in your sight,
                        and then coming hither
what sort I did again? Marriages,
                        marriages,
you begat us, and upon begetting
sent up once more the same seed, and
                        made known
fathers, brothers, children—kindred
                        blood-guiltiness—
brides, wives, mothers, and whatever
                        deeds
are most shameful that come to pass
                        among mankind.
                        —Sophocles, *Oedipus the King*

10
Through Freud
to Sophocles

CONSIDERABLE PUBLICITY has recently surrounded the accusations of Jeffrey M. Masson that "the present-day sterility of psychoanalysis throughout the world"[1] may be attributed to Freud's abandonment of his original seduction theory in favor of the Oedipus complex. Although they have garnered far less notice, similar hypotheses have been put forward independently by Marie Balmary and Marianne Krüll.[2] But whereas Balmary and Krüll explain Freud's repudiation of the seduction theory in terms of a need to shield himself from knowledge of the alleged sexual transgressions of his father Jakob, Masson traces it to Freud's desire to exculpate Fliess for his bungled operation on the nose of Emma Eckstein and, secondarily, to regain the approbation of the Viennese medical establishment.

These attempts to challenge the Oedipus complex by rehabilitating the seduction theory are relevant here because, by addressing the crucial issue in Freud's self-analysis, they invite us to reflect also on Sophocles' tragedy. Having come at the dynamic relation between Freud and Oedipus in parts 1 and 2 from the complementary perspectives of biography and intellectual history, it remains for us now to turn to the Greek play that occupies a central place in both psychoanalytic theory and nineteenth-century thought. I hope already to have shown the extent to which Freud's self-analysis is constituted by its structure as a repetition of *Oedipus the King*. In the present chapter, I propose to reverse the vector of inquiry and consider how Freud's discovery of the Oedipus complex illuminates Sophocles' tragedy. In the remainder of this part, I shall seek to integrate my reading of *Oedipus the King* into an interpretation—informed by the theoretical principles of both structuralism and psychoanalysis—of Sophocles' Oedipus cycle as a whole.

One obvious failing of Masson's book is that, in his zeal to account for Freud's theoretical change of heart in terms of the Eckstein episode, he nowhere mentions the fact that Freud's father died in October of 1896. The entire context of Freud's self-analysis is thus left out of Masson's discussion of the relative merits of the seduction theory and the Oedipus complex. Indeed, under the spell of his speculation that Fliess may have sexually abused his son Robert, Masson writes:

Freud was like a dogged detective, on the track of a great crime, communicating his hunches and approximations and at last his final discovery [i.e., the seduction theory] to his best friend, who may in fact have been the criminal.[3]

Phrased in the manner, Masson's indictment of Freud reads like a weak parody of the plot of *Oedipus the King*, which culminates in Oedipus' realization that, not he, but, let us say, Creon is the murderer of Laius.

The speculations of Krüll and Balmary that Freud's adoption of the Oedipus complex was intended to deflect blame from his ostensibly licentious father are no less far-fetched than Masson's theory of a cover-up to protect Fliess.[4] These authors, however, go beyond Masson in pursuing their disagreement with Freud into a debate over the interpretation of the Oedipus legend. In her opening chapter, "Oedipus Has Still More to Teach Us," Balmary draws attention to details from the prehistory of *Oedipus the King* that may be little known except to scholars. In particular, she stresses the incident in which Laius, having sought refuge after the death of his father with King Pelops, abducted and committed homosexual rape against Pelops' son, Chrysippus. It is this offense, according to mythological tradition, which brings down the curse on the house of Labdacus. Arguing that Freud's "inattention to the foundations of the Oedipean myth" is tied to his father's career as a "hidden Don Juan," Balmary asks rhetorically, "Would he have failed to recognize in the myth what he failed to recognize in his own family?" and further: "What made Freud retain less of Oedipus than Sophocles had?"[5]

The validity of Freud's shift in emphasis from actual sexual seduction in childhood to unconscious infantile fantasies may be defended in purely psychological terms. My interest here, however, is merely to demonstrate that Balmary goes seriously astray in believing that Freud's perspective on the Oedipus myth differs from Sophocles'. For, as E. R. Dodds expounded in a classic essay, whereas Aeschylus' trilogy on the Oedipus theme—consisting of *Laius, Oedipus,* and *Seven Against Thebes,* accompanied by the satyr-play *Sphinx* (of which only *Seven Against Thebes* survives intact)— is organized around the motif of the inherited curse, it is precisely Sophocles' originality in *Oedipus the King* to have *suppressed* any such explanatory principle.[6] All the material concerning the abduction of Chrysippus and Laius' "hidden fault," in other words, is drawn by Balmary from mythological handbooks and knowledge of other Greek sources, but *not* from Sophocles' tragedy.

The fact that Sophocles has excluded the motif of the inherited curse is of the utmost interest. On one level, it may be connected with his abandonment of trilogic form in favor of autonomous single plays, which in turn favors the emergence of individual heroes freed from the overarching providential or infernal patterns found in Aeschylus.[7] Most compelling from a psychoanalytic standpoint, however, is the realization that, by shifting attention away from the culpability of Laius—which is, specifically, for a deed of symbolic *paternal seduction*—to Oedipus' quest for his own origins, Sophocles has anticipated Freud's rejection of the seduction theory in favor of the Oedipus complex. If, as I have contended, the "age of Oedipus" could only begin when German Romantics rebelled against Seneca and French neoclassicism and asserted the primacy of *Oedipus the King,* the greatness of Sophocles' drama is itself in large measure due to his having dismissed as irrelevant the escapades of Laius and *reconceived the Oedipus myth from the point of view of the son as a tragedy of self-knowledge.*[8]

Many features of Sophocles' artistry in *Oedipus the King* may be brought into relation with his fundamental suppression of the motif of an inherited curse. Concerning oracles, for example,

whereas in *Seven Against Thebes* (ll. 742–49) the prophecy given
by Apollo to Laius takes a *conditional* form—if you wish to save
the city, then die childless—that in *Oedipus the King* given both to
Laius (ll. 711–14) and to Oedipus (ll. 787–93) is *unconditional*—
it is the fate of the father to be killed by his son, and of the son to
kill his father and marry his mother, with no possibility of escape.[9]
Thus, when, in Aeschylus, Laius succumbs to lust and has intercourse with Jocasta, he compounds his assault on Chrysippus
with a *second* "transgression" (*parbasian*) (l. 743), and thereby
insures that his moral guilt will be inherited by his progeny. By
removing any such implication of contingency or human failing
from his drama, Sophocles transforms the fatal collision of father
and son at the crossroads into an ineluctable necessity, and thereby
endows the theme of patricide with genuine universality.

The coherent nature of Sophocles' innovations in *Oedipus the
King* is shown by three apparently incidental details, all of which
have the effect of accentuating the role of Apollo in Oedipus' story.
In the first place, from the single extant fragment of Aeschylus'
Oedipus—the second play of his trilogy—it is known that he placed
the crossroads at which Oedipus kills Laius near Potniae, a region
of Boeotia sacred to the Furies.[10] In *Oedipus the King*, on the other
hand, Jocasta responds to Oedipus' question concerning the place
of Laius' murder: "The land is called Phocis, and a split /
road leads into one from Delphi and from Daulia" (ll. 733–34).
Sophocles, that is, transposes the crossroads to a place near the
Delphic oracle, from which Oedipus was returning and to which
Laius was proceeding at the time of their meeting. In thus replacing
the Furies with Apollo as the presiding deity over the crossroads
in his tragedy, Sophocles epitomizes his metamorphosis of the
Aeschylean emphasis on a family curse into his own preoccupation with self-knowledge.

Similarly, earlier versions of Oedipus' life had depicted his
exposure as an infant as taking place either in southern Boeotia
or in Sicyon, a city associated with the Furies, where he was found
and raised by shepherds. In *Oedipus the King*, however, Oedipus is
left to die on Mount Cithaeron, where he is given by the Theban
Herdsman to his Corinthian counterpart, who in turn hands him
on to the king and queen of Corinth who become his adoptive
parents. By this "slight departure from his authorities," as F. J. H.

Letters has observed, Sophocles "not only yields two distinct threads of evidence to be tied together as the plot evolves, but eliminates the Aeschylean shadow of the inherited curse symbolized by the Eumenides."[11] Finally, it seems highly probable that the Sphinx was traditionally sent to Thebes as an agent of Hera, who wished to punish Laius for his violation of the hospitality of Pelops. But in Sophocles, the Sphinx, in Alister Cameron's words, becomes unmistakably "Apollo's creature," because the riddle of human identity she poses to Oedipus "is the Delphic command 'know thyself,' in another form."[12]

Freud's self-analysis thus provides a unique vantage point for comprehension of *Oedipus the King* because its central *peripeteia*— the abandonment of the seduction theory—underscores what is most original about Sophocles' handling of the myth. But the convergence between the perspectives of Freud and Sophocles does not stop here. One of the most important paradoxes of psychoanalysis, as we have seen in chapter 3, is that whereas Freud until 1923 consistently formulated the Oedipus complex in terms of the boy's "love of the mother and jealousy of the father," in actual practice he arrived at his realization of "the universal human application of the Oedipus myth" by "doing violence to 'the old woman,'" that is, by inadvertently committing a hostile action (confusing morphine with eye lotion) against an elderly female patient who is a symbolic substitute for the mother. I have connected this pivotal incident with other manifestations of Freud's unconscious proclivity toward misogyny, including his and John's "defloration" of Pauline in early childhood, his (or his nurse's) theft of money from his mother during this same "prehistoric" period, and his conduct with patients such as Emma Eckstein, Dora, and Sabina Spielrein.

Oedipus, of course, is known as the man who killed his father and married his mother, and thereby lent his name to Freud's complex. A careful reading of *Oedipus the King*, however, shows Sophocles to have endowed Oedipus with a "complete" Oedipus complex that astonishingly replicates the ambivalence of Freud. At several points near the outset of the play, Oedipus asserts his solidarity with the dead king Laius, whose throne he occupies and whose wife he has married, and vows: "Therefore am I such an ally / with the divinity [Apollo] and with the dead man" (ll. 244–

45). Conversely, as the sequence of searing revelations builds to its climax, Oedipus is felled by the Herdsman's disclosure that it was his *mother* who exposed him as an infant: "For *she* gave him to you?" (l. 1173). Upon fitting into place this final piece in the puzzle of his personal history, which confirms that he is the son of Laius and Jocasta, Oedipus rushes into the palace.

What happens next is told in the *rhēsis* of the Second Messenger—the climax of the entire play. First, he describes how Jocasta hurtled toward her marriage bed calling on Laius; then he proceeds to tell of Oedipus:

> He roams about calling on us to provide him with a
>   sword,
> where he might find his wife and no wife, the double
> maternal field of him and of his children.
>
> (ll. 1255–57)

The decisive detail here is Oedipus' demand for a sword, for there can be no doubt that he wished to use it to *kill Jocasta,* in response to having learned that she sought to destroy him in infancy.[13] Only when he discovers that she has already hanged herself does Oedipus snatch the brooches from Jocasta's dress and put out his own eyes. Thus, although Oedipus does commit the two crimes for which his name is a byword, in the course of the play he actually shows his *love for his father* and tries to *kill his mother,* just as Freud began his self-analysis in the "close the eyes" dream by identifying with his dead father and confronted his own Oedipus complex by an assault on a mother surrogate.

It is only to take this analogy to its conclusion to suggest that the explanation for the dynamics of the "complete" Oedipus complexes found in both Freud and Oedipus is virtually the same in each case. Freud, it will be recalled, had as one of the biographical accidents contributing to his heroic destiny the presence in his household, until the age of two and a half, of two mothers—his young biological mother Amalie, and his Czech nurse. Because his "Nannie" was expelled from the family when Freud was at such a tender age, he was able to banish also his resentments against the imago of the "bad mother," and to preserve his *"mater"* as the unsullied ideal of the pure object of desire that goes into the positive Oedipus complex. Only the history of Freud's relations with women enables us to see that these hostile feelings were not banished completely, just as it is the obviously libidinal component of his many attachments to men—friends, colleagues, patients— that best documents the inadequacy of the notion of the father simply as the rival for the mother's love.

Like Freud, Oedipus had two mothers—and here I mean not the surrogate couple Polybus and Merope in Corinth, but Jocasta and the Sphinx. For the Sphinx, as we have seen in our discussion of Lévi-Strauss, may be regarded as a phallic or "bad" mother. In Mark Kanzer's words, she exemplifies

an allegory of the problems presented by female sexuality. A full-breasted woman above, a lioness below, she combines the beloved and dreaded aspects of femininity which the boy must reconcile in order to achieve genital potency.[14]

And if the Sphinx is Oedipus' "bad mother," Jocasta embodies the idealized "good mother." The underlying identity of these figures, however, is confirmed in that the suicide of Jocasta constitutes a repetition of that of the Sphinx. The defense mechanism of splitting responsible for this pattern has been clearly discerned by H. A. van der Sterren:

The Sphinx therefore is the menacing, dangerous creature, and Jocasta the attractive, loving woman. But in the background Jocasta also appears dangerous and hostile, and Oedipus is her enemy. *Vice versa*, the Sphinx is also the seducer, for the fact that every day one of the youths of Thebes had to appear before her to solve the riddle, can only mean that they were seduced by her and could not pass her by.[15]

Particularly valuable here is van der Sterren's observation that "the Sphinx is also the seducer," for Freud likewise referred to his nurse as his seductress or "primary originator" of neurosis. Thus, just as "Nannie" was removed from Freud's life in early childhood, so the Sphinx was dispatched by Oedipus in the prehistory of the play. But the ostensibly positive feelings for the "good mothers" who remain—"*mater*" and Jocasta—are belied in the cases of both heroes by the acts of aggression that reveal their unresolved ambivalence toward women.

The scene reported by the Second Messenger in which Oedipus rushes into the palace and blinds himself is replete with symbolism. It represents a culmination of the process by which

Oedipus returns to his own origins, and, as such, enacts a reentry into Jocasta's womb. This assertion is corroborated by both literary and psychological evidence. Oedipus, who addresses the assembled Theban people in the first line as "children" *(tekna),* is himself called "child" *(pai, teknon)* by the Corinthian Messenger (ll. 1008, 1030) in the latter half of the play. In this reversal from the role of father to son are distilled all the ironies by which Oedipus, initially the detective or analyst, is himself exposed as the perennial criminal or patient. Oedipus' transformation from activity to passivity, moreover, is sustained by Sophocles through three interwoven metaphors—helmsman, ploughman, and hunter—which are drawn from the "ode on man" in the first stasimon of *Antigone.*[16]

But that Oedipus, in addition to becoming a child, specifically reenters the maternal womb is intimated by Sophocles through anatomical symbolism. Oedipus in fact reaches Jocasta in two stages: first (l. 1252) he passes through the palace doors and subsequently (l. 1261) through the doors of the bedchamber, which had been slammed shut by Jocasta. What is taking place here, both in its immediate and its larger implications, has been suggestively interpreted by John Hay:

> It may be pointed out, at the risk of seeming too clinically exact, that the two doorways through which [Oedipus] passes . . . symbolize both vaginal and cervical entrances respectively, and thus *the bedchamber symbolizes precisely the womb.* Oedipus is symbolically retracing the route of his own incestuous seed, and that of his father before him, to the homosporic (same-sown) womb—there to confront his beginnings; there to die; there to be reconceived; thence to be reborn and to issue forth, once again through the same gates, transfigured.[17]

In his masterwork *Thalassa* (1923), which describes human life as being motivated by the compulsion to return to the womb, Sándor Ferenczi enumerates the "threefold manner" in which this regression takes place in the male during the sex act:

> the whole organism attains this goal by purely hallucinatory means, somewhat as in sleep; the penis, with which the organism as a whole has identified itself, attains it partially or symbolically; while only the sexual secretion possesses the prerogative, as representative of the ego and its narcissistic double, the genital, of attaining *in reality* to the womb of the mother.[18]

As we know, it was Ferenczi himself in "The Symbolic Representation of the Pleasure and Reality Principles in the Oedipus Myth" who first proposed the now canonical psychoanalytic interpretations of Oedipus' self-blinding as a displaced act of castration and of his name "Swollen Foot" as an allusion to an erect penis. If Ferenczi is indeed correct in this early essay to posit that "the myth completely identifies with a phallus the man who achieved the monstrous feat of sexual intercourse with the mother,"[19] it is only to follow the evolution of his thought to *Thalassa* to concur that Oedipus—at the point of reentering the palace and the bedchamber—becomes identified also with the "sexual secretion" and exercises its "prerogative" of "attaining *in reality* to the womb of the mother." In the decisive speech he gives when Jocasta, who has already grasped the truth from the Corinthian Messenger, withdraws into the palace, Oedipus resolves:

> Burst out what will! However small it be,
> I shall will to see my seed *(sperm' idein boulēsomai).*
>
> (ll. 1076–77)

The second sentence of this passage is translated by Jebb: "Be my race never so lowly, I must crave to learn it." Jebb is right to bring out the theme of lineage, and to translate "small" *(smikron)* as "lowly," because it is for believing he is lowborn that Oedipus mistakenly reproaches Jocasta. But Oedipus literally says he will "see my seed," and it is this that he achieves when he returns inside Jocasta's "homosporic" womb.

Anatomical symbolism similar to that subtending the scene of Oedipus' reentry inside the palace may be found in the central motif of the crossroads. The psychoanalytic pioneer to whom we are indebted in this case is Karl Abraham, who in 1922 published " 'The Trifurcation of the Road' in the Oedipus Myth."[20] Following an observation of Freud's, Abraham points out that Oedipus' encounter with Laius is said to take place both at a "narrow pass" and a "split road." For Abraham, it presents no problem to deduce that "the narrow pass is a symbol of the female genitalia" (p. 83), but the meaning of the "split road" or "trifurcation" proves more elusive. On the basis of a patient's dream, however, Abraham is able to interpret: "The two roads which merge to form a wide highway are the two thighs which join at the trunk. The junction is the site of the genitalia" (p. 85). He thus comes to the conclusion that "the trifurcation has the same meaning as the narrow pass. The former symbolizes the site of the female genitalia; the latter their shape" (p. 85). What is more, Abraham draws the illuminating distinction that whereas the trifurcation, "the place of heavy traffic, clearly represents the mother as a prostitute," the version of the narrow pass "gives expression to another fantasy, that of encountering the father inside the mother's body before birth; the fantasy of observing coitus from within the womb" (p. 85). Abraham's double interpretation of the crossroads catches exactly the way that Oedipus' reentry inside the palace symbolically portrays both his own sexual intercourse with Jocasta and "the fantasy of observing coitus from within the womb," since Jocasta has just thrown herself on the marriage bed and called on the long-dead Laius.

As the scene of Oedipus' self-blinding with Jocasta's brooches fuses the symbolism of physical and spiritual rebirth with that of sexual intercourse, it likewise brings together the opposites of death and love. Concerning the Messenger's description of the ooze pouring from Oedipus' eyes "like a black / rain and bloody hailshower" (ll. 1278–79), Kanzer has written that "in this fantasy of coitus and orgasm, the sexual act is depicted as a sadistic and castrating attack from the maternal phallus. The brooches of Jocasta are another version of the talons of the Sphinx."[21] Since Oedipus is to be imagined as stabbing both eyes simultaneously, moreover, the "gold-wrought / pins" (ll. 1268–69) of Jocasta recall also the "double prongs" (l. 809) of the stick with which Laius smote the head of Oedipus at the crossroads.[22] The self-blinding, that is, is a ghastly repetition not only of Oedipus' incest but also of his patricide. In its violent crossing of eros and thanatos Oedipus' final consummation with Jocasta is a necrophilic union, which provides a prototype both for Kleist's confusion of the "bed" and the "grave" in his double suicide with Henriette Vogel and, more immediately, for the underground *Liebestod* of Haemon and Antigone in *Antigone*.

Abraham focuses on the discrepancy between the references to the crossroads as a "narrow pass" and a "split road." Seth Benardete concentrates on the related question of whether this "split road" or "trifurcation" is in fact double or triple:

Oedipus says that he met Laius at a triple road, but Jocasta calls the meeting of the ways from Daulia and Delphi a split road (733, 800 ff., cf. 1399). A τριπλὴ ὁδός ("triple way") is the same as a σχιστὴ ὁδός ("split way"). Two is the same as three. If one is walking a road and comes to a branching of it, there are only two ways that one can go, for the third has already been traversed. If, however, one is not walking but simply looking at a map of such a branching, there appear to be three ways to take. Action sees only two where contemplation sees three.[23]

Benardete's comment that "two is the same as three" in the crossroads draws attention to a recurring motif in *Oedipus the King*. Early in the play, when the Chorus timidly speak up with reference to the murder of Laius, "The second best of the things that seem good to me I might say," Oedipus rejoins: "And if there is a third, do not omit to tell it" (ll. 282–83). By the same token, during the fateful exchange between the Corinthian Messenger, the Theban Herdsman, and Oedipus, the Messenger assures Oedipus that their reluctant interlocutor will remember the bygone times on Mount Cithaeron:

> he with double flocks, I with one
> was near this man [the Herdsman] for three whole
> six-month seasons, from spring to September.
> (ll. 1135–37)

Once again, the Messenger emphasizes the fact that the Herdsman had "double flocks" and that they spent "three whole seasons" together. The opposition between *two* and *three*, however, is here played off against that between *one* and *two* in the number of flocks tended by the two shepherds. This latter binary antithesis, taken together with the emphasis on rotating "six-month seasons" and the hint of hostility between the two ancient retainers, seems to carry an allusion to the theme of twin rulership found elsewhere in the Oedipus myth in the fraternal enmity of Eteocles and Polyneices.[24]

Like the anatomical symbolism of the palace bedchamber and the crossroads, the numerical symbolism of Sophocles' Theban plays is too pronounced to be dismissed as accidental. The most decisive confirmation of the significance of the ambiguity in the depiction of the crossroads as "split" and as "triple" is provided by the figure of the Sphinx. As we know from Nietzsche and Lévi-Strauss, the Sphinx is of *"two* species"—woman above, and animal below. On the other hand, the riddle of human identity she tells is cast in a *tripartite* form: what walks on four legs in the morning, two legs at noon, and three at night? The interplay of *two* and *three* in Sophocles' dramatization of the myth thus may be traced back to Oedipus' primordial encounter with the "complex-singing Sphinx" (l. 130).

Sophocles' use of the Sphinx's riddle in turn points to a third major respect—after the suppression of the inherited curse and the depiction of an underlying "negative" Oedipus complex— in which his treatment of the Oedipus myth prefigures that of Freud. When, in a footnote added to the *Three Essays on the Theory of Sexuality* in 1920, Freud termed the Oedipus complex "the shibboleth that distinguishes the adherents of psycho-analysis from its opponents" (*SE,* 7:226), it was particularly an acknowledgment of the *universality* of Oedipus' fate that he demanded. I have already argued in part 1 that the best defense for Freud's claim lies not in anthropological or sociological controversy but in the philosophical concept of the hermeneutic circle, with its oscillation between the poles of subject and object, self and other. It remains to be noted here that Sophocles precedes both Freud and Hegel in regarding Oedipus as a "universal individual." After his self-recognition, Oedipus is expressly deemed by the Chorus a "paradigm" *(paradeigm')* (l. 1193) of the human condition.[25] But it is above all by inscribing Oedipus' ontogenetic history within the phylogenetic pattern of the Sphinx's riddle that Sophocles affirms Oedipus' "paradigmatic" status.

The Sphinx enigmatically defines man in terms of the number of his feet and walking. The name Oedipus means, most simply, "Swollen Foot," and, because he had his ankles pierced in infancy, he lives up to his name and has difficulties in walking. As Géza Róheim puts it, in advancing his interpretation of the Sphinx's riddle as a representation of the primal scene, "In very truth only 'Swollen Foot' can solve this riddle of the feet; for he is the victorious hero of the Oedipus tragedy of all mankind."[26] No less important for the connection between Oedipus and the Sphinx is the riddle's tripartite form. Oedipus, appropriately, kills Laius at a place where *three* roads meet, since it is his own fate to become the crossroads of *three* generations. This is so, as we noted in comparing the kinship structures of Freud and Oedipus in chapter 1, because the effect of Oedipus' incest with Jocasta is to arrest the passage of time and to make him a contemporary both of his parents' and his children's generation. The doubling of Oedipus' kinship ties, moreover, as "son and husband" to Jocasta and "brother and father" of his children, causes him to replicate in his own person not only the tripartite form of the Sphinx's riddle, but also the "two species" of the Sphinx herself. Thus, the confusion of *two* and *three*, which we found both in the crossroads and in the Sphinx, is mirrored in Oedipus himself; and, as Nietzsche so profoundly recognized, Oedipus proves ultimately to be indistinguishable from the riddle he thinks he has answered.

Sophocles, it should be acknowledged, does not actually cite the Sphinx's riddle in the text of *Oedipus the King*. Yet there can be no doubt that he assumed it to be familiar to his audience and that it is deeply embedded in the dramatic action. In his initial supplication to Oedipus on behalf of the Theban people, the Priest declares:

> you see us, of what age we have come hither
> to your altars: some not yet having the strength
> to fly far; others heavy with age,
> priests, I one of Zeus; and yet others chosen
> from those unmarried. (ll. 15–19)

The Priest's tripartite division of the populace according to age— children, old men, and bachelors—confronts Oedipus from the outset with a new impression of the Sphinx's enigma, but he is unable to see that this is what lies before him.[27] Similarly, in the course of *Oedipus the King* itself Oedipus may be said to recapitulate the Sphinx's riddle in warped form: he begins the play in the prime of manhood, he returns to his infancy, and ends the play as a blind old man.[28] In more obvious fashion, when Teiresias taunts Oedipus with the riddle of his origins—"This day will beget and will destroy you" (l. 438)—he makes clear that the action of the play is to show Oedipus' unraveling in his own being the puzzle of human identity posed in abstract and impersonal form by the Sphinx.

Benardete has interestingly highlighted a sense in which Oedipus may be thought to stand outside the Sphinx's riddle. Because of the injury to his feet, he believes, Oedipus walks with a staff— that is, on three legs—even in middle age; but this defect, "by placing him outside the species-characteristic, allowed him to see the species-characteristic."[29] Whether Oedipus indeed needs a staff to aid him in walking is difficult to determine from the text of the play. But Benardete's observation is in any case complicated by an additional consideration. In the Sphinx's riddle itself, as it has come down to us from antiquity, the ages of men are not, as might be expected, given in chronological sequence:

> On two feet, yet on four, and on three,
> There treads the earth a creature of one name.
> Alone it changes shape of all that walk
> On ground or fly in air or swim the sea.
> But when it goes supported on four feet,
> Then is the speed the feeblest in its limbs.[30]

The suggestion that Oedipus' anomalous nature is what "allowed him to see the species-characteristic" would not automatically diminish his standing as a representative man. But, as it turns out, even this qualification is unnecessary, since Oedipus' disruption of linear time—both in his individual being and in the action of the play—matches that found in the Sphinx's riddle. Once again, therefore, the conclusion is confirmed that, when Freud asserted the universality of Oedipus' fate, he merely retraced and made explicit a hermeneutic circle already laid down by Sophocles in *Oedipus the King.*

Freud's discovery of the Oedipus complex, as we have seen, took place through a nearly fatal error that revealed the physician administering an injection to an elderly lady to be himself a patient in need of analysis. The inherent interminability of analytic work is confirmed by the various unconsciously motivated lapses in *The Interpretation of Dreams,* which demand to be interpreted in *The Psychopathology of Everyday Life.* These constitutive features of Freud's self-analysis have their symbolic counterparts in *Oedipus the King.* In addition to its primary meaning of "Swollen Foot" (*oidos* = swollen; *pous* = foot), the first syllable of Oedipus' name also suggests the Greek word *oida* ("I know"), and thus the whole might also be rendered "know-foot." Oedipus' entire tragedy is compressed in the double meaning of his name, in which his pretensions to knowledge are mocked by the reminders of his identity as an exposed infant.[31] Even the meaning "swollen" bears on the theme of knowledge, as well as on that of sexuality, since, as Theodore Thass-Thienemann has pointed out:

The Greek verb *oidaō* "to swell, to become swollen" denotes the physiological tumescence but refers also to the specific character trait "to be inflated," "to ferment," "to be troublesome." . . . Oedipus, the solver of riddles, is inflated and infatuated by his "knowledge," but such knowledge "puffeth up," Paul said (I Cor. 8:1–3). The logical consequence of such infatuation is stumbling and error.[32]

The significance of Oedipus' lameness, as also of Freud's lapses, is that a certain tragic "stumbling and error" must inevitably accompany—and impede—the "inflated" hero in his quest for self-knowledge.[33]

One of the manifestations of "stumbling" or repression in Freud's self-analysis, it will be recalled, is the dislocation in temporality, whereby he is both dimly aware "in advance" of his discoveries and only experiences their full impact belatedly through "deferred action." Sophocles has built a similar tension between the rhythms of haste and delay into the plot of *Oedipus the King*. Near the end of his second speech Oedipus expresses impatience that Creon has not yet returned from the oracle of Apollo:

And already when the day is measured with the time,
it vexes me what he is doing; for beyond the probable
he is gone, more than the appropriate time.

(ll. 73–75)

Even as Oedipus finishes speaking, however, the Priest announces that Creon is upon them: "But opportunely did you speak: these men just now / are signalling to me that Creon draws near" (ll. 78–79). Similarly, when the Chorus urge Oedipus to consult Teiresias, he replies: "Nor among things neglected did I leave this matter" (l. 287). And on the heels of Oedipus' declaration, "And this long time I wonder why he is not here" (l. 289), the Chorus hail the arrival of the seer "in whom / alone of men the truth is native" (ll. 298–99). These imperceptible hesitations, in which an anticipated action is found already to have taken place, exemplify the way that both present and future are engulfed by the past in the play as a whole.

The tension between antithetical movements of haste and delay is a direct expression of the self-analytic structure of *Oedipus the King*, wherein Oedipus' quest for himself is simultaneously a flight from himself. Whereas Oedipus constantly wishes to press forward with his investigation, Teiresias at his first entrance exhibits the underside of fear before the impending discovery:

> Alas, alas, how terrible to have wisdom when it brings
> no profit to him who is wise! For I know these things
> well,
> but forgot them, else I would not have come hither.
>
> (ll. 316–18)

The same contrast between Oedipus' relentless forward movement and the apprehensiveness of Teiresias recurs at a lower social level in the encounter between the Corinthian Messenger and the Theban Herdsman, Oedipus' two old rescuers.[34] The former garrulously volunteers information in ignorance of its true significance; the latter has to be coerced into revealing the truth of whose horror he is only too fully aware. The struggle that arises in Oedipus' exchanges with the various characters who seek to retard his inquiry—Teiresias, Jocasta, the Herdsman—is best understood as an externalized representation of the division existing within his own mind. That this is so is especially clear in the case of Teiresias, who, as a "blind seer" in a sense antithetical to that of Oedipus, is his uncanny opposite.[35] The reversal whereby, upon his self-blinding, Oedipus becomes indistinguishable from Teiresias is enclosed within the larger pattern in which he is shown to incarnate the Sphinx's riddle.

Because the action of *Oedipus the King* consists of Oedipus' solving of the Sphinx's riddle for a second time, the entire play is structured by "deferred action." The theme of repetition is elaborated by Sophocles with extraordinary subtlety.[36] If Teiresias may be assimilated not only to the Sphinx but also to the Delphic oracle, which sent Oedipus away "dishonored" *(atimon)* (l. 789) when he sought to learn the truth concerning his parentage, then the immediately ensuing quarrel with Creon becomes a reenactment of Oedipus' original killing of Laius, which followed his frustrated consultation of the oracle. If, moreover, we accept the idea that the play enacts Oedipus' regression to his childhood, and that his reemergence from the palace after his self-blinding is a symbolic rebirth from the womb, then his plea to be exiled on Mount Cithaeron (ll. 1451–54) is for a reenactment of the expulsion from Thebes he suffered in infancy. Even the collision with Laius at the crossroads, where Laius strikes the first blow, may be regarded as a repetition of the violence done to Oedipus in infancy. The plague on Thebes at the outset of the play—a curse of sterility emanating from the incestuous union of Oedipus and Jocasta—duplicates the earlier blight on the city imposed by the Sphinx, the penalty for Laius' and Jocasta's crime of attempted infanticide. And insofar as the deed of self-blinding fuses the symbolism of incest and patricide, it recalls the vanquishing of the Sphinx, who embodies aspects of both Laius and Jocasta. Because of the endless process of deferral and anticipation in *Oedipus the King*, one is never merely at any single point of the action, but each moment looks back or ahead to others in the myth.

A recognition that Teiresias and Oedipus embody two halves of a single psyche will enable us to take a position on the vexed question of whether Oedipus is aware of having committed the crimes of incest and patricide. The most ardent champion of the affirmative view is Philip Vellacott, who has maintained that Sophocles contrived a "hidden play" for particularly astute readers or spectators, in which a knowingly guilty but magnanimous Oedipus decides that the best way to save the city is "to have the truth brought out apparently by accident as the result of an inquiry initiated by himself."[37] Stated thus baldly, Vellacott's thesis is unconvincing, and has deservedly met with general condemnation. Nonetheless, it contains a grain of truth, which is often overlooked by those who would dismiss it completely.

To unearth that grain, it is necessary only to replace Vellacott's assumption of a deliberately self-incriminating Oedipus in an esoteric "hidden play" with the psychoanalytic tenet of unconscious knowledge. Like Freud in the course of his self-analysis, in other words, Sophocles' Oedipus possesses a "blindness of the seeing eye" and is in "the strange state of mind in which one knows and does not know a thing at the same time" (*SE*, 2:117). Certainly, after the interview with Teiresias, who explicitly tells him, "I say you are the murderer you are seeking to find" (l. 362), Oedipus is at least on one level in possession of the truth for which he continues to search. But if Teiresias speaks with the voice of Oedipus' own unconscious, it is plausible to suggest that Oedipus' repressed awareness of his condition is with him from the beginning of the play.

This line of argument has been strongly contested by Brian Vickers. According to Vickers, the "dislocation of chronology" introduced by Sophocles into his plot—turning on the presumed death of Oedipus as an infant, Oedipus' own belief that he is the child of Polybus and Merope, and the report that Laius was killed by a band of robbers—"not only makes it impossible for Oedipus to infer correctly who he is, and why, but also guarantees his innocence."[38] But though Vickers is right to draw attention to the "false premisses" governing the behavior of Oedipus and Jocasta, the conclusion he draws as to the invincibility of Oedipus' ignorance does not necessarily follow. Rather, these mistaken assumptions are better regarded in the manner of what Freud called the "false connections" that go into the formation of neurotic symptoms, as a façade of self-delusion that is gradually destroyed by the analytic work of the play.[39]

In particular, the second of these "dislocations"—Oedipus' conviction that he is the son of Polybus and Merope—does not withstand careful examination. In his narrative to Jocasta (ll. 779–99), Oedipus says that he was moved to consult the Delphic oracle because of a reproach let fly by a drunken man, who told him that he was no true son of Polybus. But upon arriving at the Delphic oracle, Oedipus is given only the prophecy that he would kill his father and marry his mother, but *not* informed who his parents are. Thus, his decision to flee as far as possible from Corinth belies the uncertainty that drove him to the oracle in the first place, and shows a crack in the façade of his ignorance.[40] It is this moment in the play that best justifies Freud's contentions in *An Outline of Psycho-Analysis* (1940):

The ignorance of Oedipus is a legitimate representation of the unconscious state into which, for adults, the whole experience has fallen; and the coercive power of the oracle, which makes or should make the hero innocent, is a recognition of the inevitability of the fate which has condemned every son to live through the Oedipus complex. (*SE*, 23:191–92)

Even for Oedipus, the "whole experience" of incest and patricide falls into an "unconscious state," and the prophecies of the oracle are thus the externalized projections of his own inadmissible desires.

To suggest that Oedipus' own desires for incest and patricide exist in a repressed form may seem paradoxical in view of the fact that he has committed these deeds in actuality. Indeed, in *The Interpretation of Dreams* Freud posits as the basis of his contrast between *Oedipus the King* and *Hamlet* the observation that in the former "the child's wishful phantasy that underlies it is brought into the open and realized as it would be in a dream," whereas in the latter "it remains repressed; and—just as in the case of a neurosis—we only learn of its existence from its inhibiting consequences" (*SE*, 4:264). Freud's argument concerning the increase of repression, as we know, is carried still further by Rank, who saw in Schiller's *Don Carlos* a third, still more attenuated, representation of the underlying oedipal fantasies.

Freud's contrast between *Oedipus the King* and *Hamlet* does possess considerable validity. Hamlet, after all, unlike Oedipus, has not actually killed his father and married his mother. Nonetheless, as even Freud's reference to dreams indicates, a rigid distinction between the plays of Sophocles and Shakespeare proves impossible to maintain. Like neurotic symptoms, dreams are compromise formations, where the illicit wishes pressing for expression are hindered by the forces of the censorship, and not unequivocal experiences of gratification. (Interestingly, Freud himself acknowledges that, just as the "two typical dreams" of the Oedipus story, "when dreamt by adults, are accompanied by feelings of repulsion, so too the legend must include horror and self-punishment" [*SE*, 4:264], but the implications of this insight are not integrated into the remainder of his discussion.) In *Oedipus the King*, by the same token, because Oedipus is depicted as having committed his deeds of incest and patricide *involuntarily*, and because it is his very attempts at avoiding his fate that cause it to come about, the play maintains a balance between the impulses of defense and desire.[41] Oedipus' self-analysis, in short, is already a *secondary* phenomenon, and—far from being "brought out into the open"—the psychological dynamics at work therein are exhibited only in a distorted form.

In a revealing application of the concept of "deferred action" to *Oedipus the King*, taking the murder of Laius as the "first scene" in the formation of a trauma and Oedipus' discovery of his guilt as the "second scene," Cynthia Chase writes: "The one person who actually enacts patricide and incest completely misses the experience—until after the fact, when parrincest is inscribed as a palimpset and becomes readable for the first time."[42] Chase's formulation remains unaffected whether we define the "first scene," as I have done, as the solving of the Sphinx's riddle or as the killing of Laius. In either case, it is possible to conclude that Oedipus, in addition to *being* the unconscious, is shown to *have* an unconscious in the course of his play.

The issue of Oedipus' awareness of his own condition in *Oedipus the King* is tied to the continuing controversy over his guilt or innocence. Clearly, having taken the position that Oedipus must be imputed unconscious knowledge of his crimes, I cannot accept the views of those critics—going back to Corneille—who insist on his complete innocence.[43] Far more satisfactory is Hegel's paradoxical notion of Oedipus' "guilt of innocence." Although Oedipus has certainly not intended his familial transgressions, and is presented as a ruler devoted to the welfare of his city, it must not be overlooked that he dominates the action at every turn. Hence the nemesis that overtakes him strikes us, not as one arbitrarily imposed from without, but rather—in Hegel's terms—as "the equal reaction of the trespasser's own deed."[44] Oedipus' culpability is underscored by the savage anger he directs at Teiresias and Creon, as well as by the skepticism he and Jocasta manifest toward divine oracles.[45] To say this is not to deny that Oedipus' suspicion of a conspiracy between Teiresias and Creon has some plausibility, especially given his conviction that he is being accused unjustly, but the excessiveness of his anger remains an indication that Oedipus is less confident of his innocence than it might appear and behaving irrationally. Perhaps the most profound commentary on the falseness of Oedipus' position has been offered by Paul Ricoeur:

At the beginning of the play Oedipus calls down curses upon the unknown person responsible for the plague, but he excludes the possibility that that person might in fact be himself. The entire drama consists in the resistance and ultimate collapse of this presumption. . . . Thus Oedipus becomes guilty precisely because of his pretension to exonerate himself from a crime that, ethically speaking, he is not in fact guilty of.[46]

Ricoeur's analysis beautifully captures the way that Oedipus can be considered innocent and guilty at the same time, and shows how it is the structure of "deferred action" in *Oedipus the King* that renders Oedipus guilty in the course of investigating a crime of which he was originally innocent.

Most critical misjudgments of *Oedipus the King* are due to an excessive tipping of the balance toward one side or the other of a dialectical equation. Just as it is necessary to see Oedipus as both innocent and guilty, so his actions are both free and determined by the gods. Complementary errors are those, on the one hand, of C. M. Bowra, who contends that "the play shows the power of the gods at every important turn in its development and leaves no doubt about the poet's theological intention,"[47] and, on the other, of Cedric Whitman, who maintains that "the action of the play itself. . . is motivated by the free will of the hero" and that Oedipus is "never considered . . . morally guilty"[48] by Sophocles. But the truth is, to adapt Hegel's remarks on *Antigone*, that both Bowra's "theological" and Whitman's "heroic humanist" Sophocles are right insofar as they articulate a partial truth and wrong to the extent that they exclude the point of view of the other. Among German Romantics, Schelling typically struck the right note in boldly affirming of *Oedipus the King* that "absolute freedom is itself absolute necessity," a paradox given more muted reformulation in Bernard Knox's recognition that "in the play which Sophocles wrote the hero's will is absolutely free and he is fully responsible for the catastrophe," and yet, "the play is a terrifying affirmation of the truth of prophecy."[49]

In Sophocles' own terms, *Oedipus the King* is a profoundly religious drama. A psychoanalytic reading of the play, however, must concentrate on man and not on the gods. Attributing the Oedipus story to "the reaction of the imagination to these two typical dreams" of incest and patricide, Freud looks upon Sophocles' dramatization of the myth as "a misconceived secondary revision of the material, which has sought to exploit it for theological purposes" (*SE*, 4:264). But though Freud simply dismisses the religious dimensions of *Oedipus the King*, I think it is both more productive and more balanced to argue that the insights apprehended in one way by psychoanalysis may be formulated in somewhat different fashion by other methods of inquiry. Concerning the workings of dramatic irony on the play, for example, Jean-Pierre Vernant observes that "the language of Oedipus thus appears as the place where two different discourses weave themselves and confront each other in the same language: a human discourse, a divine discourse."[50] Vernant's statement is valid on its own terms, and may remind us of Hölderlin's theories concerning the nature of tragedy, but it requires no violent modification to reconcile what he says about the structure of riddles with the psychoanalytic categories of conscious and unconscious knowledge. Similarly, when Karl Reinhardt asserts that *Oedipus the King* centers on the depiction of "illusion and truth as the opposing forces between which man is bound,"[51] it is again easy to correlate his Heideggerian definition of life's "opposing forces" with the dualities of Freud. Properly understood, the theological, the existential, and the psychoanalytic perspectives are all responsive to the dialectical quality of *Oedipus,* and should enhance rather than diminish one another.

In addition to approaching the play as a drama of self-analysis, however, it is the psychoanalytic contribution to insist on the irreducible importance of the incest theme to Sophocles' artistry. The doubling of kinship ties that results from Oedipus' incestuous union with Jocasta is refracted by the principle of "condensation" that governs the structure of the play as a whole.[52] For not only is Jocasta both wife and mother to Oedipus, but the Corinthian Messenger, who initially enters to bring Oedipus the news of the death of Polybus, proves also to be the man who gave Oedipus to Polybus and Merope in infancy. Similarly, the Theban Herdsman, originally summoned because he was the sole surviving witness to the murder of Laius, is also the man who took Oedipus from Jocasta and handed him to the Messenger. This double function both in the present and the past of supporting characters serves the ends of artistic economy, but also conveys the psychological truth that for Oedipus, who is at once a "son and husband," the present *is* his past.

The doctrine of the Oedipus complex holds that the woman the ordinary (male) individual chooses to marry will be *like* his mother. But Oedipus, because of the principle of "condensation" that controls his fate, transforms simile into identity and marries the woman who *is* his mother. Oedipus, that is, lacks the saving difference brought about by the passage of time, and hence experiences the repetition compulsion not figuratively but as a literal truth. But as with Freud's inability to escape the "ideal situation of childhood," the same compulsion that makes Oedipus' destiny tragic also makes it heroic, for he lives out and lays down the pattern that the rest of us replicate only in attenuated form.

11
Incest
and Burial

ANY STUDY of the interrelations among Sophocles' Theban plays must begin with the recognition that they do not form a trilogy. *Antigone,* the earliest in order of composition, was probably produced in 442 B.C. and *Oedipus the King* in about 425 during the plague in the sixth year of the Peloponnesian War; *Oedipus at Colonus,* written shortly before Sophocles' death at the age of ninety in 406, was first performed posthumously in 402.[1] The difficulties of interpretation are compounded by the fact that nothing certain is known about the other two works that were performed together with each of these plays, and which may or may not have been related to them in subject matter. It must be borne in mind, furthermore, that all three plays are independent wholes, apart from their relations to any larger sequence.[2]

These important considerations notwithstanding, I wish to press the case for the unity of the Oedipus cycle. Certainly, there are minor inconsistencies from one play to the next: the "hateful and shameful" (l. 50) death ascribed to Oedipus by Ismene in *Antigone* contradicts the miraculous account of his passing in *Oedipus at Colonus;* and in *Antigone,* Creon commends the Chorus (ll. 168–70) for their loyalty to Oedipus' sons following their father's demise and asks that they now support him, whereas in *Oedipus the King* Creon seizes power immediately, and there is no question of any claim on the part of Eteocles and Polyneices.

But these discrepancies are outweighed by the evidence for continuities linking the three plays. In *Oedipus at Colonus*, above all, it is clear that Sophocles has sought to establish connections with *Oedipus the King*. In a broad sense, the plot of *Oedipus at Colonus* constitutes a reversal and an undoing of the earlier play: instead of a movement from strength and weakness, there is movement from weakness to strength; and Oedipus, rather than attempting to circumvent the predictions of oracles, now aligns himself with the forces seeking their fulfillment.[3] The parallels between *Oedipus the King* and *Oedipus at Colonus* are announced as early as the first word, since the address of the aged Oedipus to his daughter Antigone, *teknon* ("child"), recalls that of the proud king to his assembled people, *tekna* ("children"). The speeches of Oedipus opening both plays, moreover, are each thirteen lines long and divided into units of eight and five lines, marked by the transition *alla* ("but").[4] Most significantly, Sophocles in *Oedipus at Colonus* has Oedipus allude (ll. 87–95) to his visit to the Delphic oracle recounted in *Oedipus the King* (ll. 788–93), where it had been foretold that he would kill his father and marry his mother, only Oedipus now discloses for the first time a new aspect of the prophecy—that he would find his final resting place in a grove of the Furies, whence he would become a blessing to his friends and a curse to his enemies. This direct reference to *Oedipus the King* in *Oedipus at Colonus*, and the transposition of Oedipus' fate into a new register, epitomizes the continuity between the two plays. Finally, it is noteworthy that in *Oedipus at Colonus* Sophocles attempts to smooth over the previous discrepancies in the accounts of the succession to the Theban throne, since Ismene explains (ll. 367–73) that the two sons—who, after all, were young boys at the time of Oedipus' fall—agreed *at first* to resign the throne to Creon, only to change their minds and battle with one another as they grew older. Whether one judges Sophocles' effort to obtain coherence to be skillful or maladroit is less important that the fact that he makes it at all, because the very undertaking shows his desire to preserve the unity of the Oedipus cycle.

If in *Oedipus at Colonus* Sophocles looks back to *Oedipus the King*, he also bears in mind the impending action of *Antigone*. After his futile appeal for support from Oedipus, Polyneices implores Antigone and Ismene (ll. 1409–10) to bury him if he should fall in his imminent expedition against Thebes. *Oedipus at Colonus* ends, similarly, with Antigone's request to Theseus (ll. 1767–72) to send her and Ismene back to "primeval Thebes," to try to prevent the threatened bloodshed between their brothers. Thematic parallels between *Oedipus the King* and *Antigone* are established primarily through the character of Teiresias, where the explicit reliance on the metaphor of blindness in Oedipus' case makes his collision with the prophet a more profound restaging of that involving Creon in the earlier play. Both rulers use the word *kerdos* ("profit") to impugn Teiresias' motives, and thus are shown by Sophocles to be oblivious to their own spiritual advantage.[5] *Oedipus at Colonus* is the knot that ties the Oedipus cycle together, but it seems likely that Sophocles intended his spectators to recall *Antigone* when they saw *Oedipus the King* performed in the Theater of Dionysus; and it forcefully underscores the magnitude of his achievement to realize that this interlacing between plays written at widely separated intervals is a phenomenon unique in extant Greek tragedy.[6]

Indeed, the remarkable nature of the links between Sophocles' Theban plays is better appreciated by us—modern readers in possession of written texts—than by his contemporaries in a predominantly oral culture. For, knowing as we do the sequence in which the plays were composed, as well as the fact that they narrate a continuous story, we are impelled to read them in *two* different arrangements simultaneously: the order of composition *(Antigone, Oedipus the King* and *Oedipus at Colonus)* and the order of the unfolding plot *(Oedipus the King, Oedipus at Colonus,* and *Antigone)*. It follows that the pivotal play in any discussion of the Oedipus cycle as a whole is *Antigone,* since it may be regarded either as a beginning or an ending. A further corollary is that the Oedipus cycle possesses *two* endings—*Antigone* and *Oedipus at Colonus*—which qualify and react upon one another. Recast in more theoretical terms, the implication of the double arrangement of the Theban plays is that they invite a reading that is at once *synchronic* and *diachronic*. The use of the term "Oedipus cycle" comes to seem most appropriate, because the word "cycle" is derived from the Greek *kuklos,* meaning "circle." The dual status of *Antigone* as both initial and final play, and the necessity of bearing in mind both the sequences of composition and fable, importantly distinguish Sophocles' handiwork from a typical trilogy such as the *Oresteia*.

The appropriateness of a synchronic as well as a diachronic reading justifies the bringing of structruralism to bear on the Oedipus cycle. But there is a second rationale for structuralist analysis that reinforces that derived from our knowledge of the dates at which the plays were written. As we have already observed from various standpoints, the consequence of Oedipus' incest is a doubling of kinship ties that freezes the passage of time and makes Oedipus the contemporary of both his parents' and his children's generation. Since Oedipus' children are, as it were, indistinguishable from himself, what we are given in *Antigone* is an externalized representation of the meaning of his own destiny. By virtue of the special conditions created by the purely intrinsic theme of incest, a synchronic reading of the Oedipus cycle becomes not merely possible but mandatory, and the dangers of "impressionism" and excessive arbitrariness of interpretation that mar Lévi-Strauss' own application of his method are correspondingly reduced.

Oedipus is not, of course, himself a character in *Antigone*. But insofar as the play enacts a working out of his fate, he exerts even in death a controlling influence on the action. This is the view expressed in what I take to be the most penetrating nineteenth-century interpretation of *Antigone*—that of Kierkegaard in Volume I of *Either/Or:*

That which in the Greek sense affords the tragic interest is that Oedipus' sorrowful destiny re-echoes in the brother's unhappy death, in the sister's collision with a simple prohibition; it is, so to say, the after effects, the tragic destiny of Oedipus ramifying in every branch of his family. . . . When, therefore, Antigone in defiance of the king's prohibition resolves to bury her brother, we do not see in this so much a free action on her part as a fateful necessity, which visits the sins of the fathers upon the children. There is indeed enough freedom of action in this to make us love Antigone for her sisterly affection, but in the necessity of fate there is also, as it were, a higher refrain which envelops not only the life of Oedipus but also his entire family.[7]

The chief merit of Kierkegaard's commentary is that it recognizes the centrality of the motif of the family curse to *Antigone*. Although allowing for a degree of "freedom of action" in Antigone's burial of Polyneices, Kierkegaard justly argues that the appearance of freedom must be subordinated to the "necessity of fate," and that this fate involves in particular "the after effects, the tragic destiny of Oedipus ramifying in every branch of his family."

As in so much of his thought, Kierkegaard in his reading of *Antigone* is implicitly challenging the dominant ideas of Hegel. According to Hegel, of course, *Antigone* is fundamentally a political drama, in which Antigone and Creon, as representatives of the opposition between "*divine* and *human* law, law of the nether world and law of the upper world, the one the *family*, the other *state sovereignty*" (*PM*, p. 739), are portrayed by Sophocles with even-handed sympathy. More recent critics have disputed Hegel's contention that there is a balance between Creon and Antigone, and a consensus has emerged that the moral scales are distinctly tipped in Antigone's favor.[8] Kierkegaard goes even further, however, by questioning Hegel's assumption that *Antigone* is best understood as a political tragedy.

The suggestion that *Antigone* is governed by the motif of the inherited curse gains credence from the connections between Sophocles' play and the Labdacid trilogy of Aeschylus, which garnered the first prize in 467 B.C. Although the authenticity of the final 100 lines of *Seven Against Thebes* has been disputed,[9] this controversy does not affect the fact that the last play of Aeschylus' trilogy concludes with the deaths of Eteocles and Polyneices at each other's hand in the successful Theban repulse of the Argive invasion, events which have taken place just prior to the opening of *Antigone*. In the first line of *Antigone*, Antigone addresses Ismene as *autadelphon* ("very sister"), a word apparently coined by Aeschylus in line 718 of *Seven Against Thebes* to describe the relation between Eteocles and Polyneices;[10] and in line 511 Antigone declares that there is no disgrace in honoring *tous homosplanchous* ("those of the same womb"), a word whose only other recorded usage is in line 890 of *Seven Against Thebes*. Most instructive is the similarity between the second stasimon (ll. 720–91) of *Seven Against Thebes*, where Aeschylus recapitulates the action of his entire trilogy, and the second stasimon (ll. 582–625) of *Antigone*, where the Chorus recount the history of the afflicted house of Labdacus by using the identical metaphor of a beach struck by successive waves of the sea; and both Sophocles' thought and language are directly indebted to Aeschylus.[11]

In my analysis of *Oedipus the King*, I placed considerable emphasis on the fact that Sophocles had suppressed the traditional motif of the inherited curse and constructed the drama from Oedipus' point of view. In *Antigone*, however, we see Sophocles relying extensively on this Aeschylean conception of tragedy. A comparison of the two plays suggests, first, that Sophocles—though already in his fifties and a mature artist at the time of writing *Antigone*—expresses his own vision of tragedy with greatest distinctiveness in *Oedipus the King*. But still more relevant to the present discussion is the further conclusion that, if the transgressions of Laius are not germane to *Oedipus*, but those of Oedipus are essential to *Antigone*, then the character of Oedipus is pivotal to all three plays of the Oedipus cycle. It is noteworthy that, whenever Ismene and Antigone lament the workings of the family curse in *Antigone*, they refer to the incestuous marriage of Oedipus and Jocasta, and *not* to any more distant nemesis incurred by Laius.[12] The upshot of Sophocles' manipulation of the motif of the inherited curse, in short, is to make his perspective on the entire myth *Oedipus-centered*, and thus to align it proleptically with that of Freud.

Hegel's interpretation of *Antigone* in terms of the conflicting principles of the "upper world" and the "nether world" is firmly grounded in the evidence of the text. In the speech in which Teiresias condemns Creon for his twin crimes of denying burial to Polyneices and consigning the living Antigone to a tomb, he proclaims:

> for you have first of all thrust below one of those in
>   this world,
> and dishonorably settled in a grave a living soul,
> and furthermore you keep in this world one belonging
>   to the gods below,
> a corpse unburied, unhallowed, unholy. (ll. 1068–71)

Earlier in the play, when Antigone offers to Creon her philosophical justification for disobeying his edict, she affirms:

> For Zeus was not the one who proclaimed these things
>   to me,
> nor did Justice who dwells with the gods below
> establish such laws among human beings. (ll. 450–52)

Concerning these lines, Karl Reinhardt has remarked that " 'Zeus' and 'Dike' [Justice] are the two terms of a polar expression here," and what Antigone invokes is therefore "the all-embracing, the whole, of which this deed of hers is a part."[13] A similar "polar expression" is found in Teiresias' imprecation to Oedipus in *Oedipus the King*:

> Do you know from whom you are? And you are
> ignorant that you are hateful
> to your own kin beneath and on earth above.
>
> (ll. 415–16)

Again Reinhardt's commentary is most pertinent:

"Beneath" and "on earth" are the two polar extremes which stand for the whole range of blood relationships, as in the prophecy in the *Antigone* [1068–73], where the totality of all nature is expressed by the phrases "this world" and "below," "living" and "a corpse."[14]

By returning us to Teiresias' denunciation of Creon in *Antigone*, Reinhardt points out the recurrence of the opposition between the realms of life and death throughout the Oedipus cycle.

But it is precisely the thematic connection of *Antigone* to *Oedipus the King* that reveals, not the incorrectness, but the incompleteness of a Hegelian reading. For if "polar expressions" of a similar kind persist in Sophocles' other Theban plays, a structuralist analysis suggests immediately that these "pairs of oppositions" must be seen as part of a single system. And, as it requires only the easiest transition from structuralism to psychoanalysis to note, these binary crossings of life and death may all be traced back to the primordial confusion of categories in incest.

Oedipus' self-blinding with Jocasta's brooches in *Oedipus the King*, I have had occasion to argue, makes explicit through reenactment the equation of love and death that inheres in the original act of incest. In addition to the polarity of "this world" and "the gods below," a confounding of the opposites of death and sexuality pervades *Antigone*. As she goes to her underground vault, Antigone apostrophizes: "O tomb, o wedding-chamber" (l. 891), and the Chorus allude to Danaë's imprisonment in a "sepulchral bridal-chamber" (l. 947). Similarly, the Chorus' tribute to man's awe-inspiring accomplishments in the "ode on man" is qualified only—and utterly—by the fact that "From Hades alone / he cannot devise an escape" (ll. 361–62); but in the third stasimon it is love (l. 787) from which there is no escape.[15] If, as I believe, these "polar expressions" cannot be adequately understood without reference to incest, then Hegel's attention to political themes addresses only the level of "manifest content," and needs to be supplemented by a Kierkegaardian and psychoanalytic recognition that the obsession with burial in the play is determined at the level of "latent content" by the "fateful necessity, which visits the sins of the fathers upon the children."

Both my hypotheses—that the permutations of the theme of burial are an outcome of Oedipus' forbidden return to the womb of Jocasta, and that Antigone herself is motivated by incestuous impulses—are likely to be met with considerably skepticism in some quarters. A vehement protest is that of A. J. A. Waldock:

> I would suggest that we may dismiss all ideas of Antigone as abnormal. . . . If we label her fixated, that is chiefly, I think, because we have a fancy for such fixations and a desire on principle to find them.[16]

But Waldock's objection to a psychological approach to Antigone is overcome by the evidence that she is impelled to bury Polyneices in large measure by a longing for death. Early in the play, when Creon admonishes the Chorus not to lend comfort to those who performed the treacherous deed of burial, they reply: "No one is such a fool that he loves to die" (l. 220). Unwittingly, in dismissing the idea of a person who "loves to die," the Chorus hit upon one true explanation for Antigone's conduct.[17] Throughout the prologue, Ismene seeks to dissuade Antigone from her senseless undertaking, telling her: "You have a hot heart for cold things" (l. 88). Once again, the diagnosis is entire accurate, for Antigone's "hot heart" is her passion and the "cold things" the impossible that is another name for death. Antigone herself repeatedly confirms that she belongs to the dead, as in the subsequent stichomythic exchange in which she rebuffs Ismene's plea to be allowed to share the responsibility for her action:

> Cheer up! You are alive, but my soul died
> long ago, so as to be of service to the dead.
>
> (ll. 559–60)

Antigone's living burial perpetuates her ambiguous state of death-in-life, and her statement that she "died / long ago" indicates that her twilight condition had its inception in her mother's marriage bed.

As might be expected on theoretical grounds, what may be termed the necrophilic motif of the play is intertwined at every turn with that of incest. One has only to accept at face value the meaning of the words used by Antigone to speak to her "dearest brother" *(adelphōi philtatōi)* (l. 81) Polyneices:

> It is beautiful for me to die doing this thing.
> A dear one I shall lie, with him a dear one,
> stopping at nothing to do holy deeds.   (ll. 72–74)

R. P. Winnington-Ingram has commented sensitively on the nuances of Antigone's diction:

Polyneices was her brother (21, 45), her kin—and so a *philos*. The word can, but need not, connote deep affection; the superlative *philtatos* surely must do so. . . . It can be no accident that, when she speaks of her state in death (73), she is made to use language . . . appropriate to lovers.[18]

Exactly like the English equivalent "I shall lie," the Greek original *(keisomai)* hovers in meaning between the sleep of love and the sleep of death; and in this equivocation are registered the erotic underpinnings of the motives for Antigone's action.

Antigone's speech of self-vindication to Creon, where she links "Zeus" and "Justice" in a "polar expression," continues with her famous invocation of "the unwritten and steadfast laws of the gods," which "are not of today or yesterday, but live / everlastingly, nor does anyone know when they appeared" (ll. 453–54, 456–57). Once again, these lines from *Antigone* resonate throughout the Theban plays. Antigone's "unwritten and steadfast laws" are identical with those "high-footed established laws" worshiped by the Chorus in *Oedipus the King,* in which "great is the god, nor does he grow old" (ll. 865–66, 871). In *Oedipus at Colonus,* analogously, Oedipus informs Theseus that "to the gods alone / old age does not happen, nor do they ever die" (ll. 608–9); and later he thunders his curses at Polyneices:

> Therefore they conquer your supplication and your
> thrones,

if indeed there is Justice spoken of old,
seated together with the ancient laws of Zeus.

(ll. 1380–82)

The recurrence of the same "polar expression" used some thirty-five years earlier by Antigone in Oedipus' vituperation of Polyneices is further vivid evidence for the unity of the Oedipus cycle. The impossibility of disentangling Oedipus' all too human anger at his faithless son from the workings of divine justice, moreover, suggests that a similar fusion of subjective and objective determinants is at work in Antigone's resistance to Creon. As Seth Benardete has acutely noted, the lines in which Antigone speaks of the laws "not of today or yesterday" enjoining burial "could equally serve to characterize the prohibition against incest."[19] But this initially implicit connection between Antigone's embodiment of the divine law of burial and her own incestuous origins only becomes fully articulated in her subsequent defenses of her conduct.

No portion of *Antigone* has generated more controversy than the speech containing the lines (ll. 904–20) in which the heroine declares that she would not have violated Creon's edict against burial for a son or for a husband, but only for a brother. This passage underlies Hegel's celebration of the "unmixed intransitive" bond between brother and sister:

> The brother, however, is in the eyes of a sister a being whose nature is unperturbed by desire and is ethically like her own; her recognition of him is pure and unmixed with any sexual relation. . . . The loss of a brother is thus irreparable to the sister, and her duty towards him is the highest. (*PM*, p. 477)

But though Hegel's views on kinship stem from an acute sensitivity to Sophocles' tragedy, his argument rests on the untenable assumption that sibling love is "unmixed with any sexual relation." One of the earliest to challenge this view was Goethe, in his conversation with Eckermann of March 28, 1827:

> "I would have thought," Goethe replied, "that the love of sister for sister was still purer and more asexual! For we would have to overlook that innumerable cases have been met with, where between brother and sister either knowingly or unknowingly a sensual inclination has been found."[20]

Goethe's pre-Freudian awareness of the incestuous dimension of the attachment between siblings gains authority from the fact that just such a revelation had formed the dénouement of *Wilhelm Meister's Apprenticeship* (1795–96). Ironically, Goethe himself goes astray when he proceeds to indict the pivotal lines from Antigone's speech as a "blemish" and voice the hope that they might be shown to be an interpolation, but in undoing Hegel's idealization of sibling love he points the way to a juster appreciation of *Antigone*.

Although Goethe's desire to prove the spuriousness of lines 904–20 has in the past gained a number of distinguished adherents, few scholars today would defend their excision.[21] There is, in the first place, a considerable amount of historical evidence for the authenticity of the passage. As is well known, Antigone's speech is cited by Aristotle in the *Rhetoric* (1417 a) as an example of how to present an implausible argument; thus, if there is corruption in the text, it would have had to take place in the period— less than a century—between Sophocles and Aristotle. In addition, the fact that the lines are imitated from an incident in Herodotus' *Histories* (3.119) likewise tends to confirm their genuineness, as Sophocles' work contains frequent borrowings from his friend Herodotus. (The objection that in Herodotus the woman pleading with King Darius is forced to choose which of her living relatives she wishes to save, whereas Antigone appraises her duty to bury the dead, only reflects the transposition of this motif of choice into the world of Sophocles' tragedy.) The speech, finally, contains a delicate example of ring composition, such as would be characteristic of Sophocles, as its central portion is framed by lines beginning with the words "of which law . . ." *(tinos nomou)* (l. 908) and "By this . . . law" *(toiōide . . . nomōi)* (ll. 913, 914).

But to reinforce these contextual and formal arguments, a psychoanalytic reading justifies the apparent extravagance of Antigone's loyalty to her brother on thematic grounds. In the most disputed lines—those encircled by ring composition—Antigone says:

> If on the one hand my husband were to die, there
>   would be another,
> and a child from another man, if I were to lose the
>   first;

> but on the other hand with my mother and father
> covered in Hades,
> there is no brother who might ever shoot forth.
>
> (ll. 909–12)

Jebb, who rejects this speech as the work of an interpolator, raises an objection in his note to line 910: "Why is it assumed that the first husband died before, or with, his child? The two hypotheses of loss should have been kept separate." Does it not seem that Sophocles—or his imitator—has committed a blunder? But an elegant, and highly plausible, answer to Jebb's query is proffered by Benardete. Antigone, he points out, "assumes that if her son died she would need another husband to have another son; and only one condition would make that inevitable: if her son were her husband. Antigone imagines herself another Jocasta."[22] Simply by following the logic of Sophocles' text, Benardete shows that this ostensible blemish conceals a thematic complexity, one that connects these lines to the entire Oedipus cycle.

The idea of weighing the comparative degree of intimacy of various kinship ties may seem foreign to modern readers. Walter Kaufmann, for example, commenting on Hegel's paraphrase of Antigone's argument, writes: "If we take these generalizations at face value, they are silly. One cannot rank human relationships in this way."[23] But though Kaufmann dismisses the endeavor as "silly," to fifth-century Athenians the problem of "ranking human relationships" was sufficiently urgent to be debated in tragedy. The central dilemma of Aeschylus' *Oresteia* (458 B.C.) concerns the injunction imposed on Orestes to avenge the murder of his father Agamemnon by killing his mother Clytaemestra. In the *Eumenides*, Orestes is acquitted of matricide and released from persecution by the Furies on the grounds that the killing of a husband is more heinous than the killing of a mother and, furthermore, that only the father and not the mother is the true parent of the child. Aeschylus, whose trilogy is a teleological myth accounting for the founding of the Athenian high court of the Areopagus and glorifying the rule of law, takes the view that the contractual relationship of marriage is superior to the bond between mother and child. In Lévi-Strauss' terminology, he grants priority to *affinity* over *descent*. Sophocles, by contrast, as befits a drama dominated by incest, depicts in *Antigone* a world in which *consanguinity* is of overriding importance. In so doing, he shows himself to be working within the tradition not only of Aeschylus' Labdacid trilogy but also of the *Oresteia,* and to be deliberately reverting to an archaic outlook that had been surmounted by his precursor.[24]

The most comprehensive summation of the interlocking themes of death, incest, and the inherited curse occurs during Antigone's earlier *kommos* or lyric dialogue with the Chorus. In response to the latter's unpitying judgment,

> Upon proceeding to the utmost rashness
> against the high pedestal of Justice
> you fell precipitously, child.
> And you are repaying some paternal ordeal
>
> (ll. 853–56),

Antigone pours forth her most impassioned speech:

> You have touched
> my most painful care—
> the thrice-repeated doom of my father
> and the destiny
> of us all
> the renowned Labdacids.
> Alas the maternal calamities
> of the marriage-bed and the self-engendered
> couplings of my mother with my ill-fated father—
> from such as these was I engendered wretched in mind
> toward them accursed, unmarried thus
> I go an alien.
> Alas, ill-destined brother,
> you obtained your marriage,
> dying you killed me yet living.[25]   (ll. 857–71)

Although Antigone rejects the imputation of the Chorus that her punishment is just, she accepts wholeheartedly their suggestion that her suffering stems from her father, the mention of whom releases in her the floodgates of emotion.

The language of choral passages is customarily more compressed and elliptical than that of dialogues in iambic trimeter, but Antigone's lines in lyric meter are rendered especially ambiguous by their attempt to convey the involutions of incest. In the phrase I have translated "self-engendered / couplings" *(koimēmata t' autogennēt'),* it is impossible to determine whether the words refer primarily to Jocasta and mean "intercourse with him whom she bore" or to Oedipus and mean "intercourse with her who bore him." This semantic indeterminacy corresponds to that produced by the incestuous union between mother and son. In the ensuing line, the words I have translated "from such as these" *(hoiōn . . . poth'),* taking them as personal and governed by "mother" and "father," might easily be construed as "from such couplings," if *hoiōn* is read as neuter rather than masculine plural. Antigone's origin, that is, is constituted as much by the fact of incest as it is by the individual identities of her parents.

But perhaps the most resonant ambiguity is that in the final three lines, where Antigone invokes her "ill-destined brother" who gained his marriage but in death destroys her life. Who is the brother of whom Antigone speaks? In the first instance, it is unquestionably Polyneices, who secured his command of the Argive expedition against Thebes by marrying Argeia, daughter of King Adrastus, and thereby sealed Antigone's own death. Although it is not mentioned in the text of *Antigone,* the story of Polyneices' marriage to Argeia belongs to the legendary material that would undoubtedly have been familiar to Sophocles' audience. But can Antigone also be thinking of Oedipus? Jebb will not hear of such an idea: "Not Oedipus. Such an allusion would be too repulsive here."[26]

Jebb's moralism offers no argument against the possibility that Antigone refers both to Oedipus and to Polyneices, but in order to justify this interpretation more compelling evidence in its favor is needed. Such corroboration can best be secured by carrying on with our attempt to set *Antigone* in the context of the Oedipus cycle. First of all, it is relevant to note that Oedipus explicitly characterizes himself as his daughters' brother both in *Oedipus the King* and in *Oedipus at Colonus.* "Come / to these my fraternal hands" (ll. 1480–81), he implores his daughters after his self-discovery in *Oedipus the King.* In *Oedipus at Colonus,* Oedipus has the following anguished exchange with the Chorus on the subject of his daughters:

> OEDIPUS: My two children, and curses . . .
> CHORUS: Zeus!
> OEDIPUS: They sprang from the travail of a common
> mother.

> CHORUS: They are your offspring and—
> OEDIPUS: Yes, kindred sisters of their father.
>
> (ll. 532–35)

In his realization of the double nature of his tie to his children, Oedipus confirms the truth of Teiresias' prophecy in *Oedipus the King*:

> He shall be shown to be to his own children
> at once brother and father, and of the woman
> from whom he was born son and husband, and of his
> father
> sharer of the same seed and murderer.   (ll. 457–60)

In view of Sophocles' pervasive insistence on Oedipus' identity as Antigone's brother as well as father, the balance of probability inclines rather toward including than excluding a reminder of Oedipus beneath the obvious reference to Polyneices in Antigone's appeal to her "ill-destined brother."

The climax of Teiresias' denunciation of Oedipus is one of the most stirring passages in *Oedipus the King*. In the Greek original, the effect is far stronger than in an English translation, since the words "and father," "and husband," "and murderer" fall in exactly the same place in their respective lines. Sophocles reiterates the word *kai* ("and") throughout the speech to build to a crescendo the description of the doubling that afflicts Oedipus' relations with his children, his mother, and his father. What I have been forced to render periphrastically "sharer of the same seed" is in Greek the single word *homosporos*. Teiresias' use of this word is especially powerful because it echoes an earlier speech where Oedipus explains, more truly than he knows, his motivations for seeking out the murderer of Laius:

> I have the power that he had formerly,
> and have also his marriage-bed and his wife sharing
> the same seed,
> and there would have been generated common ties of
> children in common,
> had not his race had bad luck.   (ll. 259–62)

When Oedipus alludes to the misfortunes encountered by the "race" of Laius, he means that Laius died childless, and thus prevented the two rulers of Thebes from having children by the same woman. But Laius, of course, did not die without issue; and

the word for "race" *(genos)* could equally well mean "offspring."
With consummate dramatic irony, therefore, Sophocles makes
Oedipus speak unwittingly of himself, his "bad luck" being precisely that he did *not* die. Similarly, when Oedipus specifies that
his tie to Laius consists in their possessing in Jocasta a wife "sharing the same seed" *(homosporon)*, he intends no more than that
she has been married both to his predecessor and to himself. But
the normal meaning of *homosporos* is "descended from the same
seed," and thus on Teiresias' lips it gains its full force to disclose
that Oedipus is both his father's killer and incestuously equated
with him in the maternal womb they have both inseminated.[27]

Not to be overlooked in Oedipus' statement of solidarity with
Laius is his contemplation of what he believes to be the hypothetical possibility that he and Laius might have shared "common
ties of children in common" *(koinōn te paidōn koin' av)*. Crucial here
is the iteration of the forms of *koinos*, for the same word is found
in lines 533 and 535 of Oedipus' exchange with the Chorus in
Oedipus at Colonus, where I have translated "common" and
"kindred." When it is added that *koinos* is the very first word of
Antigone—Antigone addresses Ismene as *ō koinon autadelphon Is-
mēnēs kara* ("O kindred, very sister head of Ismene")—it cannot
be doubted that it contains a buried reference to the incest of
Oedipus, and that it strikes a keynote for the entire Oedipus
cycle.[28]

One final consideration may be offered concerning Antigone's
appeal to her "ill-destined brother." In the Second Messenger's
climactic speech in *Oedipus the King*, as we have seen, we learn of
Jocasta's suicide. Tearing her hair and "hurling straight toward
the marriage / bed" (ll. 1242–43),

> she calls on the long-dead Laius of heretofore,
> remembering the ancient sowings, from which
> he died himself, and left her the mother
> to his own offspring a bearer of ill-born children.
> And she mourned the bed, wherein, wretched, double
> she bore a husband from her husband and children
>   from her child.   (ll. 1245–50)

As in Antigone's recollection of the "self-engendered / couplings"
by which she was procreated, Jocasta's memory of "ancient
sowings" fuses the act of intercourse with the children that are its

product. The word I have translated "sowings," *spermatōn*, means literally "seeds," and thus refers to actual coitions, but is frequently used in the sense of "offspring." The simple words "from which," analogously, may either be construed impersonally or personally; in the latter case, they would be masculine rather than neuter plural, and mean "by whom." Laius, that is, is killed in overdetermined fashion both by his son Oedipus and by the sexual activity at the marriage bed that is itself a crossroads.

Most noteworthy, however, is the simple fact that, at her moment of death, Jocasta thinks not of Oedipus but of her first husband Laius. It is as though, with Jocasta's realization that she is mother to Oedipus, the entire action of the play momentarily flashes backward one generation in time. In view of the synchronicity of the Oedipus cycle, it makes sense that Antigone—on the point of death in her own play—should likewise confound generations, and allow her thoughts to turn to the brother who is also her father, the "after effects" of whose marriage have destroyed her life.

12
Binary Oppositions and the "Unit of Kinship"

I_N "STRUCTURAL Analysis in Linguistics and in Anthropology," the essay in which he defines the ties of consanguinity, affinity, and descent as the minimal requirements for the formation of "the unit of kinship," Lévi-Strauss singles out the "maternal uncle" as the "necessary precondition for the structure to exist."[1] The role of the maternal uncle—the man who gives the bride away to her husband—is indispensable in kinship systems because Lévi-Strauss regards society as founded upon a process of exchange in which "a man must obtain a woman from another man who gives him a daughter or a sister." (Although he acknowledges the "theoretical possibility" that women could exchange men, Lévi-Strauss argues on "empirical grounds" that "it is the men who exchange the women, and not vice versa.") This theory of the exchange of women between exogamously related men underpins Lévi-Strauss' anthropological defense of "the universal presence of an incest taboo."

As the challenges of Masson, Balmary, and Krüll to the Oedipus complex pointed the way to our reading of *Oedipus the King*, so Lévi-Strauss' emphasis on the avunculate opens up a valuable critical perspective on *Antigone*. For Creon, as Jocasta's brother, stands in the relation of maternal uncle to Oedipus. In the present chapter I propose to amplify my previous hypothesis that the burial theme in *Antigone* depicts the working out of the confusion between life and death—womb and tomb—that inheres in the original act of incest. In particular, I shall argue that beneath the "manifest" political conflict between Antigone and Creon the play is structured by a "latent" struggle between Creon and the spirit of Oedipus for control over the family.

The importance of Creon's identity as maternal uncle of Oedipus must, however, be brought into relation with a second crucial feature of the play amenable to structuralist analysis—its obsessive concern with binary oppositions. This motif discloses itself above all in the fact that from Oedipus' marriage with Jocasta are born *two* sons and *two* daughters. The doubling of kinship ties that results from Oedipus' commission of incest, that is, is mimetically reproduced in the "third" generation of his family by this binary distribution of progeny.[2] My previously advanced contention that *Antigone* portrays an unfolding of the meaning of Oedipus' destiny is borne out by a recognition that this doubling of sons and daughters is not a random occurrence, but a direct outgrowth of his own incest. If, moreover, the action of the play is controlled by an inherited curse—originating, in Sophocles, with Oedipus—that curse has the effect of creating an *identity* between Oedipus' two sons, and a *difference* between his two daughters. Creon, however, in granting burial to Eteocles but not to Polyneices, seeks to impose a *difference* between the brothers; and in vowing to punish Ismene as well as Antigone for the crime of burial, he tries to establish an *identity* between the sisters. This attempt by Creon to undo and invert the binary pattern of identity and difference imposed by the fate of Oedipus constitutes the underlying antagonism of *Antigone*.[3]

The symmetrical distribution of sons and daughters in *Antigone* carries with it a revealing insight into the earlier history of the Oedipus legend. For in the scattered allusions to Oedipus contained in the epics of Homer and Hesiod, there are several important differences from the canonical versions of the story familiar from fifth-century tragedy. Specifically, when Odysseus descends to the underworld in Book 11 of the *Odyssey*, he meets Oedipus' mother—here named Epikaste—who relates (ll. 271–

81) that their incestuous marriage was made known "immediately" by the gods and that Oedipus, though pursued by maternal furies, continued to occupy the throne of Thebes. The word "immediately" *(aphar)* has caused difficulty at least since the time of Pausanias (2d century), who wondered (9.5.11) how the truth could have been made known *aphar,* if Oedipus had four children by Epikaste. He explains that these were children of a *second* marriage, with Euryganeia, citing as evidence the lost *Oedipodeia* from the Epic Cycle.[4] By the time of Aeschylus, however, this second marriage has been eliminated, and the children are ascribed to Oedipus' marriage with Jocasta. Thus, although the existence and even the number of these children may have been known to epic tradition, only with the transition to tragedy does their binary arrangement acquire a connection to incest. In conjunction with other narrative developments—the introduction of the self-blinding that symbolizes Oedipus' awareness of his moral pollution and the transformation of his combat with the Sphinx from the physical to the intellectual plane—this newly charged significance to his two pairs of offspring is an essential precondition for Oedipus' entry into the world of tragedy.

Binary oppositions are a stock in trade of modern structuralist analysis, but they are not therefore foreign to Sophocles' art. In the predawn conversation between sisters that opens *Antigone,* *ones* and *twos* echo like a tolling refrain. To Antigone's query whether she has learned of the latest ills to befall her family, Ismene replies:

> To me no word of our dear ones, Antigone,
> neither sweet nor painful has come since the time
> we two were deprived of two brothers
> who died on one day by a double hand.[5]

In addition to the antitheses between "sweet" and "painful" and between "one day" and "double hand," Sophocles exploits the special Greek resource of the dual number ("we two," "two brothers") to convey the solidarity between the siblings of either sex.[6] Because of Creon's edict, however, this parity between brothers has been broken, a fact indicated by Antigone through another characteristically Greek locution—the contrast between *ton men* ("the one") and *ton d'* ("the other"):

> Why, has not Creon held our two brothers of a tomb
> the one preferred, the other dishonored? (ll. 21–22)

Creon's attempted transformation of the brothers' *identity* into *difference* is distilled in Antigone's shift from the dual form ("two brothers") in line 21 to the antithetical construction ("the one," "the other") in line 22. It is, moreover, highly significant that though the sisters speak of themselves in the dual seven times in the first sixty-three lines of the play, the form is not used of them after Ismene has refused to join Antigone in the burial of Polyneices.[7]

An awareness of the avuncular relationship between Creon and Oedipus sheds light on the difficult problem of Creon's characterization throughout the Oedipus cycle. Once the tension inherent in the kinship tie between the two men is placed in the foreground, the variations in Sophocles' depiction of Creon in the three plays will seem minor in comparison with the recurrent theme of his struggle with Oedipus.[8] At the end of *Oedipus the King*, Oedipus entrusts Ismene and Antigone to the care of their "kinsman" (l. 1506) Creon, and effectively appoints him their guardian. But this surrender comes back to haunt Oedipus in *Oedipus at Colonus*, when Creon (l. 830) justifies his plot to abduct Oedipus' daughters by asserting his legal custody over them. This overt battle between Creon and Oedipus in *Oedipus at Colonus* brings to the surface their implicit collision in *Antigone*.

Even in details the consistency of Sophocles' portrait of Creon is unmistakable. In *Antigone* Creon seeks to evade responsibility for Antigone's death by means of a technicality—the leaving of a ritual portion of food in her tomb (ll. 775–76). This conduct squares with his invocation of a legalistic pretext to screen his kidnapping of Ismene and Antigone in *Oedipus at Colonus*, where it is contrasted with the genuine piety of Theseus, who interrupts his sacrifices to Poseidon to come to Oedipus' rescue. Nor is it entirely true to say, as does F. J. H. Letters, that Creon in *Oedipus at Colonus* is "simply the unscrupulous politician," whereas in *Antigone* he "at least honestly believed he was right."[9] For even in *Oedipus at Colonus* Creon insists (ll. 832, 880) on the righteousness of his cause; and, though he is clearly condemned by the action of the play, it does not follow that he is therefore unpersuaded by his own rationalizations.

Creon in *Oedipus the King* does not display the glaring villainy of *Oedipus at Colonus* and *Antigone*, but it is latent in him nonetheless. His superficiality, the absence of a "heroic temper,"[10] is common to all three plays. Part of his argument to Oedipus in *Oedipus at Colonus* (ll. 755–58) is that the latter should return to Thebes so as to hide his pollution. Similarly, at the close of *Oedipus the King* (ll. 1424–29), he urges Oedipus to conceal himself within the palace as quickly as possible. The same concern with appearances manifests itself early in the play when, upon his return from Delphi, Creon asks Oedipus (ll. 91–92) whether he is to report the oracle before all the people or the two men are to withdraw inside the palace, clearly implying his own preference for the second alternative.

In *Oedipus the King*, no less than in *Oedipus at Colonus*, there is a heated conflict between Oedipus and Creon. Although Oedipus' suspicions of a conspiracy between Creon and Teiresias are unfounded, Creon's self-satisfied protestation that he is contented with merely being second in command is sophistical and unconvincing. He avers:

> I certainly am not desirous myself
> to be a tyrant rather than to do tyrannical things,
> nor is anyone else who knows how to think soundly.
>
> (ll. 587–89)

The fallaciousness of Creon's reasoning is revealed by his abuse of the verb *sōphronein* ("to think soundly") to justify a devious preference for the substance rather than the trappings of tyranny, instead of recognizing that one who was truly *sōphrōn* would abjure tyranny altogether. In this dissembling lie the seeds of Creon's will to power, which is fully exposed only in *Oedipus at Colonus* and *Antigone*. Despite being written later than *Antigone*, *Oedipus the King* shows Creon at an earlier stage of his career; but such a capacity to move backward as well as forward in time is intrinsic to Sophocles' artistry in the Oedipus cycle.

Our knowledge of Creon's character aids in the elucidation of a troubling line at the end of *Oedipus the King*. When pressed by Oedipus to grant his request for immediate exile from Thebes, Creon replies: "For the things I do not mean I do not love to speak in vain" (l. 1520). The difficulty lies in determining whether Creon accedes to or denies Oedipus' petition, for the same verb I have translated "do not mean" *(mē phrōnō)* could equally well be rendered "do not understand." In this second case, the response would be a denial, under the pretext that the matter rested in the lap of the gods. That is, indeed, the construction given to the words in *Oedipus at Colonus*, when Oedipus—in another direct reference back to *Oedipus the King*—offers (ll. 765–71) as one of his harshest attacks on Creon the reproach that he would not grant the boon of exile when it had first been requested, but only later, after Oedipus had reaccustomed himself to living in Thebes. A sense of the irreconcilable enmity between Creon and Oedipus precludes our reading Creon's response as an outright acceptance, or seeing his conduct in the last scene of the play as wholly charitable; but it does accord with Creon's character to take the point of the line to be its equivocal phrasing, its pragmatic forestalling of the need to give a definite answer one way or the other.

Oedipus' relationship with Creon does not escape the doubling present in all his kinship ties. For, on the surface, the two men are brothers-in-law; the avuncular bond between them depends on the hidden fact that Jocasta is Oedipus' mother. Terence Turner has interestingly suggested that the ambivalent behavior of Creon and Oedipus toward each other stems from this structural ambiguity, since as a rule "the avuncular relationship is generationally asymmetrical and supportive, while the brother-in-law relationship tends to be generationally symmetrical and fraught with conflict." In this view, Creon generously offers Oedipus Jocasta's hand in marriage if he can defeat the Sphinx; but once the marriage has been consummated, Creon "as wife's brother becomes a latent rival and opponent of Oedipus."[11] Turner's effort to correlate the positive and negative poles of the Oedipus–Creon relationship with its avuncular and fraternal aspects is perhaps too neat, but it does have the advantage of allowing for displays of friendship while recognizing their fundamental antagonism. Because of the interplay of familial and political themes throughout the Oedipus cycle, moreover, it may be inferred that the recurrent contest between the unheroic nature of Creon and Oedipus' unyielding heroism centers at once on the throne of Thebes, to which they both aspire, and on the woman Jocasta who symbolizes that throne and who serves as a medium of exchange between them.[12]

As our structuralist perspective enables us to offer a coherent interpretation of the character of Creon in the three Theban plays, so it allows us to take a position on the difficult problem of the character of Antigone in her play. Although few critics would go so far as to condemn her for possessing a "tragic flaw,"[13] it is impossible to deny that, in C. M. Bowra's words, she "seems forbidding and unfriendly," particularly in her dealings with Ismene, and that "her sense of duty seems to have dried up all human feelings except love for her brother."[14] Indeed, once Ismene refuses to participate in the burial of Polyneices, as R. P. Winnington-Ingram justly observes, Antigone "uses words of enmity, of hating. Ismene is in Creon's camp, and there, for Antigone, she remains."[15] As we have noted, no dual forms are employed by either of the sisters following Ismene's demurral, and Antigone's language becomes increasingly vituperative:

> I would not urge it, if you should yet wish
> to act, nor find it pleasing should you join with *me*.
>
> (ll. 69–70)

When Ismene volunteers at least to keep silence, Antigone retorts:

> Ah, speak it out! You shall be far more hateful
> being silent, if you do not proclaim these things to all.
>
> (ll. 86–87)

Antigone taunts Ismene by tying her to Creon, because the verb "proclaim" *(kēruxēs)* is the base form of the noun "proclamation" *(kērugma)*, which she had earlier (l. 8) used to refer to Creon's edict. Antigone's most violent outburst in the prologue, after Ismene prays her not to undertake the impossible, occurs during her final speech:

> If you shall speak these things, you shall be hated by
> me,
> and shall justly obtain hatred from the dead.
>
> (ll. 93–94)

Such a reaction seems far in excess of what is called for by Ismene's gentle efforts at dissuasion, and from the prologue alone it would be difficult to tell that our sympathies are meant to lie with Antigone.

The harshness in Antigone's character is, if anything, still more in evidence in the second epeisodion, when she brushes aside Ismene's plea to share in the responsibility and hence in the punishment for her action:

> But justice will not allow you this, since
> you were not willing, nor did I make common cause.
>
> (ll. 538–39)

Most telling in this allusion to her earlier rebuff at lines 69–70 is Antigone's insistence that she did not "make common cause" *('koinōsamēn)* with Ismene, because this implies that Ismene is no longer her "kindred" *(koinon)* sister as she had been in the first line of the play. The same word appears in Antigone's verbal thrust several lines later: "Do you not die in common *(koina)* with me, nor make your own / the things you did not touch" (ll. 546–47). To Ismene's lament that she will not be able to live alone, Antigone answers: "Love Creon! For you are his protector" (l. 549). Again, as in her earlier use of the verb "proclaim," Antigone underscores her point with a verbal association, since the word for "protector" *(kēdemōn)* is normally used for the care bestowed on the sick or the dead, and thus suggests that Ismene ministers to Creon in the way that she ought to have done to the corpse of Polyneices.[16] Antigone must be taken at her word when she goes on to explain: "For you on the one hand chose to live, but I on the other to die" (l. 555); and, in light of her scathing tone throughout this exchange, it is impossible to read her injunction that Ismene "Cheer up!" (l. 559) as anything except a bitter irony.

The path to a correct interpretation of Antigone's character is not to overlook or deny its crueler features, but to seek to comprehend their inevitability. Winnington-Ingram hits the mark with his statement that Ismene is, for Antigone, "in Creon's camp." From the standpoint of my own explanatory model, since the destiny of Oedipus requires that there be a *difference* between his two daughters, Antigone must resist any attempt by Ismene to shift her allegiance from Creon to Oedipus. Only Antigone, that is, is singled out as the heir of her father's "heroic temper," and it is Ismene's fate—along with that of Eteocles and Polyneices— to be relegated to insignificance.

My analysis may, perhaps, be made clearer with the help of some simple algebraic notation. From Oedipus' point of view, the curse imposed upon Eteocles and Polyneices makes both sons *identical* and *negative* (− −). Ismene, likewise, is for Oedipus allied to Creon and opposed to Antigone, who alone acknowledges the overriding claims of consanguinity, which extend beyond Polyneices to her father/brother Oedipus. Thus, Ismene must be awarded a minus sign and only Antigone a plus sign (− +). But this pattern is, as I have argued, inverted by Creon, who seeks to impose a *difference* between the two brothers—favoring through burial the loyal Eteocles but not the traitor Polyneices (+ −). Similarly, he transforms Oedipus' *difference* between the two sisters into a *negative identity*, by striving to punish the innocent Ismene as well as the genuinely culpable Antigone (− −). The minus signs that adhere not only to Eteocles and Polyneices but also to Ismene, in Oedipus' view, exemplify the fact that all three non-heroic children are indeed "in Creon's camp," despite Creon's own unavailing efforts to distinguish between the enemy brothers. For our reading of the prologue, the implication of this structuralist model is that, although it appears that Ismene might have chosen to join Antigone in performing the forbidden burial, in reality her decision was determined in advance. Exactly this blend of seeming freedom and underlying necessity is captured by Kierkegaard in his description of the way that in Antigone's burial of Polyneices "we do not see . . . so much a free action on her part as a fateful necessity," and that the action of the entire play is enveloped by the "higher refrain" of "Oedipus' sorrowful destiny."

The Chorus recognize the extent to which Antigone is her father's daughter when they brand her "the savage offspring of a savage father" (l. 471).[17] It is a curious paradox that Antigone, who declares to Creon in one of her most famous lines, "It is not my nature to join in hating *(sunechthein)* but in loving *(sumphilein)*" (l. 523), should display such enmity toward her well-meaning sister. But it is pertinent to recall that Oedipus, who in the supremely moving conclusion of *Oedipus at Colonus* assures his daughters:

> But one word alone
> dissolves all these toils.
> For of loving [*philein*] there is no one from whom
> you will receive more than from me, deprived of whom
> you must now spend the remainder of your life
>   (ll. 1615–19),

is the same man who earlier unleashed violent storms of fury against both Creon and Polyneices. Indeed, Oedipus in his diatribe against Creon condemns the latter's blandishments as "noble in word but evil in deeds" (l. 782), an antithesis that recurs in Antigone's indictment of Ismene: "I cannot love a dear one whose dearness is in words" (l. 543). Thus, the parallel between Antigone in *Antigone* and Oedipus in *Oedipus at Colonus* is matched by that between Ismene and Creon; and in *Antigone* Ismene conspicuously shares Creon's belief in the natural inferiority of women to men (see ll. 61–62, 679–80). In addition to confirming the "fateful necessity" of Ismene's siding with Creon, this dovetailing of earlier and later plays again points up the indissoluble unity of Sophocles' conception in the Oedipus cycle.

An acceptance that the "savage" behavior of Antigone toward Ismene is motivated by her claim to be the sole heir of Oedipus' heroism—with its capacity for extremes of hatred as well as love—immediately clears up a puzzle in Antigone's final lines in the play. Addressing the Chorus, she says as she is led off the stage:

> Behold, you commanders of Thebes,
> the sole remaining royal daughter,
> what things I suffer from what men,
> for revering reverence.   (ll. 940–44)

In his note to this passage, J. C. Kamerbeek comments: "To my mind the ignoring of Ismene remains strange. . . . I feel inclined to assume a very old and deep corruption in these lines." Kamerbeek is right to draw attention to the strangeness of Antigone's denial of Ismene's existence, but his reaction—"to assume a very old and deep corruption in these lines"—duplicates the mistake of those who would excise the lines where Antigone vows that she would not have violated Creon's edict against burial except for a brother. My working hypothesis, on the contrary, is to assume the soundness of the received text, and to allow its seeming oddities to open us to radical possibilities in the domain of interpretation. In this case, the inference should be that Antigone means exactly what she says—that Ismene, having sided with Creon, is no longer a daughter of Oedipus.

The same confidence in the inner logic of the play enables us to take a no less firm position on what is, after lines 904–20, the second most problematic feature of the text of *Antigone*—the fact that Antigone nowhere refers to her betrothal to Haemon. To remedy this apparent deficiency, editors—beginning with Aldus in 1502 and followed by Jebb and others to the present day— have disregarded manuscript authority and changed the speaker of line 572, "Dearest Haemon, how your father dishonors you!" from Ismene to Antigone. In like fashion, line 574, "But will you deprive your child of this maiden?" is frequently assigned to the Chorus rather than to Ismene. A negative exemplum is in this instance supplied by H. D. F. Kitto, who, in defending the authenticity of lines 904–20, writes: "The play does in fact make perfectly good artistic sense as it stands, so that we will not require an explanation which requires us to reconstruct it."[18] Unfortunately, when Kitto comes to the attribution of line 572 he violates his own excellent dictum, for he asserts of Haemon and Antigone that "these two young people really are in love with each other," but the "implied affirmation from Antigone herself is wanting."[19]

In a familiar pattern, the emending critic justly calls attention to an undeniable peculiarity in the play—here, Antigone's silence with regard to Haemon—but incorrectly responds to it by changing the text to suit his preconceptions rather than attempting to determine what the artistic purpose of Sophocles' apparent anomaly might be. Ironically, moreover, just as the genuineness of the lines borrowed from Herodotus is somewhat more certain than most of the rest of the play, since they were quoted by Aristotle, so the reassignment of lines 572 and 574 is objectionable on formal as well as thematic grounds, since they occur in the course of a stichomythic dialogue between Ismene and Creon, which would be disrupted by the introduction of extraneous characters.

The conscious design in Antigone's failure to mention her love for Haemon becomes perceptible when it is realized that, in the lost Euripidean version of *Antigone*, Haemon assists his beloved in the burial of Polyneices, marries her, and fathers her child.[20] The reason for what Richmond Lattimore has aptly called "the refused story of star-crossed lovers"[21] in Sophocles' play is simply that, since Antigone has given her all to consanguinity, she has nothing left over for affinity. Indeed, in the very forcibleness of Ismene's appeal to "dearest Haemon"—often adduced as an argument why the line should be given to Antigone—there lies a cogent reason by Antigone cannot be the speaker, since she had already used the same superlative (*philtath'*) in line 81 of Polyneices. In the desire of Euripides and some editors and critics to create a romance between Haemon and Antigone—even going so far as to save Antigone's life—one may find a counterpart to Nahum Tate's rewriting of *King Lear*, in which Cordelia is preserved from death and marries Edgar. The more austere plots of Sophocles and Shakespeare have also this in common, that the tragic deaths of Antigone and Cordelia may be traced ultimately to their inability to escape incestuous fixations on their royal fathers.[22]

The equation between the "tomb" and the "wedding-chamber" is, as we know, made by Antigone herself, and it is central to the structure of Sophocles' drama. This theme reaches its culmination in the speech of the Messenger, who reports how Creon and his belated party of rescuers came upon Haemon in Antigone's tomb:

> In the back of the tomb,
> we saw clearly the one hanging by the neck,
> fastened by a threaded noose of fine linen,
> and the other lying beside her embracing her waist,
> loudly bewailing the destruction of his bride gone
> below,
> and his father's deeds and the wretched marriage.
>
> (ll. 1220–25)

The sexual imagery becomes even more explicit in the description of Haemon's suicide by the sword:

> And breathing hard he shoots forth a keen stream
> of bloody drops on her pale cheek.
> Corpse upon corpse he lies, having obtained
> the sorry burial rites in the halls of Hades.
>
> (ll. 1238–41)

This consummation of love in death—the counterpart of the scene of Oedipus' self-blinding with Jocasta' brooches in *Oedipus the King*—suggests immediately the Shakespearean analogue of *Romeo and Juliet*, as well as the joint deaths of Kleist and Henriette Vogel in real life. But a crucial difference separates the *Liebestod* in *Antigone* from these latter two examples. For though Haemon clearly slays himself out of hatred of his father and love for Antigone, there is no evidence that her own death by hanging has anything to do with *him*. On the contrary, Sophocles continues his "suppression of a developed erotic subplot"[23] to the end, playing off Haemon's illusion of a marriage in death against the indifference of Antigone, a sentiment born of her overwhelming attachment to her kinsmen Polyneices and Oedipus.

Several related interpretive problems center on the figure of Creon. Initially, when Creon is confronted by Antigone's unexpected avowal of her own culpability, he summarily decides also to punish Ismene:

> she and her kinswoman must not escape
> the worst of dooms: for I accuse equally the latter
> of having planned this burial.   (ll. 488–90)

Later in the play, however, after his bitter exchange with Haemon, Creon suddenly has a change of heart, and tells the Chorus that he will condemn only one sister: "Not the one who did not touch; for you speak well" (l. 771). This remark echoes lines 546–47, where Antigone admonishes Ismene not to lay claim to "the things you did not touch." Although Creon's reversal is amply motivated in naturalistic terms, since it may be seen as an inner weakening in response to his son's defiance, it has a structural explanation as well. The offhandedness with which he throws off his announcement that he plans to spare Ismene signals that he is simply yielding to a *fait accompli*, one stemming from the demand of Oedipus' destiny that there be a *difference* between his two daughters.

Matters stand differently, however, with regard to a second reversal undergone by Creon. For just as, after his encounter with Haemon, he pardons Ismene, so the scene with Teiresias terrorizes Creon into trying to release Antigone. But a curious inconsistency intrudes in Creon's actions. The Chorus implore him:

> Go, free on the one hand the girl from the chamber
> underground, build on the other a tomb for the one
>   lying dead.   (ll. 1100–1)

But when Creon finally comes to execute their behest, he does so in the *reverse* order, stopping first to cremate and bury the body of Polyneices, and only subsequently proceeding to the tomb of Antigone. As a result, he arrives too late, finding Antigone already hanged and Haemon transported by a murderous rage. Once again, Creon's catastrophic failure to adhere to the sequence of events ordained by the Chorus is explicable in several complementary ways. In the first place, it is motivated naturalistically, if Creon is assumed to recognize that Polyneices' burial is the more important action, since the unburied corpse is the source of the original pollution on the city. Second, Creon reveals himself to be subjected to a talismanic law, which dictates that knots must be undone in the order in which they were tied. He himself alludes to this principle in the aphoristic declaration," I myself bound and being present shall set free" (l. 1112), which conflates his literal imprisonment of Antigone with his violation of the cosmic order. Finally, Creon's inability to rescue Antigone may again simply be attributed to the preordained pattern that there must be a *difference* between the two sisters. Thus, just as his earlier decision to free Ismene does no more than ratify a requirement imposed by the structure of the play, that to redeem Antigone from her choice of death is doomed to failure for the same reason.

Yet a third deviation from his original intention on Creon's part is best comprehended in structuralist terms. At the same time that he relents toward Ismene, Creon alters the mode of Antigone's punishment (ll. 773–80) from death by stoning to imprisonment in an underground vault. In addition to elevating Antigone to the anomalous status of death-in-life, this shift makes her death thematically related to the confusion between "upper world" and "nether world" in the case of Polyneices, and allows the fate of both siblings to be seen as the outcome of the incest of Oedipus.

Both Creon's continual vacillations and his delay in arriving at Antigone's tomb are parodically reflected in the character of the Guard. At his first entrance (ll. 223 *ff.*), the Guard blusters apologetically for having taken so long to bring the news of Polyneices' burial, and in subsequent conversation only exasperates Creon by the long-windedness with which he delivers his message. As Benardete points out, the Guard "confesses without reason to the imaginary crime of tardiness," because Creon learns of it "only through his own admission."[24] The Guard, truly one of the few comic figures in Greek tragedy, resembles Shakespeare's clowns in the way his seemingly irrelevant banter leads directly to issues at the heart of the play.[25] For in convicting himself of lateness, the

Guard functions as a double of Creon, who will repeat the former's "crime of tardiness" in a tragic mode.

In identical fashion, when the Guard is dismissed with his life by Creon following their first interview, he vows: "There is no way you will see me coming hither" (l. 329). Only some fifty lines later, however, following the first stasimon, the Guard reenters with the captured Antigone in tow, and admits: "O lord, it is not for mortal men to deny an oath, / for afterthought falsifies the judgment" (ll. 388–89). This statement by the henchman applies equally to the master, for Creon too finds himself forced to abjure each of his oaths in the course of the drama. Indeed, such reversals are symptomatic of what might be termed the party of self-interest—headed by Creon, but to which Ismene and the Guard also belong—but Antigone's unswerving devotion knows only how to persevere stubbornly in the course of action she has originally chosen.

The character of the Guard is inextricably bound up with still another interpretive stumbling block in *Antigone*—Polyneices' "two burials." As often, unnecessary difficulties have arisen when critics have neglected the evidence of Sophocles' text. The suggestion that the first burial, reported by the Guard, may have been performed by Ismene[26] is wholly without foundation and contradicted by everything that happens in the play. The second unorthodox theory, first proposed by S. M. Adams and revived by Marsh McCall,[27] that not Antigone but the gods effected the first burial, though it cannot be discounted entirely, likewise requires modification in light of the evidence. For the Guard's statement (ll. 427–28) that Antigone cursed those who uncovered the body makes no sense unless she carried out the burial in the first place.[28]

Nonetheless, it is undeniably true that a divine aura surrounds not only the first burial of Polyneices but also the second. When the news of the first burial is announced by the Guard, and the culprit is mysteriously described as being "without a sign" (l. 252), the Chorus incense Creon by voicing the thought: "O lord, deep meditation has long deliberated in me, / whether this deed is not even something god-sent" (ll. 278–79). Subsequently, after Polyneices' body has again been stripped bare on Creon's orders, supernatural intervention is unmistakable in the dust storm—termed by the Guard a "heavenly distress" (l. 418) and a "divine sickness" (l. 421)—which arises to shroud Antigone as she returns to the corpse for a second time. At the same time that Antigone is in the grip of the family curse and prompted by intensely personal loyalties, she is the agent of divine law and justice; and the effect of the supernatural sanction for her actions is to show that these two levels of meaning are ultimately interchangeable.

In addition to its religious dimensions, the motif of double burial offers Sophocles some purely dramatic advantages. By allowing Creon to find out about the fact of Polyneices' burial before learning the identity of the perpetrator, as Kitto notes, Sophocles creates "an interval of partial knowledge"[29] that heightens the effect of the eventual disclosure of Antigone's guilt. In psychoanalytic terms, this strategic delay conforms to the theory of "deferred action," with its assumption that there must be a conjunction between a "first scene" and "second scene" in the formation of a trauma. Indeed, the very point of Polyneices burial may be thought to reside in the necessity of its repetition, given that *Antigone* is a play pervaded by doublings and binary oppositions. But it should be added that Polyneices is actually buried not twice but three times, for he is finally laid to rest by Creon near the end of the play. Although the funeral rites performed by Antigone were presumably sufficient to permit Polyneices' soul to pass to the underworld, Creon had still to attend to the burial for his own sake, to attempt to atone for his earlier transgressions. In so doing, he thereby restores the violated *identity* between Oedipus' two sons.

There is, finally, a strikingly perfunctory quality to the burials Antigone does perform. As Jebb observes in his note to line 80:

She speaks as if she hoped to give him a regular sepulture. This is ultimately done by Creon's command (l. 1203), though the rites which Antigone herself performs are only symbolical (255, 429).

When the Guard first tells of Polyneices' burial, he specifies: "for he disappeared from view, not entombed, / but fine dust was upon him, as if by one fleeing a curse" (ll. 256–57). Antigone's "only symbolical" appeasement of the obligation to bury Polyneices by coating his body with "fine dust" finds a structural counterpart in Creon's equally "symbolical" attempt to evade responsibility for Antigone's death by leaving a ritual portion of food in her tomb.

Examined in the context of the entire play, however, it is Polyneices, Ismene, and all those belonging to Creon's "camp" whose
destiny does not exceed the merely "symbolical," whereas Antigone shares with Oedipus what may be called a "full-scale" fate
of heroic proportions.

If *Antigone,* like *King Lear,* depicts a world divided into rival
"camps," which—despite the structural balance between Antigone and Creon—are in moral terms roughly those of good and
evil, the question arises: on whose side does Haemon belong? For
Haemon seems to exhibit both the capacity for reversal that characterizes the "party of self-interest" and the unwavering devotion
that would align him with Antigone. In other words, he is caught
between his conflicting roles as son and bridegroom. Upon his
first entrance in the play, when Creon demands his unquestioning
obedience, Haemon pledges: "Father, I am yours" (l. 635). During
the ensuing scene, however, Haemon gradually tacks about, reporting the whispered belief of the people that Antigone is "worthy to obtain golden honor" (l. 699), to the point where he ends
up 180 degrees from where he started. "Then she will die, and
dying will destroy another" (l. 751), he ambiguously threatens,
in words assumed by Creon to be directed against himself, but
intended by Haemon to refer to his own impending suicide.

But though Haemon does mediate between Creon and Antigone, several lines of argument converge to show that he remains
within the orbit of his father. When the Messenger describes the
scene of carnage at the tomb, he does so in a highly self-conscious
language. "Haemon *(Haimōn)* has perished; by his own hand he
is bloodied *(haimassetai)*" (l. 1175). Through an etymological pun,
the Messenger links Haemon's name with the Greek word for
blood *(haima),* thus disclosing how Creon is undone by the very
principle of consanguinity he has sought to deny.[30] There is a
further equivocation in the Messenger's line, because the word
autocheir ("by his own hand") could equally well mean "by a
kinsman's hand," these concepts not being lexically distinguished
in Greek. Thus, the Chorus are forced to ask for grammatical
clarification: "By his father's, or by his proper hand?" (l. 1176),
in order to understand exactly what has occurred. Murder and
suicide, for Sophocles no less than for Freud, are but two outcomes
of a single "narcissistic formation," in which subject and object

are blurred in an act of violence that is at once *intrapsychic* and *interpersonal*. Indeed, Haemon in his fury first attempts (ll. 1231–34) to slay his father, before turning his sword on himself. By thus ending *Antigone* with what is in effect the murder of a son by his father, Sophocles completes the pattern begun at the outset of the Oedipus cycle with the killing of a father by his son in the prehistory of *Oedipus the King*.

Creon confirms his responsibility for the deaths of Haemon as well as of his wife Eurydice in his final speech of the play:

> Would you people lead a vain man out of the way,
> who killed you, my son, unwillingly,
> and you [Eurydice] before me likewise, woe is me
> unhappy! (ll. 1339–41)

Attentiveness to the question of the apportionment of culpability helps to clear up a frequently noted oddity about the end of the play, paralleling Antigone's silence concerning Ismene in her final speech—the fact that in the last 100 lines, as Creon bemoans the deaths of his wife and son, he makes no mention of Antigone. In accordance with our principle of taking seriously apparent oddities in the text, this omission may be interpreted simply as an indication that Creon is genuinely free of guilt in the case of Antigone, who took her own life and, more importantly, is under the sway of Oedipus. As early as the first speech of the play, Antigone differentiates between those "evils derived from Oedipus" (l. 2) and "evils proceeding toward our dear ones from our enemies [i.e., Creon]" (l. 10), and this distinction is preserved throughout *Antigone*. Ironically, therefore, Creon's hypocritical device of leaving a token portion of food in the tomb *does* suffice to clear him and the city of guilt for Antigone's death. In the same way, Haemon's initial declaration, "Father, I am yours," carries unexpected oracular force, despite his subsequent reversals, and it helps indirectly to account for the completeness with which Haemon is ignored by Antigone up to the moment of her death. Even Ismene, who "chose to live" when Antigone chose death, receives her fate to the letter, for she is not mentioned again in the play following Creon's announcement at line 771 that she has been spared.

Eurydice makes no more than a fleeting appearance in *Antigone*. She speaks only nine lines, and is clearly introduced by

Sophocles to heighten the pathos endured by Creon at the close. As is so often the case, however, this naturalistic explanation for Eurydice's appearance dovetails with that supplied by structuralist analysis—here, the need to create a symmetry between the families of Creon and Oedipus. Shortly before she is led to her rocky vault, Antigone utters an imprecation against Creon:

> Well then, if these things [i.e., her punishment] are
> beautiful in the eyes of the gods,
> through suffering we might acknowledge that we have
> erred;
> but if these men are erring, may they suffer no greater
> evils
> than those they unjustly do to me.   (ll. 925–28)

Antigone's prayer that Creon might meet with "no greater evils" than her own finds a striking echo in *Oedipus at Colonus*, when the blind Oedipus curses Creon for attempting to kidnap him:

> Therefore to you yourself and to your race
> may the all-seeing god Helios grant at some time
> to grow old in life in such a way as I have done.
>   (ll. 868–70)

Both the threats of Antigone and Oedipus come true with uncanny literalness. As the Chorus in *Oedipus the King* "count [Oedipus] equal / even to those not living" (ll. 1186–88) after his fall, so at the end of *Antigone* Creon calls himself one "not being more than nothing" (l. 1325). Analogously, the Messenger brands Creon a "breathing corpse" (l. 1167), thereby discerning in him the same confusion between life and death he had inflicted on Antigone.[31] The homology between the fates of Creon and Oedipus is reinforced by the fact that both lose their wives to suicide. Indeed, the ominously silent departure of Eurydice (ll. 1244–45) in *Antigone* recalls—or prefigures—that of Jocasta (l. 1072) in *Oedipus the King*.

Sophocles accentuates the interpenetration between the families of Oedipus and Creon through the changes rung on the word *autocheir*, aptly termed by Kamerbeek in his note to line 52 "a keyword of this play." In this line, Ismene emphatically reminds Antigone of the way their father smote his eyes "himself with a self-working hand" *(autos autourgōi cheri)*. Subsequently, the word is used by Creon (l. 172) to describe the simultaneous deaths of

Eteocles and Polyneices and in his admonition to the Guard to find the "very doer" (1. 306) of Polyneices' burial; and it is spoken by Antigone (1. 900) when she takes pride in having performed the funeral rites not only for her two brothers but also for her father and mother. (In *Oedipus the King,* moreover, Oedipus applies the term *autocheir* to the murderer of Laius [ll. 231, 266] and to his own self-blinding [1. 1332)]). Thus, when Haemon is reported by the Messenger (1. 1175) to have perished *autocheir,* or Eurydice is said (1. 1315) to have pierced herself in the liver in the same fashion, the implication is clearly, as Charles Segal has written, that "Creon's house doubles with its chaotic opposite, the house of Oedipus."[32]

Unlike the "chaotic" house of Oedipus, however, that of Creon is not thrown into confusion by incest. As a result, the kinship ties surrounding Creon lack the incessant doubling that prevails in the family of Oedipus. Before her death, Eurydice curses Creon (1. 1303) not only for the death of Haemon but also for that of her *other* son Megareus, who, according to legend, voluntarily sacrificed his life to fulfill a prophecy that only by the death of a descendant of the original Spartoi would Thebes succeed in repulsing the Argive invasion.[33] On the one hand, this allusion to Megareus confirms the resemblance between Creon and Oedipus in that both suffer the loss of two sons. On the other hand, because Megareus is so shadowy a figure in the play, and because there is no connection between his death and Haemon's, it remains true that what occurs singly in the house of Creon is, as it were, refracted in duplicate in that of Oedipus.

For Lévi-Strauss, the avunculate or relationship between brothers-in-law is "the necessary axis around which the kinship structure is built," but it is only through the birth of children that "the dynamic and teleological character of the initial step, which establishes kinship on the basis of and through marriage," is validated. He continues:

The initial disequilibrium produced in one generation between the group that gives the woman and the group that receives her can be stabilized only by counterprestations in following generations. Thus, even the most elementary kinship structure exists both synchronically and diachronically.[34]

In the Oedipus cycle, the "groups" engaged in exchange are personified individually by Creon and Oedipus, and because of the entanglements produced by incest it is not possible finally to differentiate between generations. But it is assuredly true that Sophocles' three plays must be read "both synchronically and diachronically," and that the restoration of "equilibrium" through Oedipus' "counterprestations" with Creon involving the two sons and two daughters born of his marriage with Jocasta constitutes the overarching action of *Antigone*.

13

The Heroization
of Oedipus

AT THE close of *Oedipus the King*, as
Oedipus pleads with Creon to expose him for a second time on
Mount Cithaeron, he has a sudden change of heart:

> And yet I know at least this much, that neither sickness
> nor anything else might destroy me; for I would never
> have been spared from death, unless for some dread
> evil.[1]

The exact nuance of this passage depends on the meaning one
gives to the last two words, *deinōi kakōi*, which I have rendered
"dread evil." *Deinos*, it will be recalled, is the same elusive word
used to describe man in the first stasimon of *Antigone*, which
Hölderlin translates into German as *"Ungeheuer"* and Heidegger
as *"unheimlich,"* and of which the semantic field in English spans
the range of "strange," "wonderful," and "terrible." *Kakon*, as a
substantive, normally has the straightforward meaning of "evil"
or "ill." Jebb, however, translates the phrase "strange doom,"
and comments in a note that "the poet of Colonus gives Oedipus
a presentiment that his end is not to be as that of other men."[2]

Jebb perhaps goes too far in softening the tone of despair that
accords with Oedipus' state of mind at his nadir in *Oedipus the
King*, but he is nonetheless right to call attention to the "presentiment" of *Oedipus at Colonus* at the end of the earlier play. Only in

the course of the *Colonus*, where he reveals the full extent of the prophecy made to him by Apollo, does Oedipus realize that the fate for which he has been spared is not a "dread evil" but a "strange doom" that is not less, but more, exalted than that of other men. But as *Oedipus at Colonus* revises and amplifies the meaning of *Oedipus the King* as a whole, so the earlier play looks ahead to its sequel, and the unity of Sophocles' entire conception in the Theban plays is again much in evidence.

In *Oedipus at Colonus*, then, Sophocles completes and at the same time brings into existence the Oedipus cycle. But this closing of the "circle" *(kuklos)* has two interrelated aspects. On the one hand, Sophocles finishes the story of Oedipus; but on the other, he lays the groundwork for what is to come in *Antigone*. Insofar as *Oedipus at Colonus* concerns the individual destiny of its hero, that is, it is a final play; but to the extent that it concerns the whole family of Oedipus, it has a sequel in a tragedy written some forty years earlier. This double perspective on *Oedipus at Colonus* as both "middle" and "final" play is dictated by the unique tension between narrative sequence and order of composition in the Oedipus cycle.

It is illuminating for an appreciation of this hybrid quality of *Oedipus at Colonus* to examine it in relation to Aeschylus. In *Antigone*, as we have seen, Sophocles begins the Oedipus cycle strongly under Aeschylus' influence, particularly in his borrowing of the motif of the family curse from *Seven Against Thebes;* secondarily, I have argued, he revises the *Oresteia* by replacing Aeschylus' emphasis on the contractual relationship of marriage with his own insistence on the more primitive ties of consanguinity. In *Oedipus the King*, however, Sophocles radically departs from his predecessor in suppressing the inherited curse and making Oedipus a representative hero of self-knowledge. But in *Oedipus at Colonus* Sophocles again reverts to a pronouncedly Aeschylean mode and, as in *Antigone*, draws both on the Labdacid trilogy and on the *Oresteia*.

As might be expected, the impact of *Seven Against Thebes* is shown most vividly in the resurgence of the theme of the family curse, which binds *Oedipus at Colonus* to *Antigone*. In the course of the play, Oedipus purges himself of the stain of his incest and patricide, but pronounces a terrible malediction on Creon, his two sons, and the city of Thebes. In a direct echo of the second stasimon (ll. 730–34) of *Seven Against Thebes*, which is likewise a source for the account of the deaths of Eteocles and Polyneices at each other's hand in *Antigone* (ll. 143–46), Oedipus informs Creon of the legacy he has bequeathed to his two sons:

> and for my sons there is of my land
> just so much to obtain, wherein only to die.
>
> (ll. 789–90)

The same crucial Aeschylean choral passage—already evoked in a parallel description of the doomed house of Labdacus in *Antigone*—is once more imitated by Sophocles when the Chorus compare the afflictions suffered by Oedipus in old age to "some northern shore that from all sides / is agitated by the waves of winter" (ll. 1240–41).[3]

But whereas the precedent of *Seven Against Thebes* comes into play in Sophocles' representation of "primeval Thebes" (ll. 1769–70) and of the nemesis that overtakes the line of Cadmus, that of the *Oresteia* is found in the glorification of Athens and in the working out of Oedipus' fate as an individual. Most profoundly, just as the *Oresteia* begins in *Agamemnon* in the city of Argos with a curse on the house of Atreus, but concludes in the *Eumenides* with that curse transformed into a blessing for the city of Athens, so *Oedipus at Colonus* depicts a movement from Thebes to Athens, which brings about the expiation of Oedipus' pollution.[4] The role of the Furies in the final play of Aeschylus' trilogy is recalled by their function as custodians of the grove into which Oedipus wanders at the outset of *Oedipus at Colonus*.[5] In general terms, both the *Oresteia* and *Oedipus at Colonus* are teleological myths designed to confirm the providential care bestowed on the city in which they were performed: the founding of the Areopagus through the resolution of Orestes' trial in the former corresponds to the special protection vouchsafed Athens by the burial of Oedipus in the latter. But this ostensible similarity is lent immense pathos by the fact that, whereas the *Oresteia* basks in the afterglow of Athens' triumph early in the fifth century in the Persian Wars, *Oedipus at Colonus*, written barely more than fifty years later, is in effect an elegy for the city on the verge of final defeat by Sparta in the Peloponnesian War.[6]

In the double nature of Sophocles' indebtedness to Aeschylus, therefore, there is a fitting emblem for the bifold vision of *Oedipus at Colonus* itself. As critical misjudgments concerning *Oedipus the King* are regularly due to a flattening out of its dialectical quality, so those pertaining to the *Colonus* often stem from a neglect of its place in the Oedipus cycle as a whole. The most glaring example of this error is provided by C. M. Bowra's declaration: "At the end of *Oedipus at Colonus* no unresolved discords remain, no mysteries call for an answer."[7] But Bowra's neglect of the final *kommos* (ll. 1670–1750) and exodus (ll. 1751–59), which return us to the earthbound and grief-stricken perspective of Antigone and Ismene, is justly criticized by R. P. Winnington-Ingram, who points out that "Antigone walks straight out of the play to meet her tragic death in *Antigone.*"[8] The fact that *Oedipus at Colonus* is part of a larger design, and expressly connected by Sophocles to *Antigone*, in other words, deprives the play of the closure it would have if read entirely on its own and as concerned exclusively with the fate of Oedipus.

Although this contention has been resisted by some critics,[9] it must be recognized that *Oedipus at Colonus* is in all essentials a sacred drama. The focus of the mystery in the play—Oedipus' passing—has never been described better than in the words of Nietzsche's friend Erwin Rohde:

One and only one is lifted by the divine grace clear of the human fate of annihilation, and in the Grove of the Erinyes the sorely tried Oedipus is translated without seeing death out of this earthly life. So living a reality to this poet of ancient piety is the conviction that the divine miracle of translation is a literal truth, that he is ever ready to make this strange circumstance serve as the sole aim and purpose of a whole drama: a miracle which all the other scenes serve not so much to prepare as simply to postpone, and thus heighten the expectancy with which the event is awaited.[10]

There is, unquestionably, as Peter Burian has observed, much "confrontation and contest" in *Oedipus at Colonus*, particularly in the scenes with Creon and Polyneices, but he is wrong to draw the conclusion that it is "not a sacred pageant."[11] On the contrary, like Shakespeare's *Tempest*—another play that self-consciously marks the close of a career—*Oedipus at Colonus* possesses a "rich and strange" masquelike quality, due to the fact that the action is controlled ultimately by the protagonist, and thus the threats posed to Prospero and Oedipus by their respective antagonists are known by the audience from the start to be illusory and ineffectual.[12]

As we have already found in our discussion of *Oedipus the King*, psychoanalysis—as a resolute humanism—must address even religious issues in terms of their meaning for *man*. In the case of *Oedipus at Colonus*, this does not mean denying or minimizing the "divine miracle of translation" portrayed by Sophocles, but consists rather in understanding Oedipus' "heroization"—that is, the process by which he becomes a *heros*, or superhuman being, whose spirit retains after death power over the affairs of men—in terms of the inner logic of the myth.[13] More specifically, this mystery must be seen as a final unfolding of the meaning of Oedipus' incest, as it pertains both to himself and to his family, and in its larger political and religious dimensions.

Despite being the longest extant Greek tragedy (1779 lines), *Oedipus at Colonus* is distinguished by its tautness of construction. Such unexpected developments in the action as there are—as when, in the first epeisodion, Theseus' arrival is preempted by Ismene's unforeseen embassy from Thebes, or, in the fourth epeisodion, when Polyneices' entrance as a suppliant postpones for two hundred lines the apotheosis of Oedipus—all contribute to the cumulative effect, and in no way render the plot "episodic."[14] In particular, the process of heroization that is "the sole aim and purpose" of the drama is announced in the opening scene of the play. Upon being told that he has trespassed into the grove of the "all-seeing Eumenides" (l. 42), Oedipus declares that he will never allow himself to be moved from the place where he has found "the token of my fate" (l. 46). As part of his full disclosure of the prophecy made to him by Apollo in *Oedipus the King*, Oedipus foreshadows the climax of the play by announcing that his end will be accompanied by "an earthquake, or some thunder, or the lightning of Zeus" (l. 94). Because of the intimate connection between the prelude to the play and its finale, it is true that the lengthy intervening scenes which "serve not so much to prepare as to postpone" Oedipus' passing are diminished in importance.[15] As Theseus remarks when he learns that the protection afforded by Oedipus depends on his burial, "You ask indeed for the last things of life, and those in the middle / you have in forgetfulness or hold as nothing" (ll. 583–84). In its own way, therefore, *Oedipus at Colonus* imitates the "condensation" of *Oedipus the King*, which depends on a structure of overspecified poles—marriage bed and deathbed—and a collapsed or nonexistent middle.

This broad resemblance between the structures of the two plays is part of the larger pattern in which *Oedipus at Colonus* constitutes both a repetition and an undoing of *Oedipus the King*. The blind and helpless Oedipus at the start of the *Colonus* seems to have stepped directly out of the end of *Oedipus the King*, but by the close he has assumed in reality the godlike status he had falsely arrogated at the outset of the preceding play. When Oedipus dispenses, in Bernard Knox's words, "angry, merciless justice" to Creon in *Oedipus at Colonus*, he reenacts the scene in which he charges the latter with treason in *Oedipus the King*; but whereas formerly Oedipus had exemplified "the tragic inadequacy of human knowledge, certainty and justice," on this occasion he "is justified."[16] In assuring the Athenian Stranger, "However much we speak, we shall speak seeing all things" (l. 74), Oedipus confirms his identification with the prophetic role of Teiresias; and in sending Polyneices to his doom, he is in effect cursing a double of his former self.[17]

Freud himself never attempted to extend his analysis of the Oedipus myth into *Oedipus at Colonus*. Focusing on Oedipus' line in his exchange with Ismene, "When I am no more, in that moment am I a man?" (l. 393), however, Jacques Lacan argues that "Oedipus' psychoanalysis ends only at Colonus. . . . This is the essential moment which gives its whole meaning to his history."[18] What is at stake in Lacan's notion of "the *assumption* of one's history" has been expounded by Shoshana Felman in language scarcely less hermetic than Lacan's own. In *Oedipus at Colonus*, she writes, Oedipus "assumes his own *relation* to the discourse of the Other," and through this acceptance of "his radical de-centerment from his own ego, from his own self-image," he "awaits—and indeed *assumes*—his death."[19] As, moreover, Oedipus' downfall in *Oedipus the King* results from his failure to comprehend this riddling "discourse of the Other"—at once that of the gods and of the unconscious—so his regeneration in *Oedipus at Colonus* is accompanied by the infusion of oracular power into his own language. In Lacan's exegesis of Oedipus' "assumption of [his] history," we have perhaps the best available psychoanalytic equivalent to a religious account of Oedipus' "heroization"; and both theological and psychoanalytic critics can endorse Nietzsche's straightforward formulation that in *Oedipus at Colonus* "the hero attains his highest activity, extending far beyond his life, through his purely passive posture, while his conscious deeds and desires, earlier in his life, merely led him into passivity."[20]

If *Oedipus at Colonus* constitutes both a repetition and a reversal of *Oedipus the King,* it does so above all with respect to the deeds of incest and patricide. When Oedipus treads upon the hallowed ground of the Eumenides at the beginning of the play, he symbolically commits the crime of incest for a second time. In Mark Kanzer's words, "Again he horrifies the populace by wandering with his mother-daughter into a sacred region which symbolizes her genitals."[21] And as the play opens with "an effort to master the original trauma" of incest by reenacting it in attenuated form, it concludes by similarly undoing that of patricide, since the mysterious vanishing of Oedipus witnessed only by Theseus is in essence "a puberty rite in which father and son each renounce their death wishes against each other, and only one man emerges from the ceremony."[22]

Integral to the process of purifying Oedipus of the pollution of both of his primal offenses is their transposition from a *literal* to a *symbolic* register. *Oedipus at Colonus* lifts the guilt of Oedipus' incest and patricide, that is, *because* it enacts their repetition. Hence Oedipus' insatiable desire "to tell the affairs of my mother and father" (l. 268), always now with an emphasis on his own innocence.[23] He narrates relevant portions of his history to the Chorus, to Ismene, and—bitterly—to Creon and to Polyneices; but the innate dignity of Theseus is evinced by immediate identification of Oedipus as "son of Laius" (l. 553) and sparing him the necessity of such a recital. As a consequence of this shift brought about by repetition, moreover, Oedipus' forbidden knowledge undergoes a final metamorphosis from a curse back into a blessing, just as it had been immediately following his solving of the Sphinx's riddle. From the standpoint of *Oedipus at Colonus,* the downward movement of *Oedipus the King* is disclosed to be the moment of antithesis in a three-part dialectic, of which the never-represented confrontation with the Sphinx and Oedipus' equally veiled culminating apotheosis are the corresponding positive moments of thesis and synthesis.

But whereas for Oedipus as an individual repetition moves in a liberating spiral, for his descendants entrapped in the family curse repetition is experienced as a circular compulsion. The delicate links between *Oedipus at Colonus* and *Antigone* are shown by the way that Sophocles again treats Oedipus' sons and daughters as separate pairs, and highlights the contrasts between them. Drawing once more on Herodotus (2.35), as he did in Antigone's controversial lines on burial, Sophocles has Oedipus deliver a stinging indictment (ll. 337–45) of the "Egyptian" behavior of his sons, who remain "like virgins" at home in Thebes while his daughters "bear in their stead the evils / of your wretched father." Particularly noteworthy is the subtle distinction Sophocles makes between Ismene and Antigone. Both daughters are loyal to their father, but only Antigone accompanies Oedipus on his wanderings, Ismene having remained behind in Thebes. Upon being sighted as she first approaches, Ismene is described in the following terms by Antigone:

> I see a woman
> drawing nearer to us, mounted on an Etnean
> colt; and on her head a sun-protecting
> Thessalian hat hides her face.   (ll. 311–14)

As Campbell points out in his notes to this passage, the "picturesque" epithets call attention to the fact that Ismene is "well clothed and mounted," since "the one implies a horse of fine breed and the other denotes a comfortable and shady riding hat." It would be going too far to say that these trappings of luxury amount to a moral condemnation of Ismene, but to a reader familiar with *Antigone* the discrepancy between the outward circumstances of the sisters cannot help but possess a latent significance, which takes on its full meaning when viewed in the light of subsequent developments.

Sophocles is no less consistent in his depiction of Oedipus' sons than of his daughters. As has been frequently observed, he departs from tradition by specifying (ll. 375, 1294, 1422) that the exiled Polyneices is the *elder* of the two brothers. But though this innovation has sometimes been interpreted as "strengthening Polyneices' case by presenting him as the natural heir to the throne unjustly deposed by a younger rival,"[24] Jebb is surely right to contend in his note to line 375 that its effect is rather that "Eteocles has now a special fault, and so the curse on *both* sons is further justified." In other words, just as Polyneices is indubitably in the wrong in that he fights as a traitor against his city, so Eteocles is no less in the wrong in that he has unlawfully usurped the throne from his elder brother; and hence Oedipus' condemnation of both (ll. 421–30) for having consented to his exile from Thebes is vindicated. (Sophocles accentuates the equal culpability of the two sons by presenting their internecine strife [ll. 371–73] as having arisen spontaneously and prior to the formal curse of Oedipus.) Like Rosenkrantz and Guildenstern, it is the function of Eteocles and Polyneices to be indistinguishable. Each is sentenced to die at the other's hand, but both are entitled to burial on Theban soil. Thus, the motif of the family curse in *Antigone* that dictates that there be an *identity* between Oedipus' sons and an irreconcilable *difference* between his daughters is both foreshadowed and retrospectively accounted for in *Oedipus at Colonus*.

As in our reading of *Antigone*, moreover, once the importance of the pattern of familial dynamics is grasped in *Oedipus at Colonus*, an interpretation of the entire play falls into place. In particular, the most problematic episode—Oedipus' confrontation with Polyneices—loses much of its puzzling aspect. The issue here is: to what extent is Polyneices meant to be sympathetic, that is, contrasted with the obvious villainy of Creon? It may be granted that Polyneices' appearance in the posture of a suppliant sets him apart from Creon, and reinforces the degree to which he constitutes a regressive double of Oedipus. It is further true that Sophocles contrives to awaken pity for Polyneices due to his affection for his sisters and his persistence in a doomed cause.[25] But these considerations do not affect the fact that Polyneices is united with Creon in his ultimate regard for his own selfish interests and lack of any genuine compassion for Oedipus. Whatever sympathy for Oedipus he does express is, like Creon's, restricted only to such externals as the "hateful / aged filth" (ll. 1258–59) that covers his body, and part of a rhetorical strategy designed to advance his own cause. As Charles Segal has well remarked, "We pity Polyneices the man and his hopeless situation; but Sophocles is relentless in demonstrating that his doom is irradicably ingrained in his character."[26]

By the same token, when Theseus and Antigone plead with Oedipus (ll. 1175–1203) to hear Polyneices, they are acting with complete justice according to their lights, and they do sway Oedipus to the extent that he grants Polyneices an interview. But it is significant that neither Theseus nor Antigone reproaches Oedipus once he has pronounced his malediction on his sons.[27] Indeed, as we have seen, Antigone herself, who here displays the attractive human quality of mercy, takes on in her own play in her dealings with Ismene the same "daemonic, superhuman wrath"[28] directed by Oedipus against Polyneices. Like that of Oedipus in *Oedipus at Colonus*, the will of Antigone comes to coincide with the intentions of the gods; and her compassion in this play is thus a function of the limitations in her vision which are not surmounted until she undergoes her own "heroization" in *Antigone*.

The character of Theseus stands in stark contrast to both Creon and Polyneices—to Creon in his capacity as ruler, and to Polyneices in becoming a surrogate son to Oedipus. Unlike the hypocritical concentration of the latter on Oedipus' external degradation, Theseus distinguishes himself at once by his recognition of the common bond of humanity he shares with Oedipus:

> For I know myself that I was reared a stranger,
> just like you. . . .
> I know well that I am a man, and that I have
> no greater portion come tomorrow than do you.
>   (ll. 562–63; 567–68)

Central to the antitheseis between Theseus and both Creon and Polyneices is their attitude toward language. Whereas Oedipus' two antagonists use language for the purposes of deception, Theseus is thanked after his rescue of Oedipus' daughters in the following terms:

> for reverence at least
> I have found in you alone among men,
> and equity and straightness of speech.
>   (ll. 25–27)

Theseus, in turn, responds by assuring Oedipus: "indeed, it is not in words that I am eager to make / my life brilliant, but rather in deeds" (ll. 1143–44). Theseus' efficient action and "straightness of speech" are human counterparts to the godlike power of Oedipus' "purely passive posture" and oracular language in *Oedipus at Colonus*.

In large measure, the action of *Oedipus at Colonus* consists of the process by which Oedipus singles out Theseus—and by extension the city of Athens—as the recipient of his heroic legacy. The covenant between Oedipus and Theseus is sealed by the provision that only Theseus is permitted to behold "the mysteries not to be touched in speech" (l. 1526) of Oedipus' passing. The Greek word for "mysteries" here is *exagista*, truly a "primal word" in that it possesses the simultaneous meanings of "things most hallowed" and "things most accursed." Oedipus further enjoins his successor:

> But guard them yourself always, and when you come
> to the end of your life, to your foremost son alone
> disclose them, and let him always show them to the
> next.   (ll. 1530–32)

The secret that is to be passed from Oedipus to Theseus and then to a single chosen male heir in each ensuing generation is literally that of Oedipus' place of burial (ll. 1521–23), but is metaphorically knowledge of the forbidden crimes of incest and patricide. Theseus, that is, becomes the custodian of those impulses in human nature which, when released unchecked, may bring personal and collective disaster, but, properly buried and repressed, are indispensable to the well-being of both the individual and society.

Taken together, *Antigone* and *Oedipus at Colonus* depict the working out of Oedipus' destiny in the *familial* and the *political* spheres. Alone among Oedipus' four children, Antigone displays the heroic qualities that mark her as her father's equal. But because Oedipus' two sons labor under the curse of their unworthiness, he is forced to look outside the family for his male descendant. It is noteworthy in this connection that Theseus is told to transmit the royal secret to his "foremost" *(prophertatōi)* (l. 1531) son, which may mean either "eldest" or "most fitting," and thus leaves open

Greek Tragedy

the possibility that Theseus too may disregard birth in appointing his successor. The relation between father and son, the myth seems to imply, is primarily a spiritual one and proceeds by adoption, whereas that between father and daughter is natural and circumscribed by the family.

It is widely agreed that the final three hundred lines of *Oedipus at Colonus* sustain a pitch of sublimity unsurpassed in Sophocles. Central to the effect of the close is the reversal whereby Oedipus, formerly the blind man guided by others, himself becomes the guide leading Theseus and his daughters to his place of rest. "For I in turn have become / a novel guide for you twain, as you were for your father" (ll. 1542–43), Oedipus informs his daughters; and earlier he had spoken in like manner to Theseus: "I myself shall forthwith unfold, untouched by a guide, / the place on earth where it is necessary for me to die" (ll. 1520–21). Oedipus' physical transformation from weakness back to strength bears out Nietzsche's observations concerning the dialectics of activity and passivity in *Oedipus the King* and *Oedipus at Colonus*. Sophocles' final allusion to Oedipus' metamorphosis occurs in the *rhēsis* of the Messenger describing to the Chorus what happened to Oedipus after he passed from their sight:

> How he went hence, even you being present I suppose
> know well, with none of his dear ones as a guide,
> but he himself unfolded to us all;
> but when he came to the precipitous road,
> enrooted in the earth with brazen steps,
> he paused in one of the many-branching paths.
>
> (ll. 1587–92)

These lines spoken by the Messesnger contain one of Sophocles' most stunning reminiscences of *Oedipus the King*. For, as Jebb has pointed out in his note, the "one of the many branching paths" on which Oedipus halts during his last journey necessarily recalls "that σχιστὴ ὁδός [split road] in Phocis at which the misfortunes of his early manhood began."[29] That "split road," as we know, is not merely the site of Oedipus' murder of Laius but also a symbolic reference to the female genitalia, and is thus fittingly revisited by Oedipus in Theseus' company on the eve of his departure from this world. As in Antigone's conflation of the "tomb" and "wedding-chamber," as well as in the necrophilic fusion of eros and death in *Oedipus the King* when Oedipus rushes into the palace and calls for a sword to murder Jocasta, so in *Oedipus at Colonus* Oedipus' grave is inevitably in the region of the crossroads that is his mother's womb.

But though Oedipus becomes the leader of the other human characters, he himself remains the follower of the god. The Messenger reports that Oedipus' leavetaking from his daughters is interrupted by an imperious divine summons:

> For the god calls him many times and oft:
> "You there, you there, Oedipus, why do we have yet
> to move? For too long there is delaying by you."
> (ll. 1625–27)

As Karl Reinhardt has remarked, "The 'we' . . . with its terrifying yet tender kind of intimacy" between god and man in this passage "has no parallel in the entire range of divine voices"[30] heard by the dying in religious literature. Coming as it does shortly after the pealing of Zeus' thunder (l. 1606), this supernatural intervention provides conclusive proof that *Oedipus at Colonus* is indeed a sacred drama and that Oedipus' heroization may properly be called an apotheosis.[31]

In addition to its dramatic function within *Oedipus at Colonus*, the motif of divine guidance constitutes a decisive intertextual pivot within the Oedipus cycle as a whole. On the one hand, Oedipus' divinely led exodus from *Oedipus at Colonus* unmistakably forms a reprise to his entry into the palace in search of Jocasta in *Oedipus the King*, where the Messenger likewise stresses Oedipus' possession by a god:

> And some daemon signals to him raving,
> for it was none of us men, who were present nearby.
> But upon bellowing terribly, as if led by some guide,
> he sprang on the double doors. (ll. 1258–61)

But no less pertinent than this instance of unseen guidance in *Oedipus the King* is the episode of the dust storm as Antigone performs her second burial of Polyneices, about which Benardete has written: "She moved through the storm with the same assurance that the blind Oedipus displayed when he went unassisted to his sacred grave."[32] By this subterranean recollection of highly charged moments from his two earlier Theban plays, Sophocles contrives to make the resolution of Oedipus' fate in *Oedipus at Colonus* at once an undoing of *Oedipus the King* and a pendant to the divinely sanctioned action of *Antigone*.

The full extent to which the end of *Oedipus at Colonus* underpins the unity of the entire Oedipus cycle only emerges, however, when an additional detail pertaining to Oedipus' mysterious passing is brought sharply into focus. As we have already seen, Sophocles makes conspicuous use of "polar expresions" involving "Zeus" and "the gods below" in both *Antigone* and *Oedipus the King*. These "polar expressions" recur for a final time in *Oedipus at Colonus* because, as Sophocles emphasizes, Oedipus ends his life by being *divided between upper and lower worlds*. The Messenger describes Theseus' response to the fearful spectacle of Oedipus' disappearance:

> And shortly afterwards and without delay
> we see him doing reverence at once to the earth
> and the Olympus of the gods in the same address.
> (ll. 1653–55)

As best he can, the Messenger elaborates the event of which only Theseus has direct knowledge:

> but either some escort of the gods, or else the unlit
> base of the earth that holds the dead stood open in
> love.   (ll. 1661–62)

Employing structuralist principles, Segal comments perceptively on the ambiguity of Oedipus' transition to immortality: "His strange end, which brings him neither to Hades nor to Olympus, characteristically blurs the division between these opposite and mutually exclusive categories."[33] But this confounding of the "opposite and mutually exclusive categories" of "nether world" and "upper world" returns us to the central fact of incest. For just as Creon's confusions in the matter of burial in *Antigone* are ultimately "after effects" of Oedipus' crossing of love and death in incest, so Oedipus' own split into antithetical worlds in *Oedipus at Colonus* is the final overcoming of the same forbidden yoking of opposites.

This convergence between structuralist and psychoanalytic perspectives prompts some concluding speculations about the artistic unity of the Oedipus cycle. As we have already seen, it is essential to remember that Oedipus' apotheosis does not coincide with the end of *Oedipus at Colonus*, and that the return to the world of *Antigone* deprives the play of the closure it would have if read on its own. But there is a corollary to this subversion of *Oedipus at Colonus* by resurgence of the motif of the family curse in *Antigone*. For though *Antigone* taken in isolation is virtually "Euripidean" in its depiction of an unjust world where good suffers at the hands of evil, its unsparing bleakness is largely redeemed when it is replaced within the overarching framework of the Oedipus cycle. Antigone's burial alive, that is—no less senseless and arbitrary than the death of Cordelia when considered only in terms of a single play—becomes part of a providential design when it is aligned with Oedipus' bridging of Hades and Olympus in *Oedipus at Colonus*.

These speculations may be pushed still further. For if the action of the Oedipus cycle arises out of the commission of incest between Oedipus and Jocasta, it is impelled toward what might be termed the "metaphoric incest"[34] between Oedipus and Antigone. Examined in its totality, Sophocles' dramatization of the Oedipus myth thus includes not only the masculine Oedipus complex—in both its "positive" and "negative" aspects—but also what Rank has called "the second great complex, which has for its contents the erotic relations between father and daughter."[35] Incest itself becomes benign through repetition, not only in Oedipus' trespassing in the grove of the Eumenides, but also in his shifting of erotic allegiance from mother to daughter. And as the literal incest between mother and son transforms the womb from a place of life to one of death, so the "metaphoric incest" between father and daughter indeed renders the tomb into the "wedding-chamber" of the immortal Antigone.

Various details of Sophocles' texts are, I think, clarified by this hypothesis of a transcendental marriage between Oedipus and Antigone. In their dialogue in *Oedipus at Colonus*, Antigone addresses Polyneices as "child" *(pai)* (l. 1420), thereby implicitly casting herself in a maternal role. This same maternal identification is present as well in *Antigone*, not only in Antigone's imagining herself, in Benardete's phrase, "another Jocasta" when she blurs (ll. 909–12) the hypothetical deaths of her son and her husband, but also when she compares (ll. 823–33) her doom to that of

Niobe, whose seven sons and seven daughters were killed when she boasted of their superiority to Apollo and Artemis, the two children of Leto. Similarly, also in a lyric passage, the Chorus parallel Antigone both with Danaë pent up in a "sepulchral bridal-chamber" (l. 947) and with the unhappily married Cleopatra (ll. 977–87). These comparisons become intelligible when they are seen as having the function of defining Antigone as symbolically married and a mother.

Since old age is a second childhood, moreover, Oedipus as well as Polyneices is a son to Antigone. Certainly, her nurturing role in *Oedipus at Colonus*, again like that of Cordelia to her aged father in *King Lear*, would suggest as much. Both daughters become identified with what Freud, in "The Theme of the Three Caskets," called the last of the "three inevitable relations" a man has with "the figure of the mother" in the course of his lifetime— that is, after mother and wife, "the silent Goddess of Death," who alone "will take him into her arms" (*SE*, 12:301). Along similar lines, Kanzer has commented that, when Oedipus summons Theseus to perform the rescue of his daughters, this "shows that he no longer depends on the infantile omnipotence of earlier days but has delegated his powers to the father as the child ordinarily learns to do in his latency period."[36] Both Oedipus' appointed heirs undergo a reversal of generational roles—his daughter, Antigone, becomes his symbolic mother and his spiritual son, Theseus, likewise becomes his father. These two reversals are part of the larger pattern of undoing through repetition, whereby Oedipus, who in *Oedipus the King* takes upon himself the burden of "whatever deeds / are most shameful that come to pass among mankind" (ll. 1407–8), in *Oedipus at Colonus* is able to part from his daughters with the admonition only to remember the "one word" (l. 1615) of love. To borrow an analogy from another major mythical system of Western thought, if Jocasta is an Eve who initiates Oedipus into the forbidden knowledge of incest, then Antigone is a maternal Virgin Mary who redeems his Fall, and Oedipus encompasses within himself the typological figures of Adam and Christ. Freud, to complete the equation, is St. Paul, who makes explicit the universal nature of the story of Adam-Oedipus, which is only hinted at in the "Genesis" texts of Sophocles.

Having begun our interpretation of the Oedipus cycle by viewing *Oedipus the King* through the lens of Freud's self-analysis, it is only fitting to conclude by observing how the outcome of the Oedipus myth in *Oedipus at Colonus* bears an uncanny likeness to the history of the psychoanalytic movement. For not only did Freud turn outside his family for a male Theseus to whom he could entrust the future of psychoanalysis—at first inappropriately choosing Jung and later, again in vain, placing his hopes primarily on Rank—but he found his ideal female heir in his daughter Anna, who in fact assumed his position as leader of the psychoanalytic movement. Not without reason did Ernest Jones dedicate his biography of Freud to Anna Freud, "true daughter of an immortal sire." Freud himself, moreover, was aware of the mythic dimension of his attachment to his daughter, whom he termed on more than one occasion in later life his "Anna-Antigone" (*Letters,* pp. 382, 424). Nor can it surprise us that this "one daughter who," as Freud wrote to Stefan Zweig on May 18, 1936, "to a rare extent satisfies all the expectations of a father" (*Letters,* p. 429) was no more able than Cordelia or Antigone to break the spell of her incestuous fixation on her father and find a husband. As Freud's identification with Oedipus begins in the cradle, it extends to the grave, and spans both the roles of son and father.

There are indications that *Oedipus at Colonus* possessed specific personal and topical meanings for both Sophocles and the original Athenian audience. Sophocles himself was born in Colonus, and in this play written in praise of his birthplace at the close of his life, he is thus returning to his own origins. Colonus, furthermore, was in 407 B.C. the site of a battle in which a Theban force was defeated by Athenian cavalry; and it is likely that this event is being recalled when Oedipus promises Theseus that his tomb will protect Athens against the threats of enemies and, in particular, when he predicts (ll. 607–28) the advent of a conflict between Athens and Thebes. But though these and other biographical and historical determinants undoubtedly play a part in the genesis not only of *Oedipus at Colonus* but of all three Theban plays, Sophocles' dramas are not therefore deprived of their universality.[37] Rather, like that of Freud, it is the genius of Sophocles to have forged from the accidents of his personal and cultural history an Oedipus in whom is embodied the abiding riddle of the human condition.

Conclusion:
Life
in the Myth

IN THE Preface to his biography of Freud, Ernest Jones comments on the considerations that led him to undertake the "dauntingly stupendous" task of recounting Freud's life. One of these in particular merits our attention:

My having passed through the identical disciplines as Freud on the way to psychoanalysis—philosophy, neurology, disorders of speech, psychopathology, in that order—has helped me to follow the work of his pre-analytical period and its transition into the analytical one. (*LW*, 1:xiii)

Lionel Trilling's observation that Freud found in Jones "his pre-destined and wholly appropriate biographer"[1] is borne out by this remarkable parallel between their respective careers. Indeed, the relation between Freud and Jones is uncanny in the strictest sense, exhibiting as it does the phenomena of both repetition and doubling. If Freud's "hero's garb" was in the weaving at birth, a similar "predestination" governs Jones' calling to discipleship.

In his capacity as biographer, I have argued at the outset of this book, Jones exemplifies the situation of all those who, embarking on the path of psychoanalysis, must confront their trans-ferential dependence on Freud. Jones' identity as Freud's double is matched by our own role as doubles of Jones. Like him, we cannot escape the fact of our *secondariness* with respect to the founder of psychoanalysis. Above all, it is Freud's self-analysis that, as the inaugurating act of psychoanalysis, can never be duplicated. The unique standing of Freud's self-analysis has been institutionalized through the requirement that anyone wishing to practice psychoanalysis must submit to a training analysis, a rite of passage in which the fledgling analyst acknowledges his or her lineal descent from Freud.

But if, from one perspective, our belatedness in relation to Freud is incontestable, from another the matter is not so bleak. For, as we have seen, the identification with Oedipus that lies at the heart of Freud's personal "Conception of the Develoment of the Hero" is itself composed of an unending chain of "supplements." Whether examined in terms of biography, cultural history, or Greek tragedy, that is, Freud's exposition of the Oedipus complex in *The Interpretation of Dreams* and subsequent writings reveals the workings of "deferred action," and is thus likewise a *secondary* phenomenon. Indeed, precisely insofar as Freud's discovery of the Oedipus complex entails a repetition of Oedipus' quest for self-knowledge, Freud is himself belated with respect to Oedipus, and a double both of Shakespeare's Hamlet and his own two pivotal patients—E. and the man with "homicidal tendencies." To take this line of thought to its conclusion, since the action of *Oedipus the King* may be viewed as a delayed reenactment of Oedipus' encounter with the Sphinx, even Oedipus is, as it were, belated with respect to himself, and Sophocles' drama constitutes, in Derrida's phrase, "a supplement at the source."

Thus, although it is true that we ourselves are secondary in relation to Freud, there is a mature wisdom in the awareness that it is impossible to escape the condition of belatedness, and hence neither Freud nor Oedipus is any better off than we. No one has formulated more bracingly than Nietzsche the insight that, though we are "born as latecomers—there is a way of living which will erase this from memory," so that "the coming generations will only know [us] as firstcomers." Nietzsche elaborates on the "remarkable consolation" available "for the fighters who use critical history for life . . . : namely, to know that this first nature also was, at some time or other, a second nature and that every victorious second nature becomes a first."[2] Nietzsche's perspective allows us to assimilate the burden of our "anxiety of influence" in taking up psychoanalysis after Freud, while finding a way to accept our lot as "latecomers" with equanimity.

Nietzsche's exhortation to live with the courage to become "firstcomers" to our own posterity likewise enables us to offer a final rejoinder to deconstruction, with its paralyzing postmodern dogmas of the unattainability of Truth and the death of Man. All Derrida's thought departs from and returns to the idea of a "supplement," that written "trace" which marks the perpetual loss of presence or fullness of being. As Derrida aphoristically insists in *Of Grammatology: "There is nothing outside the text."* His remarks on Rousseau have a programmatic significance:

What we have tried to show by following the guiding line of the "dangerous supplement," is that in what one calls the real life of these existences "of flesh and bone" . . . there has never been anything but writing; there have never been anything but supplements, substitutive significations. . . . And thus to infinity, for we have read, *in the text*, that the absolute present, Nature, that which words like "real mother" name, have always already escaped, have never existed; that what opens meaning and language is writing as the disappearance of natural presence.[3]

The nihilism of the proposition that "there has never been anything but writing," implicit in Derrida, becomes explicit in Paul de Man's analysis of the idea of literary modernity. For de Man, the artist's aspiration to "modernity"—to have immediate access to experience or "life"—is fraught with an inherent contradiction, since when writers "assert their own modernity, they are bound to discover their dependence on similar assertions made by their literary predecessors; their claim to being a new beginning turns out to be the repetition of a claim that has always already been made." De Man draws from this knowledge of the ineluctability of repetition the mordant conclusion that "the distinctive character of literature thus becomes manifest as an inability to escape from a condition that is felt to be unbearable."[4]

Psychoanalysis shares with deconstruction a skepticism about the possibility of a "new beginning" and the conviction that human experience is structured by repetition. Indeed, it was Freud himself who formulated the theory of "deferred action" that underlies Derrida's notion of a "dangerous supplement." But, as a humanism—albeit one informed by a tragic vision—psychoanalysis cannot endorse the conclusion that Rousseau's "real mother" has "never existed" or that "writing" entails the abolition of "natural presence." What is needed is a strategy to accept and go beyond the deconstructive awareness of the textual structure of experience. With a more benign view of repetition, it may be possible to alleviate de Man's jaundiced insistence on the "unbearable" condition of both literature and life with a measure of Nietzschean joyfulness.

Just such an antidote to deconstruction is supplied by Thomas Mann in the second of his two seminal essays on Freud, "Freud and the Future" (1936).[5] Here, as in "Freud's Position in the History of Modern Culture" (1929), Mann convincingly situates Freud in the context of German Romanticism and nineteenth-century philosophy. Most importantly, however, he reflects theoretically on the problem of the relation between individual experience and mythic prototypes. Arguing that myth is "the timeless schema . . . into which life flows when it reproduces its traits out of the unconscious" (p. 422), Mann cites the example of Cleopatra, who took her own life by laying an asp on her bosom, as a historical figure who self-consciously shaped her existence to conform to a mythical model—that of the goddess Isis. Similarly, he observes, when Jesus exclaimed on the cross, *"Eli, eli, lama sabachthani?"* ("My God, my God, why hast thou forsaken me?"), far from being a "spontaneous outcry," this was a deliberate allusion to the Twenty-Second Psalm, which announces the coming of the Messiah. Thus, Mann explains, "Jesus was quoting, and the quotation meant: 'Yes, it is I!' Precisely thus did Cleopatra quote when she took the asp to her breast to die; and again the quotation meant: 'Yes, it is I'" (p. 425).

Although such "mythical identification" (p. 424) is particularly prevalent in ancient times, it has by no means disappeared in the modern period. In this connection, Mann refers to Napoleon, who is reported to have affirmed, in true antique fashion, "I am Charlemagne." But, in an essay on Freud, Mann might just as easily have instanced Freud himself, who took as his heroic exemplars Oedipus, Hannibal, Moses, and the rest, and renamed the process of "mythical identification" the "reenactment syndrome." "Significant life," therefore, now as always, is the "reconstitution of the myth in flesh and blood," and Mann proceeds to justify his belief that such life may justly be described in festive terms:

For life in the myth, life, so to speak, in quotation, is a kind of celebration, in that it is a making present of the past, it becomes a religious act, the performance by a celebrant of a prescribed procedure; it becomes a feast. For a feast is an anniversary, a renewal of the past in the present. (p. 425)

Mann's understanding of "life in quotation" exactly parallels Derrida's "dangerous supplement," but because he recognizes that "life in quotation" is also "life in the myth," he regards the necessity of repetition as cause for "celebration" and not a requiem. In their dedication to the assumption that "writing as the disappearance of natural presence" impoverishes life, the deconstructors fail to consider that there must be "a renewal of the past in the present" if the past is to continue to exist at all. The same point has been well made by Gadamer, when he writes that "tradition is not simply a precondition into which we come, but we produce it ourselves, inasmuch as we understand, participate in the evolution of tradition and hence further determine it ourselves."[6] This inability to see that the relation between past and present is a genuinely dialectical one persists in Derrida's treatment of the catgories of "life" and "text." For him, the doctrine of the "trace" suffices to dismiss the "real life of these existences 'of flesh and bone' "; but Mann again contends with greater profundity that life itself depends for its meaning on the continued "reconstitution of the myth in flesh and blood."[7]

As Mann shows, psychoanalysis is able to assimilate the teachings of deconstruction while retaining what is of permanent value in the metaphysical tradition. Life is indeed composed of "supplements," but each "second nature" has its provisional moment of incarnation, of fullness, and in turn becomes a "first nature" to those who come after it. Oedipus-Freud-Jones-Rudnytsky-the present reader: all are "traces," doubles, but there intervenes a real human existence at each stage of transmission of the myth. It is above all the myth of the hero—of the individual subject *as* hero—that psychoanalysis preserves for us. And, if every psychoanalysis is ultimately a self-analysis, is not the analyst always the Sphinx, and every (de) Man(n) the Sphinx's riddle?

Appendix:
Oedipus
and Anti-Oedipus

THIS BOOK has avowedly taken both Freud and Oedipus as its exemplars as well as its subject matter. In addition to my immediate aims—contributing to the understanding of Freud's life, of nineteenth-century intellectual history, and of Sophoclean tragedy—I hope by my work as a whole to have attested in practice to the explanatory power of psychoanalysis and to the human truth of the Oedipus myth.

Yet it must be recognized that my chosen paradigms have come under attack from various quarters. The issue, at its deepest level, is the ideological one of canon-formation—the implications of singling out certain literary texts and intellectual systems as touchstones of cultural value. Indeed, *Oedipus the King* is perhaps *the* preeminent classical text in the Western tradition. For, more than two millennia before *The Interpretation of Dreams*, Aristotle in the *Poetics* identified *Oedipus the King* as the bench mark for excellence in tragedy.

Evidently, Aristotle's grounds for admiring *Oedipus* were in many respects different from Freud's, though in point of fact the convergence between their views is deep and startling: Aristotle's emphasis on plot accords with Freud's remarks on the way the play's action "can be likened to the work of a psycho-analysis"; Aristotle's key concepts of *anagnorisis* ("recognition") and *peripeteia* ("reversal") suggest the aims and method of psychoanalytic therapy; and Aristotle shares with Freud the conviction that the most painful tragedies are those where family members are involved.[1] But overriding these specific areas of agreement is the simple fact that Aristotle joins with Freud in adopting an *Oedipus-centered* perspective, and hence in elevating Sophocles' tragedy to its unique place in the life of the Western mind. From this standpoint, the "age of Oedipus" begins not with Schiller but with the canonization of *Oedipus the King* in the *Poetics*.

Although I cannot be expected to renounce my own investment in the tradition upheld at either end by Aristotle and Freud, it is at least incumbent on me to be aware of alternative points of view. Thus, this book would not be complete without a direct encounter with those critics who have recently called into question the hegemony of the Oedipus myth. Only through such a "labor of the negative" can the continued vitality of psychoanalysis be affirmed in the face of the challenges of postmodernism. Accordingly, in the following "supplementary" discussion, I shall take up the gauntlet thrown down by four representatives of the party of "anti-Oedipus," each of whom invites us to reflect on what has been suppressed or excluded by the legacy of Sophocles. These are, in succession, the radical Marxism of Gilles Deleuze and Félix Guattari, the idiosyncratic theory of "mimetism" of René Girard, the deconstructionist reading of *Oedipus the King* by Sandor Goodhart, and the feminist critique of Freud. The tone of my remarks will necessarily be polemical, but I offer them in the spirit of dialogue rather than diatribe.

No assault on the Oedipus complex could be more violent and uncompromising than that of Deleuze and Guattari in *Anti-Oedipus: Capitalism and Schizophrenia*.[2] As their subtitle suggests, this French team of philosopher and militant analyst are concerned above all with social and political issues, and their aim is to effect a complete break from Freud by repudiating the "familialism" of psychoanalysis in favor of a Marxist-oriented "schizoanalysis." Strikingly, however, the name of Sophocles does not appear in the index to this wide-ranging book, and Deleuze and Guattari do not seek to ground their confrontation with Freud in a reappraisal of the tragedy from which he derived his inspiration.

For Deleuze and Guattari, as translator Mark Seem explains in his Introduction, Oedipus is the "figurehead of imperialism," and the endeavor of their project of liberation is to persuade mankind "to strip itself of *all* anthropomorphic and anthropological armoring, all myth and tragedy, and all existentialism, in order to perceive what is nonhuman in man" *(AO,* p. xx). To the skeptical reader, this is likely to seem a rather bizarre enterprise, because the civilizing achievements of myth and tragedy are surely preferable to "what is nonhuman in man." In their disdain for humanism, Deleuze and Guattari exemplify the painfully familiar phenomenon of revolutionaries who, in the name of freedom, impose a reign of terror worse than the old regime they have overthrown. As a representative instance of the tone in which Deleuze and Guattari conduct their "de-oedipalizing," it suffices to quote the following:

In place of the benevolent pseudo neutrality of the Oedipal analyst, who wants and understands only daddy and mommy, we must substitute a malevolent, an openly malevolent activity: your Oedipus is a fucking drag, keep it up and the analysis will be stopped, or else we'll apply a shock treatment to you. *(AO,* p. 112)

It is one thing to point out that the ideal of analytic neutrality conceals tacit ideological presuppositions, and quite another to insist on the superiority of one's own brand of "shock treatment." Michel Foucault writes in his laudatory Preface that it is an essential principle of "living counter to all forms of fascism" that one should decry "all unitary and totalizing paranoia" *(AO,* p. xiii), by which is chiefly meant the Oedipus complex; but it is rather Deleuze and Guattari whose "openly malevolent" cast of mind inclines toward fascism.

Anti-Oedipus belongs to the vanguard of the movement of *anti*psychiatry, whose noted English-speaking exponents include R. D. Laing, David Cooper, and Thomas Szasz. Rejecting neurosis as a capitulation to the norms of society, antipsychiatrists celebrate psychosis as a more intense and "anoedipal" mode of experiencing reality. Lionel Trilling has justly censured Laing on the grounds that "his theory of mental pathology rules out the possibility of pain being inherent in the process of the mind,"[3] and the same reproach applies to the authors of *Anti-Oedipus.* In "The Process," Deleuze and Guattari proclaim their gospel of the schizophrenic as hero:

The schizo knows how to leave: he has made departure into something
as simple as being born or dying. . . . These men of desire—or do they
not yet exist?—are like Zarathustra. They know incredible sufferings,
vertigos, and sicknesses. . . . But such a man produces himself as a free
man, irresponsible, solitary, and joyous, finally able to say and do something in his own name, without asking permission; a desire lacking
nothing, a flux that overcomes barriers and codes, a name that no longer
designates any ego whatever. He has simply ceased being afraid of becoming mad. (*AO*, p. 131)

The ostensible acknowledgment of the "sufferings, vertigos, and
sicknesses" of schizophrenia is undercut by Deleuze and Guattari's
portrayal of their imaginary egoless "schizo" as "free" and "joyous." Unlike the philosophers from Plato through Hegel and
Freud, for whom the human condition is characterized by the
individual's experience of desire as a *lack*, Deleuze and Guattari
opine that their fearless madman possesses "a desire lacking nothing." It is a final irony that, at the very moment when "the schizo"
announces his freedom "in his own name," Deleuze and Guattari
themselves invoke the *name* of Zarathustra.

Although seemingly minor, this latent self-contradiction
points out an even deeper problem than the "openly malevolent"
rhetoric of schizoanalysis. Despite their destructive intentions, Deleuze and Guattari reveal themselves to be entrapped by the dilemma that Geoffrey Hartman has argued is inherent in the attempt to create "a truly iconoclastic art": "The artist has a bad
conscience because of the idea that forms, structures, etc. always
reconcile or integrate, that they are conservative despite themselves."[4] The title *Anti-Oedipus*, for example, seems at first glance
to be "truly iconoclastic," to announce the authors' resolution "to
shatter the iron collar of Oedipus and discover everywhere the
force of desiring-production" (*AO*, p. 53). On closer inspection,
however, *Anti-Oedipus* ceases to mean simply "against Oedipus"
and, like the term "anti-hero," takes on a curiously positive aura,
with all the substantiality of a proper name. Indeed, in the original
French title, *L'Anti-Oedipe*, the presence of the definite article,
which might appear to be due merely to grammatical necessity,
accurately registers the fact that Deleuze and Guattari are seriously
proposing a new cultural anti-hero—that strange being known as
"the schizo," whom we might rename *"the* anti-Oedipus." De-

leuze and Guattari's virulent rhetoric, accordingly, becomes comprehensible as a symptom of their "bad conscience," caused by their discomfort at being "conservative despite themselves" in failing to escape a parodic dependence on the myth of the hero and hence on their psychoanalytic nemesis "Oedipus."

The same paradox reappears in Deleuze and Guattari's appeal to Melanie Klein's notion of "partial objects" as a theoretical support for their rejection of the "totalizing paranoia" of the Oedipus complex:

Partial objects unquestionably have a sufficient charge in and of themselves to blow up all of Oedipus and totally demolish its ridiculous claim to represent the unconscious, to triangulate the unconscious, to encompass the entire production of desire. The question that thus here arises is not at all that of the relative importance of what might be called the *pre-oedipal* in relation to Oedipus itself, since "pre-oedipal" still has a developmental or structural relationship to Oedipus. The question, rather, is that of the absolutely *anoedipal* nature of the production of desire. (*AO*, pp. 44–45)

The difficulty, however, is whether this "anoedipal" view of the "production of desire" can be consistently maintained. Klein herself, as Deleuze and Guattari are forced to admit, saw no incompatibility between her findings and the Oedipus complex. On the contrary, she used the idea of partial objects to "water Oedipus down, to miniaturize it, to find it everywhere, to extend it to the very earliest years of life" (*AO*, p. 45). There is, moreover, an aesthetic counterpart to Deleuze and Guattari's psychological anarchy. As opposed to Plato (*Phaedrus* 264 c) and Aristotle (*Poetics* 1450 b), for whom a work of art should resemble a living creature in the organic unity of the whole and the proper arrangement of its parts, our theorists exhibit a quintessentially modern preference for the *fragment*. But, as Hans-Georg Gadamer has argued, the very notion of a part or fragment is inconceivable apart from that of a larger totality, since "the movement of understanding is constantly from the whole to the part and back to the whole."[5] Gadamer's reasoning provides a hermeneutic underpinning to Klein's psychoanalytic awareness that preoedipal stages must be seen in their "developmental or structural relationship to Oedipus," and exposes by contrast the self-subverting rashness of Deleuze and Guattari.

Fundamental to the Marxist "schizoanalysis" of Deleuze and Guattari, as I have indicated, is an emphasis on the political and social realms for which the "familialism" of psychoanalysis purportedly fails to account. Concerning Freud's analysis of Schreber's memoirs, for example, they remark: "From the enormous political, social, and historical context of Schreber's delirium, *not one word is retained.* . . . Freud invokes only a sexual argument" (*AO*, p. 57). As opposed to Freud's monolithic emphasis on "the name of the father," Deleuze and Guattari wish us to think in the plural of "all the *names* of history" (*AO*, p. 56).

Although a measure of justice may be conceded to Deleuze and Guattari's indictment of the "reductionism" of psychoanalysis, a theoretical rejoinder is available. They themselves point the way when they draw attention to an apparently surprising fact— the congruence between their own views and those of Jung. They instance the "modest and practical point of disagreement" that precipitated the break between Freud and Jung: "Jung remarked that in the process of transference the psychoanalyst frequently appeared in the guise of a devil, a god, or a sorcerer, and that the roles he assumed in the patient's eyes went far beyond any sort of parental images" (*AO*, p. 46). Like Jung, that is, Deleuze and Guattari highlight the manifold variety in human dreams and fantasies. The negative corollary, however, is that they also follow Jung in neglecting to take into account the psychoanalytic principle of *repression,* which requires that one make a distinction between latent and manifest contents of psychical products.

Jung himself was explicit about his rejection of this cornerstone of psychoanalytic theory:

I was never able to agree with Freud that the dream is a "façade" behind which meaning lies hidden—a meaning already known but maliciously, so to speak, withheld from consciousness. To me dreams are a part of nature, which harbors no intention to deceive, but expresses something as best it can, just as a plant grows or an animal seeks its food as best it can.[6]

Whereas for Jung dreams are "a part of nature, which harbors no intention to deceive," for Freud they belong to the category of *language,* and display all the ambiguity and censorship characteristic of human discourse. The difference between Jung and Deleuze and Guattari on the one hand and Freud on the other is not that the former are attentive to dream contents or transference roles of which the latter was unaware, but rather that these are viewed by Freud with a *suspicion* that his critics altogether lack. If for Freud the delusions of Judge Schreber could be reduced to "the name of the father," that is because the innumerable "names of history" were not to be taken at face value.

Deleuze and Guattari express the contrast between psycho-analysis and "schizoanalysis" most starkly in their insistence that the unconscious be viewed, not as a *theater*, but as a *factory* (*AO*, p. 55). They are right to point out the extent to which Freud's "oedipalism" ties him to a notion of the unconscious which is profoundly theatrical. But Deleuze and Guattari do not acknowl-edge the degree to which Freud's "theatrical" conception of the unconscious is tied to his preoccupation with the workings of memory. Alluding to the prominence of visual elements in dreams, Freud writes in *The Psychopathology of Everyday Life:*

Visual memory accordingly preserves the type of infantile memory. In my own case the earliest childhood memories are the only ones of a visual character: they are regular scenes worked out in plastic form, comparable only to representations upon the stage. (*SE*, 6:47)

Thus, just as Deleuze and Guattari's preference for Jung over Freud entails a retreat from the psychoanalytic postulate of repression, so their mechanistic understanding of the unconscious leads also to a dismissal of Freud's probing inquiry into the persistence of "earliest childhood memories."

But it is not in fact necessary to regard Freud's model of the unconscious and that of Deleuze and Guattari as mutually exclu-sive. For when Deleuze and Guattari speak of the schizophrenic as one who "deliberately seeks out the very limit of capitalism . . . its inherent tendency brought to fulfillment" (*AO*, p. 35), there is an undoubted validity to their diagnosis. Indeed, in a rare moment of illumination, Deleuze and Guattari even allow for the possibility of a dialectical accommodation with psychoanalysis:

Yes, Oedipus is nevertheless the universal of desire, the product of uni-versal history—but on one condition, which is not met by Freud: that Oedipus be capable, at least to a certain point, of conducting its autocri-tique. (*AO*, p. 271)

I thoroughly share Deleuze and Guattari's belief that the Oedipus myth must be critically examined if it is to retain its standing as a "universal of desire." But just as psychoanalysis is far more open and self-questioning than Deleuze and Guattari recognize, so such a reappraisal cannot possibly be conducted using their incendiary rhetoric and uncompromising methods.

The pivotal question remains: can one reconcile their concept of "desiring-production" with the claims of the Oedipus complex to "triangulate the unconscious"? But such a genuine meeting of the minds is precisely what Deleuze and Guattari will not tolerate: "There is no oedipal triangle: Oedipus is always open in an open social field. Oedipus opens to the four winds, to the four corners of the social field (not even 3 + 1 but 4 + *n*)" (*AO*, p. 96). The authors of *Anti-Oedipus* force us to probe anew the psychoanalytic assumption that triangulation is inherent in human experience.

To raise the issue of triangulation is immediately to invite a comparison between the attack on psychoanalysis of Deleuze and Guattari and that of René Girard in *Violence and the Sacred*,[7] also published originally in French. Unlike Deleuze and Guattari, whose challenge to Freud is at the most general level, Girard remains much closer to orthodox psychoanalysis and engages Freud in a direct debate about the meaning of the Oedipus myth. Ironically, however, in his own essay devoted to *Anti-Oedipus*, Girard finds it necessary to insist that he, and not Deleuze and Guattari, offers the real alternative to Freud: "In my opinion, we must regret not the attack on psychoanalysis but the positions justifying it and making impossible any real confrontation with the essential Freud, any profound criticism of the psychoanalytic myth, the Oedipus complex."[8] Girard's inability to recognize the comparatively modest nature of his differences with Freud epitomizes the distortion in perspective that flaws his important and provocative work.

As in his earlier *Deceit, Desire, and the Novel*,[9] Girard presents in *Violence and the Sacred* a radical argument that human desire is necessarily structured by triangulation. His thought is founded on the two interlocking concepts of "mimetic rivalry" and "mediated desire." In Girard's view, the essential fact is that in all conceivable "varieties of desire" there may be found "not only a subject and an object, but a third presence as well: the rival. It is the rival who should be accorded the dominant role" (*VS*, p. 145). According to Girard, rivalry never arises "because of the fortuitous convergence of two desires on a single object; rather, *the subject desires the object because the rival desires it.* In desiring an object the rival alerts the subject to the desirability of the object" (*VS*, p. 145). Girard's theory further connects the experience of desire with that of violence: "By making one man's desire into a replica of another man's desire, [mimetism] invariably leads to rivalry; and rivalry in turn transforms desire into violence" (*VS*, p. 145).

It is evident that Girard's twin axioms of "mimetic rivalry" and "mediated desire" are closely allied to the Oedipus complex, and may indeed be regarded as a more general version of the latter. But so nearly does Girard approximate Freud that one may legitimately wonder in what respect he differs from psychoanalysis at all. Girard himself specifies that the crux of the dispute is the choice between his own "mimetic concept" and Freud's "full-blown patricide-incest drive":

The mimetic process detaches desire from any predetermined object, whereas the Oedipus complex fixes desire on the maternal object. The mimetic concept eliminates all conscious knowledge of patricide-incest, and even all desire for it as such; the Freudian proposition, by contrast, is based entirely on a consciousness of this desire. (*VS*, p. 180)

Girard is strangely mistaken in saying that psychoanalysis presupposes a "consciousness" of the wish for "patricide-incest"; it is rather our *unconscious* impulses to commit the crimes of Oedipus that Freud established. Nonetheless, he correctly asserts that psychoanalytic theory accords primacy to desire for the "maternal object." Like Deleuze and Guattari, therefore, in his attempt to disengage his notion of "mimetic rivalry" from parental figures, Girard in his own way issues a challenge to the "familialism" of psychoanalysis.

Girard accomplishes his revision of Freud through an intriguing displacement of psychoanalytic terminology. In place of the oedipal triangle of father, mother, and son, Girard proposes the mimetic triangle of "the model, the disciple, and the object that is disputed by both because the model's desire has made the object desirable to the disciple" (*VS*, p. 181). By thus eliminating the specifically sexual or familial dimension of the psychoanalytic paradigm, Girard believes that he has succeeded in giving it a more general applicability.

As Toril Moi has shown in a trenchant critique, however, Girard's argument breaks down in several crucial respects. In the first place, Girard's language makes clear on abundant occasions that he has not in fact abandoned the male-male-female model in constructing his triangles. "The subject does not want to win the girl decisively; if he did, he would lose the mediator and he would lose all interest in the girl,"[10] he writes in a typical passage. The sexism displayed in the use of the word "girl" is compounded by Girard's assumption that the desiring "subject" and his "mediator" or rival are both masculine. Second, although Girard's scheme places greater emphasis on the figure of the rival than on that of the loved object, he refuses to explore the homosexual components of the ambivalent relations between the male doubles. On the contrary, he assumes not only that heterosexuality is innately "prescribed by our instinctual apparatus inherited from animal life," but also that the hypothesis of a "negative" Oedipus complex is the most absurd of Freud's theories: "a passive homosexual desire for the father, a desire of being desired by the father as a homosexual object! . . . The unconscious is a stubborn concept, but this desire of the son for the father is a lot, even for the most recalcitrant of concepts."[11] Finally, as Moi astutely notes, Girard's occlusion of the role of the mother—and of the entire preoedipal period—is unavoidable, because were he to admit that the mother is the first love object for children of both sexes, he would be driven by his own theory of mediated desire to conclude that "all males would be homosexual, as a consequence of their initial imitation of the mother's desire for the father."[12]

Thus, whereas Girard's substitution of the mimetic triangle for that of the Oedipus complex appears initially to offer, as it were, a healthy Hegelian leavening of psychoanalytic theory, in actual practice his thought proves to be a reductive and inflexible application of Freud. At his worst moments, moreover, Girard gives the impression of one who believes that he is in sole possession of revealed truth, who is truly in the grip of what Deleuze and Guattari would call "totalizing paranoia":

The endless diversity of myths and rituals derives from the fact that they all seek to recollect and reproduce something they never succeed in comprehending. There is only one generative event, only one way to grasp the truth: by means of my hypothesis. On the other hand, there are innumerable ways of missing it; hence the multiplicity of religious systems. (*VS*, p. 316)

In contrast to Freud's tentativeness in defining the ontological status of his "primal scenes"—his uncertainty as to whether traumas are precipitated by fantasies or actual occurrences—Girard dogmatically insists on branding his speculations as "fact" and maintains that "there is only one way to grasp the truth." The ultimate irony of Girard's intellectual posture, however, is that he is at his strongest in those respects in which he agrees with Freud, and becomes progressively less compelling as he exaggerates the uniqueness of his own point of view.[13]

The greatest difference between Freud and Girard is that Girard seeks to abolish the psychoanalytic focus on sexuality in favor of an exclusive concentration on his own theory of "generative violence." He ventures, for example, the dismissive statement that "Psychoanalysis is wrong . . . to attribute to young children a knowledge of parental sexuality" (*VS*, p. 220). The all-embracing hypothesis Girard proposes to explain "the endless diversity of myths and rituals" is essentially Freud's idea of the "primal murder" in *Totem and Taboo*, but now stripped of any connection with the father:

If we hope to get to the root of the matter we must put the father out of our minds and concentrate on the fact that the enormous impression made on the community by the collective murder is not due to the victim's identity per se, but to his role as unifying agent. (*VS*, p. 214)

Once again, Girard promotes what is at best speculation to the status of a "fact" and does not recognize that, whereas psychoanalysis has no difficulty in accommodating his own findings about violence, he himself is unable to profit from Freud's discoveries about infantile sexuality and the role of the father in the Oedipus complex.

These objections to Girard's attempts to decouple violence from sexuality would carry less weight if he did not share the psychoanalytic assumption that *Oedipus the King* is a paradigmatic text. But precisely because of his "mimetic rivalry" with Freud, Girard is driven to assert the superiority of his own interpretation of the Oedipus myth. It is, therefore, worth recapitulating at least some of the ways in which Sophocles makes clear the symbolic identity of Oedipus' twin crimes of incest and patricide.[14] The three roads of the crossroads are matched by the conflation of three generations in the act of incest. The "gold-wrought / pins" (ll. 1268–69) of Jocasta with which Oedipus puts out his eyes recall the "double prongs" (l. 809) of the stick with which Laius attacks Oedipus in their encounter. On a purely linguistic level, when Oedipus recounts this incident at the crossroads to Jocasta, he says (in the historical present) of his retaliation against the coachman: "I strike in anger" (l. 807). The same verb "strike" *(paiein)*, which may bear the colloquial meaning "have intercourse with," recurs in compound form in the speech of the Second Messenger, who describes how Oedipus "burst in" (l. 1252) through the palace doors in search of Jocasta; it appears uncompounded several lines later in the Messenger's graphic account of the way Oedipus repeatedly "struck" *(epaisen)* (l. 1270) the sockets of his eyes. In addition, forms of the same verb "to leap on" *(enallesthai)* are used by Oedipus with reference to the ill-fated death of Laius (l. 263), by the Messenger to convey Oedipus' divinely possessed plunge through the double doors of Jocasta's bedchamber (l. 1261), and once more by Oedipus himself in lamenting the blow he has suffered at the hands of the *daimon* (l. 1311). In view of this intricate network of thematic and verbal associations between the deeds of incest, patricide, and Oedipus' self-blinding, it is possible to conclude unequivocally that Girard's endeavor to explain the workings of violence without reference to sexuality proceeds in disregard of the meaning of Sophocles' tragedy.

Indeed, nowhere are Girard's simultaneous brilliance and perversity more clearly in evidence than in his commentary on *Oedipus the King*—brilliance insofar as he confines himself to a deepening and elaboration of psychoanalytic insights, and perversity when he insists on going his own way. Girard is on solid ground when he draws attention to the function of repetition in the Oedipus myth:

All episodes of the Oedipus myth are repetitions of one another. Once we recognize this fact it becomes apparent that all the figures in various episodes are monsters and that their resemblance is far closer than appearance alone might suggest. (*VS*, p. 252)

Even here Girard's confident use of the word "fact" is troubling, but the observation itself is unexceptionable. Linked to this awareness of repetition is Girard's argument that, in the Oedipus myth, "all masculine relationships are based on reciprocal acts of violence" (*VS*, p. 48); and, more generally, that the same underlying structure is at work in all occurrences of doubling:

If violence is the great leveler of men and everybody becomes the double, or "twin," of his antagonist, it seems to follow that all the doubles are identical and that any one can at any given moment become the double of all the others; that is, the sole object of universal obsession and hatred. (*VS*, p. 79)

Because, for Girard, "tragedy envelops all human relationships in a single tragic antagonism," it is ultimately impossible to differentiate between the fraternal conflict of Eteocles and Polyneices, the father-son conflict of Laius and Oedipus, and the gnostic conflict of Oedipus and Teiresias: "The rivalry of the two prophets is indistinguishable from the rivalry between brothers" (*VS*, p. 65). But though Girard's argument about the nature of this "single tragic antagonism" is alluring, doubts begin to arise. If "all the doubles are identical" at all times, then everything is "indistinguishable" from everything else. We note, too, Girard's unwavering assumption that "reciprocal violence" is characteristic of *masculine* relationships, untroubled by the query whether such a law applies also to feminine desire.

The doubts instilled by Girard's penchant for overstatement are reinforced when he comes to apply his notion of sacrificial violence to *Oedipus the King*. When Freud writes in *The Interpretation of Dreams* that Oedipus' fate "moves us because it might have been ours—because the oracle laid the same curse upon us before our birth as upon him" (*SE*, 4:262), he anticipates Girard in recognizing that the choice of Oedipus as a *"surrogate victim"* (*VS*, p. 79) is, as it were, random or arbitrary. After all, in a moment of bravado before learning the secret of his birth, Oedipus boasts that he is "a child of Chance" (l. 1080), an account of his origins that proves true in a sense deeper than he had intended. But, in Girard's hands, this concept of arbitrariness is twisted to mean that Oedipus may be *mistakenly* accused of guilt in the play. According to Girard, the "burden of guilt" that "oscillates freely among the three protagonists"—Oedipus, Teiresias, and Creon—finally settles upon

Oedipus only because he is the victim of a successful frame-up by his two rivals:

The attribution of guilt that henceforth passes for "true" differs in no way from those attributions that will henceforth be regarded as "false," except that in the case of the "true" guilt no voice is raised to protest any aspect of the charge. A particular version of events succeeds in imposing itself; it loses its polemical nature in becoming the acknowledged basis of the myth, in becoming the myth itself. (*VS*, p. 78)

Beginning in plausibility, Girard by imperceptible steps arrives at absurdity. If Oedipus' exposure as the murderer of Laius is no more than "a particular version of events" that "succeeds in imposing itself," what then is to be made of his incest with Jocasta? Would Girard have us believe that his culpability for this transgression is likewise shared with Creon and Teiresias? Girard pays the price for his neglect of eros by allowing himself to be placed in such an untenable position. Psychoanalysis can indeed profit from a meditation on Girard's work, but before Girard concludes that he has dispensed with the Oedipus complex, he would do well to attend to the evidence of Sophocles' *plot*—that part held by Aristotle to be "both the first and most important"(*Poetics* 1450b) of a tragedy.

Before we ourselves dismiss Girard's conclusions too hastily, however, we must turn to our third representative of the forces of "anti-Oedipus." For in his essay "Ληστὰς ᾿Εφασκε [He Said 'Robbers']: Oedipus and Laius' Many Murderers"[15]—published, appropriately, in an issue of *Diacritics* devoted to the work of René Girard—Sandor Goodhart takes seriously Girard's thesis that Oedipus is only convicted of Laius' murder by conspiratorial machinations, and offers a careful reading of *Oedipus the King* in the original Greek in support of his case.

Goodhart's essay is commendable above all because he is fully aware of the issues posed by a debate over the meaning of the Oedipus myth. Because "Oedipus is part of our language in the West," he justly writes, "then what is at stake in Oedipus . . . is Western humanism at large" (p. 68). As a result of "Freud's appropriation of the 'Sophoclean legend' as the program for a scientific institution," furthermore, the consequences of what Goodhart regards as the "blindness" of traditional humanist understanding are carried "to a dangerous new level" (p. 68). Consequently, Goodhart envisions his brief for Oedipus' possible innocence as a direct challenge to "twenty-four hundred years of critical tradition" (pp. 63–64), and to psychoanalysis in particular.

What is more, Goodhart draws upon the ideas of various "anti-oedipal" theoreticians, and thereby allows us to discern their underlying affinities. Most conspicuous is his indebtedness to Girard, whose name is invoked only at the conclusion of the essay as "the critic who, more than anyone else in the contemporary context, has thought out the relation of violence to human communities" (p. 70). But in his denunciation of the way in which "the production of an 'Oedipus complex,' the 'Oedipalization' of the patient, is an enabling condition for the psychoanalytic cure" (p. 69), Goodhart does not fail to cite the *Anti-Oedipus* of Deleuze and Guattari. Finally, in his insistence that, "rather than an illustration of the myth, the play is a critique of mythogenesis, an examination of the process by which one arbitrary fiction comes to assume the value of a truth" (p. 67), Goodhart poses the problem of "truth" in a manner congruent with the recent philosophical interrogations of deconstruction; and he appropriately refers (p. 66) to Derrida in this connection. Thus, not only does Goodhart bring the attack on psychoanalysis down to a microscopic textual analysis of *Oedipus the King*, but he deserves praise for setting this problem of literary criticism in the widest possible context.

What, then, is the basis for Goodhart's revisionary reading of Sophocles? He draws attention to the fact—already castigated as an absurdity by Voltaire in the third of his *Letters on Oedipus*—that, when the old Herdsman is finally summoned into Oedipus' presence, he does not testify about the murder of Laius, of which he is the sole surviving witness, but rather unravels the mystery of Oedipus' origins by confirming that he had received him as an infant from Jocasta. As Goodhart puts it:

It is not that the Herdsman skirts the issue of the Phocal murder but that it never comes up. On the issue for which he was summoned, the issue on which the solution of the play's mystery depends, he is simply never questioned. (p. 56)

Goodhart connects this lacuna with a second crucial detail about the plot of *Oedipus the King*—the persistently circulating rumor that Laius was killed, not by a single murderer, but by a band of highwaymen. Because the evidence that convicts Oedipus remains purely "circumstantial" (p. 61), Oedipus' assumption of his own "oedipal" guilt becomes, in Goodhart's view, the paradigmatic instance of the imposition of a "mythic pattern" that Sophocles' drama itself "deconstructs":

Oedipus discovers he is guilty of patricide and incest—he translates what the Herdsman does tell him into the mythic fulfillment—less by uncovering certain hitherto obscure empirical facts than by voluntarily appropriating an oracular logic which assumes he has always already been guilty. (p. 67)

In the terms of Goodhart's Girardian analysis, the ultimate theme of *Oedipus the King* is not the "empirical issue" of "the determination of any unique culprit," but rather "the plague of scapegoat violence for which it comes to substitute" (p. 57).

Without doubt, Goodhart has performed a valuable service in redirecting attention to one of the most pivotal and time-honored problems in Sophoclean criticism. In addition to attracting the strictures of Voltaire, the discrepancy between the accounts of Laius' murder is perceived to be crucial by Tycho von Wilamowitz-Moellendorff: "The entire action of *Oedipus Rex* rests, one might say, on the poet's consciously false and ambiguous substitution of a plural for the singular."[16] But though Goodhart's interpretation of *Oedipus the King* is remarkable for its radicality and novelty, his attempt to subvert "twenty-four hundred years of critical tradition" by absolving Oedipus proves as much a mirage as that of Girard.

A demonstration of Goodhart's fallaciousness may begin by comparing his handling of the question of "Laius' many murderers" with a considerably earlier one—William Chase Greene's 1929 essay, "The Murderers of Laius."[17] In a footnote, Goodhart dismisses Greene's approach to the "paradox of number" in *Oedipus the King* as tending to "support the myth itself" by "offering us yet another example of the poet's skill at naturalistic characterization" (p. 58). In point of fact, however, Greene's supposedly naive "naturalistic" reading of *Oedipus the King* is far more astute and compelling than Goodhart's strained theory that Sophocles intended the play as a "critique of mythogenesis."

Noting that the story of Laius' death at the hands of a band of robbers originates with the Herdsman, Greene suggests that such a prevarication is consistent with what we know of the Herdsman's character. For the fact that the same retainer in Laius' household had earlier taken the baby Oedipus and given him to the Corinthian, in violation of his orders to expose the child, is "an indication that the trusty servant is not above practicing a deception" (Greene, p. 84). Thus, when he alone of Laius' party escaped Oedipus' assault, he may well "have tried to save his reputation" by the "apparently innocent deception" of exaggerating the number of his attackers, much as—the inevitable comparison is Greene's—"valiant Jack" Falstaff recounts being set upon by "eleven men in buckram" when in truth he was routed only by the disguised Prince Hal and Poins (Greene, p. 85). To be sure, Sophocles does not explicitly state that this is the reason for the Herdsman's false report, but he certainly makes it possible to draw such an inference; and I believe that our appreciation of *Oedipus the King* is enhanced by Greene's "naturalistic" interpretation.

Then there is the matter that, on at least two occasions, Oedipus reverts to the singular in speaking of Laius' murder, when in the preceding lines his interlocutor has referred to the number of assailants in the plural. When Oedipus first learns from Creon of the escaped witness' testimony—"He said robbers coming on not with a single / strength killed them, but with a multitude of hands" (ll. 122–23)—he replies: "How indeed might the *robber*" (l. 124; italics added) dare such a deed, unless impelled by bribery from the city. Similarly, to the Chorus' reminder that Laius was said to have been killed "by certain wayfarers" (l. 292), Oedipus answers: "I, too, have heard, but none sees *him* who saw" (l. 293; italics added).[18] In his note to line 294, Jebb comments that "the reversion from plural to singular is unconscious, just as in 124," a statement that gains full force if we take "unconscious" in its psychoanalytic sense. As Greene elaborates, because "embers of old memories are faintly fanned," Oedipus "pictures in his mind an individual murderer who strikes the blow, even though he can conceive of the deed only as the result of a bribe" (Greene, p. 77). To this haunting suggestion that Oedipus' use of the singular stems from a buried recollection of his own act of bloodshed, Goodhart retorts: "If Oedipus reduces Creon's account from a plurality to a

singularity, it may be less that Oedipus implicates himself unconsciously in the guilt than that much more consciously he implicates
Creon" (p. 59). Every reader is free to decide which account of
Oedipus' shift in number carriers greater conviction—indeed, as
Greene's reference to the thought of a bribe indicates, it is possible
to combine *both* explanations—but it is surely no accident that
Goodhart's emphasis on Creon closely parallels Jeffrey Masson's
portrait of Freud the "dogged detective" communicating his discovery of the seduction theory to Fliess, "his best friend, who may
have been in fact the criminal."

The longer one ponders Goodhart's denial that *Oedipus the
King* is a drama of self-analysis, the more far-fetched his arguments
come to seem. He recognizes, for example, that the vindication of
Oedipus depends upon the incrimination of Teiresias, upon showing that the position of the blind prophet is not divinely sanctioned: "Unless we privilege Teiresias *a priori* as spokesman for
the mythic pattern, we may have no confidence that the knowledge of the practicing mantic is other than professional" (p. 60).
But what reader of *Antigone* could possibly accept the characterization of Teiresias as a "practicing mantic," whose claims to superior wisdom are merely "professional"? Goodhart's exegesis
understandably proceeds without a word of reference to the other
plays of the Oedipus cycle, for it is impossible to reconcile with
Sophocles' indubitable adherence to the "mythic pattern" in *Antigone* and *Oedipus at Colonus.*

Nor does the initial attractiveness of Goodhart's hypothesis
concerning the lacuna in the Herdsman's testimony withstand
careful examination. For whereas the interpretation of *Oedipus the
King* in terms of a "critique of mythogenesis" is cumbersome at
best, a far more compact explanation for the Herdsman's shift
from the recent to the distant past is simply that Sophocles is
obeying the laws of dramatic economy. As Greene aptly remarks,
citing Jebb, the omission of any reference to the number of Laius'
murderers "is better than consistent: it is natural. A more urgent
question has thrust the other out of sight" (Greene, p. 81). To
Goodhart, such a concern with dramatic economy has perhaps
been rendered obsolete by Girard's theory of "scapegoat violence," but the heritage of "twenty-four hundred years of critical
tradition" is not to be brushed aside so easily.

Like Girard, moreover, Goodhart is completely baffled by the fact that the Oedipus myth is not simply about patricide, but also about incest. For, even according to his own reasoning, Oedipus has been shown by the Herdsman to be the son of Laius and Jocasta, and is therefore indisputably guilty of incest. Is he to be supposed to have committed one crime but not the other? As Greene again observes with complete correctness, Oedipus' "knowledge that he has indeed killed Laius is not directly established, but is inferred from the discovery of his origin and from the discovery that he has fulfilled the half of the Delphic oracle that prophesied incest" (Greene, p. 81). To use Goodhart's terminology, the fact that Oedipus convicts himself of Laius' murder "less by uncovering certain hitherto obscure empirical facts than by voluntarily appropriating an oracular logic" is the best evidence that Sophocles was working *within* the "mythic pattern," and not calling that pattern into question.

It may seem an ungrateful exercise to rebut Goodhart's reading of *Oedipus the King* in such detail. But it must be borne in mind how much is at stake in this dispute over Sophocles' drama— nothing less than "Western humanism at large," and in particular the textual foundations of psychoanalysis. For if Goodhart's supremely articulate and self-conscious "anti-oedipal" position paper can be shown to be without foundation, then Freud's appropriation of *Oedipus the King* as the "shibboleth" of psychoanalytic truth—and, by extension, the canonical position of the tragedy in Western thought since Aristotle—has withstood its most arduous challenge.

The crux of Goodhart's dispute with psychoanalysis may be expressed in the following terms: whereas for Freud the drama of *Oedipus the King* is essentially a process of "demystification"—the discovery of a hidden but nonetheless decisive truth—in Goodhart's "deconstructive" view the revelation is precisely that there is no absolute or final truth to be found. Goodhart's inability to make his case that truth is no more than an "arbitrary fiction" is thus symptomatic of the untenability of the more radical claims of deconstruction, and attests to the undiminished vitality of the traditions of Western metaphysics and humanistic introspection.

Because he does not look upon *Oedipus the King* as a tragedy of self-knowledge, Goodhart has nothing to say about the double function of the various characters—the Messenger, the Herdsman, Jocasta—both in Oedipus' present and his past, or about the breathtaking moments of reversal and recognition that occur when Oedipus unexpectedly comes upon the missing piece of a puzzle for which he did not realize he had been searching. In Karl Reinhardt's Heideggerian reading—the last great response to the play within the metaphysical tradition—*Oedipus the King* enacts "the irruption of truth into the structure of appearance," and this process occurs in two distinct stages. First, Oedipus confronts the question of who killed Laius, and then the question of his own identity. In Reinhardt's words: "For a while the second question lies hidden behind the first, then both run parallel for a time, in secret harmony, and at the end they come together."[19] No room is left in Goodhart's account for this "secret harmony" and ultimate convergence of internal and external quests; but then again, it is only the "mythic pattern."

Finally, even the matter of Sophocles' sleight of hand regarding the number of Laius' assailants may be explained—without reference to the reliability of the Herdsman—in a manner wholly at variance with Goodhart's assumptions. As Oedipus compares his own recollection of a murderous encounter at a crossroads with the rumored report of the Herdsman, he tells Jocasta that his hopes rest on the numerical discrepancy between the two versions:

> You said he spoke of robbers as the men
> who killed him. If, then, on the one hand still
> he shall say the same number, I am not the killer:
> for *one* could not be made equal to many.
> If, on the other hand, he shall name one solitary man,
> clearly the balance tips and this deed is mine.
>
> (ll. 842–47)

In an ordinary world, nothing could be clearer or more irrefutable than Oedipus' logic: either he committed the murder, or a band of robbers, but not both, "for *one* could not be made equal to many." But *Oedipus the King* does not depict an ordinary world, for Oedipus, as we know, is overwhelmed by his incest with "the burden of plural identities incapable of co-existing within one person."[20] Thus, the laws of logic and noncontradiction need not apply in this play, and Oedipus can be both one man and many. As Charles Segal has written:

Oedipus founds his innocence on a basic law of noncontradiction, the fundamental logic in man's apprehension of reality. Here, however, noncontradiction gives way to a fantastic, irrational "logic" of paradoxes in which opposites can in fact be equal and "one" can simultaneously be "many."[21]

It is fittingly ironic that, in seeking to uphold what seems to be a radical and daring reading of *Oedipus the King*, Goodhart exhibits a rigid literalism of the imagination.

Although there is truly much common ground among the three partisans of "anti-Oedipus" we have anatomized—above all, their enmity toward psychoanalysis and its "familialism"— important differences between Deleuze and Guattari and Girard lurk beneath the surface. In particular, the Marxists are at odds with Girard, not merely in the basis of their opposition to the Oedipus complex, but in their entire political outlook. Whereas Deleuze and Guattari are revolutionaries of the left, who threaten to become commissars in a dictatorship of the liberated, Girard is an equally unappealing ideologue of reaction, for whom any attempt to bring about social change is doomed from the outset.[22] For Girard, the only remedy is to turn away from the mediated world of human desire, as Don Quixote does at the end of Cervantes' novel, toward a direct communion with a transcendent God. A defense of psychoanalysis and the humanist tradition is thus also a plea for a liberal middle ground between the Marxist belief in the possibility of a withering away of the human condition and a reactionary quietism that preaches acceptance of even the most repugnant status quo.

This consideration of political issues brings us to our fourth and last challenge to the Oedipus complex, that articulated by feminist thought.[23] Two intertwined levels of inquiry need to be disentangled from the outset: Sophocles' representation of the Oedipus myth, and the use made of Sophocles by Freud. In both instances, it is possible to object that a story with a male protagonist is said to be emblematic of the human condition as a whole, and hence suppresses the perspective of women. At least in the case of Sophocles, a reply is readily available. For Sophocles does not tell only the story of Oedipus, and Jocasta is not his only representation of the female character. The Oedipus cycle begins and ends with *Antigone*, in which Antigone heroically refuses to accept the restraints on female action taken for granted by both

Creon and Ismene. And since, as we have seen, the Oedipus cycle includes the filial tragedies of both sonship and daughterhood, there seems to be little justification for reproaching Sophocles with sexist bias.

The matter is somewhat more delicate in the case of Freud. There can be no doubt that, on the basis of his own experience, he generalized the oedipal model into a universal paradigm, and for a long time remained blind to the fact that the early psychosexual development of girls was not simply a mirror image of that of boys. I have likewise shown that there is frequently an undercurrent of hostility in his personal relations with women, though it should be stressed that he always welcomed women as equals in the psychoanalytic movement. It was not until 1923, in *The Ego and the Id*, that Freud realized how involved was even the boy's Oedipus complex: "The intricacy of the problem is due to two factors: the triangular character of the Oedipus situation and the constitutional bisexuality of each individual" (*SE*, 19:31). But with this recognition of bisexuality and the dynamics of a "complete" Oedipus complex, I believe, Freud arrived at a formulation that is fundamentally applicable to members of both sexes.

At issue in the current encounter between psychoanalysis and feminism is the perennial problem of nature and nurture— how to balance the sense that there are certain constants in human experience with the evident fact of cultural diversity—particularly as this pertains to the institution of the family. Indeed, although the advent of feminism has injected a new note of urgency into the debate, the fundamental terms have not changed very much since the early part of the twentieth century, when Bronislaw Malinowski drew upon his anthropological field work among the Trobriand Islanders of New Guinea to call in doubt the hypothesis of the universality of the Oedipus complex; and Ernest Jones responded on behalf of psychoanalysis that Malinowski's observations of a boy's incestuous attraction to his sister and rivalry with his maternal uncle were but superficial displacements of the "nuclear family complex."[24]

I have myself argued as a rejoinder to Malinowski that the Oedipus complex depends for its vindication less on empirical data than on the philosophical concept of the hermeneutic circle and on the literary power of Sophocles' tragedy. But if the dispute is to be conducted on anthropological grounds, it is clear that psychoanalysis must emphasize the constants in human nature— the fact that the family is founded on the biological reality of procreation by a single mother and father, however complex and manifold the departures from this elemental model may be in actual social practice. The most forceful recent restatement of the classic psychoanalytic position is that of André Green: "To say that the Oedipus complex is universal is to say that every human being is born of two progenitors, one of a sex identical to his [or her] own, the other of a different sex." Green elaborates:

As soon as there was a family, there was the Oedipus complex. As long as there is a family, there will be an Oedipus complex. This does not mean that modifications were not introduced to it at various periods in history or that social systems did not influence the form it took. But one may well have reservations concerning this relativist attitude. The determining factors that affect the complex are of two kinds. The first are primary; they derive from the prematuration of the infant and its dependence on its parents, which is a biological and social fact. The others are secondary; they depend on the way in which the images of maternal and paternal identification are transmitted and on the way in which the parental roles are assumed by those who perform them in a given culture and period. It is easy to understand, then, that only the secondary determinations are susceptible to the influence of time, or the historico-social context.[25]

Once it is taken from granted that "every human being" includes women as well as men, it becomes truly "the fate of all of us" to repeat the drama of Oedipus. The variations noted by Malinowski and others at the *secondary* level of social institutions do not affect the inescapable *primary* experiences of desire and its interdiction. In joining both Deleuze and Guattari and Girard in their attack on the "familialism" of psychoanalysis, too many feminists lose sight of the ontological and biological priority of the "nuclear family," which does not depend on the sex of the child, and is likewise unaffected by the consideration that frequently the "parental roles" may not be assumed by the child's actual mother and father.

Such an overestimation of the importance of "secondary" sociological factors clouds one of the most perceptive feminist critiques of Freud, Nancy Chodorow's *The Reproduction of Mothering*. Chodorow's central contention is that

the psychoanalytic theory of the mother-infant relationship confounds an implicit claim for the inevitability and necessity of exclusive mothering by the biological mother with an argument for the necessity of constancy of care and a certain quality of care by some*one* or some few *persons*.[26]

As a practical matter, it may well be true that an adequate "quality of care" can be provided by individuals other than an infant's natural mother, and Chodorow's call for greater participation by men in child rearing is doubtless a healthy one. But this adaptability should not be allowed to obscure the awareness that the mother-infant bond—grounded in the biological realities of pregnancy and lactation—is the prototype, for which other arrangements are at best compensatory substitutes. To Chodorow's confidence that "a tremendous social advance"[27] can be brought about by the reforms she proposes, one may contrast the stoical acceptance of the female version of the oedipal predicament by Edna O'Brien:

If you want to know what I regard as the principal crux of female despair, it is this: in the Greek myth of Oedipus and in Freud's exploration of it, the son's desire for the mother is admitted; the infant daughter also desires its mother but it is unthinkable, either in myth, in fantasy or in fact, that that desire can be consummated.[28]

No pretense that the place of the mother can be filled "by some*one* or some few *persons*" diminishes the force of O'Brien's perception that the developmental task of women contains a hurdle not faced by men, since they must learn—if heterosexuality is to be achieved—to shift their erotic allegiance from the sex that bore them.

Notes

1. The Hero's Garb

1. The most valuable studies of Freud's life remain the psychoanalytically informed biographies of Ernest Jones, *The Life and Work of Sigmund Freud;* and Max Schur, *Freud: Living and Dying.* Also indispensable is Didier Anzieu, *L'auto-analyse de Freud et la découverte de la psychanalyse.* Ronald W. Clark's *Freud: The Man and the Cause* is a skillful retelling of the life, buttressed by new primary materials, by a professional biographer innocent of psychoanalytic sophistication. At the opposite pole from the present study, Frank J. Sulloway's *Freud: Biologist of the Mind* attempts to puncture "the mythical bubble surrounding Freud's life and achievements" (p. 5), claiming that "it seems highly unlikely that Freud's self-analysis played anything like the 'decisive' role that has so often been attributed to it in connection with the abandonment of the seduction theory" (p. 208), and that it is necessary to recover "the hidden biological roots of Freudian thought" (p. 3). Of the spate of recent books attempting to argue that Freud was fundamentally mistaken in rejecting the seduction theory in favor of the Oedipus complex perhaps the most suggestive, though least sharply focused, is Marianne Krüll's *Freud and His Father.* Peter J. Swales possesses an unrivaled knowledge of the details of Freud's life, and his hypothesis of an affair between Freud and his sister-in-law Minna Bernays deserves serious consideration. Unfortunately, his "gnostic" approach to Freud, in "Freud, Minna Bernays, and the Conquest of Rome" and other papers, is marred by his insistence that he is the first and only individual to have revealed "the *true* Freud" (p. 1). Swales further denies such psychoanalytic tenets as the unconscious, repression, and the controlling importance of infantile experience, and concurs with Sulloway in exaggerating Fliess' intellectual influence on Freud. See "Freud, Martha Bernays, and the Language of Flowers," pp. 35, 58; and "Freud, Fliess, and Fratricide," p. 5. Most recently, in a balanced and brilliant book, *Freud's Discovery of Psychoanalysis: The Politics of Hysteria,* William J. McGrath returns to the tradition of Jones and Schur by using psychoanalytic theory to explore the interrelations between the recurrent patterns of Freud's mental life and the unfolding political context in which he grew to maturity. While admitting that Freud's rejection of the seduction theory in favor of a view emphasizing the centrality of fantasy took place "for clearly personal as well as objective, scientific reasons," McGrath reasserts the classic psychoanalytic position, with which I am in complete agreement, that "this step represented an advance in both theoretical and personal insight" (p. 23).

2. Laplanche, *Life and Death in Psychoanalysis*, p. 40. See also the entry under "deferred action" in Laplanche and Pontalis, *The Language of Psychoanalysis*, pp. 111–14.

3. Laplanche, *Life and Death in Psychoanalysis*, p. 41.

4. These documents, with the exception of the *Project for a Scientific Psychology*, are at last published in *The Complete Letters of Sigmund Freud to Wilhelm Fliess 1887–1904*, Masson ed. and trans. In striving for literal fidelity to Freud's German, however, the translations in this volume often seem wooden, and whenever possible I have preferred to retain the earlier versions in *The Origins of Psychoanalysis*. The German edition used is *Aus der Anfängen der Psychoanalyse*. For an account of the recovery of these letters, and of Freud's alarmed reaction to the news of their existence, see *LW*, 1:287–89.

5. See *The Interpretation of Dreams*, *SE*, 4:142, for an editor's note listing all Freud's allusions to these lines.

6. Stanescu, "Young Freud's Letters to Silberstein," p. 196.

7. Gedo, "Freud's Self-Analysis and His Scientific Ideas," p. 296.

8. Quoted in McGrath, *Freud's Discovery of Psychoanalysis*, p. 91. Following Fritz Wittels, McGrath points to the resemblance between "On Nature" and Faust's question in Goethe's play: "Where shall I grasp thee, boundless nature? Where are your breasts from which all life doth flow?" For both Freud and Faust, he notes, "the desire to plumb nature's depths took the form of an erotic quest" *(ibid.)*.

9. See Clark, *Freud: The Man and the Cause*, p. 36, where the first use of "Sigmund" is dated to June 28, 1875.

10. Gedo and Wolf, "The 'Ich.' Letters," p. 84.

11. E. Freud, "Early Unpublished Letters," p. 424.

12. *Ibid.*, p. 423.

13. Sophocles, *Oedipus the King*, l. 33. Subsequent line numbers will be included parenthetically in the text. For documentation of the passage translated by Freud on his *Matura*, see *Sigmund Freud: His Life in Words and Pictures*, pp. 74–75.

14. The concluding speech of the Chorus, from which this line is taken, is quoted by Freud during his dicussion of *Oedipus the King* in *The Interpretation of Dreams*, *SE*, 4:263.

15. Derrida, *Of Grammatology*, p. 304.

16. Freud, "Early Unpublished Letters," p. 420.

17. Quoted in Clark, *Freud: The Man and the Cause*, p. 23.

18. *Ibid.*, p. 22. As McGrath remarks, "Freud's travels often seem to have had the effect of exposing him to regressive moods" connected particularly with "longing for a mother figure" *(Freud's Discovery of Psychoanalysis*, pp. 133, 153).

19. Quoted in Clark, *Freud: The Man and the Cause*, p. 25.

20. *Ibid.*, p. 24.

21. Since the publication of Jones' biography, archival research in Freiberg has brought to light the fact that Jakob Freud was briefly married for a *second* time to a woman named Rebekka, whose death or disappearance remains mysterious, prior to his marriage to Amalie Nathanson. See Sajner, "Sigmund Freuds Beziehungen zu seinem Geburtsort." For an assessment of the possible impact of this knowledge on Freud, see Schur, *Freud: Living and Dying*, pp. 20–21, 190–91; and the fascinating but unsound book by Marie Balmary, *Psychoanalyzing Psychoanalysis*. In *Freud and His Father*, however, Krüll holds that the case for Jakob Freud's second marriage remains unproven (p. 96).

22. Bernfeld and Bernfeld, "Freud's Early Childhood," p. 109.

23. See Shengold, "Freud and Joseph," p. 73.

24. See McGrath, *Freud's Discovery of Psychoanalysis*, for even more detailed correspondences between Freud's family constellation and that of the biblical Joseph: "Like Joseph, he was thus the favored elder son of a father named Jakob and his well-loved younger wife" (p. 33). The existence of one such pattern, of course, does not cancel out the significance of a second or a third.

25. Said, *Beginnings*, p. 170.

2. The Transference Neurosis

1. Shakespeare, *Hamlet*, 1.2.103–4, 92–93.
2. Quoted in Schur, *Freud: Living and Dying*, pp. 267–68. Freud appears to have conflated his brother's birth and death, since, according to Schur, Julius "was born sometime late in 1857 and died on April 15, 1858" (p. 21), just before Freud's second birthday.
3. For further discussion of the role of Julius in Freud's life, see Schur, *Freud: Living and Dying*; and Blum, "The Prototype of Preoedipal Reconstruction." In "A Childhood Recollection from *Dichtung und Wahrheit*" (1917), Freud seeks to account for the impact on Goethe of the deaths of several siblings in early childhood. Concerning his next-youngest sibling, Hermann Jakob, who died when Goethe was nearly ten, Freud comments: "One might feel some surprise that the autobiography does not contain a word of remembrance concerning him" (*SE*, 17:151). The true cause for "surprise," however, as Freud acknowledged in a footnote added in 1924, is that he is mistaken, for Hermann Jakob is indeed mentioned in *Dichtung und Wahrheit*. This unconsciously motivated lapse shows both Freud's desire to remake Goethe in his own image and his continuing guilt over failing to offer any public "word of remembrance" concerning Julius.
4. This use of "transference" to define the relation between the day residue and the infantile wish in dreams underlies its application to clinical setting. See the editor's note to *The Interpretation of Dreams*, *SE*, 5:562–63.
5. For confirmation of the view that Freud's self-analysis arose in response to his father's death, see Schur, "Some Additional 'Day Residues,'" pp. 68–69; and Grinstein, *Sigmund Freud's Dreams*, p. 420.
6. Anzieu, *L'auto-analyse de Freud*, 1:237. For additional discussion of the "close the eyes" dream, including comparison between the versions found in the letter to Fliess and in *The Interpretation of Dreams*, see Robert, *From Oedipus to Moses*, pp. 85–130; and Krüll, *Freud and His Father*, pp. 41–43.
7. Buxbaum, "Freud's Dream Interpretation," p. 59. Jeffrey Masson, however, inexplicably maintains that "it is not illuminating to claim, as some have done, that this intense relationship was one of transference" (Masson, p. 2).
8. Here I clearly disagree with Swales, whose judgment that Freud was "an exceedingly bizarre . . . and devious individual" ("Language of Flowers," p. 64) seems to me as reductive as the idealized portrait of Freud it is intended to correct.
9. In "Freud's Mother Conflict," Ruth Abraham suggests that Fliess may also have played the part of a mother surrogate in Freud's self-analysis. She notes that, toward both Fliess and Martha Bernays, Freud had "an attitude of extreme overvaluation which was often used as a defense against hostile and fearful feelings" (p. 488).
10. Kohut, "Creativeness, Charisma, Group Psychology," p. 393.
11. Stanescu, "Young Freud's Letters to Silberstein," pp. 205–6.
12. On the Emma Eckstein episode, see Schur's indispensable article, "Some Additional 'Day Residues'"; and Masson, *The Assault on Truth*. In her account of Masson's collision with Kurt Eissler, Janet Malcolm states that Schur's article was published "in an obscure volume" (*In the Freud Archives*, p. 44). This assertion is misleading, because *Psychoanalysis—A General Psychology*, as a *Festschrift* in honor of Heinz Hartmann, could not be considered "obscure" by anyone coversant with the field of psychoanalysis. In addition, Malcolm is unjustifiably harsh (p. 7) on the work of Paul Roazen, *Brother Animal: The Story of Freud and Tausk*, and far too uncritical in her admiration of Kurt Eissler's intemperate rebuttal, *Talent and Genius: The Fictitious Case of Tausk Contra Freud*. Whatever its failings, Roazen's is an important book, and Malcolm's conclusion that Eissler administers to Roazen "one of the most severe trouncings of one scholar by another in the annals of scholarly quarrelling" (p. 8) is so one-sided as to call her objectivity into doubt.
13. Schur, *Freud: Living and Dying*, p. 12. See also van Velzen, "Irma at the Window." The operation on Emma Eckstein had, of course, been prompted by Fliess' bizarre theory of a connection between the nose and genital organs.

14. *A Psycho-Analytic Dialogue*, p. 168.

15. Other implicit references to Julius include the use of the phrase *non vixit* ("he did not live") in place of *non vivit* ("he is not alive") and the importance of the name *Julius Caesar* in the dream.

16. On Freud's repeated involvement in disputes over priority and plagiarism, see Roazen, *Brother Animal*, pp. 59–93; and *Freud and his Followers*, pp. 190–202. In *Talent and Genius*, Eissler naively contends that Freud displayed an "unconcern with priorities" (pp. 183–87).

17. See Schur, *Freud: Living and Dying*, pp. 161, 168.

18. Rieff, *Freud: The Mind of the Moralist*, p. 195.

19. Sophocles, *Oedipus the King*, ll. 808–9. Subsequent line numbers will be included parenthetically in the text.

20. Girard, *Violence and the Sacred*, p. 48.

21. Swales, "Language of Flowers," notes that Fliess' sister was named Clara, and not Pauline, as had been previously believed (p. 39).

22. See Carotenuto, *A Secret Symmetry*, with a valuable Commentary by Bruno Bettelheim. Subsequent page references to this volume will be indicated parenthetically by the abbreviation *Symmetry*.

23. Gallop, *The Daughter's Seduction*, p. 69.

24. Rosenberg, *Why Freud Fainted*, p. 11. Italics deleted.

25. *Ibid*.

26. See Kanzer, "Sigmund and Alexander Freud on the Acropolis," pp. 272–73.

27. See Schorske, "Politics and Patricide." Useful discussions of this episode may also be found in Cuddihy, *The Ordeal of Civility*, pp. 48–57; and McGrath, "Freud as Hannibal."

28. M. Freud, *Sigmund Freud: Man and Father*, pp. 70–71. A similar anti-Semitic incident, experienced by Freud during a train ride in December 1883, is cited by McGrath, "Freud as Hannibal," p. 41; and by Cuddihy, *The Ordeal of Civility*, pp. 54–55. But the extreme nature of Freud's reaction in 1901 must qualify somewhat McGrath's assertion that, by joining B'nai B'rith in September 1897, he "renounced his unjust adolescent criticism" of his father "by choosing the same sort of restrained and dignified response to anti-Semitism that Jakob Freud had chosen" (*Freud's Discovery of Psychoanalysis*, p. 213).

29. Mahl, "Father-Son Themes in Freud's Self-Analysis," p. 59.

30. See Robert, *From Oedipus to Moses*. Concerning "The Moses of Michelangelo" (1914), moreover, Krüll remarks on the "emotional ambivalence" in Freud's fascination with Michelangelo's statue: "On the one hand, he identified himself with Moses, the self-controlled lawgiver; on the other hand, Moses was a father image of whom he was afraid" (*Freud and His Father*, p. 187).

31. Schorske, "Politics and Patricide," p. 336.

32. See Shengold, "Freud and Joseph," pp. 70–71; and Anzieu, *L'auto-analyse de Freud*, 1:329.

33. Gadamer, *Truth and Method*, p. 269.

3. In My Own Case Too

1. For clarification of the distinct identities of these two patients, and particularly for the reconstruction of the manner in which Freud arrived at his discovery of the Oedipus complex, I am indebted to Anzieu, *L'auto-analyse de Freud*, 1:326–34.

2. In *Origins*, the final sentence incorrectly reads "some puzzles in my own case." The German original in *Anfängen* is: "Da ich noch irgendein Rätsel bei meinen Fällen habe, so muß dies auch in der Selbstanalyse aufhalten" (p. 202). Masson, in his edition, renders the final sentence accurately, but goes astray in failing to insert a period after the "why" ending the second sentence. I have noticed at least two other mistakes in his edition: in

the letter of October 31, 1895, he translates the German "Bis 96" (*Anfängen*, p. 117) as "by the end of '96" (p. 148), whereas the true meaning is "by 1896"; and in the letter of January 26, 1900 the phrase "In the case of F., . . ."(p. 397) should read "In the case of E."

3. Implicit or explicit references to E. may be found in the letters of: October 31, 1895; November 2, 1895; December 6, 1896; December 17, 1896; January 3, 1897; January 12, 1897; January 24, 1897; Draft L; December 29, 1897; February 19, 1899; December 21, 1899; January 8, 1900; January 26, 1900; March 11, 1900; April 4, 1900; and April 16, 1900. This list supplements that in Anzieu, *L'auto-analyse de Freud*, 1:260. No entry for E. appears in the index of Masson's edition of the Freud-Fliess letters.

4. On E., see also the excellent article of Rosenblum, "Le premier parcours psychanalytique d'un homme."

5. On Monika Zajíc, see Sajner, "Freuds Beziehungen zu seinem Geburtsort," pp. 173–75. Citing the recent research of Sajner and Swales, however, Krüll has asserted that Freud's nanny was in fact not Monika Zajíc but Resi Wittek. See *Freud and His Father*, p. 119. This change of names, in any case, does not appear to affect anything else we know about her.

6. Krüll, *Freud and His Father*, p. 121.

7. On the relation of "Screen Memories" to Freud's wooing of Martha Bernays and his adult life generally, see Swales, "Language of Flowers."

8. See Krüll, *Freud and His Father*, p. 132.

9. See Krüll, *Freud and His Father*, p. 156; Swales, "Language of Flowers," p. 32; Anzieu, *L'auto-analyse de Freud*, 1:379; and Grinstein, *Sigmund Freud's Dreams*, pp. 56–63.

10. See Rosenblum, "Le premier parcours psychanalytique d'un homme."

11. See Wittels, *Sigmund Freud*, p. 114.

12. The death of this old lady is reported by Freud in his letter to Fliess of August 7, 1901; she likewise appears in an association to the "Irma" dream of July 24, 1895. In *The Psychopathology of Everyday Life*, Freud says that he visited her for "six years" (*SE*, 6:164).

13. Puzzlingly, however, Gedo has insisted that Freud's conduct toward Emma Eckstein and Sabina Spielrein does not "involve negative aspects of [his] infantile relations with women" ("Theban Plague," p. 256).

14. Heidegger, *Being and Time*, p. 195. See further Hoy, *The Critical Circle*.

15. Schorske, "Politics and Patricide," p. 330.

16. Swales, "Freud, Fliess, and Fratricide," p. 15.

17. *Ibid.*, p. 20.

18. Drawing on interviews with Fliess' daughter and the son of a close family friend, Swales maintains that Fliess believed that Freud actually intended to murder him at Achensee. See *ibid.*, p. 13. On the affair with Minna, see "Conquest of Rome."

19. The same dream is adduced in *The Interpretation of Dreams*, SE, 4:155–57.

20. The case that Freud was sexually involved with Minna hinges also on the assumption that her five-month stay in a Merano sanitorium, from September 1900 through February 1901, was for the purpose of having an abortion, instead of (or in addition to) treatment for tuberculosis. But this remains unproven, though Swales' circumstantial argument that Freud helped defray Minna's medical expenses is convincing. It should be added that some external corroboration for the affair exists in the form of the testimony of Jung, who more than once reported that Minna had confessed the fact to him. See "Conquest of Rome," pp. 11, 15.

21. See Krüll, *Freud and His Father*, p. 195.

22. Grinstein, *Sigmund Freud's Dreams*, p. 339.

23. Shengold, "The Metaphor of the Journey," p. 54. McGrath interprets Freud's change of compartments as an escape from "a conflict-ridden Austrian dream world" to

"an English dream world in which he was socially accepted and his revolutionary sexual theories brought fame without guilt" (*Freud's Discovery of Psychoanalysis*, p. 266).

24. See Sajner, "Freuds Beziehungen zu seinem Geburtsort," p. 172.

25. See Krüll, *Freud and His Father*, pp. 125–26.

26. Considerable controversy surrounds the motivations for Jakob Freud's departure from Freiberg. In "Screen Memories," Freud himself attributes his family's upheaval to a "catastrophe" in "the branch of industry in which my father was concerned" (*SE*, 3:312), to which Jones (*LW*, 1:12) added the further explanation of anti-Semitic outbreaks in Freiberg. But Jones' theory of hostility on the part of Czech weavers against Jewish cloth merchants such as Freud's father has been disproven by Sajner, "Freuds Beziehungen zu seinem Geburtsort," p. 176. In her effort to argue that Jakob Freud left Freiberg to conceal evidence of his mysterious second marriage, Balmary asserts that "after Sajner's work" any pretense that his family's migration was due to "antisemitism or economic catastrophe in the textile business" is "inadmissible" (*Psychoanalyzing Psychoanalysis*, p. 141). But since Sajner's research in fact contradicts only Jones' suspicion of anti-Semitism, the economic motive for the move remains valid, and Balmary's far-fetched conspiracy theory is unsubstantiated. For confirmation of the economic pressures compelling Jakob Freud to abandon Freiberg, see Gicklhorn, "The Freiberg Period of the Freud Family."

27. Marcus, *Freud and the Culture of Psychoanalysis*, p. 73.

28. Sachs, *Freud: Master and Friend*, p. 83.

29. Buxbaum, "Freud's Dream Interpretation," p. 64. Krüll connects Freud's fear of the Breslau gas lamps with the threat of castration as a punishment for masturbation, which came to seem real to him after seeing Pauline's genitals (*Freud and His Father*, p. 142).

30. See Bernfeld, "An Unknown Autobiographical Fragment."

31. A comparable example of this attitude is supplied by Kris, who contends that the discrepancy between Freud's statement in *The Interpretation of Dreams* that the "close the eyes" dream took place the night *before* his father's funeral, whereas in his November 2, 1896 letter to Fliess it is ascribed to the night after, is due to Freud's having prepared the published version "with the aid of notes" (*Origins*, p. 171). This explanation is at best disingenuous, since it seems clear that the alteration in *The Interpretation of Dreams* is a deliberate attempt to minimize his self-disclosure on Freud's part.

32. Bernfeld, "An Unknown Autobiographical Fragment," p. 28.

33. In *The Psychopathology of Everyday Life*, Freud introduces his discussion of the "*aliquis*" parapraxis by saying that last summer "I renewed my acquaintance with a certain young man of academic background" (*SE*, 6:8–9). Swales' belief that this slip is really Freud's gains support from the echo in these words of the description of the fictive patient in "Screen Memories" as "a man of university education." By affirming that he has "renewed" this acquaintance, Freud appears to be wittily referring back to his earlier disguised self-portrayal.

34. Bernfeld, "An Unknown Autobiographical Fragment," p. 27.

35. See S. C. Bernfeld, "Freud and Archaeology."

36. See Lewin, "The Train Ride," pp. 72, 82.

37. Sterba, "The Fate of the Ego in Analytic Therapy," p. 121.

38. Lacan, "Desire and the Interpretation of Desire in *Hamlet*," p. 44.

39. See the comments of Jean Starobinski quoted in Anzieu, *L'auto-analyse de Freud*, 1:329–30; and Green, "Shakespeare, Freud et le parricide."

40. See Trosman, "Freud and the Controversy over Shakespearean Authorship."

41. See Balmary, *Psychoanalyzing Psychoanalysis*, and the cautionary remarks in note 26 above. In *Freud and His Father*, moreover, Krüll makes the prudent observation that "had Jacob really wanted to conceal his alliance with Rebekka he would certainly not

have moved with Amalie to Freiberg" (p. 136) in the first place. Krüll herself, however, contributes to the implausible theories of sexual misconduct surrounding the Freud family by proposing that Freud's half-brother Philipp had an affair with Freud's mother Amalie, and that one of the reasons Jakob sent his elder sons to England was to separate Philipp and Amalie (pp. 124–28). Krüll is indecisive on the question of the reasons for the departure of the Freud family from Freiberg, first denying and then admitting the possibility of an economic motive (p. 144).

42. See Swan, *"Mater* and Nannie," p. 42.

43. See Gedo, "Freud's Self-Analysis and His Scientific Ideas," p. 301. In point of fact, as Krüll (*Freud and His Father*, p. 108) notes, Freud actually had *three* maternal figures in early childhood, if one counts also Emmanuel's wife Maria. But it is the splitting in two of the image of the mother that seems to have left the most profound effect on Freud's imagination, as in the "peasant-woman" and "children's nurse" in "Screen Memories" or his forming a household with the two sisters Martha and Minna Bernays.

44. Swan, *"Mater* and Nannie," p. 34. See also Grigg, "'All Roads Lead to Rome.'"

45. See McGrath, *Freud's Discovery of Psychoanalysis*, p. 63; and Krüll, *Freud and His Father*, p. 123.

4. Sophocles Unbound

1. Heller, "Observations on Psychoanalysis and Modern Literature," pp. 188–89.

2. See Ellenberger, *The Discovery of the Unconscious*. Ellenberger's refusal to confront "the specificity of the psychoanalytic discovery" is criticized by Anzieu, *L'auto-analyse de Freud*, 1:12.

3. Nietzsche, *The Gay Science*, sec. 34. (Book V of *The Gay Science* was added in 1887.)

4. Gay, *Freud, Jews, and Other Germans*, p. 33.

5. See Sulloway, *Freud: Biologist of the Mind*.

6. For this view of Freud, see, in addition to Heller's essay cited in note 1, Trilling, "Freud and Literature"; and the two seminal essays by Thomas Mann, "Freud's Position in the History of Modern Culture" (1929), and "Freud and the Future" (1936).

7. See McGrath, *Freud's Discovery of Psychoanalysis*, pp. 111–27. Also useful is Barclay, "Franz Brentano and Sigmund Freud," which argued for Brentano's influence on Freud before the decisive proof established by the partial publication of the Silberstein correspondence. For further judicious discussion of Brentano in light of Freud's attitudes toward philosophy, see Herzog, "The Myth of Freud as Anti-Philosopher."

8. Habermas, *Knowledge and Human Interests*, p. 228. For a vehement attack on the hermeneutic approach to psychoanalysis, and on the scientific standing of psychoanalytic theory, see Grünbaum, *The Foundations of Psychoanalysis*.

9. Steiner, *Antigones*, p. 6.

10. See Butler, *The Tyranny of Greece Over Germany*.

11. Useful information on Sophocles is scattered throughout Sandys, *A History of Classical Scholarship*. On the performance of *Oedipus the King*, translated by Giustiniani with choruses set to music by Gabrielli, at the opening of Palladio's Teatro Olimpico at Vicenza in 1585, see Schrade, *La répresentation d'Edipo Tiranno au Teatro Olimpico*. Early versions of *Oedipus*, in addition to those discussed in the text, include plays by Anguillara (1565) and Tesauro (1643).

12. Seneca, *Oedipus*, l. 909. Subsequent line numbers will be given parenthetically in the text.

13. Sophocles, *Oedipus the King*, ll. 60–61.

14. See Schönau, *Sigmund Freuds Prosa*, pp. 42–48. Like Freud, Hegel was also decisively influenced by Lessing. See Kaufmann, *Hegel: A Reinterpretation*, pp. 41–45.

15. See Butler, *The Tyranny of Greece Over Germany*, pp. 58–59.

16. Lessing, *Werke*, 6:38.

17. *Ibid.*, 4:609.

18. *Ibid.*, 4:609–10.

19. Lessing was, moreover, the author of an influential *Life of Sophocles* (1760).

20. Although my emphasis often diverges from his, I am indebted in my examination of imitations of Sophocles to Mueller, *Children of Oedipus*. An analysis of the neoclassical *Oedipus* by Dryden and Lee (1678) could easily be assimilated to those of Corneille and Voltaire offered in the text.

21. Corneille, *Oeuvres Complètes*, p. 832.

22. *Ibid.*, p. 567.

23. *Ibid.*

24. Voltaire, *Oeuvres Complètes*, 2:19, 21.

25. *Ibid.*, 2:28.

26. See Rank, *Incest-Motif*, p. 240.

27. See Besterman, *Voltaire*, pp. 20–22, 76.

28. See Trilling, *Sincerity and Authenticity*, pp. 27–28, where the influence of *Rameau's Nephew* on Marx is also noted.

29. Taylor, *Hegel*, pp. 17–18.

30. Schlegel, *Lectures on Dramatic Art and Literature*, p. 211. Ensuing page references will be given parenthetically in the text. Schlegel's more gifted brother Friedrich likewise saw in tragedy "the most excellent of Greek poetic arts" and affirmed that Sophocles "achieved the utmost aim of Greek poetry." See the remarks on Sophocles in his seminal treatise *Über das Studium der Griechischen Poesie* (1797), pp. 296–301.

31. On this nexus, see Staiger, *Der Geist der Liebe und das Schicksal*, pp. 15–30; Nauen, *Revolution, Idealism, and Human Freedom*, pp. 1–26; and Montgomery, *Hölderlin and the German Neo-Hellenic Movement*, Part 1, pp. 200–21.

32. See Kaufmann, *Hegel: A Reinterpretation*, p. 313.

33. See Serber, Introduction to Hegel, *Difference Between the Fichtean and Schellingian Systems*, pp. xxi–xxii.

34. See Nauen, *Revolution, Idealism, and Human Freedom*, p. 41.

35. Schelling, *Werke*, Buchner et al., eds., vol. 1, part 3, pp 106–7.

36. Schelling, *Sämtliche Werke*, 5:693. Ensuing page references will be included parenthetically in the text.

37. Silk and Stern, *Nietszche on Tragedy*, p. 309.

38. See Nauen, *Revolution, Idealism, and Human Freedom*, p. 4. On Hellenic influences on German thought during this period, see also, among others, Taminiaux, *La Nostalgie de la Grèce*; and Rehm, *Griechentum und Goethezeit*.

39. Schiller, *Werke: Nationalausgabe*, 29:141–42.

5. Three Romantic Case Studies

1. See Prader, *Schiller und Sophokles*; Gerhard, *Schiller und die griechische Tragödie*; and Wittrich, *Sophocles' ''König Ödipus'' und Schillers ''Braut von Messina.''*

2. Schiller, *Werke: Nationalausgabe*, 30:177. See also "The Symbol of the Veil," where E. H. Gombrich (p. 93) quotes from the second of Schiller's *Philosophical Letters* (1786): "Our philosophy is the fateful curiosity of Oedipus who never ceased asking till the terrible oracle was solved: 'may you never learn who you are.' "

3. Butler, *The Tyranny of Greece Over Germany*, p. 194.

4. My summary of *Narbonne* follows that given in Prader, *Schiller und Sophokles*, pp. 37–55.

5. Quoted in *ibid.*, p. 38.

6. Schiller, *The Bride of Messina*, ll. 961–67. Subsequent line numbers will be given parenthetically in the text.

7. Mueller, *Children of Oedipus*, pp. 137–38.

8. *Ibid.*, p. 142.

9. Rank, *Incest-Motiv*, p. 564.

10. Schiller, *Don Carlos*, ll. 276–80.

11. See Rank, *Incest-Motiv*, p. 43.

12. See Passage, Introduction to Schiller, *The Bride of Messina*, p. vii.

13. Frederick Ungar, for example, writes that "erotic forces play hardly any creative role at all in Schiller's Life" (*Schiller: An Anthology for Our Time*, p. 100). Similarly, Gilbert J. Jordan maintains that Schiller's "exceptionally productive career . . . shows hardly a note of personal experience" (Schiller, *Wilhelm Tell*, p. xi).

14. Rank, *Incest-Motiv*, p. 562.

15. See *ibid.*, p. 576.

16. See McGrath, *Freud's Discovery of Psychoanalysis*, pp. 67–77, where it is further noted of *The Robbers:* "The drama's portrayal of the beautiful young Amalia caring for the old father provided a framework into which Freud could easily fit his own family story of an old father with a young wife much desired by the brothers" (p. 69).

17. Rank, *Incest-Motiv*, p. 92.

18. Schiller, *Naive and Sentimental Poetry*, p. 100. Subsequent page references will be given parenthetically in the text.

19. Schiller, *Aesthetic Education*, p. 81. Subsequent page references will be given parenthetically in the text.

20. Nietzsche, *The Birth of Tragedy*, sec. 1. I have, however, throughout this book altered Kaufmann's translation of "Apollinian" to "Apollonian." Subsequent section numbers will be given parenthetically in the text.

21. See the editor's note to Schiller, *Aesthetic Education*, pp. 88–89.

22. Hölderlin, *Sämtliche Werke*, vol. 7, part 2, pp. 303–4.

23. See Hamburger, Introduction to Hölderlin, *Poems and Fragments*, p. 3. Unless otherwise noted, translations from Hölderlin's poetry will be taken from this bilingual edition, with page references indicated parenthetically in the text by the abbreviation "Hamburger."

24. Hayman, *Nietzsche: A Critical Life*, p. 42.

25. Hölderlin, *Hyperion*, p. 23. In vol. 3 of Beissner's edition of the *Sämtliche Werke*, there is an analytical table comparing the texts of various versions of *Hyperion*.

26. Hölderlin, *Hyperion*, p. 82.

27. Goethe, *Sorrows of Young Werther*, p. 121.

28. Hölderlin, *Sämtliche Werke*, vol. 6, part 1, p. 157.

29. *Ibid.*, p. 173.

30. See Laplanche, *Hölderlin et la question du père*, p. 55. Although Laplanche's psychobiographical study is a model of its kind, it is curious that his examination of the "question of the father" does not address Hölderlin's involvement with the Oedipus myth.

31. See *ibid.*, p. 29.

32. See Butler, *The Tyranny of Greece Over Germany*, pp. 225–34.

33. Quoted in Hamburger, Introduction to Hölderlin, *Poems and Fragments*, p. 13.

34. Reinhardt, "Hölderlin und Sophokles," p. 287. A fervent defense of Hölderlin's translations as "the most violent, deliberately extreme act of hermeneutic penetration and appropriation of which we have knowledge" is offered by Steiner in *After Babel*, pp. 322–

33. See also Steiner, *Antigones*, 66–103; Harrison, *Hölderlin and Greek Literature*, pp. 160–92; and Binder, "Hölderlin und Sophokles." A critical assessment of Hölderlin's translations is put forward in Schadewaldt, "Hölderlin's Übersetzung des Sophokles."

35. Hölderlin, *Sämtliche Werke*, 5:272. Subsequent volume and page references to the *Anmerkungen zum Oedipus* and *Anmerkungen zur Antigonae* will be indicated parenthetically in the text. See also Schrader, *Hölderlins Deutung des "Oedipus" und der "Antigone."*

36. See Else, "Sophokles the Elusive," p. 127.

37. See Green, *The Tragic Effect*, pp. 225–26. The French title of Green's book, *Un oeil en trop*, is taken from "In lovely blueness," and he offers a penetrating discussion (pp. 225–30) of Hölderlin's reflections on tragedy.

38. Butler, *The Tyranny of Greece Over Germany*, p. 235.

39. Hölderlin, *Sämtliche Werke*, vol. 7, part 3, p. 5.

40. *An Abyss Deep Enough*, pp. 205–6. Subsequent page references to this volume will be indicated parenthetically by the abbreviation *Abyss*.

41. In "The Dismantling of a Marionette Theater," Erich Heller seizes upon the excesses of a recent piece of psychoanalytic literary criticism on Kleist to dismiss the value of the method itself. Heller's polemical essay, however, does not take into account the long tradition of distinguished psychoanalytic writing on Kleist, beginning with Isidor Sadger's 1910 biographical monograph, *Heinrich von Kleist*. A portion of Sadger's research was presented to the Vienna Psychoanalytic Society, where it met with a lively and by no means uncritical reception. See *Minutes*, 2:220–26. See further Ernest Jones' 1911 paper, prompted by Sadger's work, "On 'Dying Together' "; and Kaiser, "Kleists 'Prinz von Homburg.' "

42. See Hölderlin's November 1794 letter to Neuffer in *Sämtliche Werke*, vol. 6, part 1, p. 140.

43. *Ibid.*, vol. 7, part 2, p. 109.

44. *Kleists Lebensspuren*, p. 103. For an extended discussion of Kleist's relationship with Goethe, see Mommsen, *Kleists Kampf mit Goethe*.

45. See *Kleists Nachruhm*, p. 153.

46. Nietzsche, *Schopenhauer as Educator*, p. 20.

47. On Freud and Tausk, see, in addition to the works cited in part 1, ch. 2, n. 12, Roazen's rebuttal to Eissler, "Reflections on Ethos and Authenticity in Psychoanalysis"; and Roustang, *Dire Mastery*, pp. 76–106.

48. Nietzsche, *Schopenhauer as Educator*, p. 24.

49. Quoted in Maass, *Kleist: A Biography*, p. 80.

50. See von Wädenswil, *Kleist und Sophokles*, pp. 25–47; and Stahl, "Guiscard and Oedipus."

51. See *Kleists Lebensspuren*, p. 96.

52. See von Wädenswil, *Kleist und Sophokles*, pp. 54–89; Schadewaldt, "Der 'Zerbrochene Krug' und 'König Ödipus' "; von Gordon, *Dramatische Handlung*; and Mueller, *Children of Oedipus*, pp. 115–28.

53. Kleist, *Der zerbrochene Krug*, in *Dramen Zwieter Teil*, p. 5. The words in brackets were subsequently added by Kleist and then crossed out. Unless otherwise noted, subsequent translations from Kleist's dramatic works will be taken from *Plays*, Hinderer, ed., with act and scene or scene and line numbers included parenthetically in the text. This volume contains: *The Broken Pitcher*, Swan, tr.; *Amphitryon*, Passage, tr.; *Penthesilea*, Trevelyan, tr.; and *Prince Frederick of Homburg*, Sherry, tr. In *The Broken Jug*, I have altered Swan's translation of *Licht* from "Link" to "Light."

54. Mueller, *Children of Oedius*, p. 118.

55. See Mommsen, *Kleists Kampf mit Goethe*, pp. 42–48.

56. Kleist, *Dramen Zweiter Teil*, p. 284. Here and in the ensuing discussion I follow the text of a manuscript version of *Penthesilea* included in this edition. Subsequent page references will be given parenthetically in the text.

57. Kaiser, "Kleists 'Prinz von Homburg,'" p. 236.

58. Kleist, *The Marquise of O——*, in *The Marquise of O—— and Other Stories*, p. 79.

59. For a contrasting view, see Greenberg, Introduction to *ibid.*, p. 35. On connections between *The Marquise of O——* and *Oedipus the King*, see von Wädenswil, *Kleist und Sophokles*, p. 46; and Aichele, "Kleist's Tragic Roots."

60. This and the ensuing two epigrams are quoted from Kleist, *Sämtliche Werke*, 1:22.

61. See Marcus, *Freud and the Culture of Psychoanalysis*, p. 73.

62. See Sadger, *Heinrich von Kleist*, pp. 30–31.

63. See *ibid.*, p. 62.

64. See Maass, *Kleist: A Biography*, p. 270. Despite its usefulness as a chronicle of Kleist's life, Maass' biography is vitiated by his antipathy to psychological analysis.

65. Here, as throughout this book, in drawing attention to oedipal patterns, I do not mean to deny the importance of preoedipal issues, which are especially prominent in Kleist's life and work.

66. See Maass, *Kleist: A Biography*, p. 182.

67. *Ibid.*, p. 291.

68. In my interpretation of *The Prince of Homburg*, I follow closely that given by Kaiser. On Kleist's continuing preoccupation with Goethe in this play, see Mommsen, *Kleists Kampf mit Goethe*, pp. 167–205.

69. Kaiser, "Kleists 'Prinz von Homburg,'" p. 225.

70. On Romantic reinterpretations of the myth of the Fall, see Abrams, *Natural Supernaturalism*; and Hartman, "Romanticism and Anti-Self-Consciousness."

71. See Lacan, "The Mirror Stage as Formative of the Function of the I" (1936).

6. Hegel

1. See Pöggeler, *Hegels Kritik der Romantik*.

2. Hegel, *Aesthetics*, 2:1219.

3. Hegel, *Logic*, p. 42. Subsequent page references to this volume will be indicated parenthetically by the word *Logic*.

4. On Hegel and ancient Greece, see Janicaud, *Hegel et le destin de la Grèce*; Gray, *Hegel's Hellenic Ideal*; Wolff, "Hegel und die griechische Welt"; Sichirollo, "Hegel und die griechische Welt"; Pöggeler, "Hegel und die griechische Tragödie"; Heidegger, "Hegel und die Griechen"; and Gadamer, "Hegel and the Dialectic of the Ancient Philosophers."

5. Quoted in Kaufmann, *Hegel: A Reinterpretation*, p. 10. On Hegel's early attitude to the classics, see also his "Über einige charakteristiche Unterschiede der alten Dichter [von den neueren]" (1788).

6. A full collection of these writings is to be found in *Hegels theologische Jugendschriften*; most also appear in Hegel, *Early Theological Writings*. Page references to these volumes will be indicated, respectively, by the abbreviations *HTJ* and *ETW*. See also Pöggeler, "Hegel und die griechische Tragödie," pp. 286–87.

7. Janicaud, *Hegel et le destin de la Grèce*, p. 13.

8. See Taylor, *Hegel*, pp. 51–64; and Kroner, Introduction to Hegel, *Early Theological Writings*, pp. 8–11. Less well-balanced is Kaufmann, "The Young Hegel and Religion," who broadly characterizes Hegel's early writings as "antitheological" (p. 63) and likewise (pp. 72–74) denies any affinity between Hegel and Romanticism.

9. Nietzsche, *Daybreak*, sec. 406.

10. Quotations from Baillie's translation of *The Phenomenology of Mind* have been

checked against Hegel, *Phänomenologie des Geistes*. Underlinings have been brought into conformity with the German edition.

11. Hyppolite, "Phénoménologie de Hegel et Psychanalyse," p. 18. On Hegel's relation to psychoanalysis, see also Ricoeur, *Freud and Philosophy*, pp. 375–418, 459–83; Vergote, "L'intérêt philosophique de la psychanalyse freudienne"; and de Waelhens, "Réflexions sur une problématique husserlienne."

12. Ricoeur, *Freud and Philosophy*, p. 461.

13. See Rieff, *The Triumph of the Therapeutic*.

14. Hyppolite, "The Structure of Philosophic Language," p. 165.

15. Habermas, *Knowledge and Human Interests*, p. 18.

16. See, however, Masullo, "Das Unbewußte in Hegels Philosophie."

17. See Janicaud, *Hegel et le destin de la Grèce*, pp. 327–28.

18. Auden, "Psychology and Art To-day," p. 69.

19. See Ricoeur, *Freud and Philosophy*, p. 465.

20. See Kelly, "Notes on Hegel's 'Lordship and Bondage,'" p. 195. Kelly's essay attempts to highlight the subjective or phenomenological dimension of the master-slave dialectic, slighted in Kojève's seminal *Introduction to the Reading of Hegel*.

21. Hegel, *Lectures on the Philosophy of Religion*, 2:264. Ensuing page references to this volume will be given parenthetically in the text. The English translation follows a revised edition of the *Lectures* issued in 1840.

22. Hegel, *Aesthetics*, 1:214.

23. Hegel, *Philosophy of History*, p. 10. Subsequent page references to this volume will be indicated parenthetically by the abbreviation *PH*. I have checked Sibree's translation, and frequently removed capitalizations, against Hegel, *Vorlesungen über die Philosophie der Geschichte*. Sibree's translation follows the third edition of 1843.

24. Hegel, *Philosophy of Right*, pp. 12–13.

25. *Ibid.*, p. 12.

26. White, *Metahistory*, p. 130.

27. Marcus, *Freud and the Culture of Psychoanalysis*, p. 17.

28. See Löwith, *From Hegel to Nietzsche*, pp. 14–17.

7. Between Hegel and Nietzsche

1. Ferenczi, "Symbolic Representation," pp. 214–15. Subsequent page references to this paper will be given parenthetically in the text.

2. See Bloom, *The Anxiety of Influence*.

3. See Hollingdale, Introduction to Schopenhauer, *Essays and Aphorisms*, p. 24. Subsequent page references to this volume will be indicated parenthetically by the abbreviation *EA*.

4. Nietzsche, *Beyond Good and Evil*, sec. 252. Subsequent section numbers will be given parenthetically in the text.

5. Nietzsche, *The Gay Science*, sec. 357. Subsequent section numbers will be given parenthetically in the text.

6. Nietzsche, *Ecce Homo*, "*The Birth of Tragedy*," sec. 1. Subsequent references to *Ecce Homo* by chapter title and section number will be included parenthetically in the text. *Ecce Homo* was posthumously published in 1908.

7. Nietzsche, *Schopenhauer as Educator*, p. 13. The ensuing page references to this work will be given parenthetically in the text.

8. Hollingdale, *Nietzsche*, p. 73.

9. This echo is noted by Kaufmann in his commentary, but his suggestion that Nietzsche "was no Hegel scholar" and "may not have realized" he had been anticipated in the *Phenomenology of Mind* is again disappointingly pedestrian.

10. See Whyte, *The Unconscious Before Freud*, p. 163.

11. Hall, *Founders of Modern Psychology*, p. 194.

12. Von Hartmann, *Philosophy of the Unconscious*, 3:150. Subsequent references to this work by volume and page number will be indicated parenthetically by the abbreviation *PU*.

13. In the first edition of *The Interpretation of Dreams*, Freud cites a brief passage from *Philosophy of the Unconscious* to show that von Hartmann "is probably furthest removed from the wish-fulfillment theory" (*SE*, 4:134) of dreams. In a footnote added in 1913 to chapter 7 of his work (*SE*, 5:528–29), Freud refers to a 1912 paper by N. E. Pohorilles, which reveals the similarity between his own view of unconscious purposive ideas and that espoused by von Hartmann. Nonetheless, Freud never examined closely the relations between psychoanalysis and von Hartmann's philosophy, and his declaration in "The Resistances to Psycho-Analysis" (1925) that "the overwhelming majority of philosophers regard as mental only the phenomena of consciousness" (*SE*, 19:216) ignores the many thinkers, including von Hartmann, for whom this is not the case. See also Ellenberger, *The Discovery of the Unconscious*, pp. 208–10, 311–12, 542.

14. See Baeumler, "Bachofen und Nietzsche," p. 231.

15. See Silk and Stern, *Nietzsche on Tragedy*, p. 212–14. For a full documentation of Nietzsche's antecedents in the use of these categories, see Baeumer, "Nietzsche and the Tradition of the Dionysian."

16. Bachofen, *Ancient Mortuary Symbolism*, in *Myth, Religion and Mother Right*, p. 29. Unless otherwise noted, all translations from Bachofen's works will be taken from this volume of selected writings, with page references included parenthetically in the text. Where necessary, titles of works will be indicated by the following abbreviations: *Mother Right* = *MR*; *The Myth of Tanaquil* = *MT*.

17. Quoted in Baeumer, "Nietzsche and the Tradition of the Dionysian," p. 187.

18. Nietzsche, *The Birth of Tragedy*, sec. 1. Subsequent section numbers will be indicated parenthetically in the text.

19. Ellenberger, *The Discovery of the Unconscious*, p. 542.

20. See, for example, the use made of Bachofen in Neumann, *The Origins and History of Consciousness*.

21. See Turel, *Bachofen-Freud*.

22. Deleuze, *Nietzsche and Philosophy*, p. 195. For additional perspectives on Nietzsche's relation to Hegel, see, among others, Beerling, "Hegel und Nietzsche"; Pautrat, *Versions du soleil*, pp. 213–41; and Kaufmann, *Nietzsche*, pp. 235–46.

23. See Heidegger, "The Word of Nietzsche: 'God is Dead'" (1952).

24. White, *Metahistory*, p. 339.

25. Nietzsche, *On the Advantage and Disadvantage of History*, pp. 47, 49.

26. Dannhauser, *Nietzsche's View of Socrates*, p. 227.

27. Deleuze, *Nietzsche and Philosophy*, pp. 157, 112.

28. Andreas-Salomé, *Nietzsche in seinen Werken*, p. 175.

29. Hegel, *Philosophy of History*, p. 10.

30. See White, *Metahistory*, pp. 94, 357.

31. Quoted in Silk and Stern, *Nietzsche on Tragedy*, p. 102.

32. Quoted *ibid.*

8. Nietzsche

1. *Minutes*, 2:31; 1:359.

2. In *An Autobiographical Study* (1925), Freud states that Nietzsche, like Schopenhauer, "was for a long time avoided by me" because of his anticipations of the findings of psychoanalysis, adding that "I was less concerned with the question of priority than with

keeping my mind unembarrassed" (*SE*, 20:60). Freud's purported lack of interest in the "question of priority" cannot be taken seriously. See also *On the History of the Psycho-Analytic Movement* (1914), *SE*, 14:15–16.

3. The ensuing paragraphs draw upon the excellent article by Anderson, "Freud, Nietzsche." Anderson discusses in detail Freud's appropriation of *On the Genealogy of Morals* in *Civilization and Its Discontents*. See further Holmes, "Freud, Evolution, and the Tragedy of Man"; Mazlish, "Freud and Nietzsche"; and Assoun, *Freud et Nietzsche*.

4. For a detailed study of the *Leseverein*, see McGrath, *Dionysian Art and Populist Politics*.

5. *Minutes*, 1:360.

6. See Roazen, *Freud and His Followers*, p. 412.

7. *The Letters of Freud and Zweig*, pp. 74, 78.

8. See Strong, "Oedipus as Hero: Family and Family Metaphors in Nietzsche." Its promising title notwithstanding, Strong's essay unconvincingly argues that Nietzsche "has escaped from the tyranny of the Oedipalized past" (p. 325) and "has broken the hold of Oedipus" (p. 329).

9. Mann "Nietzsche's Philosophy in the Light of Contemporary Events," p. 361.

10. Nietzsche, *The Birth of Tragedy*, sec. 9. Subsequent section numbers of this work will be given parenthetically in the text. For the original German of Nietzsche's writings, I have used Schlechta, ed.,*Werke*.

11. For a useful outline of the structure of *The Birth of Tragedy*, see Dannhauser, *Nietzsche's View of Socrates*, p. 49.

12. In *Nietzsche on Tragedy*, Silk and Stern argue that "Nietzsche's obligations toward Aeschylus inhibit him from developing his formula for tragedy on its natural Sophoclean ground" (pp. 257–58). My own formulation reverses this emphasis.

13. Nietzsche, *The Gay Science*, sec. 357. Subsequent section numbers of this work will be indicated parenthetically in the text.

14. Nietzsche, *Daybreak*, sec. 128.

15. Sophocles, *Oedipus the King*, ll. 981–82.

16. In my interpretation of *Thus Spoke Zarathustra*, I am extensively indebted to an unpublished paper by my student Michael J. McNulty, "Nietzsche, His Zarathustra, and the Discovery of Oedipus in the Unconscious." Parts 1 and 2 of *Thus Spoke Zarathustra* were published in 1883; part 3 in 1884; and part 4 in 1885.

17. Heidegger, "Who is Nietzsche's Zarathustra?" (1961), p. 73.

18. Donadio, *Nietzsche, Henry James, and the Artistic Will*, p. 36.

19. In this context, the spider upon which Zarthustra concentrates his attention may be interpreted as a symbol of the maternal genitalia. See Abraham, "The Spider as a Dream Symbol" (1922).

20. Groth, "Nietzsche's Zarathustra," p. 13.

21. Nietzsche, *Beyond Good and Evil*, sec. 1. Subsequent section numbers will be indicated parenthetically in the text.

22. Nietzsche, *Ecce Homo*, "Wise," sec. 1. Subsequent references to *Ecce Homo* by chapter title and section number will be included parenthetically in the text.

23. Quoted in Hayman, *Nietzsche: A Critical Life*, p. 251.

24. Quoted in *ibid.*, p. 18. See also Klossowski, "La consultation de l'ombre paternelle," in *Nietzsche et le cercle vicieux*, pp. 253–84, where the existence of a second version of this dream, recorded by Nietzsche at the age of seventeen, is noted and discussed.

25. See Hayman, *Nietzsche: A Critical Life*, p. 21.

26. Quoted in Hollingdale, *Nietzsche*, p. 49.

27. Nietzsche, *Werke und Briefe*, 2:369.

28. See Silk and Stern, *Nietzsche on Tragedy*, p. 45.

29. Hollingdale, *Nietzsche*, p. 47.

30. Hayman, *Nietzsche: A Critical Life*, p. 122.

31. Quoted in Kaufmann, *Nietzsche*, p. 32. As Kaufmann remarks, in equating Cosima with Ariadne, Nietzsche was identifying Wagner with the deserted Theseus and himself with the victorious Dionysus (though in the legend it is Theseus who abandons Ariadne). By claiming the identity of his preferred deity, moreover, Nietzsche was reversing the situation of 1872 when Hans von Bülow, having been rejected by Cosima, visited Nietzsche and compared himself to Theseus, Cosima to Aridane, and Wagner to Dionysus.

32. Silk and Stern, *Nietzsche on Tragedy*, p. 93.

33. See *ibid.*, pp. 104–5.

34. Quoted in Hayman, *Nietzsche: A Critical Life*, p. 253.

35. Kaufmann, *Nietzsche*, p. 37.

36. Hayman, *Nietzsche: A Critical Life*, pp. 260–61.

37. Quoted in *ibid.*, p. 251.

38. *Ibid.*, p. 285.

39. See Kaufmann, *Nietzsche*, pp. 392, 398.

40. Schiller, *Werke: Nationalausgabe*, 25:193–94.

41. See Rank *Incest-Motiv*, pp. 237–38.

42. *The Freud Journal of Lou Andreas-Salomé*, p. 163.

43. Nietzsche, *Schopenhauer as Educator*, p. 163.

44. I have restored and italicized Freud's original "why."

9. After Freud

1. Heidegger, *An Introduction to Metaphysics*, p. 84. Subsequent page references to this work will be given parenthetically in the text, indicated where necessary by the abbreviation *IM*.

2. In "The Poet and the Owl," Hoy cogently notes that "Heidegger's notion of the history of metaphysics as unified by the growing oblivion of being *(Seinsvergessenheit)* is equally as encompassing as Hegel's absolute and his notion of reason in history" (p. 405).

3. See Adorno, *The Jargon of Authenticity*.

4. Gadamer, "Hegel and Heidegger," p. 104.

5. See Spanos, "Heidegger, Kierkegaard, and the Hermeneutic Circle." For an application of Heideggerian thought to literary criticism, see Bové, *Destructive Poetics*.

6. Kierkegaard, *Repetition*, pp. 52–53.

7. Kierkegaard, *The Sickness Unto Death*, p. 164.

8. Heidegger, *Being and Time*, p. 67. The subsequent page reference to this work will be given parenthetically in the text.

9. Steiner, *Martin Heidegger*, p. 98.

10. Contrast Merleau-Ponty's recognition in *Phenomenology of Perception* (1945): "Thus the significance of psychoanalysis is less to make psychology biological than to discover a dialectical process in functions thought of as 'purely bodily,' and to reintegrate sexuality into the human being" (p. 158).

11. See Thass-Thienemann, "Oedipus and the Sphinx."

12. Heidegger, "What is Metaphysics?" p. 362.

13. Thass-Thienemann, "Oedipus and the Sphinx," p. 27. Concerning Heidegger's use of the word *alētheia* to denote "truth" or "reality," Thass-Thienemann remarks that the word "properly means 'the uncovered,' deriving from *lanthanō* 'to be hidden,' 'forgotten.' It is the otherwise hidden nakedness which can be uncovered" (p. 24).

14. See Halliburton, *Poetic Thought*, p. 122.

15. Sophocles, *Antigone*, ll. 332–33.

16. Nietzsche, *The Gay Science*, sec. 335.

17. Heidegger, ". . . Poetically Man Dwells . . . ," p. 273.

18. Lévi-Strauss, *Tristes Tropiques*, p. 33. Subsequent page references to this work will be indicated parenthetically in the text by the abbreviation *TT*.

19. Lévi-Strauss, *The Raw and the Cooked*, p. 16. Subsequent page references to this work will be indicated parenthetically by the abbreviation *RC*.

20. See Heidegger, "Letter on Humanism"; and Lévi-Strauss, "History and Dialectic," in *The Savage Mind*, pp. 245–69.

21. See Derrida, *Of Grammatology*, pp. 101–40.

22. Lévi-Strauss, "The Structural Study of Myth," pp. 216–17. Subsequent page references to this essay will be indicated parenthetically by the abbreviation "SSM." This essay was originally published in English.

23. Cameron, *The Identity of Oedipus the King*, p. vii.

24. Curiously, Freud might seem to lend support to the position I am attacking. In *The Interpretation of Dreams*, he asks why *Oedipus the King* continues to move us, whereas "modern tragedies of destiny" do not. He answers by saying that "its effect does not lie in the contrast between destiny and human will, but is to be looked for in the particular nature of the material on which that contrast is exemplified" (*SE*, 4:262). But if the power of Sophocles' play resides in "the particular nature of the material," it is indeed difficult to see how one version of the Oedipus myth may be judged superior to another. But this objection overlooks the fact that Freud's assertion was made for a polemical purpose—to differentiate Sophocles' *Oedipus* from inferior contemporary "tragedies of destiny" to which it appears to bear a resemblance. Had Freud wished to contrast Sophocles' play with Voltaire's or Seneca's, he doubtless would have looked beyond the themes of incest and patricide to consider the artistic merits of each work. Indeed, as we have seen, Freud does draw attention to the "cunning delays and ever-mounting excitement" of Sophocles' plot, and compares the action of *Oedipus the King* to "the work of a psycho-analysis" (*SE*, 4:262). In light of this responsiveness to the form of Sophocles' drama, it will not do to turn Freud into a structuralist *avant la lettre*, who inadvertently sanctions the view that the Oedipus myth "consists of all its versions."

25. On Lévi-Strauss' interpretation of the Oedipus myth, see Turner, "Oedipus: Time and Structure"; Carroll, "Lévi-Strauss on the Oedipus Myth"; Vickers, *Towards Greek Tragedy*, pp. 192–99; Kirk, *Myth*, pp. 42–83; and Pucci, "Lévi-Strauss and Classical Culture." Useful general studies include Leach, *Lévi-Strauss;* and Steiner, "Orpheus with His Myths."

26. Lévi-Strauss, "Structural Analysis," p. 46. Lévi-Strauss' most comprehensive treatment of the incest prohibition occurs in his first major treatise, *The Elementary Structures of Kinship* (1949). For a recent reappraisal of psychoanalytic and structural theories of the incest taboo, which criticizes Lévi-Strauss both for emphasizing the "classificatory" or intellectual function of totemism at the expense of its "interdictory" or affective function and for confusing the sexual act of incest with exogamy as a rule governing the institution of marriage, see Fox, *The Red Lamp of Incest*.

27. See Rank, *Incest-Motiv*, p. 267.

28. Lévi-Strauss, "Structural Analysis," p. 46.

29. Turner, "Oedipus: Time and Structure," pp. 32, 31. See also Pucci, "Lévi-Strauss and Classical Culture," p. 110.

30. Turner, "Oedipus: Time and Structure," p. 32.

31. See Carroll, "Lévi-Strauss on the Oedipus Myth," p. 810.

32. Vickers, *Towards Greek Tragedy*, p. 193.

33. Turner, "Oedipus: Time and Structure," p. 32. See also Carroll, "Lévi-Strauss on the Oedipus Myth," pp. 806–7; and Vickers, *Towards Greek Tragedy*, p. 193. As will be seen in chapter 11, I in fact share Lévi-Strauss' conviction that Antigone's burial of Polyneices displays an "overrating of blood relations" connected to Oedipus' incest. But,

as Lévi-Strauss presents no evidence in support of his assertion, the force of his detractors' objections must be recognized.

34. Turner, "Oedipus: Time and Structure," p. 30.

35. Carroll, "Lévi-Strauss on the Oedipus Myth," p. 807.

36. See Turner, "Oedipus: Time and Structure, p. 30; and Carroll, "Lévi-Strauss on the Oedipus Myth," pp. 808–9.

37. Lévi-Strauss, *The Savage Mind*, p. 277. Italics added.

38. Leach, "Genesis as Myth," pp. 9–10.

39. Lévi-Strauss, *Totemism*, p. 69.

40. Lévi-Strauss, "The Scope of Anthropology." Subsequent page references will be given parenthetically in the text.

41. See Rank, *Incest-Motiv*, p. 265.

42. Burgess, "If Oedipus Had Read His Lévi-Strauss," p. 259.

43. Nietzsche, *The Birth of Tragedy*, sec. 9.

44. Thass-Thienemann, "Oedipus and the Sphinx," p. 29.

45. Turner, "Oedipus: Time and Structure," p. 49.

46. Róheim, *The Riddle of the Sphinx*, p. 8.

47. In his polemics against Sartre in *The Savage Mind*, Lévi-Strauss mocks "the allegedly self-evident truths of introspection" and "the snare of personal identity" (p. 249). Nonetheless, as especially *Tristes Tropiques* makes clear, the subjective and self-analytic components of Lévi-Strauss' own writing cannot be discounted.

48. Lévi-Strauss, *The Savage Mind*, p. 209.

10. Through Freud to Sophocles

1. Masson, *The Assault on Truth*, p. 48

2. See Balmary, *Psychoanalyzing Psychoanalysis*; and Krüll, *Freud and His Father*, pp. 100–1. Balmary believes that Jakob Freud's sexual misdeeds revolve around his mysterious second marriage to Rebekka. Krüll, on the other hand, who remains unconvinced of the reality of this marriage, vaguely proposes possible acts of adultery, masturbation, and the mere fact of having married a much younger woman, Amalie, as the causes of Jakob's putative sexual guilt. For neither of these incompatible views is there any concrete evidence. See also chapter 1, n. 21; and chapter 3, n. 41.

3. Masson, *The Assault on Truth*, p. 142.

4. In "Freud's Self-Analysis and the Nature of Psychoanalytic Criticism," Efron argues that in his discovery of the Oedipus complex, with its emphasis on the endopsychic fantasy life of the child, Freud "blocked from consciousness those aspects which threatened to develop into a radical critique of authoritarian fathers and even of the principle of authority itself" (p. 255). In criticizing the extreme formulations of Masson, Balmary, and Krüll, I do not mean to deny that they may contain a kernel of truth, succinctly stated by Efron.

5. Balmary, *Psychoanalyzing Psychoanalysis*, pp. 6, 37, 27. Krüll, too, cities a nineteenth-century mythological handbook to bolster her claim that Freud has "stripped [the Oedipus legend] of the Laius prelude" out of a desire to shield his father (*Freud and His Father*, p. 62). The ramifications of the Chrysippus episode are discussed, along lines similar to Balmary's and Krüll's, in an extremely suggestive article by Devereux, "Why Oedipus Killed Laius."

6. See Dodds, "On Misunderstanding the *Oedipus Rex*." An unconvincing rejoinder to Dodds is offered by Lloyd-Jones, *The Justice of Zeus*, who claims (pp. 104–28) that the motif of the family curse is no less important in *Oedipus the King* than in *Antigone* or *Oedipus at Colonus*. Dodds himself concludes that the absence of an inherited curse demonstrates "the essential moral innocence of Oedipus" (p. 42), a view with which I am largely in disagreement.

7. See Knox, *The Heroic Temper*, pp. 2–3.

8. See Versényi, "Oedipus: Tragedy of Self-Knowledge"; and Opstelten, *Sophocles and Greek Pessimism:* "Sophocles' innovations here concentrate all our attention on the self-analysis of the hero" (p. 102).

9. In my translations from the Greek, I have striven for literal accuracy, when necessary at the expense of the felicity of my English renderings. All line numbers for quotations from Aeschylus and Sophocles will be included parenthetically in the text. Throughout my reading of Sophocles' Theban plays in part 3, I have consulted the editions of Campbell and Jebb, as well as the commentaries on *Oedipus Tyrannus* and *Antigone* of Kamerbeek. My understanding of *Oedipus the King* is also indebted to the translation and edition of Gould. My reading of *Seven Against Thebes* has been accompanied by Lupaş and Petre's invaluable *Commentaire*.

10, See Cameron, *The Identity of Oedipus the King*, p. 10. Cameron's first chapter, "The Maker and the Myth," pp. 3–31, is a valuable discussion of Sophocles' relation to earlier treatments of the Oedipus myth.

11. Letters, *The Life and Work of Sophocles*, p. 204.

12. Cameron, *The Identity of Oedipus the King*, p. 21. It should be stressed that the meaning of the Delphic injunction is "know you are a man and not a god." As Cameron notes, both the Delphic command and the Sphinx's riddle "are about the strength and weakness of man" (p. 21). The plague on Thebes at the opening of the play, sent by Apollo, is yet another Sophoclean innovation not found in earlier versions of the Oedipus myth.

13. See Harshbarger, *Sophocles' Oedipus*, p. 19. Psychoanalytic essays commenting on Oedipus' aggression toward Jocasta include Kanzer, "The Oedipus Trilogy"; van der Sterren, "The 'King Oedipus' of Sophocles"; and Faber, "Self-Destruction in *Oedipus Rex*," and "*Oedipus Rex:* A Psychoanalytic Interpretation." Faber stresses that Sophocles' decision to specify Jocasta and not Laius as the one who exposed Oedipus in infancy represents a departure from his sources. For useful bibliographies, see Caldwell, "Selected Bibliography on Psychoanalysis and Classical Studies"; and Edmunds and Ingber, "Psychoanalytic Writings on the Oedipus Legend."

14. Kanzer, "The Oedipus Trilogy," p. 562.

15. van der Sterren, "The 'King Oedipus' of Sophocles," p. 347.

16. See Knox, *Oedipus at Thebes* pp. 107–16. For further discussion of imagistic reversals in *Oedipus the King*, see Musurillo, "Sunken Imagery in Sophocles' *Oedipus*."

17. Hay, *Oedipus Tyrannus*, p. 103.

18. Ferenczi, *Thalassa*, p. 18. See also Hay, *Oedipus Tyrannus*, pp. 120–22.

19. Ferenczi, "Symbolic Representation," p. 222.

20. See Abraham, "'The Trifurcation of the Road.'" Page references to this paper will be given parenthetically in the text. For the relevant correspondence between Freud and Abraham, see *A Psycho-Analytic Dialogue*, pp. 324–26.

21. Kanzer, "The Oedipus Trilogy," p. 564.

22. See Harshbarger, *Sophocles' Oedipus*, p. 33; and Gould's commentary on line 809 in his edition of the play.

23. Benardete, "Sophocles' *Oedipus Tyrannus*," p. 117.

24. See Fry, "*Oedipus the King*," p. 181. To the alternation between *two* and *three*, one may compare the sequence of knocks in the Porter scene (2.3), and the mysterious appearance of the Third Murderer (3.3), in *Macbeth*.

25. See Knox, *Oedipus at Thebes*, pp. 48–49, 98, 137–38.

26. Róheim, *The Riddle of the Sphinx*, p. 8.

27. See Benardete, "Sophocles' *Oedipus Tyrannus*," p. 106.

28. See Segal, *Tragedy and Civilization*, p. 216.

29. Benardete, "Sophocles' *Oedipus Tyrannus*," p. 111.

30. Quoted in Turner, "Oedipus: Time and Structure," p. 44.

31. See Vernant, "Ambiguity and Reversal," p. 483.

32. Thass-Thienemann, "Oedipus and the Sphinx," p. 11.

33. See Hay, *Oedipus Tyrannus*, p. 108.

34. See Knox, *Oedipus at Thebes*, p. 96; and Reinhardt, *Sophocles*, p. 122.

35. On Oedipus and Teiresias, see Róheim, "Teiresias and Other Seers," p. 315; and Rado, "*Oedipus the King*," p. 228. For qualification of Róheim's equation between Oedipus and Teiresias, see the probing article of Caldwell, "The Blindness of Oedipus."

36. For the various examples of repetition cited in this paragraph, see Cameron, *The Identity of Oedipus the King*, p. 125; Kanzer, "The Oedipus Trilogy," p. 565; Segal, *Tragedy and Civilization*, p. 223; and Turner, "Oedipus: Time and Structure," p. 50. On the affinities between Laius and the Sphinx, see Reik, "Oedipus and the Sphinx," pp. 321–22; and Turner, "Oedipus: Time and Structure," p. 45.

37. Vellacott, *Sophocles and Oedipus*, p. 137.

38. Vickers, *Towards Greek Tragedy*, p. 541, n. 9.

39. On Freud's concept of "false connections," and its early use to describe the workings of the transference in analysis, see *Studies on Hysteria, SE*, 2:67–70, 302–3.

40. See Kaplan, "Dream at Thebes," p. 13; and Vellacott, *Sophocles and Oedipus*, p. 115. For an unconvincing denial that this inconsistency possesses any psychological significance, see Vernant, " 'Oedipe' sans complexe," pp. 92–93.

41. See van der Sterren, "The 'King Oedipus' of Sophocles," pp. 343–45.

42. Chase, "Oedipal Textuality," p. 58.

43. For this view, see, in addition to Dodds' "On Misunderstanding the *Oedipus Rex*"; Whitman, *Heroic Humanism*, pp. 122–45; and the lengthy three-part essay by Gould, "The Innocence of Oedipus."

44. Hegel, *The Spirit of Christianity*, in *Early Theological Writings*, p. 230.

45. For a balanced discussion of the culpable nature of the skepticism of Oedipus and Jocasta, see Winnington-Ingram, *Sophocles: An Interpretation*, pp. 179–204. On "the blinding power of Oedipus' impetuosity and self-reliance" in the scene with Creon, see Kirkwood, *A Study of Sophoclean Drama*, p. 172.

46. Ricoeur, *Freud and Philosophy*, p. 516.

47. Bowra, *Sophoclean Tragedy*, p. 175.

48. Whitman, *Heroic Humanism*, pp. 141, 124.

49. Knox, *Oedipus at Thebes*, pp. 5, 43.

50. Vernant, "Ambiguity and Reversal," p. 478. See also Dimock, "Oedipus: The Religious Issue."

51. Reinhardt, *Sophocles*, p. 134.

52. On the application of Freud's concept of "condensation" to *Oedipus the King*, see Hartman, "The Voice of the Shuttle," pp. 347–48.

11. Incest and Burial

1. Line numbers for all quotations from Aeschylus and Sophocles will appear parenthetically in the text. On the date of *Antigone*, see Ehrenberg, *Sophocles and Pericles*, pp. 135–36; and on that of *Oedipus the King*, see Knox, "The Date of the *Oedipus Tyrannus*." On *Oedipus at Colonus*, I follow Jebb's Introduction to *The Plays and Fragments*, 2:xxxix–xl.

2. On Sophocles' abandonment of trilogic form, see, in addition to Knox, *The Heroic Temper*, pp. 2–3; Lesky, *Greek Tragic Poetry*, pp. 187–88. This development makes it likely that the lost plays accompanying each of the Theban plays were *not* thematically dependent, and hence justifies the removal of the three works with which we are concerned from their individual contexts so as to consider them together. My discussion of the unity of the Oedipus cycle has profited from Mangan, "From Progression to Pattern."

3. See Adams, "Unity of Plot in the *Oedipus Coloneus*," p. 139.

4. See Burian, "Suppliant and Savior," p. 429, n. 48.

5. See Reinhardt, *Sophocles*, pp. 99–100. On the use of the metaphor of sight and blindness to set off Oedipus' encounter with Teiresias from that of Creon in *Antigone*, see Kirkwood, *A Study of Sophoclean Drama*, p. 130. The word *kerdē* ("profits") recurs in lines 92 and 578 of *Oedipus at Colonus*, where Oedipus speaks of the advantage he will bring to those who receive him. On the antithetical meanings given to *kerdos* by Antigone and Creon in *Antigone*, see Segal, "Sophocles' Praise of Man."

6. See Rosenmeyer, "The Wrath of Oedipus," pp. 92–93.

7. Kierkegaard, *Either/Or*, 1:154. I cannot deal here with the ironies entailed by Kierkegaard's use of fictive personas and literary frames. Curiously, however, he asserts that "in the Greek tragedy Antigone is not at all concerned about her father's unhappy destiny" (p. 153).

8. See, e.g., Vickers, *Towards Greek Tragedy*, pp. 526–46; Knox, *The Heroic Temper*, p. 113; Reinhardt, *Sophocles*, p. 77; Funke, "ΚΡΕΩΝ ΑΠΟΛΙΣ"; and Santirocco, "Justice in Sophocles' *Antigone*."

9. The most resolute defender of the authenticity of the ending is Lloyd-Jones, "The End of the *Seven Against Thebes*." For a rejoinder, see Dawe, "The End of *Seven Against Thebes*." As Lupaş and Petre justly observe, a judgment on the authenticity of lines 1005–78 "is not, in the final analysis, a philological demonstration, but rather a verdict of an aesthetic order" (*Commentaire*, p. 282). My own belief is that the lines are genuine.

10. See Willis, "ΑΥΤΑΔΕΛΦΟΣ in the *Antigone* and the *Eumenides*," p. 556.

11. See Lloyd-Jones, *The Justice of Zeus*, p. 113.

12. See Gould, "The Innocence of Oedipus," part 3, p. 489. The sole trace in Sophocles of the motif of Chrysippus' abduction by Laius occurs in *Oedipus at Colonus*, when Oedipus insists that the gods caused him to commit involuntarily his crimes of incest and patricide: "Perhaps they have some ancient anger against our race" (l. 965). But while confirming Sophocles' familiarity with the Chrysippus material, the obliqueness of this allusion shows how peripheral it in fact is to the Oedipus cycle.

13. Reinhardt, *Sophocles*, p. 76.

14. *Ibid.*, p. 109. I have altered the English translations of the quoted words to bring them into conformity with my own renderings.

15. See Santirocco, "Justice in Sophocles' *Antigone*," p. 191. On the "death-as-a-bridal motif" in the play, see also Goheen, *The Imagery of Sophocles' "Antigone,"* pp. 37–41.

16. Waldock, *Sophocles the Dramatist*, p. 109.

17. See Benardete, "A Reading," part 1, p. 176. My own interpretation of *Antigone* owes much to Benardete's extensive three-part commentary.

18. Winnington-Ingram, *Sophocles: An Interpretation*, p. 130. Contrast Kamerbeek's note to lines 73–75: "It is certainly preposterous to read an incestuous intention into the words."

19. Benardete, "A Reading," part 2, p. 12.

20. Eckermann, *Gespräche mit Goethe*, pp. 518–19.

21. Decisive arguments for the genuineness of this passage are contained in Agard, "*Antigone*, 904–20." Agard's comments are noted approvingly by Wilson in "The Wound and the Bow," p. 239. The first scholar to challenge these lines, only a few years before Goethe voiced the wish to see them excised, was A. Jacob in 1821; the most famous was Jebb in his edition. It is ironic that Waldock, after condemning attempts to deem Antigone "abnormal," should reject these lines, confidently assuring us that they "do not fit" her character (*Sophocles the Dramatist*, p. 142).

22. Benardete, "A Reading," part 3, p. 152.

23. Kaufmann, *Hegel: A Reinterpretation*, p. 127.

24. See Knox, *The Heroic Temper*, pp. 78–79; and Segal, *Tragedy and Civilization*, p. 184.

25. In this passage, I follow Campbell in preferring the reading of the Laurentian manuscript in line 865, δυσμόρῳ ματρός, to Pearson's δυσμόρου ματρός.

26. Contrast Benardete: "Antigone herself perhaps could not tell us whether her exclamation at her brother's ill-fated marriage refers to Oedipus' or Polyneices' " ("A Reading," part 2, p. 53). It is noteworthy that, in the analogous case of lines 756–57 of *Seven Against Thebes*, "Madness joins together / the frenzied newlyweds," it is impossible to be certain whether the couple in question is Laius and Jocasta or Oedipus and Jocasta, and a scholiast has even suggested a reference to the marriage of Polyneices and Argeia. See Lupaş and Petre, *Commentaire*, p. 238.

27. See Vernant, "Ambiguity and Reversal," pp. 492–93.

28. See Benardete, "A Reading," part 1, p. 148.

12. Binary Oppositions and the "Unit of Kinship"

1. Lévi-Strauss, "Structural Analysis," p. 46.

2. See Zeitlin, "Language, Structure, and the Son of Oedipus": "In the logic of Greek myth, incest . . . either produces no progeny (sterility), or, as in the case of Oedipus and Jocasta, it reproduces its own redundancy by the begetting of a double progeny" (p. 554). In her assertion that no other tragedy than *Seven Against Thebes* "specifically elevates the task of making and unmaking binary oppositions to the level of a crucial and explicit action of the drama" (p. 561), however, Zeitlin does not adequately consider the extent to which the same is true also of *Antigone*.

3. In *Tragedy and Civilization*, Segal likewise discusses the struggle between Antigone and Creon concerning the two brothers as involving the claims of "sameness" and "difference" (p. 186), but does not extend this to the two sisters or posit an underlying antagonism between Creon and Oedipus.

4. See Baldry, "The Dramatization of the Theban Legend," pp. 25–27; and de Kock, "The Sophoklean Oidipus and its Antecedents," pp. 15–16. In his classic work *Oidipus*, Robert argues unconvincingly (1:110) against the hypothesis of two marriages, and claims that Eurygenia is merely another name for Epikaste. Also seminal on the pre-Sophoclean history of the Oedipus legend is Delcourt, *Oedipe ou la légende du conquérant*.

5. Sophocles, *Antigone*, ll. 11–14. Line numbers for subsequent quotations from Sophocles will be included parenthetically in the text.

6. Useful on the exploitation of dual forms in the prologue is Jäkel, "Die Exposition in der Antigone." Jäkel errs, however, in asserting (p. 40) that Ismene's first use of the dual occurs at line 50, as several dual forms are already present in line 13.

7. See Knox, *The Heroic Temper*, pp. 79–80.

8. For a defense of the consistency of Creon's character in the three plays, but one which places him in too favorable a light, see Peterkin, "The Creon of Sophocles."

9. Letters, *The Life and Work of Sophocles*, p. 303.

10. See Knox, *The Heroic Temper*, p. 68 and *passim* on Creon's unheroic nature in *Antigone*.

11. Turner, "Oedipus: Time and Structure," p. 57.

12. The hypothesis that a rivalry over Jocasta between Oedipus and Creon may be found in *Oedipus the King* is proposed in the important psychoanalytic essay of Anzieu, "Oedipe avant le complexe," p. 695; and rebutted in Vernant, " 'Oedipe' sans complexe," pp. 96–97.

13. See Flickinger, *The* ἁμαρτία *of Sophocles' "Antigone."* Like Vellacott's hypothesis of a knowingly guilty and self-incriminating Oedipus in *Oedipus the King* (see chapter 10,

n. 37), Flickinger's argument concerning the "flaw" in Antigone's character is an exaggeration that contains a distorted truth.

14. Bowra, *Sophoclean Tragedy*, pp. 80, 82.

15. Winnington-Ingram, *Sophocles: An Interpretation*, p. 134.

16. See Knox, *The Heroic Temper*, p. 176.

17. I here retain the reading of the Laurentian manuscript, τὸ γέννημ' ὠμὸν, rather than the conjecture of Blaydes adopted by Pearson, τὸ γοῦν λῆμ' ὠμὸν ("at least the savage spirit").

18. Kitto, *Form and Meaning in Drama*, p. 144.

19. *Ibid.*, p. 163. In "Les fiançailles d'Haimon et d'Antigone," Roussel points out that Ismene's line 570, "Not as things are fixed between her and him," does not imply a romantic accord between Haemon and Antigone, but simply a formal betrothal (p. 66). Von Fritz, "Haimons Liebe zu Antigone," argues unpersuasively that Haemon's quarrel with Creon and death are not motivated by love for Antigone. Von Fritz does not discuss Antigone's silence with regard to Haemon.

20. See Webster, *The Tragedies of Euripides*, p. 163.

21. Lattimore, *Story Patterns in Greek Tragedy*, p. 57.

22. In the opening scene of *King Lear*, Cordelia responds to Lear's demand for a declaration of love in words reminiscent of the marriage vow: "Obey you, love you, and most honor you" (l. 98). But though she goes on to affirm that "Happily, when I shall wed, / That lord whose hand must take my plight shall carry / Half my love with him, half my care and duty" (ll. 100–2), in point of fact Cordelia's husband, France, returns to his home country, leaving her to fight with his armies on Lear's behalf. The irresistible bond between father and daughter is given consummate expression in Lear's "birds i' th' cage" (5.3.8) speech, and represented iconographically in the reverse pietá when Lear enters with Cordelia dead in his arms.

23. Goheen, *The Imagery of Sophocles' "Antigone,"* p. 138.

24. Benardete, "A Reading," part 1, p. 177.

25. See Santirocco, "Justice in Sophocles' *Antigone,"* p. 186.

26. See Rouse, "The Two Burials in *Antigone.*"

27. See Adams, "The *Antigone* of Sophocles"; and McCall, "Divine and Human Action in Sophocles."

28. See Winnington-Ingram, *Sophocles: An Interpretation*, p. 125; and Knox, *The Heroic Temper*, p. 176, n. 3.

29. Kitto, *Form and Meaning in Drama*, p. 156. See also Reinhardt, *Sophocles*, p. 76.

30. See Santirocco, "Justice in Sophocles' *Antigone,"* p. 184. Indeed, many of the names in the Oedipus myth carry etymological significance. Creon (*Kreōn*) is a generic term meaning "ruler"; Eurydice (*Eurudikē*), "wide justice," lives up to her name as Queen of the Dead; the name Polyneices contains a double pun: "many quarrels" (*neikos* = quarrel) and "many corpses" (*nekus* = corpse) (see ll. 26, 110–11); the name of Polyneices must be juxtaposed with that of Eteocles (*Eteoklēs*), "genuine glory" (*kleos* = glory) and "genuine weeping" (*klaiō* = I weep). In the enigmatic quality of their names, both sons follow in the tradition of their father, for Oedipus, as we have seen, means both "Know-foot" and "Swollen Foot." Less familiar is the fact that Antigone (*Antigonē*) means literally "generated in place of another" or "anti-generation." On various of these names, see Segal, *Tragedy and Civilization*, p. 180; Santirocco, "Justice in Sophocles' *Antigone,"* pp. 191, 193; Vernant, "Ambiguity and Reversal," p. 483; Zeitlin, "Language, Structure and the Son of Oedipus," p. 560; and Benardete, "A Reading," part 2, p. 156.

31. See Knox, *The Heroic Temper*, p. 116.

32. Segal, *Tragedy and Civilization*, p. 190.

33. This episode is preserved in Euripides' *The Phoenecian Women,* where, however, Creon's son is named Menoeceus. It seems also to be hinted at in lines 993–95 of *Antigone,* where Creon reminds Teiresias that he has heeded his counsel previously.

34. Lévi-Strauss, "Structural Analysis," pp. 46, 47.

13. The Heroization of Oedipus

1. Sophocles, *Oedipus the King,* ll. 1455–57. Line numbers for subsequent quotations from Sophocles will be included parenthetically in the text.

2. For a defense of Jebb's translation of "strange doom," see Howe, "Taboo in the Oedipus Theme," p. 139.

3. See Segal, *Tragedy and Civilization,* p. 366.

4. See *ibid.,* p. 405.

5. See Winnington-Ingram, *Sophocles: An Interpretation,* p. 264; and Whitman, *Heroic Humanism,* pp. 201–2. Valuable discussion of the relation between Oedipus and the Furies is to be found in Edmunds, "The Cults and the Legend of Oedipus"; and Henrichs, "The 'Sobriety' of Oedipus."

6. For a moving comparison between the "old Oedipus" of *Oedipus at Colonus* and "the exhausted, battered Athens of the last years of the war," see Knox, *The Heroic Temper,* pp. 143–44.

7. Bowra, *Sophoclean Tragedy,* p. 349.

8. Winnington-Ingram, *Sophocles: An Interpretation,* p. 255.

9. For misguided secular readings of the play, see Linforth, *Religion and Drama;* and Hester, "To Help One's Friends and Harm One's Enemies." Equally wide of the mark is Whitman's contention that the "heroic victory" of Oedipus or Antigone "had all its reference in the purely human sphere" *(Heroic Humanism,* p. 204).

10. Rohde, *Psyche,* pp. 430–31.

11. Burian, "Suppliant and Savior," p. 408.

12. On final plays in general, see Grene, *Reality and the Heroic Pattern.*

13. On the concept of a *heros,* see Knox, *The Heroic Temper,* p. 147; Winnington-Ingram, *Sophocles: An Interpretation,* p. 254; Bowra, *Sophoclean Tragedy,* pp. 307–9; and Whitman, *Heroic Humanism,* p. 190.

14. For a convincing defense of this view, see Adams, "Unity of Plot in the *Oedipus Coloneus";* and contrast Colchester, "Justice and Death in Sophocles."

15. See Reinhardt, *Sophocles,* p. 195; and Kirkwood, *A Study of Sophoclean Drama,* p. 150.

16. Knox, *The Heroic Temper,* pp. 147–48. See also Segal, *Tragedy and Civilization,* p. 404.

17. See Segal, *Tragedy and Civilization,* p. 384.

18. Quoted in Felman, "Beyond Oedipus," p. 1027.

19. *Ibid.,* p. 1028.

20. Nietzsche, *The Birth of Tragedy,* sec. 9.

21. Kanzer, "The 'Passing of the Oedipus Complex,' " p. 133. See also Lefcowitz, "The Inviolate Grove," p. 81; and Bacon, "Women's Two Faces," p. 18. For an early psychoanalytic essay on the play, see Lorenz, *"Ödipus auf Kolonus."*

22. Kanzer, " 'Passing of the Oedipus Complex,' " p. 133.

23. In "Beyond Oedipus," Felman stresses that *Oedipus at Colonus* is "about the *historicization* of Oedipus' destiny, through the *symbolization*—the transmutation into speech—of the Oedipal desire" (p. 1030).

24. Burian, "Suppliant and Savior," p. 424. The same view is espoused by Bowra, *Sophoclean Tragedy,* p. 326; and by Whitman, *Heroic Humanism,* p. 211.

25. For sympathetic assessments of Polyneices, see Burian, "Suppliant and Savior," p. 423; and Easterling, "Oedipus and Polyneices," p. 6. In particular, Burian's treatment of the suppliant theme brings out the extent to which Polyneices may be seen as a double of Oedipus. But the "essential falseness in Polyneices' argument" is justly emphasized by Adams, "Unity of Plot in the *Oedipus Coloneus*," p. 144.

26. Segal, *Tragedy and Civilization*, p. 387.

27. On the contrast between the human perspectives of Theseus and Antigone and the divine perspective of Oedipus, see Bowra, *Sophoclean Tragedy*, p. 330.

28. Knox, *The Heroic Temper*, p. 159.

29. See also Seidensticker, "Beziehungen zwischen den beiden Oidipusdramen," p. 274; and Segal, *Tragedy and Civilization*, p. 368. See line 733 for the "split road" in *Oedipus the King*.

30. Reinhardt, *Sophocles*, p. 223.

31. Despite his fundamentally theological approach to Sophocles, Bowra insists: "Oedipus' passing is no apotheosis. It is not accompanied by storms and thunderbolts" (*Sophoclean Tragedy*, p. 341). But though it is true that the Messenger states (ll. 1658–60) that there were no "storms or thunderbolts" at the moment of Oedipus' disappearance, Bowra's assertion is misleading unless it is qualified by a recollection of the earlier thunder at l. 1606 and of the explicit divine summoning of Oedipus. The term "apotheosis" is employed by Whitman, *Heroic Humanism*, p. 213.

32. Benardete, "A Reading," part 2, p. 3.

33. Segal, *Tragedy and Civilization*, p. 369.

34. I take this term from Willner, "The Oedipus Complex, Antigone, and Electra," p. 63. She likewise cites (p. 62) a pertinent passage from Ernest Jones: "a man who displays an abnormally strong affection for his daughter also gives evidence of a strong . . . fixation in regard to his mother. . . . In his phantasy he begets his mother . . . he becomes thus her father, and so arrives at a later identification of his real daughter with his mother."

35. Rank, *The Myth of the Birth of the Hero*, p. 77.

36. Kanzer, "'Passing of the Oedipus Complex'" p. 3. In "The 'King Oedipus' of Sophocles," van der Sterren challenges Kanzer's interpretation, pointing out that Oedipus in fact "acquires very great power" (p. 348) in the course of *Oedipus at Colonus*. But van der Sterren's justified observation does not invalidate Kanzer's insight concerning Oedipus' filial dependence on Theseus.

37. I thus cannot agree with Kanzer, "On Interpreting the Oedipus Plays," who moves from the premise that Sophocles "was expressing highly personal views on political, religious, and military problems of his time" to the conclusion that his Oedipus is "in many respects a contemporary sophisticated Athenian, and scarcely a universal dream that had acquired life" (p. 26). These two alternatives are not mutually exclusive.

Conclusion: Life in the Myth

1. Trilling, Introduction to Jones, *The Life and Work of Sigmund Freud*, abridged ed., p. xiv.

2. Nietzsche, *On the Advantage and Disadvantage of History*, pp. 49, 22.

3. Derrida, *Of Grammatology*, pp. 158–59.

4. De Man, "Literary History and Literary Modernity," pp. 161, 152.

5. Page references to this essay will be indicated parenthetically in the text. Mann takes as his point of departure Ernst Kris' 1935 article, "The Image of the Artist."

6. Gadamer, *Truth and Method*, p. 261.

7. In the discussion following his 1966 paper "Structure, Sign, and Play in the Human Sciences" read at the fabled conference on "The Languages of Criticism and the Sciences of Man" at Johns Hopkins University, Jacques Derrida responded to Serge Dubrovsky's

observation that "in as much as there is an intention of language, I inevitably find a center again. For it is not 'One' who speaks, but 'I,'" with the following remarkable words: "First of all, I didn't say that there was no center, that we could get along without the center. I believe that the center is a function, not a being—a reality, but_a function. And this function is absolutely indispensable. The subject is absolutely indispensable. I don't destroy the subject; I situate it. That is to say, I believe that at a certain level both of experience and of philosophical and scientific discourse one cannot get along without the notion of the subject. It is a question of knowing where it comes from and how it functions. Therefore I keep the concept of center, which I explained was indispensable, as well as that of the subject, and the whole system of concepts to which you have referred" (pp. 271–72).

With this passage I have no quarrel, but it should be recognized that in it Derrida defends deconstruction by surrendering to the position he has sought to refute.

Appendix: Oedipus and Anti-Oedipus

1. On the familial basis of tragedy, see *Poetics* 1453 b. For an excellent discussion of the applicability of the *Poetics* to *Oedipus the King*, which demonstrates that "recognition" for Aristotle entails specifically the discovery of kinship ties, see Else, *Aristotle's Poetics*, pp. 346–53, 378–79.

2. Page references to this work will be indicated parenthetically by the abbreviation *AO*.

3. Trilling, *Sincerity and Authenticity*, p. 160.

4. Hartman, "Toward Literary History," p. 367.

5. Gadamer, *Truth and Method*, p. 259.

6. Jung, *Memories, Dreams, Reflections*, pp. 161–62.

7. Page references to this work will be indicated parenthetically by the abbreviation *VS*.

8. Girard, "Delirium as System," p. 86.

9. See Girard, *Deceit, Desire, and the Novel*. For more recent developments in Girard's thought, see *Des choses cachées depuis la fondation du monde*.

10. Quoted in Moi, "The Missing Mother," p. 23. See also the critiques of Girard offered in Kofman, "The Narcissistic Woman"; and El Saffar, "Unbinding the Doubles."

11. Quoted in Moi, "The Missing Mother," pp. 28, 26.

12. *Ibid.*, p. 28.

13. For a similar appraisal of Girard's predicament, see Chase, "Oedipal Textuality": "He must therefore fail to recognize his own strenuous efforts at self-distinction—must decline to reckon with the significance of this very gesture in the elaboration of his own thesis" (p. 60).

14. Line numbers for quotations from *Oedipus the King* will be given parenthetically in the text. On the points covered in this paragraph, see Gould's commentary on l. 261 in his edition of *Oedipus the King*.

15. Page references to this essay will be indicated parenthetically in the text.

16. Wilamowitz-Moellendorff, *Die dramatische Technik des Sophokles*, p. 79.

17. Page references to this essay will be indicated parenthetically by the abbreviation "Greene." See also the eccentric treatment of the same problem in Harshbarger, "Who Killed Laius?"

18. I here retain the manuscript reading, ἤκουσα κἀγώ· τὸν δ' ἰδόντ' οὐδεὶς ὁρᾷ, instead of the conjecture adopted by Pearson: τὸν δε δρῶντ' οὐδεὶς ὁρᾳ ("but none sees the doer"). The unemended line preserves the fusion between the witness to Laius' murder and its perpetrator, which is surely to be reckoned a Sophoclean irony.

19. Reinhardt, *Sophocles*, pp. 100, 101.

20. Said, *Beginnings*, p. 170.

21. Segal, *Tragedy and Civilization,* p. 216.

22. Girard writes: "The more men believe they are realizing their utopias of desire, in short, the more they cling to their emancipatory ideologies, the more they, in effect, work to perfect the competitive world in the midst of which they suffocate." Quoted in Moi, "The Missing Mother," pp. 30–31.

23. Two feminist works notable for their grasp of psychoanalytic theory, the latter written from a Lacanian perspective, are Mitchell, *Psychoanalysis and Feminism;* and Gallop, *The Daughter's Seduction.*

24. See Malinowski, *Sex and Repression in Savage Society* (1927); and Jones, "Mother Right and the Sexual Ignorance of Savages" (1924). The phrase "nuclear family complex" appears on p. 169. (Jones is responding to articles published by Malinowski prior to *Sex and Repression.*)

25. Green, *The Tragic Effect,* pp. 236, 232.

26. Chodorow, *The Reproduction of Mothering,* p. 74.

27. *Ibid.,* p. 219.

28. Roth, "A Conversation with Edna O'Brien," p. 40.

Bibliography
of Works Cited

Abraham, Karl. "The Spider as a Dream Symbol." 1922. In *Selected Papers on Psycho-Analysis*, pp. 326–32. 1927. Douglas Bryan and Alix Strachey, trs. New York: Brunner/ Mazel, 1979.

—— " 'The Trifurcation of the Road' in the Oedipus Myth." Part 2 of "Two Contributions to the Study of Symbols." 1922. In *Clinical Papers and Essays on Psychoanalysis*, pp. 83– 85. Hilda Abraham and D. R. Ellison, trs. New York: Basic Books, 1955.

Abraham, Ruth. "Freud's Mother Conflict and the Formulation of the Oedipal Father." *Psychoanalytic Review* (1982), 69:441–53.

Abrams, M. H. *Natural Supernaturalism: Tradition and Revolution in Romantic Literature.* 1971. New York: Norton, 1973.

Adams, S. M. "The *Antigone* of Sophocles." *Phoenix* (1955), 9:47–62.

—— "Unity of Plot in the *Oedipus Coloneus.*" *Phoenix* (1953), 7:136–47.

Adorno, Theodor W. *The Jargon of Authenticity.* 1964. Knut Tarnowski and Frederic Will, trs. 1973. Evanston: Northwestern University Press, 1985.

Aeschylus. *Septem Quae Supersunt Tragoedias.* Denys Page, ed. 1972. Oxford: Oxford University Press, 1982.

Agard, Walter A. "*Antigone* 904–20." *Classical Philology* (1937), 32:263–65.

Aichele, Klaus. "Kleist's Tragic Roots." In *Heinrich von Kleist Studies: Hofstra University Cultural and Intercultural Studies*, 3:27–32. New York: AMS Press, 1980.

Anderson, Lorin. "Freud, Nietzsche." *Salmagundi* (Winter-Spring 1980), 47–48:3–29.

Andreas-Salomé, Lou. *Friedrich Nietzsche in seinen Werken.* 1894. Dresden: Carl Reißner, n.d.

—— *The Freud Journal of Lou Andreas-Salomé.* Stanley A. Leavy, tr. 1964. New York: Basic Books, 1976.

Anzieu, Didier. *L'auto-analyse de Freud et la découverte de la psychanalyse.* 2 vols. 1959. Paris: Presses Universitaires de France, 1975.

—— "Oedipe avant le complexe." *Les Temps Modernes* (1966), 22:675–715.

Aristotle. *Poetics.* D. W. Lucas, ed. 1968. Oxford: Clarendon Press, 1980.

Assoun, Paul Laurent. *Freud et Nietzsche.* Paris: Presses Universitaires de France, 1980.

388   *Bibliography of Works Cited*

Auden, W. H. "Psychology and Art To-day." 1935. In Perry Meisel, ed., *Freud: A Collection of Critical Essays*, pp. 61–72. Englewood Cliffs, N.J.: Prentice-Hall, 1981.

Bachofen, J. J. *Myth, Religion, and Mother Right: Selected Writings of J. J. Bachofen.* Ralph Manheim, tr. 1967. Princeton: Princeton University Press, 1973.

Bacon, Helen H. "Women's Two Faces: Sophocles' View of the Tragedy of Oedipus and His Family." *Science and Psychoanalysis* (1966), 10:10–27.

Baeumer, Max L. "Nietzsche and the Tradition of the Dionysian." Timothy L. Sellner, tr. In James C. O'Flaherty et al., eds., *Studies on Nietzsche and the Classical Tradition*, pp. 165–89. 1976. Chapel Hill: University of North Carolina Press, 1979.

Baeumler, Alfred. "Bachofen und Nietzsche." In *Studien zur deutschen Geistesgeschichte*, pp. 220–43. Berlin: Junker und Dunnhaupt Verlag, 1937.

Baldry, H. C. "The Dramatization of the Theban Legend." *Greece and Rome*, 2d Series (1956), 3:24–37.

Balmary, Marie. *Psychoanalyzing Psychoanalysis: Freud and the Hidden Fault of the Father.* 1979. Ned Lukacher, tr. Baltimore: Johns Hopkins University Press, 1982.

Barclay, James R. "Franz Brentano and Sigmund Freud." *Journal of Existentialism* (Summer 1964), 5:1–36.

Beerling, R. F. "Hegel und Nietzsche." *Hegel Studien* (1961), 1:229–46.

Benardete, Seth. "A Reading of Sophocles' *Antigone.*" *Interpretation: A Journal of Political Philosophy* (1975), 4:148–96; 5:1–55; 5:148–84.

—— "Sophocles' *Oedipus Tyrannus.*" In Thomas Woodard, ed., *Sophocles: A Collection of Critical Essays*, pp. 105–22. Englewood Cliffs, N.J.: Prentice-Hall, 1966.

Bernfeld, Siegfried. "An Unknown Autobiographical Fragment by Freud." *American Imago* (1946), 4:3–19. Rpt. in *The Yearbook of Psychoanalysis* (1947), 3:15–29.

Bernfeld, Siegfried and Suzanne Cassirer Bernfeld. "Freud's Early Childhood." *Bulletin of the Menninger Clinic* (1944), 8:107–115.

Bernfeld, Suzanne Cassirer. "Freud and Archaeology." *American Imago* (1951), 8:107–28.

Besterman, Theodore. *Voltaire.* 1969. Chicago: University of Chicago Press, 1976.

Binder, Wolfgang. "Hölderlin und Sophokles." *Hölderlin Jahrbuch* (1969-70), 16:19–37.

Bloom, Harold. *The Anxiety of Influence: A Theory of Poetry.* New York: Oxford University Press, 1973.

Blum, Harold P. "The Prototype of Preoedipal Reconstruction." In Kanzer and Glenn, eds., *Freud and His Self-Analysis*, pp. 143–63.

Bové, Paul A. *Destructive Poetics: Heidegger and Modern American Poetry.* New York: Columbia University Press, 1980.

Bowra, C. M. *Sophoclean Tragedy.* 1944. Oxford: Clarendon Press, 1967.

Burgess, Anthony. "If Oedipus Had Read His Lévi-Strauss." In *Urgent Copy: Literary Studies*, pp. 258–61. New York: Norton, 1968.

Burian, Peter. "Suppliant and Savior: *Oedipus at Colonus.*" *Phoenix* (1974), 28:408–29.

Butler, E. M. *The Tyranny of Greece Over Germany.* 1935. Boston: Beacon Press, 1958.

Buxbaum, Edith. "Freud's Dream Interpretation in the Light of His Letters to Fliess." *Bulletin of the Menninger Clinic* (1951), 15:197–212. Rpt. in *The Yearbook of Psychoanalysis* (1952), 59:56–72.

Caldwell, Richard S. "The Blindness of Oedipus." *International Review of Psycho-Analysis* (1974), 1:207–18.

—— "Selected Bibliography on Psychoanalysis and Classical Studies." *Arethusa* (1974), 7:117–34.

Cameron, Alister. *The Identity of Oedipus the King: Five Essays on the "Oedipus Tyrannus."* New York: New York University Press, 1968.

Carotenuto, Aldo. *A Secret Symmetry: Sabina Spielrein Between Jung and Freud.* 1980. Aldo Pomerans et al., trs. 1982. New York: Pantheon Books, 1984.

Carroll, Michael P. "Lévi-Strauss on the Oedipus Myth: A Reconsideration." *American Anthropologist* (1978), 80:805–14.

Chase, Cynthia. "Oedipal Textuality: Reading Freud's Reading of *Oedipus.*" *Diacritics* (Spring 1979), 9:54–68.

Chodorow, Nancy. *The Reproduction of Mothering: Psychoanalysis and the Sociology of Gender.* 1978. Berkeley: University of California Press, 1979.

Clark, Ronald W. *Freud: The Man and the Cause.* New York: Random House, 1980.

Colchester, L. S. "Justice and Death in Sophocles." *Classical Quarterly* (1942), 36:21–28.

Corneille, Pierre. *Oeuvres Complètes.* André Stegman, ed. Paris: Editions du Seuil, 1963.

Cuddihy, John Murray. *The Ordeal of Civility: Freud, Marx, Lévi-Strauss, and the Jewish Struggle with Modernity.* 1974. New York: Delta, 1976.

Dannhauser, Werner J. *Nietzsche's View of Socrates.* Ithaca: Cornell University Press, 1974.

Dawe, Roger. "The End of the *Seven Against Thebes.*" *Classical Quarterly* N.S. (1967), 17:16–28.

Delcourt, Marie. *Oedipe ou la légende du conquérant.* Paris: Librairie E. Droz, 1944.

Deleuze, Gilles. *Nietzsche and Philosophy.* 1962. Hugh Tomlinson, tr. New York: Columbia University Press, 1983.

Deleuze, Gilles and Félix Guattari. *Anti-Oedipus: Capitalism and Schizophrenia.* 1972. Robert Hurley, Mark Seem, and Helen R. Lane, trs. New York: Viking Press, 1977.

de Man, Paul. "Literary History and Literary Modernity." In *Blindness and Insight: Essays in the Rhetoric of Contemporary Criticism*, pp. 142–65. New York: Oxford University Press, 1971.

Derrida, Jacques. *Of Grammatology.* 1967. Gayatri Chakravorty Spivak, tr. Baltimore: Johns Hopkins University Press, 1976.

—— "Structure, Sign, and Play in the Human Sciences." In Macksey and Donato, eds., *The Structuralist Controversy*, pp. 247–72.

Devereux, George. "Why Oedipus Killed Laius: A Note on the Complementary Oedipus Complex in Greek Drama." *International Journal of Psycho-Analysis* (1953), 34:132–41.

Dimock, George. "Oedipus: The Religious Issue." *Hudson Review* (1968), 21:430–56.

Dodds, E. R. "On Misunderstanding the *Oedipus Rex.*" *Greece and Rome.* 2d series (1966) 13:37–49.

Donadio, Stephen. *Nietzsche, Henry James, and the Artistic Will.* New York: Oxford University Press, 1978.

Easterling, P. E. "Oedipus and Polyneices." *Proceedings of the Cambridge Philological Society* N.S. (1967), 3:1–13.

Eckermann, Johann Peter. *Gespräche mit Goethe in den letzen Jahren seines Lebens.* Berlin: Aufbau-Verlag, 1982.

Edmunds, Lowell. "The Cults and the Legend of Oedipus." *Harvard Studies in Classical Philology* (1981), 85:221–38.

Edmunds, Lowell and Richard Ingber. "Psychoanalytic Writings on the Oedipus Legend: A Bibliography." *American Imago* (1977), 34:374–86.

Efron, Arthur. "Freud's Self-Analysis and the Nature of Psychoanalytic Criticism." *International Review of Psycho-Analysis* (1977), 4:253–80.

Ehrenberg, Victor. *Sophocles and Pericles.* London: Blackwell, 1954.

Eissler, K. R. *Talent and Genius: The Fictitious Case of Tausk Contra Freud.* New York: Quadrangle Books, 1971.

Ellenberger, Henri F. *The Discovery of the Unconscious: The History and Evolution of Dynamic Psychiatry.* New York: Basic Books, 1970.

Else, Gerald F. *Aristotle's Poetics: The Argument.* Cambridge: Harvard University Press, 1963.

—— "Sophokles the Elusive." In Emery E. George, ed., *Friedrich Hölderlin: An Early Modern*, pp. 119–33. Ann Arbor: University of Michigan Press, 1972.

Faber, M. D. "*Oedipus Rex:* A Psychoanalytic Interpretation." *Psychoanalytic Review* (1975), 62:239–68.

—— "Self-Destruction in *Oedipus Rex.*" *American Imago* (1970), 27:41–51.

Felman, Shoshana. "Beyond Oedipus: The Specimen Story of Psychoanalysis." In Robert Con Davis, ed., *Lacan and Narration: The Psychoanalytic Difference in Narrative Theory,* pp. 1021–53. Baltimore: Johns Hopkins University Press, 1983.

Ferenczi, Sándor. "The Symbolic Representation of the Pleasure and Reality Principles in the Oedipus Myth." 1912. In *Sex in Psychoanalysis,* pp. 214–27. Ernest Jones, tr. New York: Dover, 1956.

—— *Thalassa: A Theory of Genitality.* 1923. Henry Alden Bunker, tr. 1933. New York: Norton, 1968.

Flickinger, Minnie Keys. *The ἁμαρτία of Sophocles' "Antigone."* Iowa Studies in Classical Philology (1935), vol. 2.

Fox, Robin. *The Red Lamp of Incest: An Enquiry into the Origins of Mind and Society.* 1980. South Bend: University of Notre Dame Press, 1983.

Freud, Ernst L. "Some Early Unpublished Letters of Freud." *International Journal of Psycho-Analysis* (1969), 50:419–27.

Freud, Ernst et al., eds. *Sigmund Freud: His Life in Words and Pictures.* Christine Trollope, tr. New York: Harcourt Brace Jovanovich, 1978.

Freud, Martin. *Sigmund Freud: Man and Father.* 1958. New York: Jacob Aronson, 1983.

Freud, Sigmund. *Aus der Anfängen der Psychoanalyse: Briefe an Wilhelm Fließ, Abhandlungen und Notizen aus den Jahren 1887–1902.* Ernst Kris et al., eds. 1950. Frankfurt: Fischer Verlag, 1962.

——*The Complete Letters of Sigmund Freud to Wilhelm Fliess, 1877–1904.* Jeffrey Moussaieff Masson, ed. and tr. Cambridge: Harvard University Press, 1985.

——*The Letters of Sigmund Freud.* Ernst L. Freud, ed; Tania and James Stern, trs. 1960. New York: Basic Books, 1975.

——*The Origins of Psycho-Analysis: Letters to Wilhelm Fliess, Drafts and Notes: 1887–1902.* Eric Mosbacher and James Strachey, trs. 1954. New York: Basic Books, 1971.

——*The Standard Edition of the Complete Psychological Works of Sigmund Freud.* 24 vols. James Strachey et al., eds. and trs. London: Hogarth Press, 1953–1974.

An Autobiographical Study. 1925. *SE,* 20:7–74.

Beyond the Pleasure Principle. 1920. *SE,* 18:7–64.

"A Childhood Recollection from *Dichtung und Wahrheit.*" 1917. *SE,* 17:147–56.

Civilization and Its Discontents. 1930. *SE,* 21:64–145.

"The Claims of Psycho-Analysis to Scientific Interest." 1913. *SE,* 13:165–90.

"A Disturbance of Memory on the Acropolis." 1936. *SE,* 22:239–48.

"The Dynamics of Transference." 1912. *SE,* 12:99–108.

"The Economic Problem of Masochism." 1924. *SE,* 19:159–70.

The Ego and the Id. 1923. *SE,* 19:12–66.

"Formulations on the Two Principles of Mental Functioning." 1911. *SE,* 12:218–26.

Fragment of an Analysis of a Case of Hysteria. 1905. *SE,* 7:7–122.

The Future of an Illusion. 1927. *SE,* 21:5–56.

"The Goethe Prize." 1930. *SE,* 21:207–12.

"The Infantile Genital Organization." 1923. *SE,* 19:141–45.

Inhibitions, Symptoms and Anxiety. 1926. *SE,* 20:87–172.

"Instincts and Their Vicissitudes." 1915. *SE,* 14:17–40.

The Interpretation of Dreams. 1900. *SE,* vols. 4 and 5.

Introductory Lectures on Psycho-Analysis. 1916–17. *SE,* vols. 15 and 16.

Jokes and Their Relation to the Unconscious. 1905. *SE,* vol. 8.

Leonardo da Vinci and a Memory of His Childhood. 1910. *SE,* 11:63–137.

"The Moses of Michelangelo." 1914. *SE,* 13:211–38.

Moses and Monotheism: Three Essays. 1939. *SE,* 23:7–137.

"Mourning and Melancholia." 1917. *SE*, 14:243–58.
New Introductory Lectures on Psycho-Analysis. 1933. *SE*, 22:7–192.
"On Beginning the Treatment." 1913. *SE*, 12:123–44.
On the History of the Psycho-Analytic Movement. 1914. *SE*, 14:7–66.
An Outline of Psycho-Analysis. 1940. *SE*, 23:144–207.
The Psychopathology of Everyday Life. 1901. *SE*, vol. 6.
"The Question of Lay Analysis." 1926. *SE*, 20:183–258.
"The Resistances to Psycho-Analysis." 1925. *SE*, 19:213–24.
"Screen Memories." 1899. *SE*, 3:303–22.
"Some Character Types Met with in Psycho-Analytic Work." 1916. *SE*, 14:311–33.
"A Special Type of Choice of Object Made by Men." 1910. *SE*, 11:165–75.
"The Theme of the Three Caskets." 1913. *SE*, 12:291–301.
Three Essays on the Theory of Sexuality. 1905. *SE*, 7:125–245.
Totem and Taboo. 1913. *SE*, 13:1–161.
"The 'Uncanny.' " 1919. *SE*, 17:219–56.
Freud, Sigmund and Karl Abraham. *A Psycho-Analytic Dialogue: The Letters of Sigmund Freud and Karl Abraham, 1907–1926*. Hilda C. Abraham and Ernst L. Freud, eds.; Bernard Marsh and Hilda C. Abraham, trs. New York: Basic Books, 1965.
Freud, Sigmund and Josef Breuer. *Studies on Hysteria*. 1895. *SE*, vol. 2.
Freud, Sigmund and Carl Jung. *The Freud/Jung Letters: The Correspondence between Sigmund Freud and C. G. Jung*. William McGuire, ed.; Ralph Manheim and R. F. C. Hull, trs. Princeton: Princeton University Press, 1974.
Freud, Sigmund and Arnold Zweig. *The Letters of Sigmund Freud and Arnold Zweig*. Ernst L. Freud, ed.; Elaine and William Robson-Scott, trs. New York: Harcourt Brace Jovanovich, 1970.
Fritz, Kurt von. "Haimons Liebe zu Antigone." *Philologus* (1934), 89:19–34.
Fry, Paul H. *"Oedipus the King."* In Michael Seidel and Edward Mendelson, eds., *Homer to Brecht: The European Epic and Dramatic Traditions*, pp. 171–90. New Haven: Yale University Press, 1977.
Funke, Hermann. "ΚΡΕΩΝ ΑΠΟΛΙΣ." *Antike und Abendland* (1966), 12:29–50.
Gadamer, Hans-Georg. "Hegel and the Dialectic of the Ancient Philosophers." 1961. In *Hegel's Dialectic: Five Hermeneutical Studies*, pp. 5–34. P. Christopher Smith, tr. New Haven: Yale University Press, 1976.
—— "Hegel and Heidegger." 1971. In *Hegel's Dialectic*, pp. 100–16.
—— *Truth and Method*. 1960. Garrett Barden and John Cumming, trs. 1975. New York: Crossroad, 1982.
Gallop, Jane. *The Daughter's Seduction: Feminism and Psychoanalysis*. Ithaca: Cornell University Press, 1982.
Gay, Peter. *Freud, Jews, and Other Germans: Masters and Victims in Modernist Culture*. New York: Oxford University Press, 1978.
Gedo, John E. "Freud's Self-Analysis and His Scientific Ideas." In Gedo and Pollock, eds., *Freud: The Fusion of Science and Humanism*, pp. 286–306.
—— "On the Origins of the Theban Plague: Assessments of Sigmund Freud's Character." In Paul E. Stepansky, ed., *Freud: Appraisals and Reappraisals. Contributions to Freud Studies*, 1:241–59. Hillsdale, N.J.: Analytic Press, 1986.
Gedo, John E. and George H. Pollock, eds. *Freud: The Fusion of Science and Humanism, The Intellectual History of Psychoanalysis*. *Psychological Issues*, vol. 9, nos. 2–3, monograph 34/35. New York: International Universities Press, 1976.
Gedo, John E. and Ernest S. Wolf. "The 'Ich.' Letters." In Gedo and Pollock, eds. *Freud: The Fusion of Science and Humanism*, pp. 71–86.

Gerhard, Melitta. *Schiller und die griechische Tragödie.* Weimar: Alexander Duncker, 1919.

Gicklhorn, Renée. "The Freiberg Period of the Freud Family." *Journal of the History of Medicine* (1969), 24:37–43.

Girard, René. *Deceit, Desire, and the Novel: Self and Other in Literary Structure.* 1961. Yvonne Freccero, tr. Baltimore: Johns Hopkins University Press, 1965.

—— "Delirium as System." In *"To Double Business Bound": Essays on Literature, Mimesis, and Anthropology,* pp. 84–20. Baltimore: Johns Hopkins University Press, 1978.

—— *Des choses cachées depuis la fondation du monde: Recherches avec Michel Oughourlian et Guy Lefort.* Paris: Editions Bernard Grasset, 1978.

—— *Violence and the Sacred.* 1972. Patrick Gregory, tr. Baltimore: Johns Hopkins University Press, 1977.

Goethe, Johann Wolfgang von. *The Sorrows of Young Werther and Selected Writings.* Catherine Hutter, tr. 1962. New York: Signet Classics, 1982.

Goheen, Robert F. *The Imagery of Sophocles' "Antigone": A Study of Poetic Language and Structure.* Princeton: Princeton University Press, 1951.

Gombrich, E. H. "The Symbol of the Veil: Psychological Reflections on Schiller's Poetry." In Peregrine Horden, ed., *Freud and the Humanities,* pp. 75–109. New York: St. Martin's Press, 1985.

Goodhart, Sandor. "Ληστὰς ἔφασκε: Oedipus and Laius' Many Murderers." *Diacritics* (Spring 1978), 8:55–71.

Gordon, Wolff von. *Die Dramatische Handlung in Sophokles "König Oidipus" und Kleists "Der zerbrochene Krug."* Halle: Karras, Kröber, and Nietschmann, 1926.

Gould, Thomas. "The Innocence of Oedipus: The Philosophers on *Oedipus the King.*" *Arion.* (1965), 4:363–86; 582–611; (1966) 5:478–525.

Gray, J. Glenn. *Hegel's Hellenic Ideal.* New York: King's Crown Press, 1941.

Green, André. "Shakespeare, Freud, et le parricide." *La nef* (1967), 31:64–82.

—— *The Tragic Effect: The Oedipus Complex in Tragedy.* 1969. Alan Sheridan, tr. Cambridge: Cambridge University Press, 1979.

Greene, William Chase. "The Murderers of Laius." *Transactions of the American Philological Association* (1929), 60:75–86.

Grene, David. *Reality and the Heroic Pattern: Last Plays of Ibsen, Shakespeare and Sophocles.* Chicago: University of Chicago Press, 1967.

Grigg, Kenneth A. " 'All Roads Lead to Rome': The Role of the Nursemaid in Freud's Dreams." *Journal of the American Psychoanalytic Association* (1973), 21:108–34.

Grinstein, Alexander. *Sigmund Freud's Dreams.* 1968. New York: International Universities Press, 1980.

Groth, H. Miles. "Nietzsche's Zarathustra: His Breakdown." *American Imago* (1982), 39:1–20.

Grünbaum, Adolf. *The Foundations of Psychoanalysis: A Philosophical Critique.* Berkeley: University of California Press, 1984.

Habermas, Jürgen. *Knowledge and Human Interests.* 1968. Jeremy J. Shapiro, tr. 1971. Boston: Beacon Press, 1972.

Hall, Stanley. *Founders of Modern Psychology.* New York: Appleton, 1912.

Halliburton, David. *Poetic Thought: An Approach to Heidegger.* Chicago: University of Chicago Press, 1981.

Harrison. R. B. *Hölderlin and Greek Literature.* Oxford: Clarendon Press, 1975.

Harshbarger, Karl. *Sophocles' Oedipus.* Washington: University Press of America, 1979.

—— "Who Killed Laius?" *Tulane Drama Review* (1965), 9:120–31.

Hartman, Geoffrey H. "Romanticism and Anti-Self-Consciousness." In *Beyond Formalism:*

Literary Essays 1958–1970, pp. 298–310. 1970. New Haven: Yale University Press, 1975.

——— "Toward Literary History." In *Beyond Formalism*, pp. 356–86.

——— "The Voice of the Shuttle: Language from the Point of View of Literature." In *Beyond Formalism*, pp. 337–55.

Hartmann, Eduard von. *Philosophy of the Unconscious: Speculative Results According to the Inductive Method of Physical Science*. 1868. 3 vols. William Chatterton Coupland, tr. 1931. London: Routledge and Kegan Paul, 1950.

Hay, John. *Oedipus Tyrannus: Lame Knowledge and the Homosporic Womb*. Washington: University Press of America, 1979.

Hayman, Ronald. *Nietzsche: A Critical Life*. New York: Oxford University Press, 1980.

Hegel, G. W. F. *Aesthetics: Lectures on Fine Art*. 1835. 2 vols. T. M. Knox, tr. Oxford: Clarendon Press, 1975.

——— *The Difference Between the Fichtean and Schellingian Systems of Philosophy*. 1801. Jere Paul Serber, tr. Roseda, Calif.: Ridgeview, 1978.

——— *Early Theological Writings*. T. M. Knox, tr. 1948. Philadelphia: University of Pennsylvania Press, 1979.

——— *Hegels theologische Jugendschriften*. Herman Nohl, ed. Tübingen: Mohr, 1907.

——— *Lectures on the Philosophy of Religion*. 1832. 3 vols. E. B. Speirs and J. Burdon Sanderson, trs. 1895. London: Routledge and Kegan Paul, 1968.

——— *Logic*. 1817. William Wallace, tr. 1873. Oxford: Clarendon Press, 1978.

——— *Phänomenologie des Geistes*. 1970. Frankfurt: Suhrkamp Verlag, 1981.

——— *The Phenomenology of Mind*. 1807. J. B. Baillie, tr. 1910. New York: Harper Torchbooks, 1967.

——— *The Philosophy of History*. 1837. J. Sibree, tr. 1899. New York: Dover Publications, 1956.

——— *Philosophy of Right*. 1821. T. M. Knox, tr. 1952. London: Oxford University Press, 1981.

——— "Über einige charakteristische Unterschiede der alten Dichter [von den neueren]." 1788. In Johannes Hoffmister, ed., *Dokumente zu Hegels Entwicklung*, pp. 48–51. Stuttgart: Frommanns, 1936.

——— *Vorlesungen über die Philosophie der Geschichte*. Hermann Glockner, ed. Stuttgart: Frommanns, 1928.

Heidegger, Martin. *Being and Time*. 1927. John Macquarrie and Edward Robinson, trs. 1962. Oxford: Basil Blackwell, 1973.

——— "Hegel und die Griechen." In Dieter Henrich et al., eds., *Die Gegenwart der Griechen im neueren Denken: Festschrift für Hans-Georg Gadamer zum 60. Geburtstag*, pp. 43–57. Tübingen: Mohr, 1960.

——— *An Introduction to Metaphysics*. 1935. Ralph Manheim, tr. New Haven: Yale University Press, 1959.

——— "Letter on Humanism." 1946. William Barrett and Henry D. Aiken, eds., *Philosophy in the Twentieth Century*, 3:270–302. 4 vols. New York: Random House, 1962.

——— ". . . Poetically Man Dwells . . ." In *Poetry, Language, Thought*, pp. 213–29. Albert Hofstader, tr. 1971. New York: Harper Colophon Books, 1975.

——— "What is Metaphysics?" 1929. In Werner Brock, ed., *Existence and Being*, pp. 355–99. Douglas Scott, tr. Chicago: Regnery, 1950.

——— "Who Is Nietzsche's Zarathustra?" 1961. Bernd Magnus, tr. In David B. Allison, ed., *The New Nietzsche: Contemporary Styles of Interpretation*, pp. 64–79. 1977. New York: Delta, 1979.

—— "The Word of Nietzsche: 'God is Dead.'" 1952. In *The Question Concerning Technology and Other Essays*, pp. 53–112. William Lovitt, tr. New York: Harper Torchbooks, 1977.

Heller, Erich. "The Dismantling of a Marionette Theatre; or, Psychology and the Misinterpretation of Literature." In *In the Age of Prose: Literary and Philosophical Essays*, pp. 195–213. Cambridge: Cambridge University Press, 1974.

—— "Observations on Psychoanalysis and Modern Literature." In *In the Age of Prose*, pp. 179–91.

Henrichs, Albert. "The 'Sobriety' of Oedipus: Sophocles' *OC* 100 Misunderstood." *Harvard Studies in Classical Philology* (1983), 87:87–100.

Herzog, Patricia. "The Myth of Freud as Anti-Philosopher." In Paul E. Stepansky, ed., *Freud: Appraisals and Reappraisals. Contributions to Freud Studies*, vol. 2. Hillsdale, N.J.: Analytic Press, 1987. Forthcoming.

Hester, D. A. "To Help One's Friends and Harm One's Enemies: A Study in the *Oedipus at Colonus.*" *Antichthon* (1971), 11:22–41.

Hölderlin, Friedrich. *Hyperion; or, The Hermit in Greece*. 1799. Willard R. Trask, tr. 1959. New York: Ungar, 1965.

—— *Poems and Fragments*. Michael Hamburger, tr. 1966. Cambridge: Cambridge University Press, 1980.

—— *Sämtliche Werke*. 7 vols. Friedrich Beissner, ed. Stuttgart: W. Kohlhammer, 1946– 1977.

Hollingdale, R. J. *Nietzsche*. London: Routledge and Kegan Paul, 1973.

Holmes, Kim R. "Freud, Evolution, and the Tragedy of Man." *Journal of the American Psychoanalytic Association* (1983), 31:187–210.

Howe, Thalia Phillies. "Taboo in the Oedipus Theme." *Transactions of the American Philological Association* (1962), 93:124–43.

Hoy, David Couzens. *The Critical Circle: Literature, History, and Philosophical Hermeneutics*. 1978. Berkeley: University of California Press, 1982.

—— "The Poet and the Owl: Heidegger's Critique of Hegel." *boundary 2* (1976), 4:393– 410.

Hyppolite, Jean. "Phénoménologie de Hegel et Psychanalyse." *La Psychanalyse* (1957), 3:2–32.

—— "The Structure of Philosophical Language According to the 'Preface' to Hegel's *Phenomenology of the Mind.*" In Macksey and Donato, eds., *The Structuralist Controversy*, pp. 157–85.

Jäkel, Werner. "Die Exposition in der Antigone des Sophokles." *Gymnasium* (1961), 68:34–55.

Janicaud, Dominique. *Hegel et le destin de la Grèce*. Paris: Librairie Philosophique J. Vrin, 1975.

Jones, Ernest. *Essays in Applied Psychoanalysis*. 3d. ed. 2 vols. London: Hogarth Press, 1964.

—— *The Life and Work of Sigmund Freud*. 3 vols. New York: Basic Books, 1953–1957.

—— "Mother Right and the Sexual Ignorance of Savages." 1924. In *Essays in Applied Psychoanalysis*, 2:145–73.

—— "On 'Dying Together': With Special Reference to Heinrich von Kleist's Suicide." 1911. In *Essays in Applied Psychoanalysis*, 1:9–15.

Jung, C. G. *Memories, Dreams, Reflections*. Aniela Jaffe, ed.; Richard and Clara Winston, trs. 1961. New York: Vintage, 1965.

Kaiser, Hellmuth. "Kleists 'Prinz von Homburg.'" *Imago* (1930), 16:219–37.

Kamerbeek, J. C. *The Plays of Sophocles: Commentaries*. 5 vols. Leiden: Brill, 1953–1978. Vol. 3: *Antigone*; vol. 4: *Oedipus Tyrannus*.

Kanzer, Mark. "On Interpreting the Oedipus Plays." *Psychoanalytic Study of Society* (1962), 3:26–38.

—— "The Oedipus Trilogy." *Psychoanalytic Quarterly* (1950), 19:561–72.

—— "The 'Passing of the Oedipus Complex' in Greek Drama." *International Journal of Psycho-Analysis* (1948), 29:131–4.

—— "Sigmund and Alexander Freud on the Acropolis." In Kanzer and Glenn, eds., *Freud and His Self-Analysis*, pp. 259–84.

Kanzer, Mark and Jules Glenn, eds., *Freud and His Self-Analysis*. New York and London: Jacob Aronson, 1979.

Kaplan, Morton. "Dream at Thebes." *Literature and Psychology* (1961), 11:12–19.

Kaufmann, Walter. *Hegel: A Reinterpretation*. 1965. Notre Dame: University of Notre Dame Press, 1978.

—— *Nietzsche: Philosopher, Psychologist, Antichrist*, 1950. Princeton: Princeton University Press, 1974.

—— "The Young Hegel and Religion." In MacIntyre, ed., *Hegel: A Collection of Critical Essays*, pp. 61–99.

Kelly, George Armstrong. "Notes on Hegel's 'Lordship and Bondage.'" In MacIntyre, ed., *Hegel: A Collection of Critical Essays*, pp. 189–217.

Kierkegaard, Søren. *Either/Or*. 1843. 2 vols. David F. Swenson and Lillian Marvin Swenson, trs. 1944. Princeton: Princeton University Press, 1971.

—— *The Sickness Unto Death*. 1849. In *Fear and Trembling and The Sickness Unto Death*. Walter Lowrie, tr. 1941. Princeton: Princeton University Press, 1974.

—— *Repetition: An Essay in Experimental Psychology*. 1843. Walter Lowrie, tr. 1941. New York: Harper Torchbooks, 1964.

Kirk, G. S. *Myth: Its Meaning and Functions in Ancient and Other Cultures*. 1970. Cambridge: Cambridge University Press, 1973.

Kirkwood, G. M. *A Study of Sophoclean Drama*. Ithaca: Cornell University Press, 1958.

Kitto, H. D. F. *Form and Meaning in Drama*. 1956. London: Methuen, 1971.

Kleist, Heinrich von. *An Abyss Deep Enough: Letters of Heinrich von Kleist with a Selection of Essays and Anecdotes*. Philip B. Miller, ed. and tr. New York: Dutton, 1982.

—— *Der zerbrochene Krug*. In *Dramen Zweiter Teil*. 1964. Munich: Deutschen Taschenbuch Verlag, 1974.

—— *Heinrich von Kleists Lebensspuren: Dokumente und Berichte der Zeitgenossen*. Helmut Sembdner, ed. Bremen: Carl Schünemann, 1964.

—— *Heinrich von Kleists Nachruhm: Eine Wirkungsgeschichte in Dokumenten*. Helmut Sembdner, ed. Bremen: Carl Schünemann, 1967.

—— *The Marquise of O—— and Other Stories*. Martin Greenberg, tr. 1960. New York: Ungar, 1979.

—— *Plays*. Walter Hinderer, ed. New York: Continuum, 1982

—— *Sämtliche Werke in vier Bänden*. Helmut Sembdner, ed. 1977. Munich: Carl Hanser Verlag, 1982.

Klossowski, Pierre. *Nietzsche et le circle vicieux*. Paris: Mercure de France, 1969.

Knox, Bernard M. W. "The Date of the *Oedipus Tyrannus* of Sophocles." *American Journal of Philology* (1956), 77:133–47.

—— *The Heroic Temper: Studies in Sophoclean Tragedy*. 1964. Berkeley: University of California Press, 1983.

—— *Oedipus at Thebes: Sophocles' Tragic Hero and His Time*. 1957. New York: Norton Library, 1971.

Kock, E. L. de. "The Sophoklean Oidipus and its Antecedents." *Acta Classica* (1961), 4:7–28.

Kofman, Sara. "The Narcissistic Woman: Freud and Girard." *Diacritics* (Fall 1980), 10:36–45.

Kohut, Heinz. "Creativeness, Charisma, Group Psychology: Reflections on the Self-Analysis of Freud." In Gedo and Pollock, eds., *Freud: The Fusion of Science and Humanism*, pp. 379–425.

Kojève, Alexandre. *Introduction to the Reading of Hegel.* 1947. Allan Bloom, ed.; James H. Nichols, Jr., tr. 1969. Ithaca: Cornell University Press, 1980.

Kris, Ernst. "The Image of the Artist: A Psychological Study of the Role of Tradition in Ancient Biographies." 1935. In *Psychoanalytic Explorations in Art*, pp. 64–84. 1952. New York: Schocken Books, 1971.

Krüll, Marianne. *Freud and His Father.* 1979. Arnold J. Pomerans, tr. New York and London: Norton, 1986.

Lacan, Jacques. "Desire and the Interpretation of Desire in *Hamlet*." James Hulbert, tr. In Shoshana Felman, ed., *Literature and Psychoanalysis. Yale French Studies* (1977), 55/56:11–52.

—— "The Mirror Stage as Formative of the Function of the I." 1936. In *Ecrits: A Selection*, pp. 1–7. Alan Sheridan, tr. New York: Norton, 1977.

Laplanche, Jean. *Hölderlin et la question du père.* Paris: Presses Universitaires de France, 1961.

—— *Life and Death in Psychoanalysis.* 1970. Jeffrey Mehlman, tr. Baltimore: Johns Hopkins University Press, 1976.

Laplanche, Jean and J. B. Pontalis. *The Language of Psychoanalysis.* 1967. Donald Nicholson-Smith, tr. New York: Norton, 1973.

Lattimore, Richmond. *Story Patterns in Greek Tragedy.* 1964. Ann Arbor: University of Michigan Press, 1969.

Leach, Edmund. "Genesis as Myth." In *Genesis as Myth and Other Essays*, pp. 7–23. London: Jonathan Cape, 1971.

—— *Lévi-Strauss.* 1970. London: Fontana Modern Masters, 1972.

Lefcowitz, Barbara. "The Inviolate Grove: Metamorphosis of a Symbol in *Oedipus at Colonus*." *Literature and Psychology* (1967), 17:78–86.

Lesky, Albin. *Greek Tragic Poetry.* 3d ed. 1972. Matthew Dillon, tr. New Haven: Yale University Press, 1983.

Lessing, Gotthold Ephraim, *Werke.* Herbert G. Göpfert et al., eds. 8 vols. Munich: Carl Hanser, 1970–1979.

Letters, F. J. H. *The Life and Work of Sophocles.* London: Sheed and Ward, 1953.

Lévi-Strauss, Claude. *The Elementary Structures of Kinship.* 1949. James Harle Bell and John Richard von Sturmer, trs. Rev. ed. Boston: Beacon Press, 1969.

—— *The Raw and the Cooked: Introduction to a Science of Mythology.* 1964. John and Doreen Weightman, trs. 1969. Chicago: University of Chicago Press, 1983.

—— *The Savage Mind.* 1962. George Weidenfeld, tr. Chicago: University of Chicago Press, 1966.

—— "The Scope of Anthropology." In *Structural Anthropology*, 2:3–32. Monique Layton, tr. New York: Basic Books, 1976.

—— "Structural Analysis in Linguistics and in Anthropology," In *Structural Anthropology*, pp. 31–54. Claire Jacobson and Brooke Grundfest Schoepf, trs. Harmondsworth: Penguin University Books, 1972.

—— "The Structural Study of Myth," In *Structural Anthropology*, pp. 206–31.

—— *Totemism.* 1962. Rodney Needham, tr. Boston: Beacon Press, 1963.

—— *Tristes Tropiques.* 1955. John and Doreen Weightman, trs. 1973. New York: Pocket Books, 1977.

Lewin, Bertram D. "The Train Ride: A Study of One of Freud's Figures of Speech." *Psychoanalytic Quarterly* (1970), 39:71–88.
Linforth, Ivan M. *Religion and Drama in "Oedipus at Colonus." University of California Publications in Classical Philology* (1951), 14:75–191.
Lloyd-Jones, Hugh. "The End of *Seven Against Thebes." Classical Quarterly* N.S. (1967), 17:16–28.
—— *The Justice of Zeus.* Berkeley: University of California Press, 1971.
Lorenz, Emil. *"Oedipus auf Kolonus." Imago* (1916), 4:22–40.
Löwith, Karl. *From Hegel to Nietzsche: The Revolution in Nineteenth-Century Thought.* 1941. David F. Green, tr. New York: Holt, Reinhart, and Winston, 1974.
Lupaş, Liana and Zoe Petre. *Commentaire aux "Sept contre Thèbes" d'Eschyle.* Paris: Les Belles Lettres, 1981.
Maass, Joachim. *Kleist: A Biography.* 1957. Ralph Manheim, tr. New York: Farrar, Straus, and Giroux, 1983.
McCall, Marsh. "Divine and Human Action in Sophocles: The Two Burials of the *Antigone." Yale Classical Studies* (1972), 22:103–17.
McGrath, William J. *Dionysian Art and Populist Politics in Austria.* New Haven: Yale University Press, 1974.
—— "Freud as Hannibal: The Politics of the Brother Band." *Central European History* (1974), 7:31–57.
—— *Freud's Discovery of Psychoanalysis: The Politics of Hysteria.* Ithaca: Cornell University Press, 1985.
MacIntyre, Alasdair, ed. *Hegel: A Collection of Critical Essays.* 1972. Notre Dame: University of Notre Dame Press, 1976.
Macksey, Richard and Eugenio Donato, eds. *The Structuralist Controversy: The Languages of Criticism and the Sciences of Man.* Baltimore: Johns Hopkins University Press, 1972.
McNulty, Michael J. "Nietzsche, His Zarathustra, and the Discovery of Oedipus in the Unconscious." Manuscript.
Mahl, George F. "Father-Son Themes in Freud's Self-Analysis." In Stanley H. Cath et al., eds., *Father and Child: Developmental and Clinical Perspectives,* pp. 33–64. Boston: Little, Brown, 1982.
Malcolm, Janet. *In the Freud Archives.* 1984. New York: Vintage Books, 1985.
Malinowski, Bronislaw. *Sex and Repression in Savage Society.* 1927. New York: New American Library, 1955.
Mangan, John W. "From Progression to Pattern: *Oedipus Coloneus* and the Unity of Sophocles' Theban Plays." M.A. essay, Columbia University, 1982.
Mann, Thomas. "Freud and the Future." 1936. In *Essays of Three Decades,* pp. 411–28. H. T. Lowe-Porter, tr. New York: Knopf, 1947.
—— "Freud's Position in the History of Modern Culture." 1929. H. T. Lowe-Porter, tr. In Hendrik M. Ruitenbeck, ed., *Freud as We Knew Him,* pp. 65–89. Detroit: Wayne State University Press, 1973.
—— "Nietzsche's Philosophy in the Light of Contemporary Events." 1947. Abr. in Robert C. Solomon, ed., *Nietzsche: A Collection of Critical Essays,* pp. 358–70. 1973. Notre Dame: University of Notre Dame Press, 1980.
Marcus, Steven, *Freud and the Culture of Psychoanalysis: Studies in the Transition from Victorian Humanism to Modernity.* Boston: Allen and Unwin, 1984.
Masson, Jeffrey Moussaieff. *The Assault on Truth: Freud's Suppression of the Seduction Theory.* New York: Farrar, Straus, and Giroux, 1984.
Masullo, Aldo. "Das Unbewußte in Hegels Philosophie des subjektiven Geistes." *Hegel-Studien, Beiheft* (1979), 19:27–63.

Mazlish, Bruce. "Freud and Nietzsche." *Psychoanalytic Review* (1968–69), 55:360–75.

Merleau-Ponty, M. *Phenomenology of Perception*. 1945. Colin Smith, tr. London: Routledge and Kegan Paul, 1962.

Mitchell, Juliet. *Psychoanalysis and Feminism: Freud, Reich, Laing, and Women*. 1974. New York: Vintage, 1975.

Moi, Toril. "The Missing Mother: The Oedipal Rivalries of René Girard." *Diacritics* (Summer 1982), 12:21–31.

Mommsen, Katharina. *Kleists Kampf mit Goethe*. 1974. Frankfurt: Suhrkamp. 1979.

Montgomery, Marshall. *Friedrich Hölderlin and the German Neo-Hellenic Movement*, Part I. London: Oxford University Press, 1923.

Mueller, Martin. *Children of Oedipus and Other Essays on the Imitation of Greek Tragedy, 1500–1800*. Toronto: University of Toronto Press, 1980.

Musurillo, Herbert. "Sunken Imagery in Sophocles' *Oedipus*." *American Journal of Philology* (1957), 78:36–51.

Nauen, Franz Gabriel. *Revolution, Idealism, and Human Freedom: Schelling, Hölderlin, and Hegel and the Crisis of Early German Idealism*. The Hague: Martinus Nijhoff, 1971.

Neumann, Erich. *The Origins and History of Consciousness*. 1949. Princeton: Princeton University Press, 1973.

Nietzsche, Friedrich. *Beyond Good and Evil: Prelude to a Philosophy of the Future*. 1886. Walter Kaufmann, tr. New York: Vintage Books, 1966.

—— *The Birth of Tragedy*. 1872. In *The Birth of Tragedy and The Case of Wagner*. Walter Kaufmann, tr. New York: Vintage, 1967.

—— *Daybreak: Thoughts on the Prejudices of Morality*. 1881. R. J. Hollingdale, tr. Cambridge: Cambridge University Press, 1982.

—— *The Gay Science*. 1882. Walter Kaufmann, tr. New York: Vintage Books, 1974.

—— *On the Advantage and Disadvantage of History for Life*. 1874. Peter Preuss, tr. Indianapolis: Hackett, 1980.

—— *On the Genealogy of Morals and Ecce Homo*. 1887 and 1908. Walter Kaufmann and R. J. Hollingdale, trs. 1967. New York: Vintage 1969.

—— *Schopenhauer as Educator*. 1874. James W. Hillesheim and Malcolm R. Simpson, trs. South Bend: Regnery and Gateway, 1965.

—— *Selected Letters of Friedrich Nietzsche*. Christopher Middleton, ed. and tr. Chicago: University of Chicago Press, 1969.

—— *The Portable Nietzsche*. Walter Kaufmann, ed. and tr. 1954. New York: Viking, 1967.

—— *Werke*. 5 vols. Karl Schlechta, ed. 1969. Frankfurt: Ullstein Materialien, 1980.

—— *Werke und Briefe*. 9 vols. Hans Joachim Mette, ed. Munich: Beck, 1934.

Nunberg, Herman and Ernst Federn, eds. *Minutes of the Vienna Psychoanalytic Society*. 4 vols. M. Nunberg, tr. New York: International Universities Press, 1962–1975.

Opstelten, J. C. *Sophocles and Greek Pessimism*. J. A. Ross, tr. Amsterdam: North-Holland, 1952.

Pautrat, Bernard. *Versions du soleil: Figures et système de Nietzsche*. Paris: Editions du Seuil, 1971.

Peterkin, L. Denis. "The Creon of Sophocles." *Classical Philology* (1929), 24:263–73.

Pöggeler, Otto. *Hegels Kritik der Romantik*. Bonn: Bouvier, 1956.

—— "Hegel und die griechische Tragödie." *Hegel-Studien, Beiheft* (1964), 1:285-306.

Prader, Florian. *Schiller und Sophokles*. Zurich: Atlantis, 1954.

Pucci, Pietro. "Lévi-Strauss and Classical Culture." *Arethusa* (1971), 4:103–17.

Rado, Charles. "*Oedipus the King.*" *Psychoanalytic Review* (1956), 43:228–34.

Rank, Otto. *Das Incest-Motiv in Dichtung und Sage: Grundzüge einer Psychologie des dichterichen Schaffens.* Leipzig: Franz Deuticke, 1912.
—— *The Myth of the Birth of the Hero: A Psychological Interpretation of Mythology.* 1909. F. Robbins and Smith Ely Jelliffe, trs. New York: Journal of Nervous and Mental Disease Publishing Co., 1914.
Rehm, Walter. *Griechentum und Goethezeit: Geschichte eines Glaubens.* 1936. Bern: Francke Verlag, 1968.
Reik, Theodor. "Oedipus and the Sphinx." 1920. In *Dogma and Compulsion: Psychoanalytic Studies of Religion and Myths,* pp. 289–332. Bernard Miall, tr. New York: International Universities Press, 1951.
Reinhardt, Karl. "Hölderlin und Sophokles." In Alfred Kelletat, ed., *Hölderlin: Beiträge zu seinem Verständnis in unserem Jahrhundert,* pp. 287–303. Tübingen: Mohr, 1961.
—— *Sophocles.* 1933. Hazel and David Harvey, trs. Oxford: Basil Blackwell, 1979.
Ricoeur, Paul. *Freud and Philosophy: An Essay on Interpretation.* Denis Savage, tr. New Haven: Yale University Press, 1970.
Rieff, Philip. *Freud: The Mind of the Moralist.* 1959. Chicago: University of Chicago Press, 1979.
—— *The Triumph of the Therapeutic: Uses of Faith After Freud.* New York: Harper and Row, 1966.
Roazen, Paul. *Brother Animal: The Story of Freud and Tausk.* New York: Knopf, 1969.
—— *Freud and His Followers.* 1971. New York: New American Library, 1976.
—— "Reflections on Ethos and Authenticity in Psychoanalysis." *The Human Context* (1972), 4:577–87.
Robert, Carl, *Oidipus: Geschichte eines poetischen Stoffs im griechischen Altertum.* 2 vols. Berlin: Weidmannische Buchhandlung, 1915.
Robert, Marthe. *From Oedipus to Moses: Freud's Jewish Identity.* 1974. Ralph Manheim, tr. Garden City, N.Y.: Anchor Books, 1976.
Rohde, Erwin. *Psyche: The Cult of Souls and Belief in Immortality among the Greeks.* 1893. W. B. Hillis, tr. New York: Harcourt, Brace, 1925.
Róheim, Géza. *The Riddle of the Sphinx; or Human Origins.* R. Money-Kyrle, tr. 1934. New York: Harper Torchbooks, 1974.
—— "Teiresias and Other Seers." *Psychoanalytic Review* (1946), 33:314–34.
Rosenberg, Samuel. *Why Freud Fainted.* Indianapolis: Bobbs-Merrill, 1978.
Rosenblum, Eva. "Le premier parcours psychanalytique d'un homme, relaté par Freud: apport à son auto-analyse." *Etudes psychotherapiques* (1973), 4:51–58.
Rosenmeyer, T. G. "The Wrath of Oedipus." *Phoenix* (1952), 6:92–112.
Roth, Philp. "A Conversation with Edna O'Brien: 'The Body Contains the Life Story,'" *New York Times Book Review,* November 18, 1984, pp. 38–40.
Rouse, W. D. "The Two Burials in *Antigone.*" *Classical Review* (1911), 25:40–42.
Roussel, P. "Les fiançailles d'Haimon et d'Antigone." *Revue des Etudes Grecques* (1922), 35:63–81.
Roustang, François. *Dire Mastery: Discipleship from Freud to Lacan.* 1976. Ned Lukacher, tr. Baltimore: Johns Hopkins University Press, 1982.
Sachs, Hanns. *Freud: Master and Friend.* 1944. Cambridge: Harvard University Press, 1945.
Sadger, Isidor. *Heinrich von Kleist: Eine pathographisch-psychologische Studie.* Wiesbaden: J. F. Bergmann, 1910.
Saffar, Ruth El. "Unbinding the Doubles: Reflections on Love and Culture in the Work of René Girard." *Denver Quarterly* (Winter 1984), 18:6–22.

Said, Edward W. *Beginnings: Intention and Method.* New York: Basic Books, 1975.

Sajner, Josef. "Sigmund Freud's Beziehungen zu seinem Geburtsort Freiberg (Príbor) und zu Mähren." *Clio Medica* (1968), 3:167–80.

Sandys, John Edwin. *A History of Classical Scholarship.* 3 vols. 3d. ed. Cambridge: Cambridge University Press, 1921.

Santirocco, Matthew S. "Justice in Sophocles' *Antigone.*" *Philosophy and Literature* (1980), 4:180–98.

Schadewaldt, Wolfgang. "Der 'Zerbrochene Krug' von Heinrich von Kleist und Sophokles' 'König Odipus.'" *Schweizer Monatshefte* (1957–58), 37:311–18.

—— "Hölderlins Ubersetzung des Sophokles." In Jochen Schmidt, ed., *Uber Hölderlin,* pp. 237–93. Frankfurt: Insel, 1970.

Schelling, Friedrich von. *Sämtliche Werke.* 14 vols. Stuttgart: Cotta, 1856–61.

—— *Werke.* 3 vols. Hartmut Buchner et al., eds. Stuttgart: Fromann-Holzboog, 1976–82.

Schiller, Friedrich. *An Anthology for Our Time.* Frederick Ungar, ed. and tr. New York: Ungar, 1959.

—— *The Bride of Messina, William Tell, and Demetrius.* 1803, 1804, and 1805. Charles E. Passage, tr. New York: Ungar, 1962.

—— *Don Carlos: Infante of Spain.* 1788. Charles E. Passage, tr. 1959. New York: Ungar, 1980.

—— *Naive and Sentimental Poetry and On the Sublime.* 1795–96 and 1801. Julius A. Elias, tr. 1966. New York: Ungar, 1975.

—— *On the Aesthetic Education of Man.* 1793. Reginald Snell, tr. 1965. New York: Ungar, 1974.

—— *Werke: Nationalausgabe.* 38 vols. Julius Petersen et al., eds. Weimar: Hermann Böhlaus Nachfolger, 1946–77.

—— *Wilhelm Tell.* 1804. Gilbert Jordan, tr. New York: Bobbs-Merrill, 1964.

Schlegel, August von. *A Course of Lectures on Dramatic Art and Literature.* 1808. John Black, tr. London: Bohm, 1846.

Schlegel, Friedrich. *Uber das Studium der Griechischen Poesie.* 1797. In *Studien des Klassichen Altertums,* pp. 203–367. Ernst Behler, ed. Paderborn: Ferdinand Schöningh, 1979.

Schönau, Walter. *Sigmund Freud's Prosa: Literarische Elemente seines Stils.* Suttgart: Metzlerische Verlagsbuchhandlung, 1968.

Schopenhauer, Arthur. *Essays and Aphorisms.* R. J. Hollingdale, tr. 1970. Harmondsworth: Penguin Books, 1978.

Schorske, Carl E. "Politics and Patricide in Freud's *Interpretation of Dreams.*" *American Historical Review* (1973), 78:328–47.

Schrade, Leo. *La représentation d'Edipo Tiranno au Teatro Olimpico.* Paris: Editions du Centre National de la Recherche Scientifique, 1960.

Schrader, Hans. *Hölderlins Deutung des "Oedipus" und der "Antigone."* *Mnemosyne* (1933), vol. 10.

Schur, Max. *Freud: Living and Dying.* New York: International Universities Press, 1972.

—— "Some Additional 'Day Residues' of 'The Specimen Dream of Psychoanalysis.'" In Rudolph M. Loewenstein et al., eds., *Psychoanalysis: A General Psychology: Essays in Honor of Heinz Hartmann,* pp. 45–85. New York: International Universities Press, 1966.

Segal, Charles Paul. "Sophocles' Praise of Men and the Conflicts of the *Antigone.*" *Arion* (1964), 3–2:46–66.

—— *Tragedy and Civilization: An Interpretation of Sophocles.* Cambridge: Harvard University Press, 1981.

Seidensticker, Bernd. "Beziehungen zwischen den beiden Oidipusdramen des Sophokles." *Hermes* (1972), 100:255–75.

Seneca. *Oedipus.* In *Tragedies I.* Frank Justus Miller, tr. 1917. Cambridge: Loeb Classical Library, 1979.
Shakespeare, William. *The Riverside Shakespeare.* G. Blakemore Evans et al., eds. Boston: Houghton Mifflin, 1974.
Shengold, Leonard. "Freud and Joseph." In Kanzer and Glenn, eds., *Freud and His Self-Analysis,* pp. 67–86.
—— "The Metaphor of the Journey in the *Interpretation of Dreams.*" In Kanzer and Glenn, eds. *Freud and His Self-Analysis,* 51–65.
Sichirollo, Livio. "Hegel und die griechische Welt. Nachleben der Antike und Entstehung der 'Philosophie der Weltgeschichte.'" *Hegel-Studien, Beiheft* (1964), 1:263–84.
Silk, M. S. and J. P. Stern. *Nietzsche on Tragedy.* Cambridge: Cambridge University Press, 1981.
Sophocles. *Fabulae.* A. C. Pearson, ed. 1924. Oxford: Oxford University Press, 1974.
—— *Oedipus the King.* Thomas Gould, ed. and tr. Englewood Cliffs, N.J.: Prentice-Hall, 1970.
—— *Plays and Fragments.* 2 vols. Lewis Campbell, ed. Oxford: Clarendon Press, 1889. Vol. 1: *Oedipus Tyrannus, Oedipus Coloneus, Antigone.*
—— *The Plays and Fragments.* 7 vols. R. C. Jebb, ed. Cambridge: Cambridge University Press, 1889–1903. Vol. 1: *Oedipus Tyrannus;* vol. 2: *Oedipus Coloneus;* vol. 3: *Antigone.*
Spanos, William V. "Heidegger, Kierkegaard, and the Hermeneutic Circle: Toward a Postmodern Theory of Interpretation as Dis-closure." *boundary 2* (Winter 1976), 4:455–88.
Stahl, E. L. "Guiscard and Oedipus." *Tulane Drama Review* (1962), 6:172–77.
Staiger, Emil. *Der Geist der Liebe und das Schcksal: Schelling, Hegel und Hölderlin.* Frauenfeld: Huber, 1935.
Stanescu, H. "Young Freud's Letters to his Rumanian Friend, Silberstein." *The Israel Annals of Psychiatry and Related Disciplines* (1971), 9:195–207.
Steiner, George. *After Babel: Aspects of Language and Translation.* New York: Oxford University Press, 1975.
—— *Antigones.* New York: Oxford University Press, 1984.
—— *Martin Heidegger.* 1979. Harmondsworth: Penguin Books, 1982.
—— "Orpheus with His Myths: Claude Lévi-Strauss." In *Language and Silence: Essays on Language, Literature, and the Inhuman,* pp. 239–50. 1967. New York: Atheneum, 1974.
Sterba, Richard. "The Fate of the Ego in Analytic Therapy." *International Journal of Psycho-Analysis.* (1934), 15:117–26.
Sterren, H. A. van der. "The 'King Oedipus' of Sophocles." *International Journal of Psycho-Analysis* (1952), 33:343–50.
Strong, Tracy B. "Oedipus as Hero: Family and Family Metaphors in Nietzsche." *boundary 2* (Spring-Fall 1981), 2:311–35.
Sulloway, Frank J. *Freud: Biologist of the Mind.* New York: Basic Books, 1979.
Swales, Peter J. "Freud, Fliess, and Fratricide; The Role of Fliess in Freud's Conception of Paranoia." Privately published by the author, 1982.
—— "Freud, Minna Bernays, and the Conquest of Rome." *New American Review* (Spring/Summer 1982), 1:1–23.
—— "Freud, Martha Bernays, and the Language of Flowers." Privately published by the author, 1982.
Swan, Jim. "*Mater* and Nannie: Freud's Two Mothers and the Discovery of the Oedipus Complex." *American Imago* (1974), 31:1–64.
Taminiaux, Jacques. *La Nostalgie de la Grèce à l'aube de l'idealisme allemand: Kant et les Grecs*

dans l'itinéraire de Schiller, de Hölderlin et de Hegel. The Hague: Martinus Nijhoff, 1977.
Taylor, Charles. *Hegel*. 1975. Cambridge: Cambridge University Press, 1978.
Thass-Thienemann, Theodore. "Oedipus and the Sphinx: The Linguistic Approach to Unconscious Fantasies." *Psychoanalytic Review* (1957), 44:10–33.
Trilling, Lionel. "Freud and Literature." In *The Liberal Imagination: Essays on Literature and Society*, pp. 32–54. 1950. New York: Anchor Books, 1953.
—— Introduction to Ernest Jones, *The Life and Work of Sigmund Freud*. Abr. by Lionel Trilling and Steven Marcus. 1961. Garden City, N.Y.: Anchor Books, 1963.
—— *Sincerity and Authenticity*. 1972. New York: Oxford University Press, 1974.
Trosman, Harry. "Freud and the Controversy over Shakespearean Authorship." In Gedo and Pollock, eds., *Freud: The Fusion of Science and Humanism*, pp. 307–31.
Turel, Adrien. *Bachofen-Freud: zur Emanzipation des Mannes vom Reich der Mutter*. Bern: Verlag Hans Huber, 1939.
Turner, Terence S. "Oedipus: Time and Structure in Narrative Form." In Robert F. Spencer, ed., *Forms of Symbolic Action*, pp. 26–68. Seattle: University of Washington Press, 1969.
Vellacott, Philip. *Sophocles and Oedipus*. London: Macmillan, 1971.
Velzen, H. U. E. Thoden van. "Irma at the Window. The Fourth Script." *American Imago* (1984), 41:245-93.
Vergote, Antoine. "L'intérêt philosophique de la psychanalyse freudienne." *Archives de Philosophie* (1958), 21:26–59.
Vernant, Jean-Pierre. "Ambiguity and Reversal: On the Enigmatic Structure of *Oedipus Rex*." Page du Bois, tr. *New Literary History* (1978), 9:475–501.
—— "'Oedipe' sans complexe." In Vernant and Pierre Vidal-Naquet, *Mythe et tragédie en Grèce ancienne*, pp. 77–98. 1972. Paris: François Maspero, 1980.
Versényi, Laszlo. "Oedipus: Tragedy of Self-Knowledge." *Arion* (1962), 1–3:20–30.
Vickers, Brian. *Towards Greek Tragedy: Drama, Myth, Society*. 1973. London: Longmans, 1979.
Voltaire. *Oeuvres Complètes*. 52 vols. Louis Moland, ed. Paris: Garniers Frères, 1877–85.
Wädenswil, Margit Schoch von. *Kleist und Sophokles*. Zurich: Aschmann and Scheller, 1952.
Waelhens, Alphonse de. "Réflexions sur une problématique husserlienne de l'inconscient, Husserl et Hegel." In *Edmund Husserl 1859–1959*, pp. 221–37. The Hague: Martinus Nijhoff, 1959.
Waldock, J. A. *Sophocles the Dramatist*. 1951. Cambridge: Cambridge University Press, 1966.
Webster, T. B. L. *The Tragedies of Euripides*. London: Methuen, 1967.
White, Hayden. *Metahistory: The Historical Imagination in Nineteenth-Century Europe*. 1973. Baltimore: Johns Hopkins University Press, 1975.
Whitman, Cedric H. *Sophocles: A Study of Heroic Humanism*. Cambridge: Harvard University Press, 1951.
Whyte, Lancelot Law. *The Unconscious Before Freud*. 1960. New York: St. Martin's Press, 1978.
Wilamowitz-Moellendorff, Tycho von. *Die dramatische Technik des Sophokles*. Ernest Kapp, ed. Berlin: Weidmannsche Buchhandlung, 1917.
Willis, William H. "ΑΥΤΑΔΕΛΦΟΣ in the *Antigone* and the *Eumenides*" In George E. Mylonas and Doris Raymond, eds., *Studies Presented to David Moore Robinson*, 2:553–58. 2 vols. St. Louis: Washington University Press, 1953.
Willner, Dorothy. "The Oedipus Complex, Antigone, and Electra: The Woman as Hero and Victim." *American Anthropologist* (1982), 84:58–78.
Wilson, Edmund. "Philoctetes: The Wound and the Bow." In *The Wound and the Bow: Seven Studies in Literature*, pp. 223–42. 1929. New York: Oxford University Press, 1965.

Winnington-Ingram, R. P. *Sophocles: An Interpretation.* Cambridge: Cambridge University Press, 1980.

Wittels, Fritz. *Sigmund Freud: His Personality, His Teaching, and His School.* Eden and Cedar Paul, trs. London: Allen and Unwin, 1924.

Wittrich, Wilhelm. *Sophokles' "König Odipus" und Schillers "Braut von Messina."* Cassel: Joseph Has, 1887.

Wolff, Emil. "Hegel und die griechische Welt." *Antike und Abendland* (1944), 1:163–81.

Zeitlin, Froma I. "Language, Structure, and the Son of Oedipus in Aeschylus' *Seven Against Thebes.*" In Stephen Kresic, ed., *Contemporary Literary Hermeneutics and the Interpretation of Classical Texts,* pp. 549–66. Ottawa: Ottawa University Press, 1981.

Index

416

Index